# RIGHT TO EDUCATION IN INDIA

This is one of the first volumes to comprehensively discuss the resource constraints and institutional challenges in realizing the fundamental Right to Education (RTE) in India. It looks at various aspects of the *Sarva Shiksha Abhiyan* (SSA), the primary vehicle to implement RTE and a flagship programme to universalize elementary education in the country. The book presents a comparative perspective across regions and states and evaluates the effective delivery of SSA at the grassroots level. Using rich empirical data, not yet available in the public domain, it provides valuable lessons for the planning and financing arrangements of SSA–RTE between the centre and the states, and towards understanding access, equity and quality of education.

The work will be a major resource for scholars and researchers of education, economics, public policy, development studies and politics.

**Praveen Jha** is Professor of Economics and Chairperson at the Centre for Economic Studies and Planning, and is Adjunct Professor at the Centre for Informal Sector and Labor Studies, School of Social Sciences, Jawaharlal Nehru University, New Delhi. He is also honorary Visiting Professor at Rhodes University, Grahamstown, South Africa, and the African Institute of Agrarian Studies, Harare, Zimbabwe.

**P. Geetha Rani** is Associate Professor at the Department of Educational Finance at the National University of Educational Planning and Administration, New Delhi. She has contributed to the financial memorandum for the Right to Education Bill under the Central Advisory Board on Education (CABE), constituted by the Ministry of Human Resources Development.

'Despite a substantial increase over the past decade, low levels of public spending and institutional bottlenecks have been both causes of and exacerbating factors in large inequities, poor quality, high dropout rates and sub-optimal learning outcomes that characterize elementary education in India. The refreshingly in-depth and analytical essays in this book identify various centre–state fiscal issues and financial constraints at different levels of government that limit the efficiency of public spending on elementary education. Assuring children the right to education will depend critically on how effectively education administrators across Indian states respond to and address the shortfalls and deficiencies in financing so aptly identified by the contributors to this book.'

A. K. Shiva Kumar, economist and policy advisor, New Delhi, India

# RIGHT TO EDUCATION IN INDIA

## Resources, institutions and public policy

*Edited by Praveen Jha and P. Geetha Rani*

Routledge
Taylor & Francis Group
LONDON AND NEW YORK

First published 2016 by Routledge

2 Park Square, Milton Park, Abingdon, Oxfordshire OX14 4RN
711 Third Avenue, New York, NY 10017

*Routledge is an imprint of the Taylor & Francis Group, an informa business*

First issued in paperback 2017



*British Library Cataloguing-in-Publication Data*
A catalogue record for this book is available from the British Library

*Library of Congress Cataloging-in-Publication Data*
A catalog record has been requested for this book

ISBN: 978-1-138-94748-1 (hbk)
ISBN: 978-0-8153-9587-4 (pbk)

Typeset in Goudy
by Apex CoVantage, LLC

# CONTENTS

# FIGURES

# TABLES

# CONTRIBUTORS

**Nilachala Acharya** holds an MPhil degree in economics and pursuing his PhD (economics) from Jawaharlal Nehru University, New Delhi, India. He is a senior research officer, Centre for Budget and Governance Accountability, New Delhi.

**Nesar Ahmad** is the coordinator of Budget Analysis Rajasthan Centre (BARC), India.

**C.E. Ajith Kumar** is associated with the NRPPD project at the Centre for Development Studies, Thiruvananthapuram, Kerala.

**K. Anji Reddy** is an assistant professor of economics, Mahatma Gandhi University, Nalgonda, Telangana.

**Jaswinder S. Brar** is a professor of economics, Centre for Research in Economic Change, Punjabi University, Patiala.

**Sailabala Debi** is a professor and former director of CMDR, Dharwad, Karnataka. At present, she is a professor (adjunct), KIIT School of Management, KIIT University, Krishna Campus, Bhubaneswar. She is also consultant to CCS, UNICEF, KIIT University.

**Avani Kapur** is currently senior research and programme analyst at the Accountability Initiative (AI), Centre for Policy Research, New Delhi.

**M. Lathika** is an associate professor of economics in NSS College for Women, Neeramankara, Thiruvananthapuram, Kerala.

**Surya N. Mishra** is the deputy director, Teacher Training and Pedagogy at Orissa Primary Education Programme Agency. He is also the Nodal officer, State Institute of Educational Management and Training, Odisha.

**Siba S. Mohanty** is faculty member at Doon University, Uttarakhand.

**Anit N. Mukherjee** is IDRC Fellow at the Centre for Global Development, Washington, DC.

**Madhu Paranjape** has taught statistics for 33 years at the undergraduate level in Kirti College, affiliated to University of Mumbai. At present, she is a guest faculty at the Maharashtra Institute of Labour Studies, Mumbai.

**Pooja Parvati** is a development practitioner currently with Oxfam India and manages their research.

**Archita Pramanik** is a doctoral candidate at Zakir Husain Centre for Educational Studies, JNU.

**Mahendra S. Rao** is associated with Budget Analysis Rajasthan Centre (BARC), Jaipur, Rajasthan, as a budget analyst since April 2009.

**B. Shiva Reddy** was professor in the Department of Economics, Osmania University, Hyderabad, till his retirement in June 2014.

**Bansi L. Shukla** is a finance controller in Pradhan Mantri Gramin Sadak Yojna (HPPWD) Shimla.

**Satadru Sikdar** is a research associate at National Institute of Public Finance and Policy, New Delhi.

**Sukhwinder Singh** is a professor of economics, Centre for Research in Economic Change, Punjabi University, Patiala.

**Hariom Soni** is a social activist and programme coordinator of Education Resource unit, Astha Sansthan, Udaipur.

# 1

# INTRODUCTION

## Setting the context

*Praveen Jha and P. Geetha Rani*

*Education costs money, but then so does ignorance.*

– Sir Claus Moses

### Introduction

Public spending on basic services notably basic education and basic health care is found to reach the poor almost universally. Broad-based education of good quality is among the most powerful instruments known to reduce poverty and inequality. In India, the constitutional obligation of universal elementary education (UEE) and its emphasis laid by the international community on Education for All (EFA) paved way for its renewed interest in UEE, neglected for decades. Despite, achieving UEE genuinely remains obscure being on the agenda of public policy since independence. The first national strategy to attain UEE in India was to provide free and compulsory education up to the age of 14 within a period of 10 years under the Constitution of India (1950), Article (45). Increased attention to education was on the anvil after the adoption of National Policy on Education (1986) (Government of India 1986). Even though, central government played an advisory role in matters relating to education, it assumed greater significance when education was shifted to concurrent list in 1976[1] and later the 86th Amendment of the Constitution in 2002 making education a fundamental right. Its role in the development of education is manifested by way of Centrally Sponsored Schemes (CSS). These schemes are designed by the line ministry, Ministry of Human Resource Development (MHRD), and implemented jointly by Education Departments of the State Governments. The first centrally sponsored scheme with an objective to achieve UEE was the scheme on non-formal education. The primary objective of the scheme was to cover the non-school going children of the age group 6–14. It was initiated in 1978 in nine educationally backward states, namely Andhra Pradesh, Assam, Bihar, Jammu and Kashmir, Madhya Pradesh, Orissa, Rajasthan, Uttar Pradesh and West Bengal. Incidentally, Literacy Mission was initiated to improve adult literacy around the same time.

The impetus of universalizing elementary education began with the National Policy on Education (1986). Operation Blackboard was an offshoot of this, as the National Policy on Education identified that the condition of educational infrastructure in elementary schools was dismal to achieve universal elementary education. This first nationwide centrally sponsored scheme was initiated in 1987 to improve educational infrastructure in all government primary schools. It aimed at improvising three critical components of educational development, namely class rooms, teachers and teaching–learning equipment. Around this time another important nationwide CSS was initiated, on teacher education, that is, establishing District Institutes of Education and Training (DIET).

During early 1990s, after macroeconomic reform policies were initiated in India, external funding for primary education appeared through the District[2] Primary Education Programme (DPEP). This programme was launched as a social safety net measure in 1994 to offset the adverse impact of structural adjustment policies adopted since 1990s. It is the largest externally funded programme in education focusing on districts with below female literacy rates. Indeed, the decentralized planning got operationalized with the endeavours under DPEP (Varghese 1996; Tilak 2002). *Sarva Shiksha Abhiyan* (SSA) builds on but differs from DPEP that SSA has nationwide coverage, encompassing most of the previous CSS under a single programme and launched in 2001.

Parallelly, significance of universal elementary education was reinvigorated at the global level with a pledge to achieve universal primary education by 2000 at the World Conference on Education for All (EFA) in 1990, at Jomtien. The EFA assessment at the World Education Forum held at Dakar after 10 years in 2000 culminated in the adoption of Dakar Framework for Action, which embodies a revitalized collective commitment to achieve Education for All by 2015. These global promises made by various participating governments at international forums in 1990s and later in 2000 combined with domestic pressures accelerated the impetus towards adoption of national strategies to achieve EFA by a number of developing countries including India. As a follow-up, SSA, the largest development programme in the world was initiated in 2001. Its aim is attaining UEE by 2010, and implemented by Department of School Education and Literacy under Ministry of Human Resource Development (MHRD) in partnership with states with fund sharing arrangements. The relative contribution of centre and state government changed over time. The funding for SSA is routed through State Implementing Agencies.

Shifting from a programme to policy mode, the fundamental right to education, enshrined in the Constitution, was strengthened by the Right of Children to Free and Compulsory Education (RTE) Act, 2009, and came into effect from 1st April 2010. SSA norms were transformed to align with RTE Act, and SSA was geared up as an implementation vehicle of RTE. In terms of resource allocation, reference to Finance Commission in section 7(4) of the RTE Act imply that on the basis of a reference by the central government through the President, the Finance Commission could sanction monies directly to states for the Act, which would be in addition to the sharing ratio of CSS. It provides an additional window for central funds to be allocated to states that need them most. The 13th Finance Commission has made allocations of Rs. 24,068 crores over a five-year period specifically for elementary education (discussed in Chapter 11). This will help states meet some finances, but would be inadequate to meet the RTE requirements.

Thrust of SSA is on bridging gender and social gaps and total retention of all children in schools by 2010. This has resulted in significant improvements in the provision of key physical inputs such as buildings and other basic school infrastructure. One of the strategies of SSA is mainstreaming out-of-school children through diverse mechanisms such as residential, non-residential bridge courses, summer camps, etc. Human resources have been provided through its provision and inputs such as teacher training. However, all these inputs have not reflected in terms of learning levels of children as per Annual Survey of Education Report (ASER 2013).

Accomplishing the goals of SSA–RTE would be meaningfully translated only if required funds are available and spent effectively resulting in better learning outcomes. Twelfth five-year plan takes ahead with implementing the RTE Act using SSA. As per the union budget 2013–14, Rs. 27,258 crores is allocated for RTE–SSA representing an increase of 6.6 per cent over 2012–13. This is in contrast to an increase of 21.7 per cent in 2012–13 over 2011–12. However, there has been tremendous increase in the outlay for SSA since its inception in 2001–02 which started with an outlay of Rs. 500 crores. Though it appears that it is a huge increase, yet the amount available under SSA from the centre is less compared to the need. It is in this context, the central concern of the volume is the resource constraints and institutional challenges in realizing RTE, the continuing long walk. It attempts to examine the centre–state relations in financing elementary education, challenges and issues of funding the CSS focusing on the principles of financing education, namely adequacy, predictability, timing and absorption capacity.

Further, it explores the process of flow of resources drawing evidence from select states, districts and up to schools. The book deals with issues in participation, learning levels vis- à-vis allocation of funds, its flow and utilization. Rarely any analytical studies have been carried out to examine the several processes and problems involved in the fund flow pattern and identify the factors responsible for it at sub-state level. Any analytical studies have been carried out to understand intra-state variations in fund utilization and their impact on certain key outcomes such as infrastructure, school participation and learning. The present volume makes an attempt to fill this vacuum by a humble beginning.

## Public financing of education

Government resources available for education in India are financed from both central and state governments. The method of public financing in general and education in particular is a complex process. Government expenditure on any activity, whether economic or social, is to be looked at in plan and non-plan expenditures in the Indian context. Plan expenditures are financed through Planning Commission transfers by and large. Such plan expenditures are intended for developmental expenditures resulting in new initiatives, innovations, building infrastructure, etc. While non-plan expenditures are for non-developmental/committed expenditures which are in the nature of maintenance expenditures. They are met out from Finance Commission transfers. Third channel of transfers is discretionary transfers through line Ministries apart from the Planning and Finance Commission transfers. The discretionary transfers are for financing the central sector schemes or the CSS. The discussion that follows is on trends in financing education covering total public expenditure on education at national level.

Resource requirement for education has been estimated as 6 per cent of GDP in 1966 and reiterated in NPE, 1986. It has been repeated in 6 per cent GDP committee (MHRD 2005). It remained on public agenda for almost five decades since 1966. The expenditure on education as percentage of GDP was 0.6 per cent during 1950–51 and improved to around 3 per cent in 1980–81. Since then it hovers around 3 to 4 per cent and touched its peak in 2000–01 with 4.28 per cent (Table 1.1). Underinvestment in education has been a perennial problem in India as argued by many

*Table 1.1* Government expenditure on education in India

| | *Govt. expenditure on education as a % of GDP* | *Govt. expenditure on education as a % of revenue expenditures* | *Govt. expenditure onelementary education as a % of GDP* | *Govt. expenditure on elementary education as a % of revenue expenditures* |
|---|---|---|---|---|
| 1951–52 | 0.64 | 7.9 | 0.29 | 3.65 |
| 1960–61 | 1.48 | 12.0 | 0.55 | 4.46 |
| 1970–71 | 2.11 | 10.2 | 0.88 | 4.23 |
| 1980–81 | 2.98 | 10.7 | 1.18 | 4.22 |
| 1990–91 | 3.84 | 9.23 | 1.51 | 4.06 |
| 2000–01 | 4.28 | 14.4 | 1.55 | 5.20 |
| 2005–06 | 3.34 | 12.7 | 1.48 | 5.64 |
| 2009–10 | 3.95 | 13.9 | 1.56 | 5.51 |
| 2011–12(BE) | 4.17 | 15.6 | 1.69 | 6.32 |

*Source:* Analysis of Budgeted Expenditure on Education, various issues.

including Dreze and Sen (2013). In terms of government's commitment to financing education, it can be gauged by its share of education expenditure to total government expenditure. This has improved to around 10 per cent share during pre-1990 period to 14 per cent in post 1990s. While government expenditure on elementary education was less than 1 per cent during pre-1970s, it improved to around 1.5 per cent but stagnated till 1990–91. Post-1990s exhibited higher financial allocations for education in general and elementary education in particular.

The pattern and size of intra-sectoral allocation within education sector indicates the relative priority assigned to different levels of education. Pattern of intra-sectoral allocation of resources reflects an unbalanced nature of educational development. Share of elementary education has been above 45 per cent and improved to 53 per cent in 2005–06 and remained at around 50 per cent of total expenditure on education. It is due to SSA and implementation of the RTE Act. The share of expenditure on secondary education ranged between 29 and 33 per cent. Indeed, secondary education has been the neglected subsector of education till recently. However, the introduction of the *Rashtriya Madhyamik Shiksha Abhiyan (RMSA)* improved the allocation and planning for secondary education in a big way. The intra-sectoral allocations towards higher education ranged between 11 and 14 per cent, while the same in technical education ranged between 2 and 5 per cent (Table 1.2).

*Table 1.2* Budgeted expenditure on education by levels of education in India (%)

| | *Elementary* | *Secondary* | *University and higher* | *Technical* | *General education** |
|---|---|---|---|---|---|
| 1970–71 | 41.67 | 29.13 | 12.28 | 5.40 | 892 |
| 1980–81 | 45.56 | 30.73 | 14.33 | 4.06 | 3,374 |
| 1990–91 | 49.71 | 33.08 | 11.81 | 2.86 | 15,550 |
| 2000–01 | 47.61 | 31.59 | 14.71 | 4.04 | 62,498 |
| 2005–06 | 53.11 | 29.43 | 11.66 | 3.87 | 94,484 |
| 2009–10 | 50.27 | 31.28 | 11.96 | 4.91 | 190,136 |
| 2012–13(BE) | 50.36 | 30.04 | 13.12 | 5.02 | 323,849 |

*Source:* Analysis of Budgeted Expenditure on Education, various issues.

*Note:* *Expenditure on education by Education Department (Rs. in 10 millions).

### *Role of centre and states in financing education*

India is one of the largest and the most diverse democracy with a federal form of government. The fiscal arrangements in India have evolved in a quasi-federal system to meet the requirements of centralized planning in a mixed framework. During the pre-reform phase, Rao and Chellaiah (1991) justify the inter-governmental transfers on grounds such as: (i) adoption of planning as a techniques of development and the formulation of five-year plans by the Planning Commission, which would cover both central and state development activities; (ii) the institution of large central grants earmarked for specific schemes; and (iii) the political accident of the same party being in power at the centre and in states. With economic reforms, liberalization and globalization have necessitated greater fiscal decentralization. In the political frontage too, India is moving away from an era of cooperative federalism towards competitive federalism, due to multiparty polity, and predominance of regional parties at the state level, and coalition governments at the centre. Such shifts in economic and political arena, however, have led to a trend towards greater decentralization. It is argued that existence of such competition brings in the importance of transaction cost of coordinating policies and their implementation (a) vertically between different levels of government and (b) horizontally between different units within each of the levels (Rao and Sen 2011).

Nonetheless, intergovernmental transfers assume importance in the efficient and equitable provision of public services such as education and health. Besides equity and justice, from the perspective of human capital theory, cost and benefit pertaining to investment in education have important social implications. The social cost of education therefore includes the subsidy provided by the government as this reflects the resources dedicated to the provision of education on behalf of the society and the cost incurred by the individuals. Similarly benefits from education accrue not only to individual but also to society as a whole (McMahon 2004). These externalities constitute a powerful justification for public subsidies. And spillover benefits of education are felt beyond the boundaries of the states in a federal nation, indeed, beyond nations. In the absence of public support, social investment in education would be suboptimal.

The case for intergovernmental transfers is emphasized further on the basis that own resources of the state governments are not adequate to finance education. Since economic liberalization, the States were expected to perform functions on a scale larger than before, but their access to tax powers and borrowing remained limited. For instance in 2004–05, the states on average raised about 39 per cent of combined government revenues, but incurred about 66 per cent of expenditures. Transfers from the centre, including tax-sharing, grants and loans made up most of the difference, with states also borrowing moderately from other sources. To counter the possible ill effects on fiscal discipline, conditionality or fiscal discipline was sought to be imposed on state governments by tying debt relief to enactment of fiscal responsibility laws. The Fiscal Responsibility and Budget Management–induced fiscal discipline has constrained the fiscal space to the states reducing their options (Jha *et al.* 2008). The role of the centre has been further justified on the ground that there are regional imbalances in educational development, and states themselves constrained by their own inadequate financial resources cannot reduce those disparities.

### *Trends in centre and state allocations in elementary education*

In India, education particularly elementary education is financed by the 'state' (central and state governments). State governments owe the major responsibility of financing elementary education. Almost 90 per cent of total expenditure on elementary education was met out by states during 1990s. Expenditure on elementary education by the centre under District Primary Education Project and SSA steadily increased since 1994–95. However, the share of centre has increased to a double digit share of 11 per cent in 2001–02. Since then the centre's share steadily increased to 22.67 per cent in 2010–11 (Figure 1.1).

Starting from 2001 to 2002, there has been a paradigm shift in financing elementary education across states. Since then the centre's share steadily increased, for instance it rose to its peak 27.8 per cent during 2006–07, though fluctuated later on. Further, the central government's significant

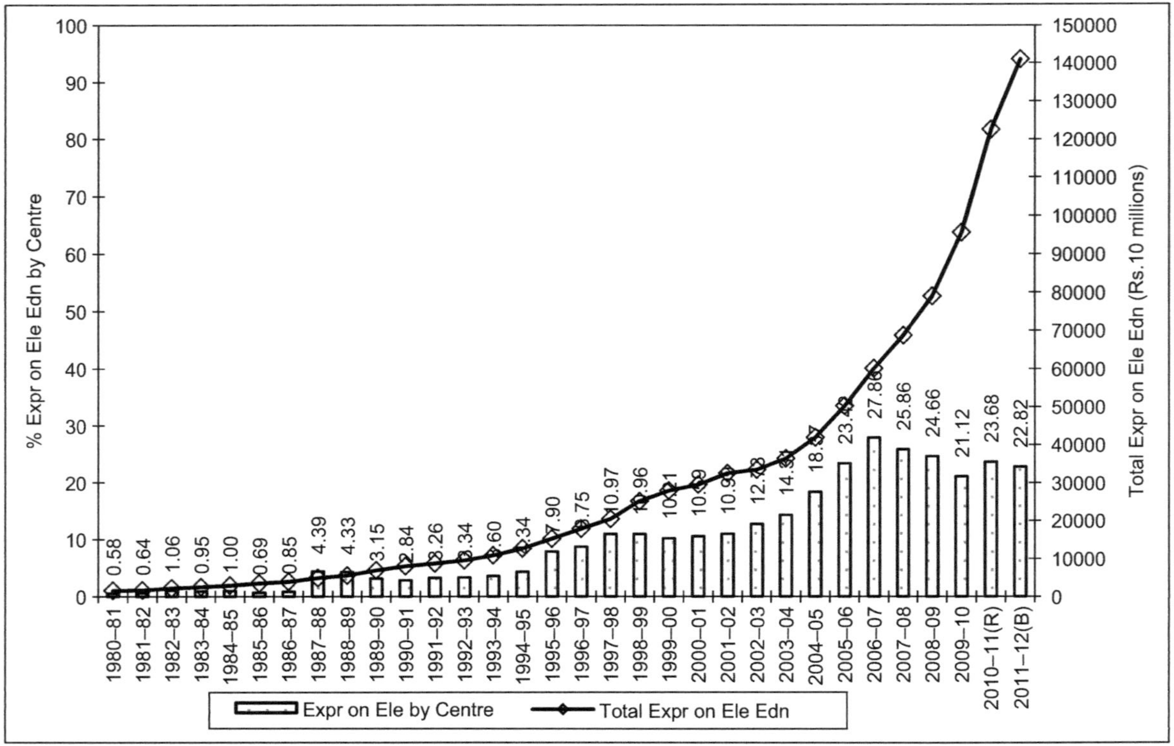


*Figure 1.1* Role of centre and states in financing elementary education in India

*Source:* Analysis of Budgeted Expenditure on Education, MHRD, various issues.

*Note:* Total (centre and states) expenditure on elementary education (Rs. in 10 millions).

role in financing elementary education is reflected in its increasing allocation towards elementary education (secondary y-axis in Figure 1.1). The increase was phenomenal from Rs. 1537.14 crores in 1980–81 to Rs. 140,900.96 crores by 2011–12 with an annual growth rate of 14 per cent. However, the overwhelming part of the cost of providing education, salaries of teachers remained by and large the responsibility of state governments.

Much of central assistance is in the form of non-plan assistance – grants to states determined by the Planning Commission to implement the CSS, like SSA. Hence the allocation of grants from Planning Commission for SSA is routed through MHRD, in principle plan account, to State Implementing Societies (SIS) bypassing the state treasury. It transformed the way in which elementary education was financed during the pre-DPEP period. Role of the centre in financing elementary education since 1980s has been increasing tremendously in the plan expenditures (Table 1.1). The main arguments for creating these parallel structures are to expedite the fund flow from centre to states. Despite, the delay in fund transfer persists under SSA.

Every decade from the 1980s to 2000s witnessed a 20 per cent point jump in central shares. By late 1990s, the central share contributed more than 50 per cent of total expenditures. Such shift is due to the number of CSS in elementary education. Besides SSA, MDM, NPGEL and KGBV are the major contributing schemes. During the later part of 1990s, the central share has been around 46 per cent of elementary expenditures in plan account among states. This has been improvised to almost 68 per cent by 2005–06 resulting in a correspondingly lesser share by states (Table 1.3).

*Table 1.3* Share of central and state governments in plan expenditures on elementary education

| | *Centre* | *States* | *Total (Rs. in crores)* |
|---|---|---|---|
| 1980–81 | 5.3 | 94.7 | 90.96 |
| 1985–86 | 8.6 | 91.4 | 266.67 |
| ***1980s average*** | **21.5** | **78.5** | **371.72** |
| 1990–91 | 28.0 | 72.0 | 803.90 |
| 1995–96 | 43.9 | 56.1 | 2,736.87 |
| ***1990s average*** | **46.7** | **53.3** | **2,647.29** |
| 2000–01 | 55.7 | 44.3 | 5,599.29 |
| 2005–06 | 68.7 | 31.3 | 17,101.32 |
| 2010–11(RE) | 61.7 | 38.3 | 46,998.45 |
| ***2000s average*** | **65.6** | **34.4** | **19,233.59** |

*Source:* Analysis of Budgeted Expenditure on Education, MHRD, various issues.

In recent times, central government's (MHRD) role and financing mechanism of education has been increasingly in the mode of CSS, namely SSA, mid-day meals (MDM), etc. In total central government expenditures, two flagship programmes SSA and MDM occupy a major share. An upward trend in shares of SSA has picked up from 2003 to 2004 onwards. SSA combined with MDM occupied more than 90 per cent of total central expenditures on elementary education from 2005–06 till 2011–12 (Table 1.4). During early 2000s, schemes such as DPEP, Operation Blackboard and non-formal education occupied the major share of central government expenditure on elementary education, besides few other schemes.

During 2003–04 and 2004–05, a number of state-specific CSS such as *Shiksha Karmi* Project in Rajasthan, *Lok Jumbish*/Rajasthan and NCTE Bihar Education Project occupy the major share besides the nationwide *Kasturba Gandhi Swatantra Vidyalaya* scheme, which later was included as part of SSA. The *Kasturba Gandhi Balika Vidyalaya* and Support to One year Pre-Primary in government local body were few other schemes besides SSA and MDM during 2005–06 and 2006–07. Since 2007–08, other schemes include Teachers Training (Strengthening of Teachers Training Institutions), National Bal Bhawan Society, *Mahila Samakhya*, DPEP, Scheme for providing Quality Education in Madrasas and

*Table 1.4* Distribution of central governmental expenditures on elementary education

| | *SSA* | *MDM* | *Other schemes*# | *Total expenditures** |
|---|---|---|---|---|
| 2001–02 | 14.00 | 28.9 | 57.13 | 3,569 |
| 2002–03 | 36.81 | 25.8 | 37.37 | 4,258 |
| 2003–04 | 52.50 | 26.4 | 21.06 | 5,201 |
| 2004–05 | 66.57 | 20.7 | 12.78 | 7,692 |
| 2005–06 | 64.13 | 27.1 | 8.78 | 11,751 |
| 2006–07 | 65.04 | 31.3 | 3.71 | 16,735 |
| 2007–08 | 64.59 | 32.8 | 2.59 | 17,770 |
| 2008–09 | 64.88 | 33.5 | 1.60 | 19,482 |
| 2009–10 | 63.53 | 34.3 | 2.14 | 20,188 |
| 2010–11(RE) | 65.49 | 32.5 | 1.97 | 29,011 |
| 2011–12(BE) | 65.32 | 32.3 | 2.40 | 32,150 |

*Source:* Analysis of Budgeted Expenditure on Education, MHRD, various issues.

*Note:* * Rs. in crores; #Other schemes include many schemes; varied during the last 10 years.

Infrastructure Development in Minority Institution. Though a number of central schemes keep evolving, they were converged into two major schemes, SSA and MDM, which sustained. This is one of the achievements of SSA which could encompass various schemes and innovations though encountering various planning and implementation shortfalls. This highlights the political commitment rather political incentive over these schemes.

## Source of finances for SSA

Analysis on sources and uses of funds under SSA offer another perspective of financing elementary education. At inception, SSA was funded from gross budgetary support along with matching shares from states like any CSS. Since 2004–05, education cess is levied at the rate of 2 per cent surcharge on the total payable taxes. It is levied on all major central direct and indirect taxes, namely income tax, corporation tax, excise and customs duties and service tax to help finance the government's commitment to UEE. Elementary Education Fund, known as *Prarambhik Shiksha Kosh (PSK)*, was established as a dedicated non-lapsable fund to receive the proceeds of cess. The collection under PSK is to be spent exclusively on SSA and MDM. It was increased by 1 per cent to cover secondary and higher education, called secondary and higher education cess since 2007–08.

Now the moot question is: what is the additionality of PSK over and above gross budgetary support in funding these two schemes? The allocations from the two sources that of gross budgetary support and PSK over a period of 2006–07 to 2013–14 indicate PSK being more a substitute rather than a complementary. The share of gross budgetary support in funding SSA has been on the decline from 42.5 per cent during 2006–07 to 32.9 per cent by 2013–14. Almost a similar trend can be found in the case of MDM (see Table 1.5).

Alternatively, the issue of substitute or complement can be examined by estimating the expenditure and revenue gap of funding these two programmes. Expenditure gap is the excess of total expenditures over expenditure on SSA and MDM financed from PSK. Education cess is rapidly outstripping the budget allocations for SSA and MDM. Total allocation under both schemes indicate an increasing share of funds from PSK (implicitly) from 58.5 per cent during 2006–07 to 67.1 per cent by 2013–14. Revenue gap is excess of expenditures over revenues collected under education cess (see Table 1.6).

Shifting the burden to education cess has fallen from 45 per cent of GBS in 2006–07 to 15 per cent by 2013–14. Although overall allocations increased,

*Table 1.5* Sources of financing of SSA and MDM: gross budgetary support (GBS) versus *Prarambhik Shiksha Kosh* (PSK)

| | *SSA* | | | *MDM* | | |
|---|---|---|---|---|---|---|
| | *GBS* | *PSK* | *Total* | *GBS* | *PSK* | *Total* |
| 2006–07 (R) | 42.5 | 57.5 | 14,959 | 39.4 | 60.6 | 4,813 |
| 2007–08 (R) | 30.8 | 69.2 | 18,024 | 53.2 | 46.8 | 6,004 |
| 2008–09 (R) | 39.0 | 61.0 | 19,140 | 32.6 | 67.4 | 7,200 |
| 2009–10 (R) | 29.5 | 70.5 | 21,064 | 38.5 | 61.5 | 9,131 |
| 2010–11 | 52.0 | 48.0 | 28,496 | 28.1 | 71.9 | 8,859 |
| 2011–12 | 43.2 | 56.8 | 30,601 | 36.8 | 63.2 | 9,759 |
| 2012–13 (R) | 34.3 | 65.7 | 31,571 | 34.9 | 65.1 | 10,241 |
| 2013–14 (B) | 32.9 | 67.1 | 36,425 | 32.9 | 67.1 | 11,893 |

*Source:* Expenditure Budget, Union Budget, various years, available at http://indiabudget.nic.in.

*Note:* Total Rs. in crores; R – revised estimates[3]; B – budget estimates.

*Table 1.6* Gross budgetary support from total expenditures and revenues under education cess on SSA and MDM in India (Rs. in crores)

| | *Total expr. on SSA and MDM* | *Expr. on SSA and MDM financed from PSK* | *Expenditures gap (%)* | *Revenue under education cess* | *Revenue gap (%)* |
|---|---|---|---|---|---|
| 2004–05 (R) | 6,261 | 0 | – | 5,010 | 20.0 |
| 2005–06 (R) | 10,177 | 0 | – | 7,032 | 30.9 |
| 2006–07 (R) | 14,959 | 8,746 | 58.5 | 8,186 | 45.3 |
| 2007–08 (R) | 18,024 | 11,128 | 61.7 | 12,998 | 27.9 |
| 2008–09 (R) | 19,140 | 12,134 | 63.4 | 14,219 | 25.7 |
| 2009–10 (R) | 21,064 | 14,029 | 66.6 | 16,813 | 20.2 |
| 2010–11 | 28,496 | 15,805 | 55.5 | 21,335 | 25.1 |
| 2011–12 | 30,601 | 18,006 | 58.8 | 23,070 | 24.6 |
| 2012–13 (R) | 31,571 | 20,667 | 65.5 | 26,151 | 17.2 |
| 2013–14 (B) | 36,425 | 24,428 | 67.1 | 30,841 | 15.3 |

*Source:* Union Budget, Expenditure and Revenue Budgets, various years, available at http://indiabudget.nic.in.

*Note:* R – revised estimates; B – budget estimates.

*Table 1.7* External aid to elementary education (Rs. in 10 millions)

| | *External aid** | *Total expenditure on elementary education#* | *% of external aid in total expr. on elementary education* |
|---|---|---|---|
| 2000–01 | 948.0 | 29,450 | 3.22 |
| 2001–02 | 1,212.3 | 32,494 | 3.73 |
| 2002–03 | 1,383.1 | 33,474 | 4.13 |
| 2003–04 | 939.6 | 36,366 | 2.58 |
| 2004–05 | 683.5 | 41,874 | 1.63 |
| 2005–06 | 1,996.5 | 50,182 | 3.98 |
| 2006–07 | 1,647.0 | 60,063 | 2.74 |
| 2007–08 | 1,677.6 | 68,710 | 2.44 |
| 2008–09 | 1,584.0 | 79,001 | 2.01 |
| 2009–10 | 1,476.9 | 95,573 | 1.55 |
| 2010–11 | 1,064.4 | 122,504 | 0.87 |
| 2011–12 | 1,935.0 | 140,901 | 1.37 |

*Source:* *Colclough and De (2013); #includes centre, states and UTs Analysis of Budgeted Expenditure on Education.

share of GBS has been on the decline. Two per cent education cess was levied ostensibly to ensure more money flow into elementary education as promised in UPA government's common minimum programme. A moot question is: whether education cess serves as a substitute or supplement?

Besides the national resources allocated for elementary education, external aid forms a tiny share in funding SSA. The contributors are World Bank, European Commission and UK Department for International Development (DFID) since 2004.[4] The share of external aid in total expenditure on elementary education ranged between 0.87 and 3.7 per cent. On an average, external aid remained around 2 per cent of SSA's total funding during 2000s (Table 1.7).

## Allocation of funds under SSA

Funds under SSA is allocated on the basis of the gap in physical infrastructure and human resources to meet benchmarks of service delivery such as distance criterion, ratio of pupils to teachers and number of students per classroom. These can be broadly grouped into four critical inputs. Development of physical facilities in terms of civil works are earmarked for constructing either new schools or additional classrooms in order to ensure the distance criterion of 1.5 kilometre radius in primary and 3 kilometres in upper primary schools and to some extent indirectly address to adhere to the pupil teacher ratio of 1:40. Besides, it also caters to fill the existing gap in the physical provision of drinking water, toilets, boundary walls, etc.

The next category of expenditures is under the maintenance of established physical resources over the decades, such as school grants, maintenance and repairing, etc. Third category of quality-related interventions include a number of expenditure heads earmarked for improving the teaching learning process in schools, namely teacher grants, Block Resource Centre (BRC), Cluster Resource Centre (CRC), teacher training, innovations, community training, research and evaluation. The rest of the expenditure heads are for ensuring equity in the provision of incentives such as free text books to socially deprived (SC/ST) students, Integration of Education of the disadvantaged children, girls' education under NPGEL and KGBV. The allocation, approval and release of funds are based as per norms and guidelines laid down by the MHRD (2004, 2009). These various expenditure heads are to cater to the four primary goals of SSA – covering all children in the age group 6–14 by 2010, bridging the social and gender gap in enrolment, universal retention by 2010 and improve the quality of education. These critical inputs fall under 21 expenditure heads and are tied grants.

## Fund flow channel under SSA

The funds under SSA get allocated via the new channels created under DPEP, known as State Implementing Societies (SIS). The same societies continue to get funds transferred from both centre and states under SSA. In a three-tier fiscal federal structure, fund flow under SSA (which is almost the same as DPEP) is decentralized up to the school level. The GOI would release funds directly to SIS in two instalments in a year, once in April and another in September. The funds thus released will be credited to the bank account of the SIS. The second instalment shall be released based on the progress in expenditure and the quality of implementation. Further instalments would be released to the society only after the state government has transferred its matching funds to the society and expenditure of at least 50 per cent of the funds transferred (centre and states) has been incurred. This is to ensure that states fully utilize the allocation for the purpose of elementary education. The utilization certificates, however, will only need to be submitted one year after the release of an instalment and further release is stalled if utilization certificates are not submitted as per the schedule.

(i) GOI to SIS: The funds released by GOI will be credited to the joint signatory bank account established by SIS in any nationalized or scheduled bank. The state society should open a separate savings joint signatory bank account for operation of funds of NPGEL. Since the amounts are deposited into the accounts of SIS, unspent balances at the end of the financial year need not be refunded to GOI and shall be carried forward for utilization in the subsequent year with proper approval. In principle, any state or district fully expending the advance through implementation of a high order could receive adequate second advance commensurate with projected activities.

(ii) State government to SIS: The financial norms of the programme envisage that the participating state contributes its agreed ratio of the programme cost within 30 days of the central contribution. It would, therefore, be necessary to make suitable provision in the state budget to facilitate the release of its share of programme cost to the SIS. The release of funds by the state government to the society would also be deposited in the same joint signatory bank account of the society in which the funds of GOI are deposited under SSA and NEPGEL. Any unspent balance from out of the state government share of funds shall be carried forward by the society for utilization in the next financial year with the approval of the state government.

(iii) SIS to districts, block, village, school: Each entity would open joint signatory bank account in any nationalized or scheduled bank at the district level and any nationalized or scheduled bank or post office at the block and village level. SIS will release funds to districts within 15 days of its receipt from GOI and state government. All funds to be used for up-gradation/maintenance/repair of school and teaching learning material/equipment and local management must be transferred to VEC/School Management Committees/gram panchayat/ or any other village/school level arrangement for decentralization adopted by the state. Districts would advance funds on the basis of the annual work plans as approved by the Project Approval Board (PAB) at the national level within 15 days of receipt from the state society. Similar to fund transfer from centre to states, fund transfer from SIS to district and sub-district would be advanced in two instalments annually, the first instalment at the beginning of the financial year and the second instalment after ensuring that the first instalment has been satisfactorily utilized. The release of the second instalment is subject to expenditure statement being rendered to the extent of at least 50 per cent of the funds be advanced to districts through banking channel to district level bank account and to block and village level SSA institutions also by banking channel.

In order to reduce the time lapse, new institutional arrangements bypass the state treasury, so that, the fund could directly flow to the SIS and also bypass the sub-district government administration and seek to involve the local community. It is easier to create new structures and institutions than reform and improve existing ones. But the parallel structures create risk unless the regular educational administration absorbs the main features of the programme in the long run. That is what is being realized while implementing the RTE now. This structure in addition to creation of parallel structures, especially in DPEP states and districts, led to creation and simultaneous operation of two societies – one for implementing district primary education and another for district upper primary education. But the evidence from this collection of papers confirm the problems of delays in disbursal, lack of flexibility to respond to local situations, maximum disbursal in last quarter, etc., which have crept into this fund flow mechanism as well. Realizing this the current proposal is channelling around 80 per cent of the allocation under CSS through state budget.

Two societies for implementing the same programme SSA at district level would create chaos rather than facilitate the implementing activities. DPEP, operational in 270 districts in 18 states in all three phases, had a potential of creating commotion. For instance in West Bengal, there are a number of institutions like the West Bengal Board of Primary Education, and the West Bengal Board of Secondary Education which covers upper primary level. Both boards have an SSA cell which gives direction and support to the programme in addition to State Council of Educational Research and Training and state implementing society. There is a need to ensure that all pull in the same direction to work coherently (MHRD 2005).

### *Fund allocation under SSA*

As discussed, funds for SSA flow from the Planning Commission to MHRD. MHRD then allocates the resources (central shares) to the state implementing societies. MHRD releases funds based upon the approved annual plans of the states and districts. The releases are to be in two instalments. The first release is to be made soon after the approval of annual plan. The matching share under SSA between centre and states was 85:15 during ninth five-year plan (1997–2002), which was the same in DPEP. However, during the 10th five-year plan (2002–07), the matching share was changed to 75:25. Considering a 75:25 sharing arrangement between the central and state governments, the first instalment is half of centre's share (i.e. 37.5 per cent). An equal share of 50:50 is followed during 11th plan (p. 5–6, GoI, undated). Since many states are in no position to sustain SSA at this ratio, hence changed ratios are 65:35 since 2007–08 and continue in 12th plan.

Approved outlay by MHRD under SSA has been increasing exponentially over a decade (column 1 of Table 1.8). As states have gained considerable experience in the preparation of district plans, almost all districts are involved in the preparation of DEEP, resulting in higher amount of approved outlay in subsequent years. Even though centre's allocations under SSA increase over time, it boosted since 2004–05 with revenues flowing from education cess earmarked for SSA via PSK. But the Union Budget has provided Rs. 10,671 crores to SSA during 2007–08, which is a plunge in the allocation of Rs. 329 crores even in nominal prices (column 2 of Table 1.8). Further, during the years 2008–09 and 2009–10 the GoI's allocation remained the same and showed marginal improvement in 2010–11 budget. Actual funds released by MHRD are in consonance with the GoI's allocations (columns 2 and 3, Table 1.8).[5]

*Table 1.8* Share of GoI's budgetary allocation to MHRD and funds released by MHRD to state implementing societies under SSA (Rs. in crores)

| | *Approved outlay by MHRD under SSA* | *GoI's allocation** | *Funds released by MHRD under SSA* | *Funds released as % of approved outlay* |
|---|---|---|---|---|
| 2000–01 | – | 325 | – | – |
| 2001–02 | 1,138 | 500 | 500 | 43.94 |
| 2002–03 | 3,080 | 1,567 | 1,569 | 50.93 |
| 2003–04 | 8,335 | 2,732 | 2,733 | 32.79 |
| 2004–05 | 11,019 | 4,754# | 11,015 | 99.97 |
| 2005–06 | 12,931 | 7,156 | 8,741 | 67.60 |
| 2006–07 | 20,085 | 10,041 | 13,318 | 66.31 |
| 2007–08 | 20,060 | 10,671 | 15,039 | 74.97 |
| 2008–09 | 24,609 | 13,100 | 12,612 | 51.25 |
| 2009–10 | 27,588 | 12,825 | 12,482 | 45.24 |
| 2010–11 | 45,705 | 19,000 | 19,331 | 42.30 |
| 2011–12 | 61,839 | 21,000 | 34,321 | 55.50 |
| 2012–13 | 69,982 | 25,555 | 48,081 | 68.70 |
| 2013–14 | 47,753 | 27,258 | 32,431 | 67.91 |

*Source:* Analysis of Budgeted Expenditure on Education, various issues; www.education.nic downloaded as on 17.3.06; 13.3.10; MHRD (2005); MHRD (2006); Ed Cil – TSG, various JRM reports.

*Note:* * includes external assistance; #Rs. 3,075 million enhanced to Rs. 4,754 million during 2004–05.

So, the approved outlay by MHRD may be as per SSA norms, but actual fund release is determined by the availability of financial resources in a year, that are distributed to states. In this process of fund flow from the GoI to MHRD, approved outlay by MHRD based on appraisal of District Elementary Education Plans has become *notional* (Geetha Rani 2007). *The design of the programme itself leads to such inconsistency between planning and financing of resources under SSA, let alone implementation.* It is important to note that in any of the previous 12 years, except during 2004–05, never there was adequate fund available from the centre to MHRD for funding approved outlays.

SSA is based on the premise that financing of elementary education interventions has to be sustainable. This calls for a long-term perspective on financial partnership between the central and state governments. It clearly emerges from the analyses that public expenditure for UEE has been inadequate. It is to be noted that the approved outlay of the districts and states by MHRD is arrived at following the norms of SSA which are the most conservative financial requirements. Given the inadequacies in the system and large number of out-of-school children, the Central Advisory Board on Education (CABE 2005) suggested that the allocation to elementary education needs to be doubled as a percentage of national income (CABE 2005). Estimates by NUEPA (2009) to implement the RTE works out to be Rs. 171,778 crores, which is about three times higher than current GOI allocations. Adequacy of resources is to be adhered under SSA. Though adequate financing may not solve all problems of UEE, it could have certainly addressed at least the quantitative pressures. Indeed, this long overdue persists under SSA.

Before we conclude, the principles of adequacy and internal efficiency of expenditures is examined. Adequacy is examined in terms of whether expenditures on elementary education kept pace with increase in enrolment. Per-student expenditures on elementary education at current prices increased from Rs. 375 during 1980s to Rs. 3,619 during 2000s (Table 1.9).

It exhibited a phenomenal growth of about 11.8 per cent on an average annually during 1980–81 to 2010–11. But, the same in constant (2004–05) prices grew only by 4 per cent. It is not only per-student budgeted expenditures on elementary education grew at 4 per cent but also per capita net national product at 2004–05 prices also grew at the same rate. Interestingly, proportion of per-student expenditure on elementary education in per capita net national product remained around 11.94 per cent during 1980s; increased to 12.09 per cent during 1990s and declined to 11.80 per cent during 2000s. Though it appears that expenditure per student improved phenomenally but not so if looked at in terms of either in constant prices or as a proportion of per capita income.

*Table 1.9* Per-student government expenditures on elementary education in India

| | *Per-student govt. expenditures* | | *Per capita net national income* | *% of per-student govt. expenditures in per capita net national income* | *GER upper primary* | *Dropout at elementary* |
|---|---|---|---|---|---|---|
| | *current prices* | *2004–05 prices* | | | | |
| 1980–81 | 195 | 1,135 | 1,852 | 10.53 | 40.0 | 72.7 |
| 1985–86 | 355 | 1,368 | 3,128 | 11.34 | 52.0 | |
| ***1980s average*** | **375** | **1,420** | **3,138** | **11.94** | – | – |
| 1990–91 | 722 | 1,833 | 5,621 | 12.85 | 60.1 | 60.9 |
| 1995–96 | 1,197 | 1,864 | 10,695 | 11.20 | 67.6 | 58.8 |
| ***1990s average*** | **1,260** | **1,974** | **10,429** | **12.09** | – | – |
| 2000–01 | 2,250 | 2,650 | 17,295 | 13.01 | 58.6 | 53.7 |
| 2005–06 | 3,199 | 3,069 | 27,131 | 11.79 | 71.0 | 48.8 |
| 2010–11(RE) | 6,207 | 4,217 | 54,151 | 11.46 | 85.5 | 40.6 |
| ***2000s average*** | **3,660** | **3,212** | **30,601** | **11.96** | – | – |
| Growth rates | 11.86 | 4.21 | 11.66 | – | – | – |

*Source*: Analysis of Budgeted Expenditure on Education, MHRD, various issues; Selected Educational Statistics, Central Statistical Organization.

Transfers in themselves are neither good nor bad; what matters from a policy perspective are their effects on the outcomes of interest such as allocative efficiency, distributional equity and macroeconomic stability (Shah 1991). In the present context in the case of non-economic well-being indictors – in elementary education – two indicators namely input level indicator of enrolment ratio in upper primary education and the process level indictor of cumulative dropouts at elementary level indicate a gloomy picture that the gross enrolment ratio in upper primary education improved from 40 to 85 per cent over three decades. Simultaneously, the children dropped out-of-school system improved from 72 to 40 per cent during the same period. The point to be noted that though we claim that enrolment ratio has reached almost universal but the dropout rates are also equally very high. It is like inflation robbing away income growth.

The major challenge the country faces today is on the outcomes of elementary education or improving the quality of public expenditure on education. The virtues of demographic dividend resulting in more working age people will mean more workers, especially in the productive age groups, more incomes, more savings, more capital per worker and more growth. All this goes well as long as this implicit assumption that the more working age people are with minimum satisfactory level of skills. Quality provision of school education is critical whether the country wants to reap the demographic dividend or going to face a demographic disaster depends on to what extent and to what proportion of these young children move up to secondary levels of education and have acquired certain minimum level of skills, so that the graduates of secondary education would be '*trainable*' in the labour market. Lewin and Caillods (2001) stress that an indirect demand for secondary education is generated due to the increasing demand for highly skilled labour force in the global economy.

In the knowledge-driven global economy, demand for graduates of secondary education is high as secondary graduates as labour force are trainable for the requirements of the globalized market. It is because effective secondary schooling introduces them to formal reasoning, abstract problem solving skills and critical thinking as well as its occupationally relevant content. Secondary education promotes the development of a skilled and knowledgeable citizenry with access not only to national but also to global economy. On the contrary, the publicly provided services in school education are of poor quality. As discussed in this volume, the increase in education investments under SSA has not resulted in satisfactory learning levels of children. Major reason being the dismal quality of public schooling as children and parents not interested in studies and direct and indirect cost of education as indicated in many household surveys.

### *An overview of the chapters*

The chapters cover a diversity of issues in financing elementary education in India. Together, the volume provides a rich collection of varied experience across states, districts and schools in the financing and implementing of one of the major development programmes in recent decades. As we discuss the issues, some common points of concern from the planning, allocation and implementation of the programme come into sharp relief. Two distinct trends are apparent in education spending. First, an increasing proportion of the resources is coming from central government, making states more reliant on centre. The allocation to education in general and elementary education in particular increased in absolute terms but as percentage of total budget and GSDP was on a decline. However, the funding to elementary education increased under plan accounts due to SSA–RTE, but crippled with issues of adequacy of funding, quality of spending, low absorption, etc. These resource constraints add to institutional bottlenecks in planning, preparing budget outlays, bureaucratic procedures and delays of approval, allocation and eventual release of money. It is evidenced that both allocation and fund flow pattern under SSA cripples with issues such as delay in receiving the funds from centre and states which abstain the whole process of implementation.

Starting with DPEP, SSA further continued to set up its own structures for transfer of funds to states primarily to avoid the delays. But evidence from various papers suggests that despite this, the usual problems of government funding (delays in disbursal, lack of flexibility to respond to local situations, maximum disbursal in last quarter, etc.) have crept into this as well. This raises the question on the effectiveness of these new fund flow channel under SSA.

The collection of papers is diverse in terms of coverage of states. They include educationally and economically backward states – Bihar, Chhattisgarh, Orissa, Rajasthan, Uttar Pradesh and West Bengal; economically prosperous agricultural state Punjab and a similar economically prosperous but an industrial state Maharashtra; both economically and educationally growing Andhra Pradesh and Uttarakhand; and educationally advanced states Himachal Pradesh and Kerala. Not only the volume covers diverse states but also varying issues and problems. The first two chapters provide the central theme and underlying assumptions of the book. Jha and Geetha Rani argue that the goals of the SSA and RTE will be meaningfully translated if funds are available and lead to better learning outcomes. From this follow the questions around what the resource constraints are and what are the institutional challenges in meeting this. Jha, Geetha Rani, Sikdar and Parvati locate this in another way, 'in our judgment key to good quality universal education is adequate public provisioning'.

This resource-based argument is stressed by Reddy and Reddy in Andhra Pradesh. That one of the major reasons for not matching plans approved and expenditure incurred is non-release of matching grant by the state to the SIS. In turn SIS is not releasing to the districts and then district to the schools. They also bring to light the high levels of misappropriation of funds under SSA. Besides, under-utilization of SSA funds across states has drawn considerable amount of attention in recent years. Brar and Singh highlight the problem of under-utilization becoming more serious in the situation of under-allocation on one side and also under-release of the committed funds. In case of some components the funds utilized were either very low or nil. Further, the best results of any project could be realized only in the situation of releasing the budgeted funds on all the components and heads of spending in Punjab. Under-expenditure on any one or more head of spending adversely affects the efficiency and performance of other sub-programmes as they are interrelated. Brar and Singh highlight the participation issues such as declining gross enrolment of girls, and enrolment shifting away from government to private schools in Punjab, which highlight inequality in participation and quality learning. They argue that no discernible pattern of spending emerge either across state, districts or schools or over more than 10 years during the implementation of the programme. That flow of funds within a district shows considerable yearly variations that the block which occupied the first rank during one year slipped to last rank in the subsequent year.

Jha and Parvati compare two districts – one in Uttar Pradesh and one in Chhattisgarh and point to various aspects of poor implementation including inflexibility. The highest proportion of expenditure was made on civil works followed by teacher's salaries. These two together consume about three-fourth of the total expenditure and the rest was on other items. Inter-component variations in the absorptive captivity brought out that in majority of the cases quality-related allocations particularly teacher training, filling up of vacancies by qualified trained Teachers and Master Trainers in BRCs/CRCs were to a large extent unspent besides equity and access-related interventions. This holds good at the national level, across states and in sample districts. They attempt to decipher out the constraints for full utilization of funds under SSA.

Debi and Mishra find low utilization and lack of funds being a barrier in Odisha. The major reason being allocation of funds is planned as per specified norm while expenditure is made as per the need. This mismatch results in bulk of unspent money. They also bring out that allocation of funds for elementary education across geographical units does not really consider their needs. For instance some developed districts are able to get more SSA funds and backward districts utilize more. Pramanik shares such similar concerns at Bankura in West Bengal, and finds inadequate attention given to Muslims. She argues that Bankura, a backward district with high SC population, faces lack of infrastructure and untimely receipt of funds.

Kapur and Mukherjee explicate the problems in having national norms with an approach of *one size fits for all* in such a vast and diverse country do not seem to work and they express the need to respond to diverse needs using the field data from Nalanda, Bihar. They question the norm of SSA that how can one justify same size of school grants for all schools without considering the size of enrolment. Such uniformity in norms induce disparity unless provided with a level-playing field. There are ample evidences which the book illustrates. For instance, even in following simple logistics, transfer of funds shifted over from issuing cheques to e-transfers to reduce the time involved in the transfer. Reddy and Reddy describe the situation in Andhra Pradesh of how e-transfer is processed via one designated bank without considering local specific spread of banks.

Mohanty and Acharya show a better Gender Parity Index (GPI) in hilly areas even though infrastructure deficits are higher in Uttarakhand. They highlight the glaring gaps in provision and distributional aspects of RTE that the state has lagged behind the nation in progressing towards RTE in terms of building infrastructure support for the efforts as well as the minimum norms stipulated under RTE. They also bring out the implementation gap across regions, plain versus hilly districts, wherein the imbalances have been reported to be widened during the years under RTE.

In terms of impact of SSA–RTE spending outcomes seems to be mixed. There is some progress in terms of increase in number of schools, infrastructure, enrolment and enrolment ratios across states. However, there seems to be positive relationship between money spent on per student and achievement test in language and numeracy across districts over the SSA period. On the contrary, no relationship was found between absorptive rates under SSA and achievement results across districts in few papers. However, quality of education and achievement tests portray one of the serious concerns. As the government institutional provision of elementary education is of unsatisfactory quality, the private sector provision of basic education has been on the rise across states. Expanding private sector is a serious cause for concern which further widens the educational inequality not only between the haves and have-nots but also across gender as many household surveys find that at the intra-household allocation, fee-paying private schools are preferred for boys than girls when resources are limited at the family level. Adding to this, widespread private tuition across both public and private schools indicates both poor quality on the one hand and the aspirations of the growing young India on the other.

Declining birth rate coupled with enrolment trend in government schools leading to closure of schools is similar in Kerala and Himachal Pradesh. This brings out an important lesson for other states in similar demographic transition to plan for their expansion in a more strategic manner. Despite this, in many states small schools are found to be economically unviable. Geetha Rani and Shukla argue that this is particularly true if new schools are opened in habitations having less population and few school-going children. Such newly opened schools particularly after 1995 have less number of children than schools opened before. They point out that in Himachal, the expenditure per child is seen as exceeding Rs. 20,000 per year (against a national average of Rs. 9766), and expenditure has been continuously increasing, and yet enrolment has been falling. Not only are these schools viable financially but also inaccessible for real learning and post-basic level of education. These schools are often single-teacher schools officially, but implying partially functioning schools in reality. As this single teacher would be involved in many of the administrative activities or absent, the schools during such circumstances are as good as non-functioning schools.

As Govinda (2011) argues that it is important to find out whether the school-specific grants have helped in improving the functioning of schools. Kapur and Mukherjee found that delay in the fund flow in the third and/or fourth quarter of the financial year lead to less than optimal utilization of such school grants in Bihar. Uniform norms, similar to that of a tied grant, do not facilitate the utilization of the respective grants. Rather if it is an untied grant would serve the requirement on the ground enduring *de facto* expenditure powers to school authorities. It is to be noted that this is similar to that of the system being followed in UK's formula-based funding since 1990. The essence of the Local Management of Schools (LMS) is that the money, once received within the school, can be deployed according to the priorities of the school as judged by the head teacher and the governing body. The only restriction is that capital funding can normally be used for capital expenditure (Levacic and Downes 2004). It is important to note that the mainstream funding is not earmarked or tied in UK unlike in the case of SSA–RTE allocation in India, which provides autonomy to the head teacher to decide on which item to spend depending on the priority and the need of that specific school. Hence, they argue that schools will be able to provide inputs in a more cost-effective manner if funds and decision-making authority were to be actually devolved to them. This leads to inefficiency in targeting of inputs while funds are allocated as per centrally designed uniform norms in a vast country like India having more than one million primary schools.

Another major concern is the *ad hoc* manner of identifying 'out-of-school children', and the informal arrangements made to run classes under EGS and managing through para-teachers instead of regularly appointed staff. Yet another fact overlooked is that the persistent dropouts each year are adding to the number of OSCs and this truth is revealed by many NSSO surveys. This holds good across states irrespective of their educational development. Lathika and Ajit Kumar categorically bring out the way in which out-of-school children are estimated and how this intensifies educational disparity in mostly children of fishermen, agricultural labourers, workers of traditional unorganized sectors, or the people of socially deprived sections like SC/ST or Muslim community in Kerala. Though it appears that Kerala had tackled the first-generation problems, the evaluation found that the state SSA machinery could not yet categorically count the children remaining out-of-school. Similar is the concern shared by Paranjape as found in Maharashtra. She also compares fund allocation in two districts, points out hurdles in timely release, etc.

Various estimates on out-of-school children published in recent years have differed not only with respect to their results but also in terms of definitions. The concern of a very low figure reported as 'out-of-school' is disturbing and indeed detracts the attention from the need for addressing a much larger number of children who may not be really in schools. The class-wise transition and dropout rates would clearly bring out the inadequacy of the system. In reality, many schools cannot accommodate if all enrolled children continue through elementary schooling. The existing teaching arrangements and other schooling requirements would be grossly inadequate. To this extent the system is not fully geared up to meet the RTE requirements.

SSA–RTE calls for greater community participation, monitoring and supervision. In the chapter on Community Monitoring on RTE, Ahmad, Rao and Soni elucidate an initiative by *Astha Sansthan*, which is rich with grass root experience and evidence. The authors examine four aspects of community monitoring of schools as per RTE, namely the functionary (SMC, its constitution and function); infrastructure (establishment and maintenance); functioning of schools (role and contribution of SMCs and PTAs) and social audits of *Astha* in Udaipur, Rajasthan. The chapter describes the monitoring of implementation of RTE act by the community in Southern Rajasthan, a tribal dominated region in the state, most of it coming under fifth scheduled area. This chapter tries to understand the monitoring process through various activities by the community and a civil society organization *Astha* based in Udaipur. In a comparative perspective from the baseline data, the process and outcomes convey a number of improvements over the community monitoring and functioning of schools in the study area. Sustainability of these efforts without *Astha* however needs to be examined in the medium to long run for effective community monitoring on a self-sustained basis.

The political economy plays an important role as better endowed regions could secure more budget with the support of political leadership, well supported bureaucrats at the highest level of administration and other pressure groups from these state/districts. Geetha Rani elucidates how financing for universal elementary education has induced inter-state disparity, as a result of the 'accumulated initial advantage of better off states with uniform financing norms'. This results in *perverse effects* that children and schools located in backward and deprived regions who are in greater need of support and supplies are in effect actually getting the least. Such fund allocation bias favour schools operating in better locations and catering to children from comparatively better-off families. Having said this, though it is difficult to explain the differences, there is a need to look into the overall development of the regions in education and other sectors.

It is hoped that the collections of papers as a whole will make significant contribution to a wider discussion and more specifically review the norms and mechanisms through which the funds are being allocated under SSA and now harmonized SSA–RTE for not only improved absorptive capacity of resources but also for improving the participation and learning levels of poor children of India.

## Notes

1 Education was transferred to concurrent list in 1976.
2 District is an administrative unit under states.
3 Revised estimates and the actual are available for many years except for 2010–11 and 2011–12.
4 These development partners were supporters of DPEP as well DFID (2010).
5 However, in 2003–04, gap between centre's budget allocation and fund released by MHRD was Rs. 3,010 millions, which is reflected in higher fund release than budget allocation in 2004–05.

## References

ASER, 2013. Annual Survey of Education Reports, Pratham, New Delhi.

CABE, 2005. Central Advisory Board on Education: Right to Education Bill, Ministry of Human Resource Development, prepared by NUEPA, New Delhi.

Colclough, C. and Anuradha De, 2013. The Emergence and Evolution of *Sarva Shiksha Abhiyan*: A New Approach to Elementary Education Provision in India, DFID, New Delhi.

DFID, 2010. Internal Audit Department, August 2010, available at https://www.gov.uk/government/uploads/system/uploads/attachment_data/file/67666/India-SSA-Inquiry-Final-Report.pdf (accessed on 18 January 2014).

Geetha Rani, P., 2007. 'Every Child in School: The Challenges of Attaining and Financing Education for All in India' in *Education for All: Global Promises, National Challenges*, Alex Wiseman and David Baker (eds), International Perspectives on Education and Society, Elsevier, 8: 207–264.

Govinda, R., 2011. Who Goes to School? Exploring Exclusion in Indian Education (ed.), Oxford University Press, New Delhi.

Jean, Dreze and A.K. Sen, 2013. The Uncertain Glory: India and its Contradictions, Allan Lane, New Delhi.

Jha, Praveen, Subrat Das, Siba Sankar Mohanty, and Nandan Kumar Jha, 2008. Public Provisioning for Elementary Education in India, Sage, New Delhi.

Levacic, R. and P. Downes, 2004. Formula Funding of Schools, Decentralization and Corruption: A Comparative Analysis, International Institute of Educational Planning, Paris.

Lewin, K and F. Caillods, 2001. Financing Secondary Education in Developing Countries: Strategies for Sustainable Growth, UNESCO, International Institute for Educational Planning, France.

McMahon, W., 2004. 'The Social and External Benefits of Education' in *International Handbook of Economics of Education*, Johnes and Johnes (eds), Edward Elgar Publishing, UK.

MHRD, 2004. *Sarva Shiksha Abhiyan: A Programme for Universal Elementary Education; Manual on Financial Management and Procurement*, Department of Elementary Education and Literacy, Ministry of Human Resources Development, Government of India, New Delhi.

MHRD, 2005. Report of Committee on National Common Minimum Programmes Commitment of Six Per cent of GDP to Education, National Institute of Educational Planning and Administration, New Delhi.

MHRD, 2006. Report of Fourth Joint Review Mission of Sarva Shiksha Abhiyan, Government of India, 17–27 July 2006, New Delhi.

MHRD, 2009. *Sarva Shiksha Abhiyan A Programme for Universal Elementary Education; Manual on Financial Management and Procurement*, Revised, Department of Elementary Education and Literacy, Ministry of Human Resources Development, Government of India, New Delhi.

National Policy on Education, 1986. National Policy on Education, Government of India, New Delhi.

NUEPA, 2009. Financial Implications for Implementing the Right of Children to Free and Compulsory Education, National University of Educational Planning and Administration, New Delhi.

Rao, Govinda and Raja Chellaiah, 1991. *Fiscal Federalism in India: Principles and Practices*, Oxford University Press, New Delhi.

Rao, Govinda and Tapas K. Sen, 2011. Federalism and Fiscal Reform in India, Working Paper No. 2011-84, National Institute of Public Finance and Policy, New Delhi, available at http://www.nipfp.org.in.

Shah, A., 1991. Perspectives on the Design of Intergovernmental Fiscal Relations, *Policy, Research and External Affairs Working Papers*, No.726, World Bank, Washington, DC.

Tilak, J.G., 2002. 'Financing of Elementary Education in India' in *India Education Report*, R. Govinda (ed.), Oxford University Press, New Delhi.

Varghese, N.V., 1996. 'Decentralization of Educational Planning in India: The Case of the District Primary Education Programme', *International Journal of Educational Development*, 16(4): 355–365.

# 2

# SHIFTING TERRAIN OF PUBLIC POLICY DISCOURSES FOR FINANCING OF SCHOOL EDUCATION

## An overview

*Praveen Jha, P. Geetha Rani, Satadru Sikdar and Pooja Parvati*

### Introduction

In almost seven decades since independence, one of the most disappointing aspects of India's development story has been its notable failure to rise up to the challenge of adequate financing for elementary education. Way back in 1966, the Kothari commission had recommended an expenditure norm of 6 per cent of GDP on education, which has not been achieved yet. With the rise of neoliberalism in recent decades, the so-called 'public services' such as education and health have increasingly been subjected to the logic of the market. As with most countries across the globe, neoliberal India has to contend with major challenges due to a transition in its overall macro-economic policy regime as regards provisioning of basic services. With respect to education, where the situation in any case was seriously worrisome even in the *digitised* era, the overall situation seems to be worsening and critical concerns relating to inclusion and equity need to be examined and addressed afresh.

It is obvious that adequate public expenditure is a crucial aspect of any architecture of public provisioning, a point which has been frequently acknowledged at various national and international fora. For instance, Dakar framework emphasized that on basic education alone governments need to spend close to 6 per cent of GDP.[1] India's expenditure on education has been well below such a suggested target all through since independence till the recent period even after the enactment of RTE Act, 2009.

In this chapter, our focus is on public provisioning for school education, in particular, at the elementary level in India. First section provides a brief sketch of India's public provisioning on school education in an international context. Second section is in the nature of a brief historical excursus highlighting some of the milestones in the relevant policy discourse both during the last stage of the British colonial rule and since independence. Third section provides a snapshot of a few indicators relating to progress in elementary education in recent years. Fourth section presents a mapping of budgetary allocation and financing pattern between the union and state government, along with discussions on recent policy initiatives towards school education in India. Fifth section provides an overview of educational outcome vis-à-vis some indicators of quality of education. Final section concludes the argument.

### *Importance of public provisioning in financing of school education*

Importance of public spending on education is almost universally accepted. Education through its multidimensional 'instrumental' and 'intrinsic' roles contributes to the overall economic and social development of any society. Also, it is quite clear that in a developing country like India, with huge deficits in terms of quantity and quality, the state has to shoulder the primary responsibility for provisioning of education. Thus, it is a matter of great concern that, given the diktats of the neoliberal policy frame, we are witnessing weakening of public policy commitments, which in any case had been indifferent at best even in the pre-reform era, towards good quality universal education in critical ways. The central tenets of a neoliberal policy regime are to facilitate ascendency of markets not only in what may be considered its 'traditional' domains but in almost every walk of economy/society; it is not only the arena of material production and consumption but also the so-called social sectors and services such as education and health, which are subjected to the logic of the market. In other words, the period since the early 1990s, characterized by a strong push to a neoliberal reforms programme, has fundamentally altered the role of government intervention in the economy and society in India, with far-reaching and pervasive implications. Like other arenas, the social sectors have also undergone significant changes, often organically linked with the neoliberal policies.

Adequate public provisioning for basic education is a major factor in contributing towards its adequacy, equity and efficiency. Developed countries, almost without exception, spend substantial portion of their expenditure on

*Table 2.1* Per-child government expenditure at primary level (in $ ppp) by years

| | *1999* | *2000–02* | *2003–05* | *2006–08* | *2009–11* |
|---|---|---|---|---|---|
| **High-income country** | | | | | |
| France | 4,220 | 4,788 | 5,153 | 5,916 | 6,486 |
| Japan | 5,060 | 5,573 | 6,283 | 6,923 | 7,758 |
| Netherlands | 4,082 | 5,073 | 6,111 | 6,972 | 7,800 |
| USA | 5,898 | 7,170 | 8,090 | 9,861 | 10,467 |
| **Middle-income country** | | | | | |
| Brazil | 725 | 745 | 1,170 | 1,799 | 2,206 |
| Costa Rica | 1,101 | 1,110 | 1,421 | 1,291 | 1,602 |
| Malaysia | – | 1,561 | 1,744 | 1,644 | 2,348 |
| Indonesia | – | – | – | 426 | 463 |
| Philippines | – | 280 | 271 | 316 | – |
| South Africa | 918 | 941 | 1,022 | 1,338 | 1,683 |
| **Low-income country** | | | | | |
| Bangladesh | – | – | – | 122 | 129 |
| Bhutan | – | – | 295 | 328 | 447 |
| **India** | **162** | **211** | **187** | – | **225** |
| Mongolia | – | – | 303 | 483 | 679 |
| Kenya | – | 241 | 281 | 300 | – |
| Nepal | 66 | 97 | 96 | 158 | 196 |
| Sri Lanka | – | – | – | – | 321 |

*Source:* UNESCO, web link: http://data.uis.unesco.org; retrieved on 15th September, 2014.
*Note:* 2000–02; 2003–04; 2006–08; 2009–11 average for three triennium.

basic education. For instance, among the high-income countries, France, Netherlands and USA have been very consistent in their spending on education over the time period 2000–10 (close to 6 per cent) (Table A2.1). It is interesting to compare the profile of public spending levels of different countries from different income groups, by comparing the public spending per child on primary education, in terms of US dollars, adjusted for purchasing power parity (Table 2.1). *USA spent almost 50 times more than India, per child, on primary education for the year 2010*. Even middle income countries like South Africa and Brazil, in whose company India happens to be as part of BRICS, also spend 7 to 10 times higher than India, per child, on primary education. Even for several low income countries such as Bhutan, Mongolia, Sri Lanka, etc., the relevant figures are higher than India.

Even after seven decades of independence, India has not been able to wipe out illiteracy and has the dubious distinction that every third illiterate in the world is an Indian. As per the most recent decennial Census, conducted in 2011, the literacy[2] at the national level is still 74 per cent below the world average literacy rate of 84 per cent. Female literacy is even lower, around 65.5 per cent, which goes down further in rural areas to 58.8 per cent. Taking rural and the urban areas together, female literacy falls short of 60 per cent in seven states, namely, Andhra Pradesh, Arunachal Pradesh, Bihar, Jharkhand, Jammu and Kashmir, Rajasthan and Uttar Pradesh. If female literacy rates in the rural areas alone were to be considered, three states Rajasthan, Jharkhand, Bihar fall below 50 per cent and another 10 states would get added to this list of less than 60 per cent. The simple inescapable point underscored by these numbers is that the deficit is still a huge one even in terms of crude quantitative indicators.

It is well known that quite a few countries in Asia such as Sri Lanka, Indonesia or China, who were roughly at comparable levels around the middle of the twentieth century, have done much better than India (Table 2.2). It would seem that India as a nation has paid scant regard for the well-being of its children over generations.

*Table 2.2* Literate adult (15+) population in select countries for various years (%)

| *Years/countries* | | *China* | *Indonesia* | *Sri Lanka* | *India* |
|---|---|---|---|---|---|
| 1981 | Female | 56.0 | 60.8 | 80.0 | 25.7 |
| | Male | 80.0 | 80.0 | 91.2 | 54.8 |
| | Total | 68.0 | 70.0 | 85.6 | 40.8 |
| 1991 | Female | 70.0 | 73.5 | 85.1 | 33.7 |
| | Male | 87.8 | 87.3 | 93.0 | 61.6 |
| | Total | 79.0 | 80.3 | 89.0 | 48.2 |
| 2001 | Female | 78.8 | 82.7 | 89.3 | 47.8 |
| | Male | 92.5 | 92.1 | 94.5 | 73.4 |
| | Total | 86.0 | 87.3 | 91.9 | 61.0 |
| 2011 | Female | 92.7 | 90.1 | 90.0 | 59.26 |
| | Male | 97.5 | 95.6 | 92.6 | 78.84 |
| | Total | 95.1 | 92.8 | 91.2 | 69.28 |

*Source:* World Bank and UNESCO data (2014), India figures of 2011 are from Census of India.

## Public provisioning in India: a brief historical excursus

The roots relating to the so-called modern education system in India is normally traced to the British colonial period, and justifiably and so are the discourses on public provisioning. Tables A2.2a and A2.2b in the annexure provide a very brief overview of some of the milestones in this respect. Demand for compulsory basic education was raised by Nationalist leader soon after the Indian National Congress was born. For instance, Annie Besant made a strong pitch for nation-wide school education in 1906 and subsequently Gopal Krishna Gokhale prepared the resolution for compulsory primary education in 1910; as per Gokhale's resolution, 'free and compulsory' primary education should be made available to all children in the 6–10 year age group and the cost could be shared in the ratio of 2:1 (66.67 and 33.33 per cent) between provincial governments and local bodies. The said resolution, presented as the Gokhale's Bill of 1911, in the Legislative Council, was initially rejected on financial grounds. However, soon after King George V declared a donation of 50 lakh in 1912 for this purpose, the Government of India passed the bill in 1913 which resulted in 0073ome expansion of primary education.[3] *Wardha Education Conference* of 1937 was another landmark which reiterated the principle of 'free and compulsory' education for all children between 7 and 14 year age group, with the objective of the 'development of ideal citizenship rather than only literacy'.

After independence, possibly the most high-profile commission was the Education Commission (1964–66), also popularly known as the Kothari Commission, as it was headed by D. S. Kothari. After an in-depth examination of the relevant issues, the Commission suggested a roadmap and made detailed recommendations for the next 20 years. One of its famous recommendations happens to be that the government should reach a spending of 6 per cent to GDP for education by 1986 and it strongly advocated for the removal of tuition fees and provision of free education at the primary stage. For lower secondary education, the Commission suggested that the tuition fees could continue but with an adequate and suitable grants and exemptions for needy students; however, it recommended to make it free for the government-aided institutions, preferably before the end of fifth five-year plan period. The Kothari commission also highlighted the importance of quality of education, need of common schools system and equalization of teacher salary across different type of schools. The National Policy on Education (NPE), 1968, tried to follow the recommendation of Kothari commission and implemented them in the fourth five-year plan period (1969–74). It had prioritized expansion of elementary schools, especially in the backward areas and among girls. Teacher training came under focus during the period to improve the quality of education.

As per the 42nd Constitutional Amendment, in 1976 education came to the concurrent list, which resulted in lot more active intervention from the union government. The National Policy on Education (NPE), 1986, in principle was an attempt to deepen and widen the policies and programmes pursued hitherto and there was considerable emphasis on equality and universalizing education among women, Scheduled Caste, Scheduled Tribes and other backward groups and areas. The subsequent policy intents have continued to be largely on the same track; however, from mid-1980s onwards the overall policy framework towards provisioning of education tended to become more market friendly and there was a weakening of the spirit of public provisioning. Gradually, along with privatization, there was a growing informalization across the entire education system and we have discussed these in detail elsewhere (Jha *et al.* 2008). It took almost five decades for enacting RTE (Efforts towards RTE reported in annexure Table A.2.2c). The adoption of the 'Right to Education' (RTE) Act, 2009, by the Country's Parliament, which came into effect on 1 April 2010, of course generated much hope, but there are serious problems, both in the Act and with its implementation.

## Progress in elementary education: select indicators

Before we look at some of the output and outcome indicators, a scrutiny of the shortfalls in outlays is in order as it helps contextualize the gap in terms of translating outlays into outcomes. Table A2.1 presents a comparison of the level of spending on education in India with some developed and developing countries and reveals the need for greater government spending.

It is also useful to flag here that even in just the last six years, enrolment patterns reveal a shift away from government schools to privately run schools.[4] Whether this is directly related to the gradual but steady decline in adequate financing of government apparatus and thereby starving it to perform poorly is debatable and will be explored in the subsequent sections. Tables A2.3a and A2.3b report the status of some key outputs with regard to elementary education. It becomes clear that while some progress has been made, the overall situation continues to be grim.

Independent surveys also corroborate this situation: Annual Status of Education Report reveals the gaps in terms of actual provision and proposed entitlements. A four-year comparison from 2010 to 2013 shows that the situation has not changed much in terms of adhering to the RTE norms with regard to basic provisions such as building, drinking water, toilets, library and mid-day meal (Table A2.3b).

Findings from the ground reiterate the concerns and throw up additional questions for scrutiny. Table A2.3c summarizes the findings emerging from an annual national exercise undertaken by the Right to Education (RTE) Forum to take stock of the implementation of the Act since the last three years of its being. The Forum's 2013 Annual Stocktaking Report compiles information related to implementation of the RTE Act in 2191 schools covering 17 states under five broad heads: Access to Elementary Education; Quality of Infrastructure; Teachers; Community Participation and Social Exclusion.

## Budgetary allocation

Before discussing the issues of fund utilization, an assessment of the budgetary allocations on elementary education is useful. Government spending on education as a proportion of GDP at 3.5 per cent in 2010–11[5] continues to be way below the recommendation made by the first Education Commission in 1966. Not only was it adopted in the subsequent National Policies on Education, but many political parties also adopted it as a key commitment. Figures 2.1 and 2.2 highlight spending patterns on education by the

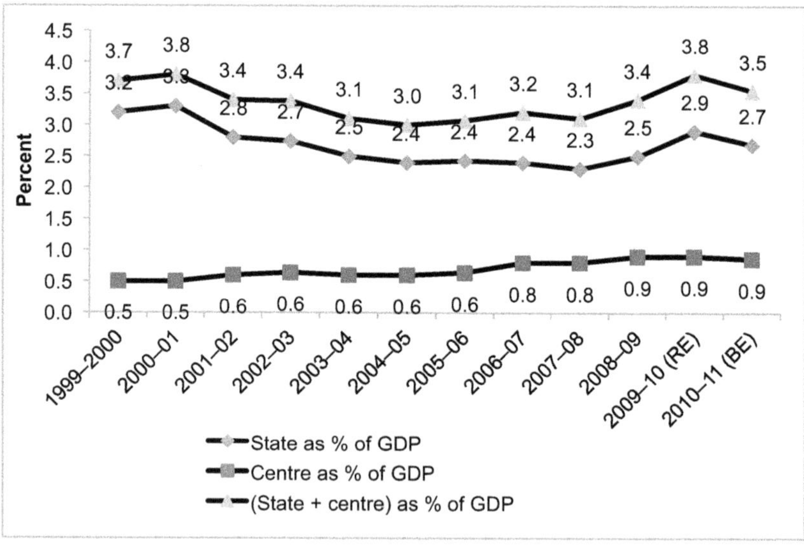


*Figure 2.1* Government spending on education as percentage of GDP

*Source:* Ministry of Human Resource and Development, Government of India (2012). GDP figures (market price at current price) from Handbook of Statistics on Indian Economy, 2011–12.

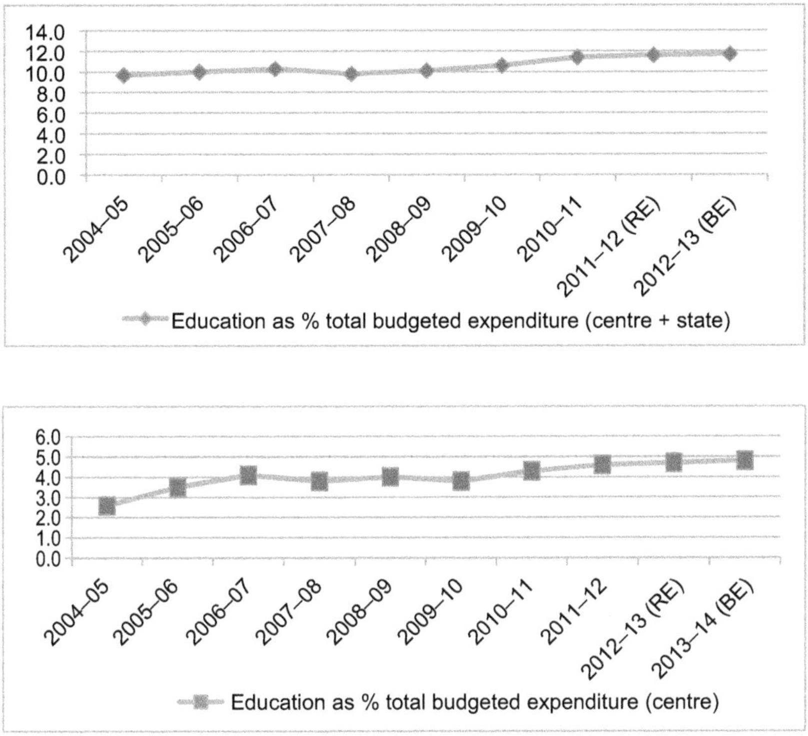


*Figure 2.2* Government spending on education as percentage of total expenditure

*Source:* How Has the Dice Rolled? Response to Union Budget 2013–14, CBGA (2013) and Economic Survey Government of India.

union and state governments as a proportion of GDP and total budgetary expenditure.

It is worthwhile to note here that comprehensive data on education expenditure is a complex terrain, because of several difficulties, which we have discussed in detail elsewhere (Jha *et al.* 2008). In this chapter, we have collected the expenditure data from 'State Finance Accounts' and 'Union Finance Accounts' published by the Comptroller and Auditor General of India. The study has focused on elementary level of school education, which is for 6–14 years age group. Statewise population data for this age group for 1991, 2001 and 2011 are from the Census of India. For estimating annual population of children projection from the decennial growth rate has been used and accordingly per-child public expenditure has been worked out. The changing pattern of per-child expenditure can be seen from Annexure Table A2.4, where it can be seen that, per-child expenditure in real terms has increased since 1991–92 to 2011–12; but it has reduced since 2009–10 to 2011–12 for some of the states, like Arunachal Pradesh, Bihar, Chhattisgarh, Jharkhand, Rajasthan, Sikkim and Uttarakhand. Also, noticeable inter-state disparity is that, in 2011–12, Himachal Pradesh spends 11 times higher than Bihar. States like Andhra Pradesh, Uttar Pradesh, Rajasthan, Orissa, Jharkhand, Madhya Pradesh, West Bengal, Punjab and Chhattisgarh are spending below national average. Annexure Table A2.5 shows although the per-child expenditure has increased in recent period; it has increased almost at a similar rate of state domestic product or national product.

Composition of public expenditure on education for the last few years reveals that elementary sector gets the priority in allocation. Elementary Education accounted for 1.64 per cent of GDP on education in 2011–12 (BE), followed by Secondary Education, which was 0.97 per cent. The share of University and Higher Education and Technical Education was 0.71 and 0.55 per cent, respectively (Figure 2.3).

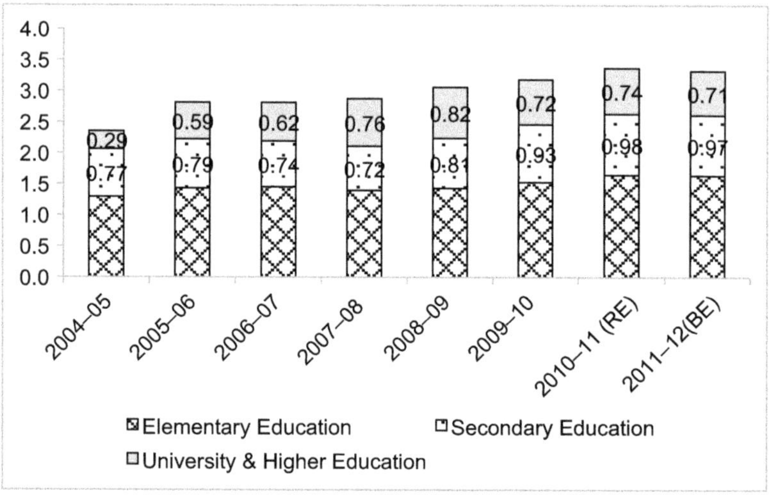


*Figure 2.3* Composition of public expenditure on education

*Source:* Analysis of Budgeted Expenditure on Education 2009–10 to 2011–12, Planning and Monitoring Unit, Department of Higher Education, MHRD (2013); GDP figures are from National Accounts Statistics, 2014, CSO.

*Note:* GDP figures are at current market price.

Tables A2.6a and A2.6b estimate the total outlays on elementary education by the union government from 2005–06 to 2012–13. While there has been substantial increase in allocation at the elementary level, capital outlays are either sporadic or completely absent.

One critical issue in the context of adequate financing is of appropriate benchmark and unit costs, which has been a sleeper terrain. Further the problem is compounded by a massive heterogeneity in the overall structure of schooling in India. With respect to typology of schools, usually the classification is by the type of management (government, local body, private-aided and private unaided) with the assumption of equal fees and facilities among these types of schools. Cost and quality varies within these groups, examples within Government school, for example, Kendriya Vidyalaya is different in its nature from Sarvodaya Vidyalaya; similarly government-aided schools in metropolitan areas are significantly different in its cost and quality, compared to other government-aided schools located in suburban areas. Differences with private unaided schools are highly noticeable, for example, recognized and unrecognized private schools are providing their services in a different manner. Numbers of participation in these different types of schools, within these categories, are not available easily.

Although per-child expenditure is not necessarily a good indicator of quality, yet it can be of some help given the management type, for instance within non-residential government schools (i.e. day school), Kendriya Vidyalaya is considered to be relatively better than the rest. Kendriya Vidyalaya, especially made for government employees, had 1,148,340 students as on 31 March 2014; considering Rs. 2554.17 crore of expenditure on 2013–14 (RE), per-child allocation was Rs. 22,242 per annum. Whereas, average per-child expenditure on education by various departments of states and including grants from union government towards state (including mid-day meal) was Rs. 5091 per annum.[6] This difference also exists among private schools. According to latest All India School Education Survey (8th AISES, 2008–09) number of unrecognized schools was 39,015 with an enrolment of more than 3 million children (2,373,201 at primary stage and 790,683 at upper primary stage); whereas number of primary and upper primary school in rural India was 979,916 at the same period. Within recognized private unaided school, fees structure also varies from Rs. 1500 to Rs. 0.1 million per annum. A comparison among 20 private unaided schools in Delhi has been done by author, which is not any representative, shows that annual charges vary from Rs. 10,000 per annum to Rs. 0.15 million per annum.[7]

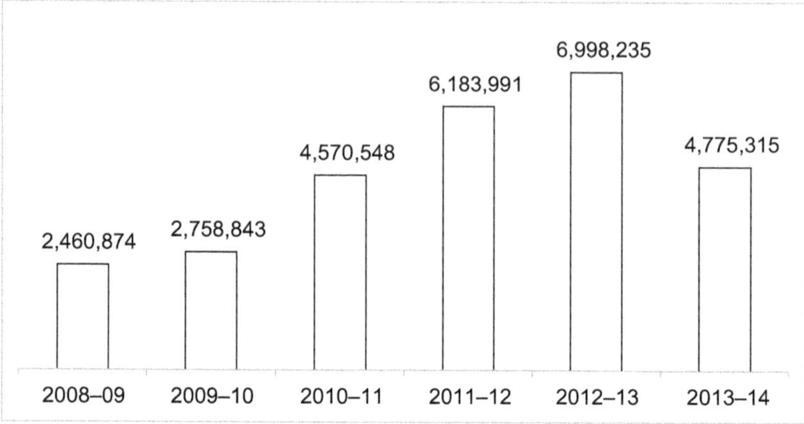


*Figure 2.4* Approved outlays for SSA

*Source:* Statement showing outlay approved to States/UTs during 2008–09 to 2013–14 under SSA; accessible from http://ssa.nic.in/page_portletlinks?foldername=financial-management.

Moving from the overall elementary education spending, Figure 2.4 presents the total approved outlays for SSA for the last six years (2008–09 to 2013–14). In the first three years of the RTE Act's implementation, SSA outlays witnessed an upward trend but this has been checked in 2013–14 (Table A2.7). However, standalone outlays do not reveal the extent of shortfalls, for which, we need to compare actual outlays to available benchmarks. There are very few benchmarks to assess the adequacy of public spending on the development schemes in the country; the five-year plan recommended outlays could be treated as some such benchmarks, even though the quality parameters to arrive at these benchmarks are not quite satisfactory.

In the case of SSA (as in many other Centrally Sponsored Schemes), we find that the budgetary outlays do not comply with the proposed plan allocations. Comparing the 11th five-year plan proposed allocations for SSA to actual budgetary outlays made; we find that allocations picked up only in the fourth year of the five-year plan period (Figure 2.4). Instead of a trend reversal, the picture we get from the first three years of the 12th plan period seems to have become more skewed with the third year allocation still nowhere near 60 per cent of the proposed plan outlays. The problem of poor planning and inadequate outlays is worsened with institutional and systemic constraints that lead to poor outcomes. The next section examines some of these implementation challenges.

### Relation between expenditure and quality of education

Apart from access and equity, quality of education also depends upon public provision on education. It hardly needs emphasis that 'quality' of education cannot be reduced to some simple metric or a given set of variables. Rather, it needs to be assessed along a whole spectrum of indicators, only some of which are amenable to measurement. The common sense judgment often links it to economic betterment through higher prospects of earning, which is a kind of limited *instrumental* yardstick; of course there is lot more to quality of education, both in *instrumental* and *intrinsic* ways connected with the lives of individuals and society at large.

There are several ongoing studies and surveys across the globe, focusing on some of the aspects of quality of school education[8]. In India, some of the recent initiatives in this respect include Annual Status of Education Report (ASER) by PRATHAM, National Achievement Survey (NAS) by National Council of Education Research and Training (NCERT) and Educational Development Index (EDI) by NUEPA using DISE data.[9] Apart from these, Indian Human Development Survey (IHDS-I in 2004–05 and IHDS-II in 2011–12) and EDWATCH survey by National Coalition for Education also provide important insights to the understanding of quality of education.

Annual Status of Education Report (ASER) collects information from their surveys conducted in rural areas across India, every year since 2005. In 2013, they covered 568 districts in India. It defines quality of education as 'Reading and Calculation proficiency of students from Class I–VIII'. While the indicators might be debatable, they provide an assessment of statewise and districtwise performances. The survey reports provide learning levels information with the help of their reading and arithmetic tool asked to the surveyed children. Since 2005, it is providing learning levels among Standard 3 to 5 level and since 2012 it is also providing learning level among children in Standard 6 to 8.

We have done a small exercise with these learning level indicators of quality of education provided by ASER and per-child expenditure on elementary education by states. As stated earlier, 'quality' of education depends on a whole range of factors; however in our judgment, key to good quality universal education is adequate public provisioning of appropriate resources based on a realistic assessment of infrastructure for decent education. These data show a positive relationship of reading and mathematical learning capability positively related with per-child total expenditure (union government and state). Annexure Figures A2.1 and A2.2 show positive relationship between reading and writing capability with per-child expenditure on elementary education from 2005–06 to 2011–12. The upswing trend line can be seen in each year for both the reading and mathematical learning capability, and these are highly related in 2005, 2007, 2010 and in 2011.[10]

## Conclusion

One of the critical factors underlying failure of public policy with respect to quality is inadequacy of resources. Even during the pre-reform period, it tended to be well below the norms suggested by various commissions and expert groups. Further, inadequate spending over time has only meant that the state responsibility to finance quality education has moved to a forever-shifting future date. However, given the worsening condition of state governments' finances and inadequate devolution of funds from centre to states, expenditures on education incurred by the centre become crucial to augment total allocations for this sector. However, the low increases in the centre's expenditure on education, on a base that is already quite small, have not been able to compensate for the declining (per capita real) expenditure on education by states.

Inadequate financing is organically connected with the systemic weaknesses of poor infrastructure. Lack of basic infrastructure, that is, buildings for schools, BRCs, CRCs and district institutes of education and training (DIETs), is one of the important factors responsible for the poor education indicators of states. Many of the deadlines for compliance to the RTE norms expired on 30 March 2013 and it becomes clear that with inadequate financial provision, skewed progress on outputs, a flawed design that attempts to 'subsume' the Act within the confines of rigid and unrealistic unit costs, and scant regard for inclusion, the fulfilment of this critical entitlement for so many children remains a distant dream.

# APPENDIX

*Table A2.1* Government spending on education as percentage of GDP

| *HDI Rank 2013* | *Countries* | *2000* | *2005–10** |
|---|---|---|---|
| 1 | Norway | 6.6 | 7.3 |
| 2 | Australia | 4.7 | 5.1 |
| 3 | United States of America | – | 5.4 |
| 6 | New Zealand | – | 7.2 |
| 7 | Sweden | 7.2 | 7.3 |
| 10 | Japan | 3.7 | 3.8 |
| 20 | France | 5.7 | 5.9 |
| 25 | Italy | 4.4 | 4.7 |
| 26 | United Kingdom | 4.5 | 5.6 |
| 40 | Chile | 3.9 | 4.5 |
| 45 | Argentina | 4.6 | 6.0 |
| 59 | Cuba | 7.7 | 12.9 |
| 61 | Mexico | 4.9 | 5.3 |
| 64 | Malaysia | 6.0 | 5.8 |
| 85 | Brazil | 4.0 | 5.7 |
| 92 | Sri Lanka | – | 2.1 |
| 94 | Tunisia | 6.2 | 6.3 |
| 121 | South Africa | 5.6 | 6.0 |
| 121 | Indonesia | – | 3.0 |
| 127 | Vietnam | – | 5.3 |
| **136** | ***India*** | **4.4** | **3.1** |
| 140 | Bhutan | 5.8 | 4.0 |
| 146 | Pakistan | 1.8 | 2.4 |
| 146 | Bangladesh | 2.4 | 2.2 |
| 157 | Nepal | 3.0 | 4.7 |
| | **World average** | – | **4.9** |

*Source: UNDP (2013) Human Development Report 2013 – The Rise of the South: Human Progress in a Diverse World. Pg 162–165. Data sourced from World Development Indicators 2012.* Washington, DC. Available at http://data.worldbank.org.

*Note:* *Data refer to the most recent year available during the period specified.

*Table A2.2a* Overview of education policies in the pre-independence period

| *Education policy/committee* | *Year* | *Recommendations* |
|---|---|---|
| General Committee of Public Instruction (GCOPI) | 1823 | Proposed to setting up English School in each district |
| Wood's Despatch | 1854 | Setting up at least one government school in each district, and a Department of Education in each province. Teaching in mother tongues. Restructured the levels of education in primary, middle and secondary. Condition-based grants towards schools was recommended by Wood's Despatch and the conditions were (i) fees for student, (ii) must provide secular education, (iii) good management, (iv) agree to state inspections. The Department of Education |
| Hunter Commission | 1882 | Emphasis on backward districts. Provide one-third of the total expenditure to the local bodies by each province and also maintain a separate fund for primary education by the District and Municipal Board and maintenance should be met from local fund. |
| Gokhale's Bill | 1911 | Free and Compulsory Education for 6–10 years age group.<br>Cost should be shared in 2:1 ratio by Provincial Government and Local Bodies.<br>PTR should be between 30 and 40. |
| Hartog Committee | 1929 | Recommended the administration of primary education through union government and its Education Department; opposed the authority of local bodies. |
| Wardha Educational Conference | 1937 | Resolutions for 'free and compulsory' basic education for all children between 7 and 14 years age group. |
| Kher Committee | 1939 | Pointed out the issues of financing, as Zakir Hussain Committee doubted on self-supporting basic education and expressed the opinion that running expenses and other educational expenditure should be covered by other sources of funding from public and private. |
| Sargent Scheme for Education | 1944 | Proposed implication of pre-primary education for 3–6 year age group, and universal compulsory and free primary or basic education for all children between the ages 6–11 (junior basic) and 11–14 (senior basic); and high school education for six years for selected children between the years 11–17.<br>Proposed for liquidation of adult illiteracy by next 40 years, i.e. by 1984. |

*Table A2.2b* Overview of education policies in the post-independence period

| *Education policy/committee* | *Year* | *Recommendations* |
|---|---|---|
| Kher Committee | 1948–49 | Decision power shifted to local bodies and expenditure share proposed as 10:20:70 basis among union, state and local bodies. |
| Kothari Commission | 1964–66 | Recommended government spending of 6 per cent to GDP for education.<br>Emphasized basic education for all.<br>Advocated for removing tuition fees in primary stage;<br>and continue fees in case of lower secondary education, but with adequate and suitable grants and exemptions for needy students; and also recommended to make it free for government-aided institutions preferably before the end of fifth plan period. |
| National Education Policy | 1968 | Increase in investment on education to reach 6 per cent to GDP.<br>Common 10+2+3 structure across all states in India. |
| 42nd Constitutional amendment | 1976 | School education again shifted under the jurisdiction of state and union government. |
| National Education Policy | 1986 (with revisions in 1992) | Government need to spend more than 6 per cent of GDP.<br>Reduce the disparities across different socioeconomic groups.<br>Focus toward universalization of elementary education. |
| 73rd and 74th Constitutional amendment | 1992 | Increase the power of decision and responsibilities upon local bodies on elementary education. |
| Saikia Committee | 1996 | More than 50 per cent of allocation on education should be spent on elementary education. |
| Tapas Majumdar Committee | 1999 | Suggested to spend 1.37 lakh crore rupees by the government, from 1998 to 2007 towards achieving universal education. |
| 86th Constitutional amendment | 2002 | Compulsory education should be provided by states among all children between 6 and 14 years age. |
| National Common Minimum Programme of UPA Government | 2004 | Increase the government spending towards education at least 6 per cent of GDP and spend 50 per cent towards primary and secondary education.<br>Introduction of education cess, for achieving universalization of elementary education. |

(*Continued*)

Table A2.2b (Continued)

| | | |
|---|---|---|
| CABE Committee | 2006 | Recommended the share of elementary, secondary and higher secondary should be 3, 2 and 1 per cent of GDP, respectively. |
| Right to Education Act, 2009 | 2010 | Pass the RTE bill for compulsory universalization of elementary education, on 1 April, 2010. |
| Committee on Implementation of the Right of Children to Free and Compulsory Education Act, 2009, and the Resultant Revamp of Sarva Shiksha Abhiyan, Bordia Commission | 2010 | For SSA funding, central–state share should be 75:25, which finally decided to 65:35. |

*Source:* Compiled from Various documents of Ministry of Human Resource and Development; De and Endow (2008).

*Table A2.2c* Timeline on the efforts towards right to education in India

| *Year* | *Efforts towards right to education in India* |
|---|---|
| 1950 | Article 45 of the Constitutions of India – Free and Compulsory education for all children in the age group 6–14 years. |
| 1976 | Education shifted to the concurrent list. |
| 1986 | National Policy on Education. |
| 1993 | Unnikrishnan Judgment as right to education is a fundamental right that flows from the Right to life in Article 21 of the Constitution. |
| 1997 | Saikia Committee submitted its report, and following its recommendations, the 93rd Constitutional Amendment Bill was introduced in Parliament in 1997 to make right to education from 6–14 years a fundamental right. |
| 1999 | Expert Group submitted its report on financial requirements for making elementary education a fundamental right. |
| 2002 | 86th Constitutional Amendment passed in 2002 under Article 21A (Part III) seeks to make free and compulsory education a fundamental right for all children in the age group 6–14 years. |
| 2004 | Central Advisory Board of Education (CABE) was reconstituted to draft the 'Right to Education' Bill. |
| 2005 | CABE submitted its report on Right to Education Bill, 2005, along with the financial memorandum. |
| 2006 | Model Bill circulated to states and UTs. |
| 2007 | Revised financial estimates based on the population projections as available from the Census of India in December 2006. |
| 2008 | Constitution of a high-level group to look into the financial implications of the Bill. |
| 2009 | Right of Children to Free and Compulsory Education (RTE) Act, 2009, w.e.f. 1st April 2010. |

*Source:* Compiled from various documents of MHRD.

*Table A2.3a* Select output indicators in elementary education (%)

| | *All schools* | | | | | *Primary schools* | | | | |
|---|---|---|---|---|---|---|---|---|---|---|
| | 2009–10 | 2010–11 | 2011–12 | 2012–13 | 2013–14 | 2009–10 | 2010–11 | 2011–12 | 2012–13 | 2013–14 |
| % of single-teacher schools | 9.33 | 8.86 | 8.31 | 8.65 | 8.32 | 12.26 | 11.8 | 10.8 | 11.79 | 11.46 |
| | *All government schools* | | | | | *All unaided schools* | | | | |
| Average number of teachers per school | 3.8 | 4 | 4 | 4.2 | 4.2 | 7.3 | 7.6 | 7.3 | 8.1 | 8.8 |
| | *All schools* | | | | | *Government schools* | | | | |
| PTR >30 at primary | | 42.44 | 40.84 | – | 29.90 | | 42.81 | 40.97 | – | |
| PTR >35 at upper primary | | 31.32 | 30.77 | – | 15.35 | | 33.20 | 32.03 | – | 16.64 |
| | *Regular* | | | | | *Contractual* | | | | |
| % of professionally trained teachers | 78.66 | – | 79.58 | 78.58 | 80.06 | 49.37 | – | 62.02 | 54.01 | 55.55 |
| % of teachers receiving in–service training during previous academic year (all schools) | | | | | | 35.03 | 29.59 | 34.23 | 25.75 | 22.03 |
| % of teachers involved in non–teaching assignments* | | | | | | 9.55 | 9.06 | 10.13 | 5.49 | 2.48 |

*Source:* District Information on School Education, National University of Education Planning and Administration, and various years.

*Note:* * (including contractual) during previous academic year.

*Table A2.3b* Shortfalls in key educational inputs

| | *All government schools* | | | | | *All private schools* | | | | |
|---|---|---|---|---|---|---|---|---|---|---|
| | *2009–10* | *2010–11* | *2011–12* | *2012–13* | *2013–14* | *2009–10* | *2010–11* | *2011–12* | *2012–13* | *2013–14* |
| Average number of classrooms | 3.7 | 3.8 | 3.8 | 3.8 | 4.0 | 7.8 | 8.0 | 7.9 | 7.1 | 7.8 |
| | *SCR >30 at primary level* | | | | | *SCR >35 at Upper primary level* | | | | |
| | | 36.74 | 37.16 | 33.53 | 30.18 | | 34.42 | 33.17 | 32.18 | 30.76 |
| | *All schools* | | | | | *Primary schools* | | | | |
| % schools with drinking water | 92.6 | 92.71 | 94.45 | 94.87 | 95.31 | 91.51 | 93.15 | | 93.73 | 94.09 |
| | *With boys toilet* | | *With functional boys toilet in all schools* | | *With girls toilet* | | *With functional girls toilet in all schools* | | | |
| | *All schools* | *Primary schools* | | | *All schools* | *Primary schools* | | | | |
| % schools with toilet (2013–14) | 94.45 | 92.93 | 92.67 | | 84.63 | 80.85 | 91.62 | | | |
| % schools with boundary wall (all schools) | | | | | | 51.45 | 55.41 | 58.16 | 59.48 | 61.87 |
| | *All schools* | | | | | *Primary schools* | | | | |
| % schools with computers | 16.65 | 18.7 | 20.53 | 22.09 | 23.3 | | 6.99 | 7.59 | 8.69 | 9.25 |
| | | | | | | *Upper primary schools* | | | | |
| schools | | | | | | | 36.8 | 40.14 | 41.96 | 43.75 |
| | *All schools* | | | | | *Primary schools* | | | | |
| % schools with ramps | 47.09 | 50.39 | 53.43 | 79.25 | 82.33 | 45.86 | 49.71 | 53.28 | 81.53 | 84.09 |
| % schools with playground | | | | | | 55.03 | | 56.1 | 56.58 | 58.05 |
| | | | *All schools* | | | *Primary schools* | | | | |
| % schools with kitchen shed (govt. and aided management) | | | 40.95 | 60.43 | 74.92 | | | 46.3 | 62.64 | 63.64 |
| % schools providing mid-day meal (govt. and aided management) | | | | | | | 88.24 | 92.06 | 94.83 | 88.6 |
| | *All schools* | | | | | *Primary schools* | | | | |
| % schools having electricity connection | 38.98 | 43.14 | 47.11 | 49.92 | 51.74 | 27.7 | 32.2 | 36.34 | 39.95 | 41.85 |

*Source:* Elementary Education in India: Progress towards UEE, Flash Statistics DISE, NUEPA, Govt. of India, various years.

*Table A2.3c* Independent survey results for implementation of RTE Act, 2013

| *Indicators to assess implementation of RTE Act* | *Figures in %* |
|---|---|
| **I. Access to elementary education** | |
| a. Child mapping carried out in schools | 61 |
| b. School functioning for less than 200 days (as per RTE norms) | 15 |
| **II. Quality of infrastructure** | |
| a. All-weather building with at least one classroom for every teacher and an office-cum-store-cum-head teacher room | 79 |
| b. Children with special needs (CWSN) friendly access in schools | 9.2 |
| c. Drinking water facility for all children | 77.8 |
| d. Kitchen where MDM is cooked | 68.8 |
| e. Playground | 60 |
| f. Arrangement for secured school building | 50 |
| g. Teaching Learning Material (TLM) provided to each class as required | 80 |
| h. Library with provisions for newspapers, magazines, books, including story books | 55 |
| i. Play material, sports and games material | 55 |
| **III. Teachers** | |
| a. Para-teachers (% teachers) | 33.8 |
| b. Proxy teachers (% teachers) | 10 |
| c. Pupil–Teacher Ratio (PTR) | 56.6 |
| d. Separate subject and language teachers (% schools) | 33 |
| e. Special educators/counsellors for CWSN (% teachers) | 33 |
| f. Teachers involved in non-educational activities (% teachers) | 47 |
| g. Distance travelled by teachers to reach schools (over 20 kms) | 25 |
| h. In-service training for teachers (% teachers) | 20 |
| **IV. Community participation** | |
| a. School Management Committee (SMC) constituted | 79 |
| b. SMC constituted through election | 49.8 |
| c. SMC preparing school development plans | 54 |
| d. Schools having SMCs monitoring functioning of plans | 66.3 |
| e. Schools having SMCs monitoring utilization of school grants | 61.2 |
| f. Involvement of PRIs/ULBs in school management | 59 |
| **V. Social exclusion** | |
| a. Age-appropriate education offered in schools | 13.6 |
| b. SCs not allowed to sit on benches | 9.4 |
| c. STs not allowed to sit on benches | 5 |
| d. Muslims not allowed to sit on benches | 7.3 |
| e. CWSN not allowed to sit on benches | 7.7 |
| f. Girls denied class monitorship | 8 |
| g. Grievance redress mechanism | 52.8 |
| h. Grievances referred to PRI / ULB (as per RTE Act) | 0.6 |
| i. Assistive devices for CWSN | 11.6 |
| j. Transport for CWSN | 3.3 |
| **VI. Implementation of 25% reservation for EWS and socially disadvantaged sections in private unaided schools** | 34.8 |

*Source:* RTE Forum Annual Stocktaking Report, 2013.

*Table A2.4* Statewise per-child expenditure on elementary education in Rs. (at 2004–05 prices)

| *State name* | *1991–92* | *1992–93* | *1993–94* | *1994–95* | *1995–96* | *1996–97* | *1997–98* | *1998–99* | *1999–2000* | *2000–2001* |
|---|---|---|---|---|---|---|---|---|---|---|
| Andhra Pradesh | 849.0 | 861.9 | 783.3 | 829.9 | 762.9 | 786.3 | 815.9 | 817.9 | 970.0 | 1,054.4 |
| Arunachal Pradesh | 2,664.4 | 2,289.0 | 2,284.7 | 2,135.6 | 2,255.7 | 2,154.4 | 2,140.9 | 2,037.3 | 1,972.3 | 2,081.8 |
| Assam | 1,608.9 | 1,532.3 | 1,660.8 | 1,407.8 | 1,527.8 | 1,554.8 | 1,566.1 | 1,624.3 | 1,501.1 | 1,671.2 |
| Bihar | 670.8 | 685.6 | 1,018.1 | 1,067.3 | 1,193.7 | 1,213.5 | 1,262.0 | 1,111.7 | 1,428.7 | 1,202.9 |
| Chhattisgarh | – | – | – | – | – | – | – | – | – | 424.4 |
| Goa | 2,747.8 | 2,924.0 | 2,597.0 | 2,544.8 | 2,759.3 | 3,098.0 | 3,587.6 | 4,285.7 | 4,165.4 | 3,761.4 |
| Gujarat | 1,517.8 | 1,540.9 | 1,516.9 | 1,579.9 | 1,687.4 | 1,783.3 | 1,835.4 | 2,340.3 | 2,116.7 | 2,307.7 |
| Haryana | 1,055.4 | 1,136.2 | 1,006.2 | 1,007.4 | 1,053.6 | 1,198.9 | 1,228.2 | 1,560.3 | 1,370.4 | 1,315.9 |
| Himachal Pradesh | 2,262.9 | 2,490.8 | 2,273.2 | 2,150.3 | 2,353.1 | 2,476.8 | 2,671.1 | 3,348.7 | 3,209.6 | 3,028.3 |
| Jammu & Kashmir | 1,623.1 | 2,261.0 | 1,359.1 | 1,404.8 | 1,465.8 | 1,544.2 | 1,623.0 | 1,698.5 | 1,638.7 | 1,614.4 |
| Jharkhand | – | – | – | – | – | – | – | – | – | 400.7 |
| Karnataka | 1,152.6 | 1,195.9 | 1,152.9 | 1,158.3 | 1,161.4 | 1,244.3 | 1,432.7 | 1,507.8 | 1,537.4 | 1,582.1 |
| Kerala | 2,411.9 | 2,378.2 | 2,347.5 | 2,604.3 | 2,305.9 | 2,327.8 | 2,359.0 | 2,504.2 | 3,069.7 | 2,938.4 |
| Madhya Pradesh | 741.6 | 775.3 | 915.3 | 914.9 | 1,041.5 | 1,070.6 | 1,131.6 | 1,422.8 | 1,362.7 | 1,293.3 |
| Maharashtra | 1,294.9 | 1,312.6 | 1,299.3 | 1,231.6 | 1,362.7 | 1,452.3 | 1,697.1 | 1,768.0 | 1,640.6 | 3,046.2 |
| Manipur | 3,496.4 | 3,179.1 | 2,816.2 | 3,010.5 | 2,943.6 | 3,321.6 | 3,429.4 | 2,490.8 | 4,084.8 | 3,317.6 |
| Meghalaya | 2,300.9 | 2,135.4 | 1,472.8 | 1,728.0 | 1,596.6 | 1,536.7 | 1,639.6 | 1,920.8 | 2,321.6 | 1,952.7 |
| Mizoram | – | – | – | – | – | – | – | – | 4,331.7 | 4,287.7 |
| Nagaland | 3,386.9 | 1,224.3 | 433.6 | 2,259.0 | 2,981.8 | 2,869.6 | 1,963.8 | 2,918.9 | 2,589.0 | 2,977.7 |
| Orissa | 1,239.4 | 1,343.6 | 1,285.8 | 1,233.1 | 1,192.1 | 1,300.0 | 1,339.1 | 1,480.9 | 1,794.2 | 1,593.6 |
| Punjab | 1,012.5 | 1,001.8 | 1,019.8 | 948.8 | 1,015.5 | 1,104.4 | 1,187.4 | 1,491.2 | 1,284.8 | 1,127.6 |
| Rajasthan | 1,036.3 | 1,219.3 | 1,038.0 | 1,070.7 | 1,101.4 | 1,109.0 | 1,326.8 | 1,496.2 | 1,470.2 | 1,453.0 |
| Sikkim | – | – | 2,606.6 | 3,031.3 | 3,393.4 | 3,133.0 | 3,200.5 | 5,559.1 | 5,326.9 | 5,239.9 |
| Tamil Nadu | 1,832.3 | 1,679.9 | 1,478.2 | 1,542.9 | 1,557.3 | 1,651.8 | 1,820.8 | 2,302.6 | 2,327.7 | 2,182.5 |
| Tripura | 1,957.9 | 1,923.7 | 1,573.4 | 1,496.5 | 1,543.1 | 1,549.4 | 1,694.5 | 1,697.4 | 2,002.3 | 2,142.1 |
| Uttarakhand | – | – | – | – | – | – | – | – | – | – |
| Uttar Pradesh | 692.1 | 663.5 | 584.9 | 655.7 | 723.9 | 719.4 | 686.4 | 909.0 | 846.8 | 930.6 |
| West Bengal | 753.1 | 721.8 | 675.8 | 667.4 | 681.3 | 750.1 | 695.2 | 726.9 | 897.7 | 950.5 |
| Union Govt.* | 14.1 | 13.7 | 12.8 | 16.1 | 59.0 | 77.3 | 115.4 | 136.4 | 129.7 | 127.9 |

| 2001–2002 | 2002–2003 | 2003–2004 | 2004–2005 | 2005–2006 | 2006–2007 | 2007–2008 | 2008–2009 | 2009–2010 | 2010–2011 | 2011–2012 |
|---|---|---|---|---|---|---|---|---|---|---|
| 1,041.3 | 1,012.1 | 1,157.2 | 1,141.2 | 1301.1 | 1,411.6 | 1,438.7 | 1,447.5 | 1,459.2 | 1,862.3 | 2,052.3 |
| 1,917.1 | 1,857.5 | 2,064.0 | 1,649.8 | 1,684.7 | 1,814.7 | 1,914.0 | 3,803.5 | 6,456.3 | 4,301.6 | 4,375.9 |
| 1,571.8 | 1,594.8 | 2,026.8 | 2,060.7 | 1,850.8 | 1,975.9 | 2,047.4 | 2,284.2 | 2,629.5 | 2,837.3 | 2,862.0 |
| 806.6 | 825.4 | 747.9 | 712.2 | 923.4 | 887.0 | 1,077.5 | 840.4 | 1,029.9 | 634.8 | 786.5 |
| 1,139.3 | 1,016.2 | 1,024.8 | 887.2 | 858.5 | 833.2 | 850.3 | 798.2 | 1,057.2 | 928.5 | 929.7 |
| 3,882.6 | 3,697.0 | 3,083.6 | 2,777.8 | 2,760.9 | 2,861.1 | 2,870.3 | 3,417.1 | 4,426.3 | 4,598.7 | – |
| 2,002.2 | 2,117.3 | 1,871.6 | 1,898.7 | 1,969.9 | 2,054.7 | 2,199.7 | 2,178.7 | 2,965.0 | 3,765.5 | 3,664.0 |
| 1,391.9 | 1,478.8 | 1,444.6 | 1,495.7 | 1,600.7 | 1,654.7 | 1,640.8 | 2,192.4 | 2,635.8 | 2,749.5 | 2,730.2 |
| 2,831.3 | 2,859.0 | 4,373.7 | 4,272.1 | 4,587.1 | 5,406.2 | 6,448.6 | 7,071.8 | 7,295.0 | 8,488.4 | 8,576.9 |
| 1,499.3 | 1,434.2 | 1,468.6 | 1,292.2 | 1,308.5 | 1,481.3 | 1,523.1 | 1,842.8 | 2,215.3 | 2,378.7 | 2,657.2 |
| 1,355.0 | 1,259.7 | 1,158.6 | 1,108.3 | 1,157.2 | 1,115.4 | 1,174.9 | 1,498.8 | 1,797.8 | 1,648.2 | 1,769.4 |
| 1,505.0 | 1,690.4 | 1,773.9 | 1,656.7 | 1,744.3 | 1,972.4 | 2,414.5 | 2,832.8 | 2,638.5 | 2,697.7 | 2,975.6 |
| 2,566.0 | 2,918.0 | 2,909.2 | 2,673.6 | 2,654.9 | 3,028.2 | 3,315.3 | 3,450.6 | 3,585.9 | 3,814.7 | 5,115.3 |
| 984.2 | 1,021.5 | 990.1 | 1,026.0 | 968.8 | 1,043.6 | 1,030.7 | 1,233.3 | 1,449.4 | 1,618.1 | 1,758.7 |
| 3,179.9 | 2,512.8 | 2,412.8 | 2,307.6 | 2,352.2 | 2,554.1 | 2,673.1 | 3,080.8 | 4,033.9 | 4,310.3 | 4,486.2 |
| 4,111.5 | 3,311.6 | 3,466.4 | 2,857.0 | 3,122.7 | 2,980.1 | 3,016.7 | 3,373.0 | 2,414.2 | 3,164.0 | 3,167.3 |
| 1,976.9 | 1,854.1 | 1,854.0 | 1,611.3 | 1,635.6 | 1,559.2 | 1,549.8 | 1,654.5 | 2,011.8 | 3,078.6 | 3,124.2 |
| 4,112.8 | 4,165.1 | 4,255.9 | 3,921.0 | 3,775.3 | 3,789.6 | 4,304.7 | 4,651.1 | 6,159.8 | 7,198.6 | 6,382.8 |
| 2,822.7 | 2,692.7 | 2,835.4 | 2,537.6 | 3,053.4 | 3,305.3 | 3,890.9 | 432.9 | 1,369.2 | 4,839.0 | 5,373.4 |
| 1,537.3 | 1,564.3 | 1,515.2 | 1,370.5 | 1,500.4 | 1,563.1 | 1,643.5 | 1,834.6 | 2,001.1 | 1,895.5 | 1,824.6 |
| 985.1 | 1,102.8 | 1,074.1 | 1,004.9 | 993.1 | 908.9 | 931.5 | 727.5 | 836.9 | 870.3 | 1,176.0 |
| 1,421.4 | 1,453.7 | 1,551.1 | 1,386.7 | 1,563.2 | 1,515.0 | 1,548.6 | 1,944.1 | 2,168.2 | 1,976.6 | 1,843.8 |
| 5,170.8 | 4,373.4 | 4,365.8 | 4,356.9 | 4,702.1 | 4,802.6 | 4,967.8 | 5,103.0 | 7,445.0 | 8,392.8 | 6,916.8 |
| 2,102.5 | 1,889.9 | 1,733.3 | 1,675.9 | 1,682.6 | 2,037.5 | 2,113.8 | 2,550.0 | 2,853.1 | 3,257.4 | 3,469.4 |
| 2,564.9 | 2,981.0 | 3,000.3 | 3,040.9 | 2346.7 | 2,389.3 | 2,766.0 | 2,862.6 | 3,979.6 | 3,892.9 | 3,986.2 |
| 1,252.6 | 2,415.5 | 2,523 | 2,382.4 | 2289.7 | 2,352.1 | 2,259.3 | 2,503.0 | 4,356.0 | 3,912.7 | 4,084.3 |
| 969.6 | 877.1 | 880.3 | 849.8 | 923.4 | 982.2 | 1,058.6 | 1,107.3 | 1,260.7 | 1,377.7 | 1,831.8 |
| 937.8 | 871.6 | 857.0 | 909.3 | 945.2 | 907.9 | 980.5 | 984.2 | 1,298.1 | 1,374.1 | – |
| 125.4 | 200.1 | 237.8 | 333.0 | 406.4 | 583.4 | 563.2 | 662.4 | 565.8 | 772.2 | 744.4 |

*Note:* Spending on Elementary education has been considered under State Finance Accounts under sub-major head 01 of major head 2202; and population has added child population between 6 and 14 years age, population has been projected from 1991, 2001 and 2011 figures, J &K figure was not available for 1991 census, for which, we have used same growth rate between 2001 and 2011. In 1991 census population available for 7–14 years; for making consistency, we have added population in seven years as population with six years.

*Union Government indicates expenditure exclusively by union government, not by any state.

*Table A2.5* Compound annual growth rate of per-child expenditure on education and per capita gross state domestic product (at 2004–05 prices)

| | *Per-child expenditure on education* | | *Per capita GSDP* | |
|---|---|---|---|---|
| | CAGR *1991–92 to 2001–02* | CAGR *2001–02 to 2011–12* | CAGR *1991–92 to 2001–02* | CAGR *2001–02 to 2011–12* |
| Andhra Pradesh | 2.190 | 7.020 | 3.813 | 7.035 |
| Arunachal Pradesh | −2.437 | 8.603 | 2.773 | 3.906 |
| Assam | 0.381 | 6.176 | 0.220 | 4.324 |
| Bihar | 6.013 | −0.251 | 2.600 | 6.339 |
| Chhattisgarh | – | −2.012 | – | 5.745 |
| Goa | 3.190 | 1.899** | 4.564 | 8.346 |
| Gujarat | 4.279 | 6.230 | 5.226 | 7.780 |
| Haryana | 2.230 | 6.969 | 2.526 | 6.869 |
| Himachal Pradesh | 2.956 | 11.721 | 4.924 | 6.937 |
| Jammu & Kashmir | −0.054 | 5.890 | 0.616 | 5.264 |
| Jharkhand | – | 2.704 | – | 5.038 |
| Karnataka | 3.218 | 7.055 | 4.050 | 5.638 |
| Kerala | 1.994 | 7.143 | 4.740 | 6.991 |
| Madhya Pradesh | 5.719 | 5.977 | 5.750 | 5.021 |
| Maharashtra | 8.931 | 3.502 | 4.401 | 6.595 |
| Manipur | −0.524 | −2.575 | 1.514 | 4.529 |
| Meghalaya | −1.628 | 4.683 | 2.369 | 5.333 |
| Mizoram | – | 4.493 | – | 5.540 |
| Nagaland | −1.279 | 6.649 | 1.096 | 8.406 |
| Orissa | 2.545 | 1.728 | 1.968 | 6.061 |
| Punjab | 1.083 | 1.787 | 2.104 | 4.044 |
| Rajasthan | 3.438 | 2.636 | 3.466 | 4.857 |
| Sikkim | 9.120* | 2.952 | 3.851* | 12.205 |
| Tamil Nadu | 1.765 | 5.136 | 4.352 | 8.072 |
| Tripura | 0.903 | 4.508 | 6.145 | 7.249 |
| Uttarakhand | – | 5.538 | – | 10.525 |
| Uttar Pradesh | 3.006 | 7.983 | 4.661 | 5.639 |
| West Bengal | 2.355 | 4.336** | 5.677 | 5.961 |
| Centre's Share | 24.708 | 19.499 | 3.735 | 6.256 |

*Note:* CAGR calculated with the formula $[\{(X_{t+n})/X_t\}^{(1/n)} - 1\}*100]$; $X_t$ is GSDP at period t, and $X_{t+n}$ is GSDP at period (t+n).

* Calculated for 8 years and ** for 9 years, rest are for 10 years.

*Table A2.6a* Elementary education outlays by Ministry of Human Resource Development from 2005–06 to 2012–13 (in Rs. million)

| *Ministry/dept.* | 2005–06 | | | 2006–07 | | | 2007–08 | | | 2008–09 | | |
|---|---|---|---|---|---|---|---|---|---|---|---|---|
| *School education & literacy* | *Plan* | *Non-plan* | *Total* | *Plan* | *Non-plan* | *Total* | *Plan* | *Non-plan* | *Total* | *Plan* | *Non-plan* | *Total* |
| Total | **119,795** | **45** | **119,841** | **168,929** | **45** | **168,975** | **199,426** | **100,012** | **209,427** | **228,465** | **15,244.6** | **243,709** |
| Revenue | 119,795 | 45 | 119,841 | 168,929 | 45 | 168,929 | 199,426 | 100,012 | 209,427 | 227,380 | 15,244.6 | 242,625 |
| Capital | – | – | – | – | – | – | – | – | – | 1,085 | | 1,084.6 |

*Source:* Expenditure Budget, Volume I, Union Budget Documents, Government of India, various years.

*Table A2.6b* Elementary education outlays by Ministry of Human Resource Development from 2005–06 to 2012–13 (in Rs. million)

| *Ministry/dept.* | *2009–10* | | | *2010–11* | | | *2011–12* | | | *2012–13* | | |
|---|---|---|---|---|---|---|---|---|---|---|---|---|
| *School education and literacy* | *Plan* | *Non-plan* | *Total* | *Plan* | *Non-plan* | *Total* | *Plan* | *Non-plan* | *Total* | *Plan* | *Non-plan* | *Total* |
| Total | 218,586 | 26,074.8 | 244,661 | 341,293 | 23,032.4 | 364,325 | 380,796 | 25,618 | 406,414 | 428,214 | 28,100.8 | 456,314 |
| Revenue | 216,086 | 26,074.8 | 242,161 | 341,293 | 23,032.4 | 364,325 | 380,796 | 25,618 | 406,414 | 428,214 | 28,100.8 | 456,314 |
| Capital | 2,500 | – | 2,500 | – | – | – | – | – | – | – | – | – |

*Source:* Expenditure Budget, Volume I, Union Budget Documents, Government of India, various years.

*Table A2.7* Disproportionate SSA budget outlays and plan allocations

| *Union budget outlays made during five-year plans* | *1st year* | *2nd year* | *3rd year* | *4th year* | *5th year* |
|---|---|---|---|---|---|
| Total outlays as % of 11th Plan allocations | 18.6 | 37.0 | 55.5 | 82.2 | 111.8 |
| Union budget outlays as % of 12th Plan allocations | 12.4 | 27.0 | 40.9 | | |

*Source:* Compiled from 11th and 12th Five Year Plan documents; Union Budget, Expenditure Budget, Volume II, various years.

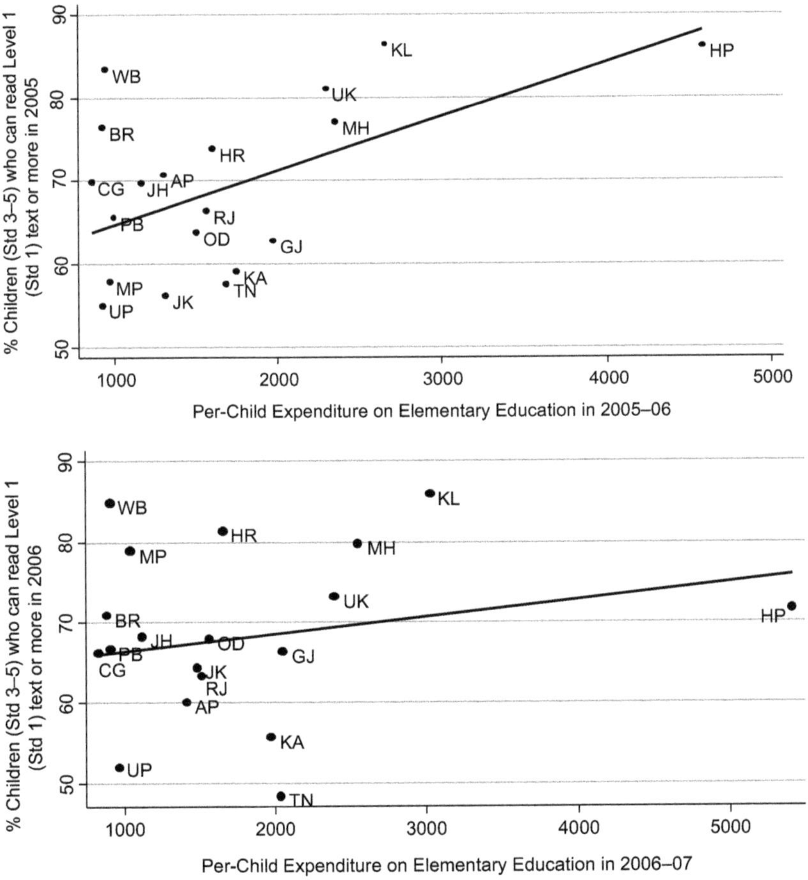


*Figure A2.1* Per-child expenditure on elementary education 2005–06 to 2011–12 and proportion of children (Std 3–5) who can read Level 1 (Std 1) text or more in the same year, collected by ASER.

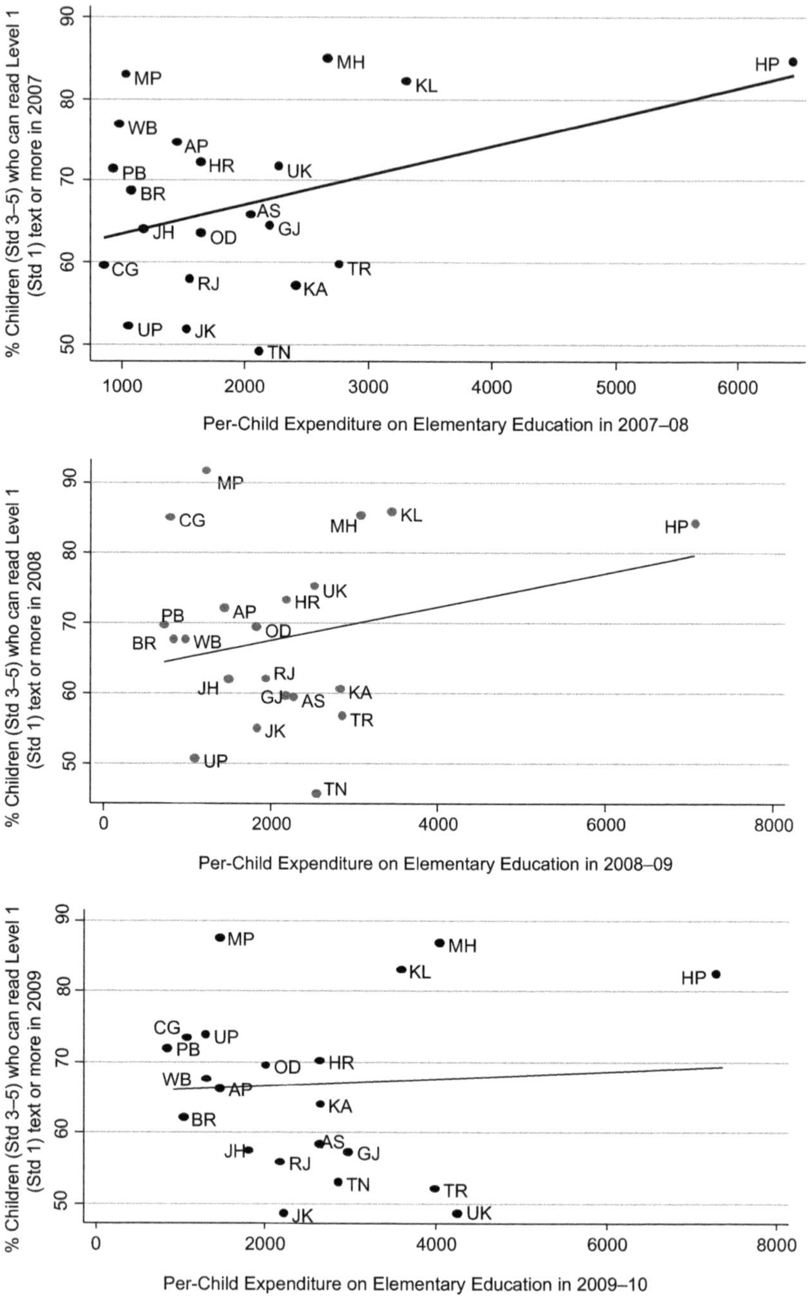


*Figure A2.1* (Continued)

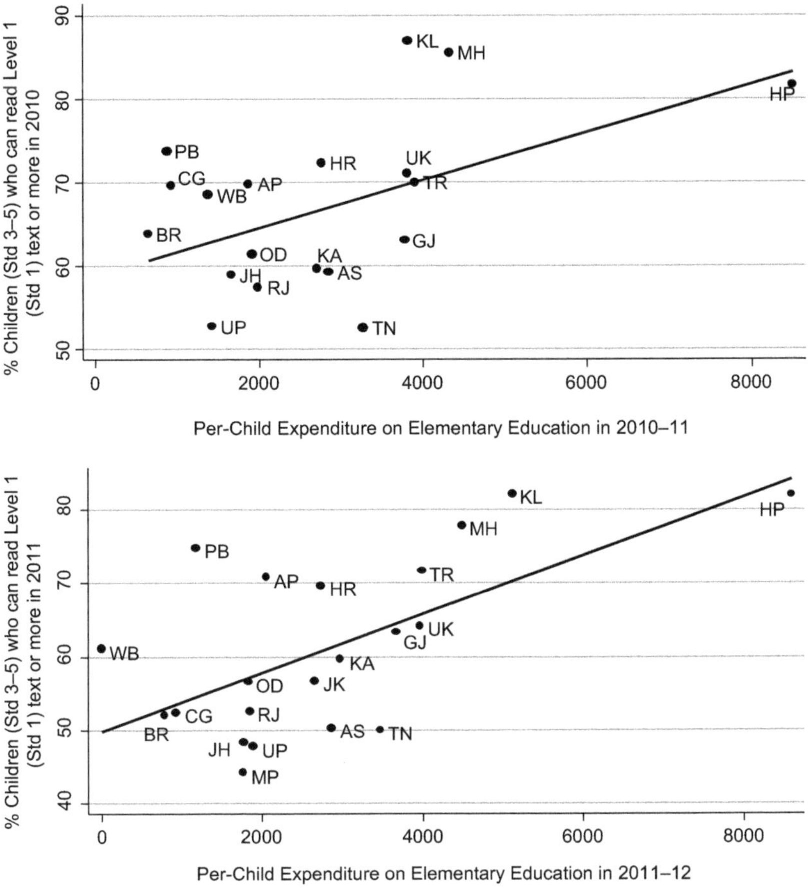


*Figure A2.1* (Continued)

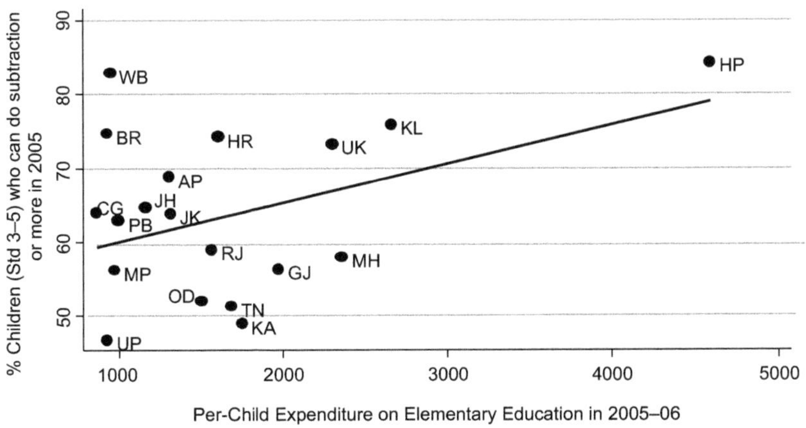


*Figure A2.2* Per-child expenditure on elementary education 2005–06 to 2011–12 and proportion of children (Std 3–5) who can do subtraction or more in the same year, collected by ASER.

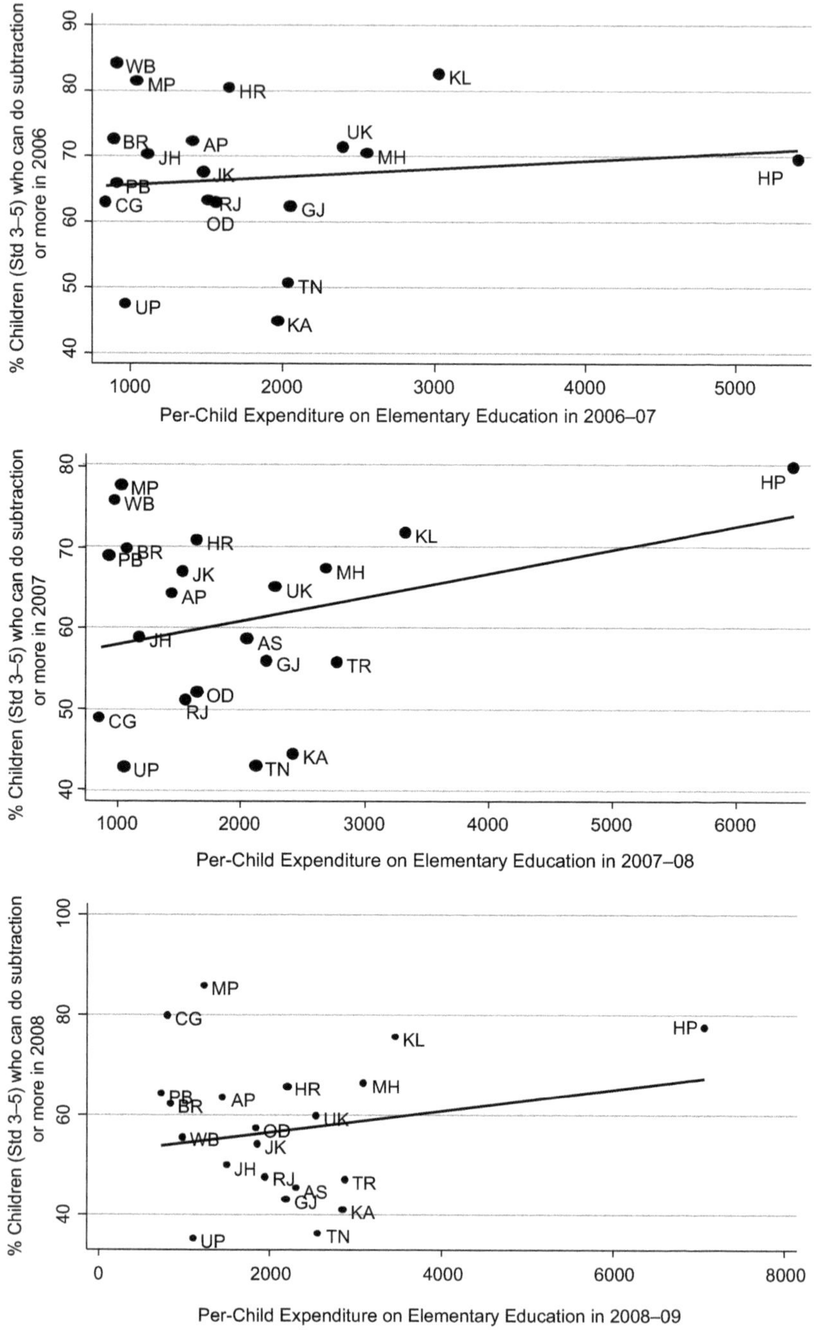


*Figure A2.2* (Continued)

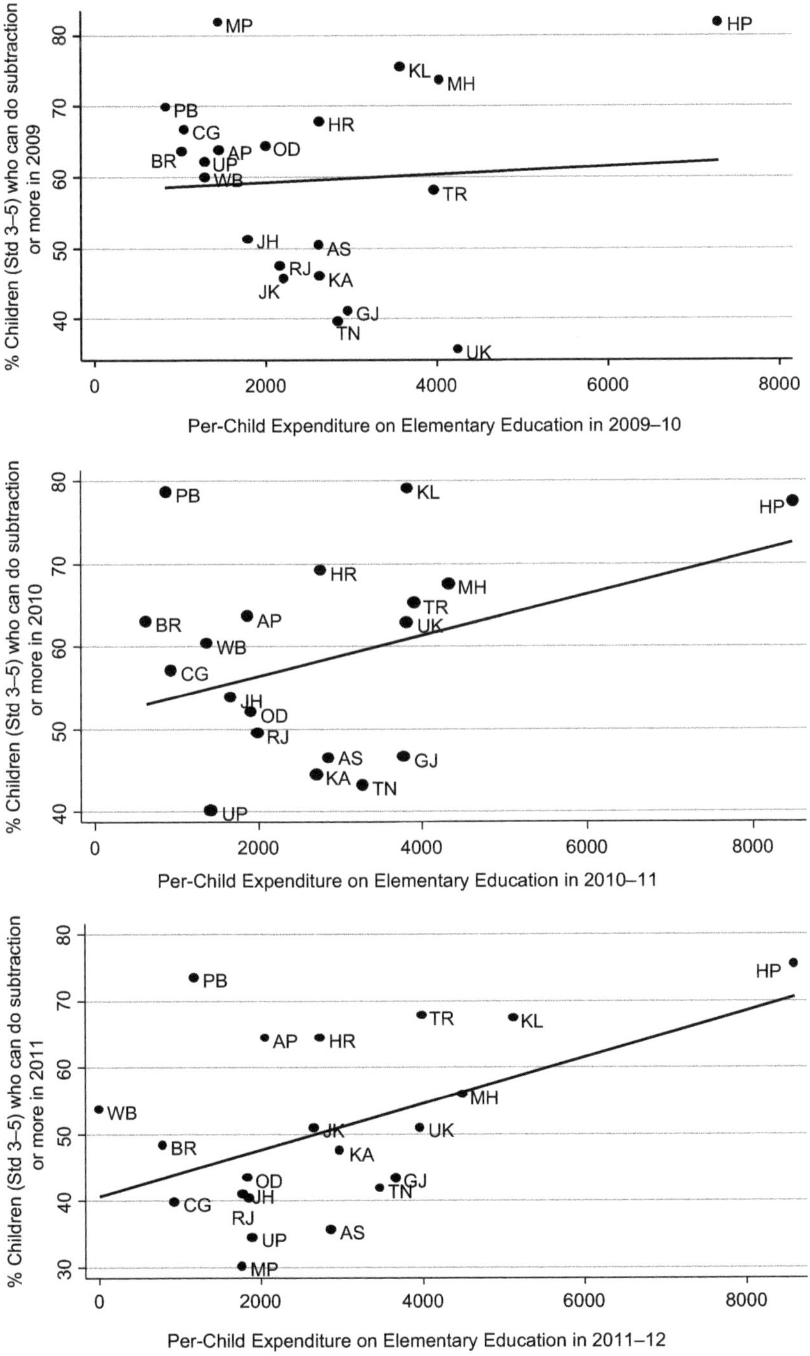


*Figure A2.2* (Continued)

## Notes

1 'The priority of education as a key instrument for development should be expressed by the commitment to gradually increase investment in the sector to at least 6 per cent of GDP in order to achieve universal coverage of basic education and to overcome current deficits', The Dakar Framework for Action, Adopted by the World Education Forum Dakar, Senegal, 26–28 April 2000; page 40.

2 The definition of a 'literate person' according to the Census Directorate of India is 'a person (belonging to the population above 7 years of age) should be able to read and write with understanding in any language. The person may or may not have received any formal education.' Conducted once in 10 years starting from 1872, the Directorate of Census operating in India has been collecting data, among other demographic features, on literacy. Till 1941 the estimates were based on the entire population. In the 1951, 1961 and 1971 Censuses the population of 5 years and above was taken. From the 1981 Census, literacy rates are being calculated for population above 7 years. The estimates are based on the response given by individuals to the enumerator's question: 'Are you literate? Can you read and write?'

3 It is interesting to note that as per the Gokhale's Bill, the pupil–teacher ratio was supposed to be in the range of 30–40.

4 Jha, Praveen and PoojaParvati, 2014. 'Assessing Progress on Universal Elementary Education in India: A Note on Some Key Constraints', *Economic and Political Weekly*, XIIX(16): 45.

5 Ministry of Human Resource and Development, Government of India (2012) GDP figures (market price at current price) from Handbook of Statistics on Indian Economy, 2011–12.

6 Calculated by 2202–01/pop, and SSA per-child exp.

7 This is done by looking at by an examination of fees paid by the parents of who are working in one particular institution of Delhi.

8 Further, among these there are quite a few multicountry studies which include: (i) Early Grade Reading Assessment (EGRA) in 44 countries, (ii) Early Development Instrument (EDI) in 24 countries, (iii) Young Lives in 4 countries, (iv) Multiple Indicator Cluster Survey (MICS) in 55 countries, (v) UWEZO in 3 developing countries, (vi) Annual Status of Education Report (ASER) in 2 countries, (vii) Literacy Boost in 9 countries, (viii) Early Grade Math Assessment (EGMA) in 11 countries, (ix) Programme for International Student Assessment (PISA) in 32 OECD countries and some partner countries, (x) Analysis Programme of the CONFEMEN Education System (PASEC) in 13 countries, (xi) Progress in International Reading Literacy Study (PIRLS) in 49 countries, (xii) Pre-PIRLS in 3 countries, (xiii) Trends in International Mathematics and Science Study (TIMSS) in 63 countries, (xiv) The Southern and Eastern Africa Consortium for Monitoring Educational Quality (SACMEQ) in 14 countries, (xv) Latin American Laboratory for Assessment of the Quality of Education (LLECE) in 16 countries and (xvi) Literacy Assessment Monitoring Programme (LAMP) in 12 countries. Most of these studies collect information on reading and simple

arithmetic proficiencies. Some other studies like MICS and Early Development Instrument concentrated also in physical, social, emotional situation of children (Simons Kate Anderson 2012). Further, among these cross countries studies three studies have been conducted in India, e.g. ASER, Young Lives (in Andhra Pradesh), PISA (in Himachal Pradesh and Tamil Nadu only in the year 2009).

9 District Information System for Education (DISE) provides Education Development Index (EDI) measurement across all states with 24 variables covering four dimensions. The four dimensions are (i) access, (ii) infrastructure, (iii) teachers and (iv) outcomes. EDI calculates overall state-wise performance ranking on the basis of these four dimensions, which cannot be considered as quality of education.

10 Although ASER data are available for every districts, we have not done this exercise for districts as because information on district-wise public expenditure on education is not available.

## References


CAG, 1993 to 2014. State Finance Accounts, Comptroller and Auditor General of India.

De, Anuradha and Tanuka Endow, 2008. Public Expenditure on Education in India: Recent Trends and Outcomes, RECOUP Working Paper No. 18, May 2008.

Jha, Praveen and Pooja Parvati, 2014., 'Assessing Progress on Universal Elementary Education in India: A Note on Some Key Constraints', *Economic and Political Weekly*, XlIX(16): 45.

Jha, Praveen, Subrat Das, Siba Sankar Mohanty and Nandan Kumar Jha, 2008. *Public Provisioning for Elementary Education in India*, SAGE India, New Delhi.

MHRD, 2012, 2013. Analysis of Budgeted Expenditure on Education 2009–10 to 2011–12, Planning and Monitoring Unit, Ministry of Human Resource and Development, Government of India.

MoF, 2006 to 2014. Expenditure Budget, Volumes I and II, Union Budget Documents, Ministry of Finance, Government of India.

NCERT, 2013. All India School Education Survey (8th AISES, 2008–09), National Council of Educational Research and Training.

NUEPA, 2010, 2011, 2012. Elementary Education: State Report Cards, DISE, National University of Education Planning and Administration.

NUEPA, 2010, 2011, 2012. Elementary Education in India: Progress towards UEE, Flash Statistics DISE, National University of Education Planning and Administration.

Planning Commission, 2013. Twelfth Five Year Plan, 2012–2017. Faster, More Inclusive and Sustainable Growth, Planning Commission, Government of India, SAGE, New Delhi.

Planning Commission, 2008. Eleventh Five Year Plan 2007–12. Inclusive Growth, Planning Commission, Government of India, Oxford University Press, New Delhi.
Pratham, 2006, 2007, 2008, 2009, 2010, 2011, 2012. Annual Status of Education Report (Rural) ASER Centre, New Delhi, India.
RBI, 2013. Handbook of Statistics on Indian Economy, 2011–12.
UNDP, 2013. Human Development Report 2013 – The Rise of the South: Human Progress in a Diverse World.

# 3

# FINANCING ELEMENTARY EDUCATION IN ANDHRA PRADESH UNDER SARVA SHIKSHA ABHIYAN

## A study on fund flow pattern and utilization of resources

*B. Shiva Reddy and K. Anji Reddy*

### Introduction

Andhra Pradesh (AP) is one of the states growing faster during the reform periods compared to many other states. But such an economic growth has not yet translated in terms of the human development of the state especially in terms of the many goals of Sarva Shiksha Abhiyan (SSA). Economic growth is higher in the last two decades but inclusive growth or equitable development has been missing in AP. Examining inclusive growth by considering agricultural growth, employment generation and poverty reduction, social sector (health and education) and reduction in regional and other disparities, Dev (2007) found that there seems to be some 'turn around' in the gross state domestic product (GSDP) of AP in the early years of the new millennium. Despite this, AP may not achieve millennium development goals in crucial indicators of *education*, health and sanitation at current rates of progress. The progress in MDGs for some regions and socially deprived sections like SCs and STs has been slower than the state average. Economic growth may be improving but AP is lagging behind in agriculture, employment, human development and in reducing regional disparities.

On the EE front, AP is known for the introduction of many initiatives for improving access and quality of Elementary Education (EE) since the middle of 1980s. They include among others Operation Blackboard (OBB),

AP Primary Education Project (APPEP), District Primary Education Programme (DPEP) and SSA. The extent and scope of funding and also their effect on improving access and quality of EE varied. SSA is the latest and ongoing flagship programme for improving access and quality of EE.

In this chapter an attempt is made to analyse the financing of EE under SSA with a focus on fund flow pattern and utilization of resources. Before we discuss on the fund flow pattern and utilization of resources a brief presentation on the progress of EE is made in the second section. This section directly and indirectly throws some light on the impact of the earlier programmes like OBB, APPEP and DPEP. While tracing the progress of EE in the state, this section also brings out the growing private sector participation and briefly outlines the trends in financing EE. In the third section trends in financing of EE under SSA is discussed followed by the fund flow pattern. Fourth section deals with misappropriation of funding under SSA and explores the reasons for such an episode. Fifth section examines the finances under SSA across districts. The subsequent section compares fund flow pattern and utilization of resources in two districts, viz., Nalgonda and Ranga Reddy districts. The last section summarizes the findings and draws some conclusions.

## Progress of EE in AP

Education especially at the elementary level has shown a remarkable growth since independence in our country. It is mandatory on the part of the government at the centre and the states to provide education to the children in the age group of 6–14 years. The successive governments at the centre and states made effort to provide educational facilities in the country through five year plans with the result, the number of schools established for providing EE and enrolment in India has increased many folds during the last six decades. The state of AP is no exception to these developments.

Many new schools at primary stage were opened under DPEP, even in habitations having small population. Due to upgradation of many primary schools into upper primary and upper primary into secondary schools in the last few years, particularly since 1995, accessibility to upper primary stage (Classes VI–VII) and also to secondary stage (Classes VIII–X) increased along with access to primary stage (Classes I–V). Earlier it was thought that reducing the distance by opening primary schools helps in increasing the enrolment. Parents' decision to send or not to send the child, particularly the girl child to school, depended upon the availability of schooling facility within the habitation. The habitations/villages having less population and hence no school were at a disadvantage compared to more populated habitations/villages. Keeping this in view the new schools were opened in habitations having less population and few school-going children. The newly opened schools, particularly after 1995, had less number of children than schools opened before. Micro planning exercise done in the AP indicated that 95.8 per cent of habitations were covered with a primary school/section in 2009–10 (GoAP 2010).

Hence, primary schools were opened in almost all the habitations to provide access to school. Wherever it was not possible to open a primary school an alternative school was provided, with a result that 99.59 per cent of habitations were covered with primary school/section. Subsequently, some of the new primary schools remained without any enrolment or a single teacher in the school for some time. There are about 0.7 per cent of primary schools with zero enrolment and another 13.6 per cent of schools with less than enrolment of 20 children (see Table 3.1). Together, about 14 per cent of schools have become financially non-viable to be run by the government in 2013–14. Compared to 2009–10 there is some improvement.

Consequently, on increase in the number of schools at various levels, the number of children attending school also increased tremendously. Due to demographic transition and minimization of under/over aged children, the enrolment at primary stage declined in the last few years. Among the different levels of education, secondary education increased more rapidly than other levels of education. Due to the emphasis on Universalization of EE (UEE) earlier, the demand for secondary education increased enormously

*Table 3.1* Trends in budget expenditure on education in AP

| *Year* | *BEE (Rs. in crores)* | | *BEE as % of* | |
|---|---|---|---|---|
| | *Current* | *Constant@* | *TRE* | *NSDP* |
| 1960–61 | 17 | 310 | 20.45 | 1.77 |
| 1970–71 | 62 | 625 | 20.92 | 2.46 |
| 1980–81 | 226 | 1,113 | 19.50 | 3.09 |
| 1990–91 | 988 | 2,170 | 17.96 | 3.28 |
| 2000–01 | 3,696 | 3,558 | 16.02 | 2.94 |
| 2008–09** | 10,520 | 7,108 | 15.00 | 3.18 |
| CAGR (%) | 14.3 | 6.7 | – | – |

*Source:* (1) MHRD (1995), (2) Tilak (1998), (3) GoAP (2002), (4) Budget in brief for various years of AP, (5) SDP of AP, DE&S, GoAP (2008).

*Note:* *Revised estimates; **Budget estimates. (@1999–2000 prices).

in the last few years. During 1959–60 and 2013–14 the enrolment at secondary stage increased at an annual growth of 6.4 per cent when compared to 2.5 per cent at primary and 5.2 per cent at upper primary stage. This is a welcome development because majority enrolled at primary stage are not only completing upper primary stage (Classes VI–VII) but also reaching secondary stage (Selected Educational Statistics, GoAP).

Along with increase in the enrolment, the proportion of students successfully completing each grade also increased. The transition rate, which gives an idea of how many enrolled in a particular class reaches next grade, increased significantly.

There are improvements in the completion of successive stages in the last decade when compared to late 1970s and early 1980s. More than three-fourth are able to complete primary stage; more than half the elementary stage and more than two-fifth are able to reach class X now than before. These suggest that increase in transition rates at a lower stage leads to increase in demand for latter stages. These improvements, however, cannot stop from looking into the inadequacies of the system in retaining more children than the present situation. To achieve UEE all children enrolled in class I should reach class VIII. Not more than two-thirds are able to complete this stage. The wastage is as much as one-third, quite high at any standards. Whether the resources are also wasted to that extent? It is yes if the provision is made for all the children. While planning for school places the dropout rates are already taken into account, indirectly. Many of the existing schools cannot have sufficient accommodation if all the children enrolled in class I successively continue in all the classes. The existing teaching arrangements either become inadequate or irrelevant. To this extent the system is not fully geared up to meet the challenges posed by the recent Amendment to the Constitution, where by EE is made a fundamental right.

Due to increase in both number of schools and enrolment the proportion of children attending the school also increased significantly in the last few years. The GER shows that almost all the children in the age group 6–10 are attending the school. About two-thirds of the children in the age group are reported to be studying in upper primary stage. The GER at secondary stage also increased. Thus GERs suggest that there is a significant increase in the demand for school education.

The quality of EE in terms of inputs like teacher availability increased significantly in the last four decades in AP. The Pupil Teacher Ratio (PTR), though increased initially exceeding the norm, declined since 1990s due to recruitment of teachers on large scale. At present the PTR is less than the norm.

However, the distribution of teachers across schools is not uniform. About 0.36 per cent of schools are running without a teacher and 11.0 per cent of schools are running with a single teacher in 2013–14. One can understand a school may be run without a building but not without a teacher. So, the schools running without a teacher may be considered as non-functioning schools and single-teacher schools may be considered as partial functioning schools. With a result though the school is physically accessible to the children education is inaccessible to all those children studying in these zero teacher or single-teacher schools. There are teachers working in schools having no student or very few students. There are schools having more enrolment but with few teachers. Further, there are schools with low enrolment but with more teachers. However, compared to 2009–10 there is some improvement in 2013–14 as GoAP has taken steps to rationalization of teacher deployment.

Pass percentage at the common examination (end of Grade-VII) has been quite high and above 90 per cent with some inter-district variations. There are no gender differences. The successful candidates in this examination are the inputs for secondary education. There is a substantial difference in the number of candidates passing class VII and the number of students in class VIII. The difference is mainly due to non-availability of facility, particularly, for those completing class VII in an UP school. Though class VIII is a part of EE at the national level, it is not so at the state level till the implementation of RTE Act. In order to meet the Constitutional requirement, UP schools having minimum 40 students in classes VI/VII (together) added class VIII. However, the pass percentage is not really measuring the quality of education in terms of learning levels. The recent evidence suggests that learning levels of children in EE is far from satisfactory despite the existence of quality improvement programmes like SSA (Rajiv Vidya Mission).

### *Private and public participation in education*

Though no clear cut policy resolution was adopted at the national level with regard to the role of private initiative in the development and financing of education, some states like AP have encouraged private initiative. At the school stage the percentage of schools under private management has increased sharply in the last few years. At the time of state formation the private unaided primary schools were negligible but they crossed single digit now. They account for more than one-eighth of the primary schools and two-fifth of upper primary schools. It is even more in the case of secondary schools because the increased demand for secondary education is being largely met by private schools.

Increased participation of private sector and public demand for up-gradation of UPS schools into secondary schools has resulted in the increase of private unaided and local body schools. In order to encourage the local bodies to upgrade the upper primary schools in rural area into secondary schools, GoAP relaxed the payment of corpus fund. It may be noted that there are marginal management-wise differences in the enrolment of girls except in the private-aided institutions where it is almost 50 per cent. This may be due to more number of girls' schools under this management and also having urban concentration. The proportion of girls in private unaided is less compared to government schools, indicating some bias towards boys (Selected Educational Statistics, GoAP 2001 and 2005).

### *Financing of EE*

The importance given to education depends on the overall budgetary position and the competing demand for funds from other sectors. Since the formation of the state budget expenditure on education (BEE) has increased significantly in AP, both in absolute and in per capita terms (Table 3.1). During the period 1960–61 and 2008–09 the BEE increased from Rs. 170 million to Rs. 105,200 million in 2008–09, thus registering an annual growth rate of 14.3 per cent. But in real terms the increase was 6.7 per cent only. The priority given to education can be judged by the ratio of BEE to Total Revenue Expenditure (TRE) and State Domestic Product (SDP). The ratio of BEE to TRE increased from 20.45 per cent in 1960–01 to a maximum of 22.84 per cent in 1994–95 but declined thereafter reaching a minimum of 15.0 per cent in the last year. The decline is more in recent years than earlier. As the ratio of SDP, BEE also increased from 1.73 per cent in 1960–61 to 3.95 per cent in 1986–87. Thereafter it declined and reached 3.18 per cent in 2008–09. The Education Commission's recommendation of allocating 6 per cent of GDP has remained unfulfilled not only at the national level but also at the state level.

In AP, the expenditure on education is incurred by several departments of GoAP, though Education Department is the main funding department. A significant part of the budgets of Social Welfare Department and Tribal Welfare Department is allocated to educational programmes. Expenditure on education incurred by departments other than Education Department accounts for about 10 to 15 per cent. Social Welfare Department and Tribal Welfare Department spend considerable amount on school education as they provide grants to APSWREIS and TWREIS. There are changes in the inter-sectoral allocation of BEE among different levels/types of education

*Table 3.2* Inter-sectoral distribution of BEE (revenue account)

| *Year* | *Elementary* | *Secondary* | *Higher* | *Technical* | *Others* | *Total* |
|---|---|---|---|---|---|---|
| 1960–61 | 49.18 | 25.22 | 9.56 | – | 16.04 | 100 |
| 1970–71 | 43.21 | 33.09 | 13.25 | 3.38 | 7.07 | 100 |
| 1980–81 | 44.77 | 29.49 | 19.59 | 3.08 | 3.30 | 100 |
| 1990–91 | 45.98 | 28.20 | 21.32 | 2.84 | 1.66 | 100 |
| 2000–01 | 42.90 | 30.10 | 23.40 | 2.40 | 1.20 | 100 |
| 2008–09* | 44.35 | 22.26 | 15.02 | 2.23 | 16.13 | 100 |

*Source:* Government of AP, Budget Estimates for various years.

*Note:* *Budget Estimates.

in the last four decades (Table 3.2). The budget allocations to EE varied between 40 and 50 per cent. Initially the share was around 50 per cent but declined later reaching a minimum of 32.90 per cent in 1994–95. But in last few years the share has increased considerably due to emphasis on UEE. Secondary education budget also varied between 25 and 35 per cent of BEE. Initially it increased gradually till 1980s but again declined in the last few years. It is very difficult to identify the reasons for these fluctuations.

When compared to school education, higher education received a favourable treatment in the budget allocation till recently. The proportion of BEE to higher education increased from around 10 per cent in 1960–61 to 22.3 per cent in 2008–09. However, there were some fluctuations during this period. Because of policy decision to restrict higher education in the public sector the allocations have declined in the last two years. The allocations to technical education, which is dominated by private sector also declined in the recent years.

## Funding of EE under SSA

As seen in Table 3.2, the allocation to EE as a percentage of BEE declined over a period of time. However, there is an increase in its share in the recent years due to introduction of plan schemes. The plan expenditure which accounted for less than 10 per cent earlier now increased to more than 10 per cent in recent years. There is gap between budget estimates, revised estimates and actual expenditure. The latter is less than the former indicating that what is proposed is not spent. This is true for both plan and non-plan budget. One of the reasons for increase in the plan budget for primary education is the centrally sponsored schemes. The ongoing scheme is the SSA. The allocation for this scheme increased significantly in the last two years from Rs. 3,500 million in 2010–11 to Rs. 6,500 million in 2011–12. AP is one of the states receiving funding continuously under one programme or the other. During 1980s the state received funding from DFID (UK) under APPEP for improving the quality of primary education. Later the funding came from the centre under OBB scheme. From mid 1990s the state received funding under the DPEP. From early part of 2000 the state is receiving funding from the centre under SSA. The extent of funding and coverage of activities varied from one scheme to the other.

### *Allocation to EE under SSA*

As SSA is a centrally sponsored programme, both the central government and state government fund it. The ratio of central share to state share changes with passing of years. It was 75:25 in the beginning of the programme and 50:50 at the end of the programme. However, there was some change in the arrangement with centre's share more than 50 per cent till 2010–11. Table 3.3 gives details about the central and state governments share in SSA funds.

As per the guidelines the Central Government releases funds directly to Rajiv Vidya Mission (hereafter referred as Society), the State Implementing Society in AP. The Society is supposed to receive funds from the centre in two instalments – in April for the first two quarters of the financial year and in September for the third and last quarter. As can be seen from

*Table 3.3* Funding of SSA by centre and state government in AP (Rs. in lakhs)

| *Year* | *Outlay approved by PAB* | *Centre released amount* | *State released amount* | *Total releases* | *% of state share in total releases* | *Total released as % to approved* | *% of centre share to outlay* | *% of state share to outlay* |
|---|---|---|---|---|---|---|---|---|
| 2001–02 | 5,376 | 1,955 | 345 | 2,300 | 15.0 | 42.8 | 36.4 | 6.4 |
| 2002–03 | 20,930 | 8,556 | 58 | 8,614 | 0.7 | 41.2 | 40.9 | 0.3 |
| 2004–05 | 49,520 | 25,000 | 8,233 | 33,233 | 24.8 | 67.1 | 50.5 | 16.6 |
| 2005–06 | 64,887 | 35,999 | 12,000 | 47,999 | 25.0 | 74.0 | 55.5 | 18.5 |
| 2009–10 | 101,369 | 13,570 | 9,047 | 22,617 | 40.0 | 22.3 | 13.4 | 8.9 |
| 2008–09 | 155,353 | 71,032 | 20,996 | 92,027 | 22.8 | 59.2 | 45.7 | 22.8 |
| 2010–11 | 226,437 | 81,000 | 65,309 | 146,309 | 44.6 | 64.6 | 35.8 | 44.6 |
| 2013–14 | 308,848 | 179,715 | 115,161 | 294,877 | 39.1 | 95.5 | 58.2 | 39.1 |

*Source*: SSA Unpublished Records.

*Table 3.4* Date-wise release of centre and state shares in AP

| *Year* | *Central government* | | *State government* | |
|---|---|---|---|---|
| | *Date of release* | *Date of receipt by Society* | *Date of release* | *Date of receipt by Society* |
| 2001–02 | 22–08–2001 | 24–11–2001 | 16–10–2001 | 12–12–2001 |
| | 19–09–2001 | 12–12–2001 | | |
| 2002–03 | 14–03–2002 | 19–12–2002 | 15–07–2002 | 19–12–2002 |
| | 03–09–2002 | 16–10–2002 | | |
| | 20–01–2003 | 14–02–2003 | 28–12–2002 | 04–06–2003 |
| 2003–04 | 27–08–2003 | 17–09–2003 | 11–03–2003 | 04–06–2003 |
| | 23–03–2004 | | 19–12–2003 | 31–03–2004 |
| | | | 23–10–2004 | 16–12–2004 |
| 2004–05 | 18–05–2004 | 16–06–2004 | 01–01–2005 | 22–01–2005 |
| | 09–08–2004 | 08–09–2004 | 19–02–2005 | |
| | 18–01–2005 | 11–02–2005 | 22–03–2005 | |
| 2005–06 | 26–05–2005 | 23–06–2005 | 27–09–2005 | 17–02–2006 |
| | 07–06–2005 | 29–06–2005 | 22–03–2006 | 31–03–2006 |
| | 05–09–2005 | 24–10–2005 | | |
| | 23–12–2005 | 16–01–2006 | 20–12–2006 | 07–03–2007 |
| 2006–07 | 14–06–2006 | 27–07–2006 | 20–01–2007 | 19–02–2007 |
| | 21–08–2006 | 06–11–2006 | 10–08–2007 | 06–12–2007 |
| | 29–03–2007 | 04–04–2007 | 12–10–2007 | 17–12–2007 |
| 2007–08 | 07–08–2007 | 29–08–2007 | 22–10–2007 | 04–03–2008 |
| | 25–02–2008 | 28–02–2008 | 15–03–2008 | 03–04–2008 |
| | | | 07–07–2008 | 17–09–2008 |
| 2008–09 | 23–05–2008 | 27–06–2008 | 17–10–2008 | 23–03–2009 |
| | 02–11–2008 | 25–02–2009 | | |
| 2009–10 | 02–06–2009 | 06–06–2009 | 08–10–2009 | 04–12–2009 |

*Source*: SSA Unpublished Records.

Table 3.4, very rarely this is followed. The centre released first instalment sometime in August/September. There is a time gap between the date of release by the centre and the date of receipt by the Society.

### *Flow of funds under SSA*

Similarly there is also delay in the release of funds from the state government. There is a lengthy procedure in the release of state share. Therefore, there is a long gap between the date of release and the date of receipt by the Society. The state government releases its share to the Rajeev Vidya Mission (RVM) as a last priority subject to it; the other important subjects are Jalayagnam (Construction of Irrigation projects), Self-help groups, Employment guarantee programme, old age pensions, etc. After releasing budgets to all these programmes the remaining is released to the Rajeev Vidya Mission. Therefore, there is a delay in release of state government share every year and in every quarter of releases (see Table 3.4).

As there is a delay in releases and less time is left to the district authorities to spend the amount by following government lengthy procedures, so, there is every scope to flout the government procedures and spend the amount to reach the targets within less time or no time. The activities planned under SSA remain incomplete almost every year and result in still out of school children and low quality of education in government run schools. The delay in release of funds from the centre and the state automatically leads to the delay in the release of funds from the Society to the districts. Table 3.5 gives some idea about the date and amount of release of SSA funds by the Society to the districts. The major amount is released in the second half of the financial year. For the first few months the released amount is less and mainly to meet the salary component. More than 20 per cent of the budget is to be spent in the last month itself which is difficult for many districts.

*Table 3.5* Instalment-wise release of funds to the districts in AP, 2008–09

| *Instalment* | *Date* | *Amount (Rs. in lakhs)* | *Per cent* |
|---|---|---|---|
| 1st instalment | 14.05.08 | 2,097.9 | 2.49 |
| 2nd instalment | 26.06.08 | 9,000 | 10.69 |
| 3rd instalment | 09.07.08 | 8,471.72 | 10.06 |
| 4th instalment | 28.08.08 | 14,320.54 | 17.01 |
| 5th instalment | – | 10,544 | 12.52 |
| 6th instalment | – | 1,328.6 | 15.78 |
| 7th instalment | – | 15,665 | 18.61 |
| 8th instalment | – | 5,207.5 | 6.18 |
| 9th instalment | 25.02.09 | 15,256.32 | 18.12 |
| 10th instalment | 23.03.09 | 2,305.68 | 2.74 |
| Total | - | 84,197.26 | 100.00 |

*Source:* SSA Unpublished Records.

## Misappropriation of DPEP/SSA funds

Though certain irregularities are reported in utilizing the funds under different schemes, the misappropriation of funds under DPEP/SSA is worth noting. It reached such a proportion that Government had to appoint a Commission (Go AP 2008) to look into the irregularities. Though unofficial sources say more, the amount of misappropriation is about Rs.15 crores. The Commission in its Report has come out with interesting and useful findings about the lapses in the monitoring of fund flows and mechanism by which funds are misappropriated. Funds from many districts are diverted when the district officials refunded the unutilized amount through Demand Drafts/Cheques to the head office at Hyderabad.

### *Reasons for under-utilization and misappropriation of DPEP/SSA funds*

As we have seen funds allotted to EE under SSA are not fully utilized. Further, there is misappropriation of DPEP/SSA funds. There are several reasons for it. Some of them are briefly explained below:

- **Appointment of non-education cadre officials as project officers**: In many districts the project officers of SSA are on deputation from various services other than education service. Since they have to work with education officials like DEO, MEOs there is lack of coordination between them. At the higher level also there is no coordination between Commissioner and Director of School Education and State Project Officer. The former is unwilling to depute education officials to work in SSA programme.
- Further, for spending on certain activities it is necessary to involve the education officials. For example, the education department has to permit teachers to attend the teacher training organized under SSA. In some cases the permission is not given and hence the funds allocated for teacher training is not fully utilized.
- **Delay in release of instalments:** As we have seen the amount earmarked under SSA is released to the districts in instalments. For example, in the last year the amount is released in 10 instalments. Initially the amount was released to meet the salary component. For carrying activities the amount is released very late. As a result there is little time to spend the money. For example, in the last year the last instalment is released in the month of March.

- **No proper maintenance of records:** As per the guidelines 22 records are necessary for proper monitoring of funds. The Report and also Audit Statement suggest that they are not maintained. Lack of maintenance also gives scope for misuse of public funds as happened with DPEP/SSA funds.
- **Office staff from other departments:** Since project office is established for implementation of the scheme which is time bound limited period of regular office staff was not recruited but taken on deputation from other departments including education. But majority of these staff have come to this office with some mollifying intentions because of huge amount of funds flow in time bound manner.

## Fund allocation, release and expenditures at district level

Wide disparities in the level of development have been observed in different districts. For instance based on the composite index, the district of West Godavari was ranked first in overall socio-economic development and the district of Guntur was found on the first position in respect of agricultural development. Wide disparities were observed in the level of development among different districts. Infrastructural facilities were found to be positively associated with the level of developments in agricultural sector and overall socio-economic field. Agricultural development was influencing the overall socio-economic development in the positive direction (Narain *et al.* 2009). Further in a district level analysis, it was found that growth rates in district domestic product (DDP) and per capita DDP shows that seven districts of Telangana (Ranga Reddy, Nizamabad, Khammam, Hyderabad, Mahbubnagar, Warangal and Medak) and two districts of North Coastal (Visakhapatnam and Srikakulam) recorded higher growth rates than that of state average. On the other hand, all the districts in South Coastal and Rayalaseema and three districts of Telangana and one district of North Coastal showed lower growth than that of state average. However, one has to see the quality of growth in Telangana and Rayalaseema districts (Dev 2007).

An attempt is made here to examine, to what extent SSA allocations have been made considering the levels of development requirements of the districts. The state allocated an amount of Rs. 37,370 million till 2007–08 (Table 3.6). The allocated amount is not released. Only about 58 per cent is released. Even the released amount is not spent in some years. On an average 96 per cent of the released amount is spent. The expenditure to

*Table 3.6* District-wise funding under SSA in AP (cumulative up to 2007–08) (Rs. in lakhs)

| *S. No* | *District* | *Allocation* | *Releases* | *Expenditure* | *% of utilization of fund* | *% of releases out of allocations* | *Exp/releases* |
|---|---|---|---|---|---|---|---|
| 1 | Srikakulam | 12,997 | 7,772 | 7,971 | 61.3 | 59.8 | 102.6 |
| 2 | Vizianagaram | 11,848 | 6,821 | 6,890 | 58.2 | 57.6 | 101.0 |
| 3 | Visakhapatnam | 17,747 | 8,920 | 8,836 | 49.8 | 50.3 | 99.1 |
| 4 | East Godavari | 23,122 | 16,807 | 16,794 | 72.6 | 72.7 | 99.9 |
| 5 | West Godavari | 19,263 | 11,927 | 12,441 | 64.6 | 61.9 | 104.3 |
| 6 | Krishna | 20,517 | 12,629 | 12,421 | 60.5 | 61.6 | 98.4 |
| 7 | Guntur | 14,134 | 8,007 | 7,917 | 56.0 | 56.7 | 98.9 |
| 8 | Prakasham | 13,463 | 7,594 | 7,929 | 58.9 | 56.4 | 104.4 |
| 9 | Nellore | 11,214 | 7,094 | 7,409 | 66.1 | 63.3 | 104.4 |
| 10 | Chittoor | 20,783 | 10,682 | 10,499 | 50.5 | 51.4 | 98.3 |
| 11 | Kadapa | 13,336 | 7,723 | 6,895 | 51.7 | 57.9 | 89.3 |
| 12 | Anantapur | 23,715 | 10,893 | 10,521 | 44.4 | 45.9 | 96.6 |
| 13 | Kurnool | 18,717 | 9,285 | 9,861 | 52.7 | 49.6 | 106.2 |
| 14 | Mahabubnagar | 19,532 | 11,361 | 11,403 | 58.4 | 58.2 | 100.4 |
| 15 | Hyderabad | 15,205 | 9,196 | 8,013 | 52.7 | 60.5 | 87.1 |
| 16 | Rangareddy | 13,092 | 6,571 | 4,696 | 35.9 | 50.2 | 71.5 |
| 17 | Medak | 13,573 | 7,967 | 8,255 | 60.8 | 58.7 | 103.6 |
| 18 | Nizamabad | 10,788 | 6,224 | 6,202 | 57.5 | 57.7 | 99.6 |
| 19 | Adilabad | 16,197 | 8,898 | 8,736 | 53.9 | 54.9 | 98.2 |
| 20 | Karimnagar | 11,887 | 6,472 | 6,786 | 57.1 | 54.5 | 104.9 |
| 21 | Warangal | 14,722 | 7,003 | 6,422 | 43.6 | 47.6 | 91.7 |
| 22 | Khammam | 14,789 | 9,020 | 8,379 | 56.7 | 61.0 | 92.9 |
| 23 | Nalgonda | 16,406 | 8,869 | 9,528 | 58.1 | 54.1 | 107.4 |
| 24 | SPO | 6,695 | 8,860 | 3,135 | 46.8 | 132.3 | 35.4 |
| 25 | Total | 373,743 | 216,594 | 207,939 | 55.6 | 58.0 | 96.0 |

*Source*: Geetha Rani (2010); SSA AP Annual Report 2008–09.

allocation is little above half (55.6 per cent to be precise). Out of 23 districts 10 districts have spent more than what is released by the state government, i.e. more than 100 per cent. These districts could have spent that amount from the previous unspent balance returned by the schools and other agencies. That means these districts might have spent less in the previous financial year than what they have shown in the records. Other than this there is no source of funds for SSA at the district level. Whatever funds comes to the SSA office of any district it has to come from state government only except the donations made by any philanthropists. Even those donations are very nominal donated by philanthropists here and there. Therefore, the districts spent more than 100 per cent of releases definitely from the balances remaining of the previous financial years returned in that particular year by the school authorities or other agencies.

Data presented in Table 3.6 show the huge gap between approved budget and actual expenditure incurred not only at the state level but also at the district level. In some districts such as Anantapur the gap is wide where less than half of the approved budget is released and spent. On the extreme there are some districts like East Godavari where more than 70 per cent is spent.

In some districts the actual expenditure by the districts exceeded the amount released. It is not clear how and from what other sources the excess amount is drawn. The Report (2008) also points out that no proper mechanism is adopted in spending more than the amount earmarked. The inter-district differences not only exist in the allocation and expenditure but also in per-student expenditure and proportion of students (Table 3.7). There are differences between proportion of SSA funds and proportion of students. It appears that some developed districts are able to get more SSA funds and also able to utilize more. Though it is difficult to explain the differences, there is a need to look into the overall development of the districts in education and other sectors.

The expenditure per student is supposed to be high in backward districts than developed districts due to special needs but the expenditure figures show the contrary picture. The backward districts like Mahaboobnagar, Medak, Warangal, Ranga Reddy, Prakasham, Srikakulam, Vizianagaram and Visakhapatnam have received less share of budget than their share of enrolment in the state during the last seven years period of time. On the other hand the developed districts like Krishna, East Godavari, West Godavari, Nellore and Kadapa have received more budget than share of enrolment in the state (see Table 3.7). Developed districts could secure more budget with the support of political leadership, well supported bureaucrats at the highest level of administration and other pressure groups from these districts.

*Table 3.7* District-wise expenditure under SSA and enrolment in EE, 2002–03 to 2008–09

| *S. No* | *District* | *Avg exp per student (Rs.)* | *Total expenditure* | *Share of enrolment* | *Share of exp* |
|---|---|---|---|---|---|
| 1 | Srikakulam | 3,256 | 2,990 | 3.8 | 3.9 |
| 2 | Vizianagaram | 3,296 | 2,546 | 3.2 | 3.4 |
| 3 | Visakhapatnam | 3,065 | 3,479 | 4.9 | 4.7 |
| 4 | East Godavari | 3,331 | 3,237 | 6.3 | 6.6 |
| 5 | West Godavari | 3,451 | 3,355 | 4.8 | 5.2 |
| 6 | Krishna | 3,816 | 3,670 | 4.5 | 5.5 |
| 7 | Guntur | 2,627 | 4,089 | 5.0 | 4.2 |
| 8 | Prakasham | 2,973 | 3,248 | 4.1 | 3.8 |
| 9 | Nellore | 3,647 | 3,283 | 3.3 | 3.8 |
| 10 | Chittoor | 3,374 | 4,664 | 5.1 | 5.5 |
| 11 | Kadapa | 3,974 | 2,582 | 3.0 | 3.8 |
| 12 | Anantapur | 3,511 | 4,593 | 5.0 | 5.6 |
| 13 | Kurnool | 2,859 | 4,634 | 5.5 | 5.0 |
| 14 | Mahabub Nagar | 3,066 | 3,892 | 5.7 | 5.5 |
| 15 | Ranga Reddy | 2,311 | 2,401 | 4.4 | 3.2 |
| 16 | Hyderabad | 3,417 | 1,463 | 2.7 | 2.9 |
| 17 | Medak | 2,919 | 2,837 | 4.3 | 4.0 |
| 18 | Nizamabad | 2,841 | 2,213 | 3.4 | 3.0 |
| 19 | Adilabad | 3,495 | 3,414 | 4.1 | 4.5 |
| 20 | Karimnagar | 2,478 | 2,302 | 4.4 | 3.4 |
| 21 | Warangal | 2,815 | 3,635 | 4.3 | 3.9 |
| 22 | Khammam | 3,576 | 2,860 | 3.9 | 4.4 |
| 23 | Nalgonda | 2,929 | 3,385 | 4.5 | 4.2 |
| | AP | 3,154 | 74,771 | 100.0 | 100.0 |

*Source:* Government of AP (2009); APSSA Annual Report 2008–09.

## Comparative study of Ranga Reddy and Nalgonda districts

The two districts of AP are taken for detailed analysis of fund flow and resource use under SSA. They are Nalgonda and Ranga Reddy districts. It may be noted that Ranga Reddy district has more urban area when compared to Nalgonda district. This district is found to be in low developed category in agricultural sector, infrastructural facilities and overall socioeconomic sector (Narain *et al.* 2009). Nalgonda district is backward compared to the Ranga Reddy. Ranga Reddy district was formed (1978) after formation of the state but Nalgonda district was in existence before the state was formed. Educationally Ranga Reddy is more developed as it is closer to capital city and in fact the capital city is surrounded by it from all sides. However, there are some parts of the district that are backward both economically and educationally. The population of Ranga Reddy is 52.96 lakhs which is 6.25 per cent of the total population of the state whereas Nalgonda population is 34.83 lakhs with 4.11 per cent of the state population. In case of density of population again Nalgonda has lesser (245) than state (308) density of population and Ranga Reddy district has higher (707) density of population. According to 2011 Census the literacy rate in Nalgonda (65.05 per cent) is less than state average (67.66 per cent) and Ranga Reddy (78.05 per cent). Even in male and female literacy rates Ranga Reddy district is ahead of state but Nalgonda is backward on both the counts.

The basic statistics related to primary education indicates that number of primary schools increased in both the districts in the last decade (Table 3.8). But the increase is more in Ranga Reddy district than in Nalgonda. The enrolment in Nalgonda showed declining trend whereas it increased in Ranga Reddy district. The GERs are more than 100 per cent in both the districts though it is less in Nalgonda than in Ranga Reddy. The dropout rates are more in Nalgonda when compared to Ranga Reddy.

The approved outlay increased during the last few years in both Nalgonda and Ranga Reddy (Table 3.9). However, the approved outlay is rarely released and as a result there is a large difference between the actual

*Table 3.8* Primary education in Nalgonda and Ranga Reddy districts

| | *Primary schools* | *Enrolment I–V* | *No. of teachers* | *GER* | *Dropout rate I–V* | *Teacher/ pupil ratio* |
|---|---|---|---|---|---|---|
| **Nalgonda** | | | | | | |
| 2001–02 | 2,450 | 416,583 | 5,093 | 128.1 | 38.5 | 39 |
| 2005–06 | 2,816 | 340,910 | 8,087 | 119.78 | 38.5 | 28 |
| 2009–10 | 2,975 | 307,782 | 7,577 | 100.2 | 29.2 | 29 |
| **Ranga Reddy** | | | | | | |
| 2001–02 | 1,760 | 482,320 | 2,916 | 137 | 42.0 | 43 |
| 2005–06 | 2,438 | 481,480 | 9,599 | 153.7 | 31.4 | 35 |
| 2009–10 | 2,561 | 540,960 | 9,780 | 160.0 | 13.5 | 32 |

*Source:* Educational Statistics of AP, for the relevant years.

*Table 3.9* SSA outlay and expenditure in Nalgonda and Ranga Reddy districts (Rs. in lakhs)

| *Year* | *Approved outlay* | *Expenditure* | *Exp. as % of approved outlay* | *Approved outlay* | *Expenditure* | *Exp. as % of approved outlay* |
|---|---|---|---|---|---|---|
| | **Nalgonda** | | | **Ranga Reddy** | | |
| 2002–03 | 1,625 | 710 | 43.7 | 1,249 | 298 | 23.9 |
| 2003–04 | 942 | 612 | 65 | 927 | 422 | 45.5 |
| 2008–09 | 5,367 | 3,385 | 63.1 | 5,065 | 2,940 | 58.1 |
| 2010–11 | 8,048 | 4,867 | 60.5 | 7,539 | 1,391 | 18.5 |
| 2012–13 | 18,737 | 10,954 | 58.5 | 20,683 | 13,877 | 67.1 |
| 2013–14 | 13,562 | 5,193 | 38.3 | 12,665 | 6,845 | 54 |

*Source:* Unpublished Records of SSA – Nalgonda and Ranga Reddy districts.

expenditure and outlay in both Nalgonda and Ranga Reddy. The district level information on utilization of resources released to the district of Nalgonda and Ranga Reddy shows that more than 90 per cent of released resources are utilized with few exceptions. But it is less than their proposals or approved outlay in all the years. These districts have succeeded to spend about 50 per cent of the amount approved by the Planning Appraisal Board (PAB) at New Delhi and much less than what they have planned to implement in the districts to achieve the desired results. Though marginally increased the utilization rate is quite low and the average utilization rate is about 50 per cent in Nalgonda and 42 per cent in Ranga Reddy.

The expenditure in Ranga Reddy has increased gradually over period of time but the expenditure in Nalgonda district has not increased consistently. During the initial years there was a sudden increase but declined and increased faster. This is mainly due to the capabilities of implementing authorities and political interference in implementation of the activities. The political interference was observed mainly in activities like running Residential Bridge Courses for out-of-school children and civil works. The political awareness is more in Nalgonda District. In Ranga Reddy District people are having less concern with school activities. Besides, the project officer posted in the Ranga Reddy district generally enjoys the support of state administration and guidance from time to time in implementation. The SSA office of Ranga Reddy district is situated just besides the state office so the state administration closely monitors the district officers who enable the district to implement the programmes more effectively.

Till 2005–06 fund flow was from the state to district, from district to sub-district and then to school in AP. During this period the state has to give cheque or Demand Draft for the amount released and concerned districts have to deposit it in their accounts. Thereafter the banks send the cheque for clearance to the cheque issuing bank. This process used to take three to four weeks. After receiving funds the district administration start the process to release funds to various activities with the approval of the district collector and chairman of the SSA society at district level. Again the district administration has to release the funds through cheques to the sub-district authorities for various activities. The sub-district administration has to do the same process that has been done at the district level. This has consumed a lot of time in transfer of funds from state to school to take up activities planned in SSA.

To avoid the delay in release of funds the state has decided to release the funds directly to the districts through online without any time lapse as the banks have introduced online funds transfer system. This has reduced time gap in release of funds. But according to the central government instruction the bank accounts should be opened only in Canara Bank so that the central government can ascertain the fund flow to the districts and balance of funds available with state project office from time to time. This facility has facilitated the central and state project offices to monitor the fund flow from centre to state offices and state to district offices, but the condition of opening accounts only in Canara bank has created certain problems to the school authorities. The Canara bank branches are not available in all the places where the schools are located or at block headquarters for opening accounts and having the transactions. In AP, State Bank of Hyderabad (SBH) has more number of branches than any other Bank. The state government operates almost all the transactions through SBH branches for payments like salaries to employees and pensions to retired employees or receipts like license fee, fine and other fee.

Since the teachers receive their salaries through bank accounts all the schools have opened accounts in State Bank of Hyderabad only. Now for the sake of SSA funds schools are forced to open accounts in Canara Bank only and schools have opened accounts but it has become difficult for school authorities to operate transactions in Canara Bank as the Branches are not available within their locality of all the schools. The school authority has to travel a long distance for any small transaction in Bank which is waste of time and money. So, there is a problem of free flow of SSA funds from district authorities to school authorities which ultimately resulted in spending the money according to the convenience of school authority that may not satisfy school requirement but may satisfy school authority.

During the discussions with district officials and school authorities they have unanimously expressed their opinion that the funds transfer in AP state should be done through State Bank of Hyderabad not through Canara Bank which will facilitate them with easy access to the bank and have the transactions. This would support for effective implementation of SSA activities to achieve the goals.

Activity-wise/intervention-wise details are not common for the districts. Even for the same districts also there is some variation in the items and order of the items. Therefore, strict comparison of activity-wise/intervention-wise across the districts and over a period of time is difficult. However, some observations can be made on the basis of the information presented in the Table 3.10. Intervention-wise/activity-wise details show that civil works continue to be one of the main items in the SSA budgets of both the districts. Even in this case also the utilization rate is quite low which varied from year to year.

The major components of the SSA Budget are civil works, teacher salary, teacher training, out-of-school children and quality of education. As

*Table 3.10* Aggregate intervention-wise approvals and achievement under SSA in Nalgonda district, 2002–03 to 2008–09

| *S. No* | *Intervention* | *Aggregate (2002–03 to 2008–09)* | | *Achievement out of approval* | *Share of each intervention in the total expenditure* |
|---|---|---|---|---|---|
| | | *Approval* | *Expend* | | |
| 1 | Civil works | 8,443 | 5,299 | 62.8 | 42.9 |
| 2 | Research, evaluation | 248 | 118 | 47.8 | 1.0 |
| 3 | Maintenance and MIS | 728 | 541 | 74.3 | 4.4 |
| 4 | CWSN | 291 | 143 | 49.1 | 1.2 |
| 5 | Out-of-school children | 1,620 | 878 | 54.2 | 7.1 |
| 6 | Teachers training | 1,097 | 514 | 46.9 | 4.2 |
| 7 | Community mobilization | 154 | 49 | 31.7 | 0.4 |
| 8 | School grant | 429 | 361 | 84.0 | 2.9 |
| 9 | Teacher grant | 239 | 126 | 52.8 | 1.0 |
| 10 | BRC | 987 | 259 | 26.2 | 2.1 |
| 11 | CRC | 358 | 78 | 21.7 | 0.6 |

(*Continued*)

*Table 3.10* (Continued)

| *S. No* | *Intervention* | *Aggregate (2002–03 to 2008–09)* | | *Achievement out of approval* | *Share of each intervention in the total expenditure* |
|---|---|---|---|---|---|
| | | *Approval* | *Expend* | | |
| 12 | Free textbooks | 63 | 21 | 33.8 | 0.2 |
| 13 | Maintenance grant | 792 | 480 | 60.6 | 3.9 |
| 14 | Teacher salary | 6,541 | 2,360 | 36.1 | 19.1 |
| 15 | Equipment | 306 | 246 | 80.4 | 2.0 |
| 16 | Remedial teaching | 36 | 28 | 77.7 | 0.2 |
| 17 | Innovative activity for disabled | 287 | 174 | 60.6 | 1.4 |
| 18 | Girls education | 82 | 13 | 15.9 | 0.1 |
| 19 | Planning and management | 10 | 1 | 7.5 | 0.0 |
| 20 | Project management | 119 | 92 | 77.1 | 0.7 |
| 21 | Distance education | 6 | 0 | 1.1 | 0.0 |
| 22 | Focus areas by groups | 272 | 257 | 94.6 | 2.1 |
| 23 | Pedagogical school improvement | 778 | 315 | 40.5 | 2.6 |
| | Total | 23,886 | 12,353 | 51.72 | — |

*Source:* Office of DPO SSA, Nalgonda.

per the SSA guideline the proportion of allocation in budget should not exceed 33 per cent for Civil Works. The aggregate expenditure incurred on civil works shows that the Nalgonda district has incurred more than stipulated ceiling expenditure on civil works but the Ranga Reddy district expenditure on civil works is within the limits. The Nalgonda district expenditure is 42.90 per cent and Ranga Reddy expenditure is 32.00 per cent.

Aggregate expenditure of civil works in Nalgonda district is about 63 per cent of the approved budget and Ranga Reddy district is 65.39 per cent. Though the achievement of aggregate expenditure on civil works in Nalgonda district is less than the achievement of Ranga Reddy district of approved budget but the share of Nalgonda district is greater than the share of Ranga Reddy district (see Table 3.11). The target is not achieved due

*Table 3.11* Aggregate intervention-wise approvals and achievement under SSA in Ranga Reddy district, 2002–03 to 2008–09

| *S. No* | | *Aggregate (2002–03 to 2008–09)* | | *Achievement out of approval* | *Share of each intervention in the total expenditure* |
|---|---|---|---|---|---|
| | | *Approved* | *Expenditure* | | |
| 1 | Civil works | 4,836 | 3,162 | 65.4 | 32.0 |
| 2 | Research and evaluation | 180 | 63 | 35.2 | 0.6 |
| 3 | CWSN | 297 | 145 | 48.9 | 1.5 |
| 4 | Girls education | 35 | 35 | 100.0 | 0.4 |
| 5 | Management and MIS | 385 | 353 | 91.6 | 3.6 |
| 6 | Teacher training | 1,345 | 894 | 66.5 | 9.1 |
| 7 | ECCE | 84 | 81 | 95.6 | 0.8 |
| 8 | Community mobilization | 147 | 73 | 49.6 | 0.7 |
| 9 | Teachers salary (recurring) | 3,498 | 1,894 | 54.2 | 19.2 |
| 10 | Teachers grant | 306 | 193 | 63.2 | 2.0 |
| 11 | School grant | 338 | 332 | 98.0 | 3.4 |
| 12 | Maintenance grant | 394 | 286 | 72.6 | 2.9 |
| 13 | Black resource centre | 283 | 54 | 18.9 | 0.5 |
| 14 | School complex centre | 41 | 41 | 100.0 | 0.4 |
| 15 | Interventions for OOSC | 1,354 | 675 | 49.9 | 6.8 |
| 16 | Media | 11 | 11 | 95.2 | 0.1 |
| 17 | Free textbooks | 230 | 4 | 1.5 | 0.0 |
| 18 | Community training | 180 | 96 | 53.5 | 1.0 |
| 19 | Remedial teaching | 49 | 49 | 101.2 | 0.5 |
| 20 | SC/ST | 126 | 93 | 74.2 | 0.9 |
| 21 | Computer education | 50 | 48 | 96.0 | 0.5 |

(*Continued*)

*Table 3.11* (Continued)

| *S. No* | | *Aggregate (2002–03 to 2008–09)* | | *Achievement out of approval* | *Share of each intervention in the total expenditure* |
|---|---|---|---|---|---|
| | | *Approved* | *Expenditure* | | |
| 22 | Learning enhancement programme (LEP) | 542 | 539 | 99.5 | 5.5 |
| 23 | Monitoring and supervision | 14 | 6 | 42.2 | 0.1 |
| 24 | Innovation | 309 | 312 | 101.1 | 3.2 |
| 25 | Planning and management | 0 | 0 | 100.0 | 0.0 |
| 26 | Equipment | 469 | 28 | 6.0 | 0.3 |
| 27 | Furniture | 33 | 2 | 6.1 | 0.0 |
| 28 | Vehicles | 31 | 11 | 33.7 | 0.1 |
| 29 | Distance education | 90 | 90 | 100.0 | 0.9 |
| 30 | Workshops and seminars | 47 | 0 | 0.5 | 0.0 |
| 31 | Honorarium | 25 | 298 | 1,193.7 | 3.0 |
| 32 | Consumables | 31 | 10 | 32.2 | 0.1 |
| | Total | 15,763 | 9,880 | 62.7 | 100.0 |

*Source:* Office of DPO SSA, Nalgonda.

to the cost escalations of construction works, non-availability of technical persons for execution of the works, timely non-release of grants and political problems. This is mainly due to the provision (25 per cent of plan proposal) made in the plan for regular appointment of teachers but recruitment of teachers is not done. The other items are teacher trainings and innovative activities not happening as per the plan proposed because of administrative problems, teacher union problems, lack of cooperation from the community, etc.

The items which were utilized fully or major part of them are school grant, maintenance grant and teacher grant. But they form small percentage of total expenditure in both districts. Maintenance grants are used for some repairs, etc., whereas school maintenance grants are used for getting electricity connection and provision of fans, etc. Teacher grants are used for acquiring some teaching learning material, etc. Though there is some improvement reported in the learning levels that can be attributed partly to SSA funding still there is a large gap between the actual and expected performance levels. Many primary schools are reported to be C-grade schools (40–60 per cent performance). There is hardly any government school with A-grade and there are very few B-grade schools. This indicates that funding is a necessary condition but not sufficient to enhance learning levels of the child. There are other factors which are also required to be addressed.

## Summary and conclusion

In this paper an attempt is made to examine the financing of EE under SSA in AP. AP received funds under various programmes to finance EE. In case of SSA there is difference in the approved budget and funds actually utilized. There is a delay in the release of funds both by the centre and state governments. As a result there is not only delay in the release of funds to the districts but it is released in several instalments which continue till the last month of the financial year. Lack of co-ordination, appointment of non-education officials and delay in release of funds are some of the important reasons leading to under-utilization of funds allocated. There are inter-district differences in the allocation and utilization of funds. Further, there is a misappropriation of DPEP/SSA funds in the state. The status of districts of Nalgonda and Ranga Reddy are not much different from rest of the districts. The actual expenditure is about 50 per cent or less of the approved ones. The activity-wise utilization varies from activity to activity, but overall utilization is less in Nalgonda than Ranga Reddy.

## References

Dev, S. Mahendra, 2007. 'Inclusive Growth in AP: Challenges in Agriculture, Poverty, Social Sector and Regional Disparities', Centre For Economic And Social Studies, Working Paper No. 71, Hyderabad.

GoAP, 2001. Selected Educational Statistics, Commissioner and Director of School Education, Government of Andhra Pradesh, Hyderabad.

GoAP, 2002. Selected Educational Statistics, Commissioner and Director of School Education, Government of Andhra Pradesh, Hyderabad.

GoAP, 2005. Selected Educational Statistics, Commissioner and Director of School Education, Government of Andhra Pradesh, Hyderabad.

GoAP, 2008. Selected Educational Statistics, Commissioner and Director of School Education, Government of Andhra Pradesh, Hyderabad.

GoAP, 2009. Selected Educational Statistics, 2008–09, Commissioner and Director of School Education, Hyderabad.

GoAP, 2010b. Educational Statistics, Commissioner and Director of School Education, Andhra Pradesh, Hyderabad.

GoAP, 2010a. Outcome Budget: 2010–11, Department of School Education, Hyderabad.

Government of India, 2010a. Sarva Shiksha Abhiyan – A Programme for Universal EE: Manual on Financial Management and Procurement, Department of EE and Literacy, Ministry of Human Resource Development.

Government of India, 2010b. Evaluation Report on Sarva Shiksha Abhiyan, Planning Commission, New Delhi.

MHRD, 1995. Analysis of Budget Expenditure on Education in India, Government of India, New Delhi.

Narain, Prem, S.D. Sharma, S.C. Rai and V.K. Bhatia, 2009. 'Inter-District Variation of Socio-economic Development in AP', *Journal of Indian Society of Agricultural Statistics*, 63(1): 35–42.

NSSO, 2009. Employment and Unemployment Situation among Social Groups in India 2004–05, Report 516, Ministry of Statistics and Programme Implementation, New Delhi.

Rajiv Vidya Mission (a): Annual Reports for various years.

Rajiv Vidya Mission (b): SSA Unpublished Records for various years.

Rani, Geetha P, 2010. Financing EE in States: Funds Flow Pattern and Utilisation of Resources under SSA, Background Paper presented in the National Seminar on Financing EE in States: Funds Flow Pattern and Utilisation of Resources under SSA at NUEPA, New Delhi, 18–20 March 2010.

Report of Sri Justice A. Venkat Ram Reddy Commission of Inquiry (To inquire into misappropriation of DPEP and SSA funds), Government of AP, Hyderabad, 2008.

Tilak, J.B.G., 1998. Public Expenditure on Education in Andhra Pradesh, Unpublished Report submitted to the State Project Director, District Primary Education Programme, Andhra Pradesh, Hyderabad.

# 4

# SARVA SHIKSHA ABHIYAN IN PUNJAB

## Overall allocations, composition and utilization of funds

*Jaswinder S. Brar and Sukhwinder Singh*

### Introduction

Sarva Shiksha Abhiyan (SSA) or 'Education for All' is a serious effort formulated in project mode to attain UEE. Central thrust of SSA has been to effectively improve education delivery mechanism in schools by providing all relevant physical, financial, organizational and human inputs by involving all stakeholders. SSA envisages the effective involvement of community in control and management of schools. Community participation has been attempted through various forums such as Panchayats, School Management Committees, Village and Urban Slum Level Committees, Parent–Teacher Associations and Mother–Teacher Associations, etc. SSA has also been viewed as a concrete response to growing demand for quality basic education all over the country (PROBE 1999). It is also considered as a political expression of promoting social justice through basic education in addition to growing requirements of human capital formation in the country. SSA involves multiplicity of efforts in order to impart reasonable quality education by resorting to all round steps which include institutional reforms, sustainable financing, decentralized administration, community-based monitoring with transparency and accountability, bottom up approach to planning, institutional capacity building, focus on special groups of population, regular academic support to teachers and habitation as a unit of planning, etc. SSA is a comprehensive approach based and designed with strong academic and research input in order to realize the desired objectives (GOP 2010:10–15).

SSA envisages the financial contribution from centre and concerned state government as discussed earlier. According to SSA provisions, after fulfilment of certain conditions the union ministry will release project funds in two instalments every year, i.e. April and September. One of the essential conditions is that state governments will maintain its investment on elementary education at a level not less than that of its level during financial year1999–2000. Further, the concerned state will provide its share within a month after release of central share. Various provisions and checks have been incorporated with an objective to ensure the timely availability and utilization of funds. SSA has in fact been designed into some sort of business model by taking into account all the possible details in order to make it a success. But, instead of crystal clear framework of funding, responsibilities, commitments, monitoring and feedback mechanism the SSA funds remained under-utilized in many states.

Punjab falls in the category of those states which could not make SSA as the case of full utilization of funds. Therefore, the present paper focuses exclusively upon numerous aspects of flow of SSA funds in Punjab. The next section deals with various aspects of elementary education sector by focusing upon its critical dimensions related to educational outcomes, general effectiveness and level and behaviour of funding. Third section deals with the relative contribution of centre and state governments in funding SSA. Fourth section provides the details of overall and district-wise break up of expenditure. Fifth section deals with the district-wise allocation and utilization of funds for various components. The last section sums up the major findings.

## Educational outcomes and budget in Punjab

Educational scenario in Punjab presents a picture which is full of adverse features and unhealthy tendencies. Educational indicators show mismatch with overall prosperity of the state particularly that of its having continuously higher level of per capita income for about four decades after the advent of green revolution since mid-1960s. The educational progress and expansion is uneven in terms of gender, regions, classes, social categories and locations (HDR 2004). The proportion of illiterate population was about 30 per cent during 2001; and 23 per cent during 2011. It was higher in case of females, rural females, SC females, etc. Moreover, as per Census-2001, literacy rank of Punjab was 16th from above among all 35 states and union territories (UTs). But, it has declined to 21st rank as per Census-2011. It means during the period between 2001 and 2011 literacy progression was comparatively slower as compared to other states.

Importantly, four states and UTs (West Bengal, Gujarat, Sikkim, Dadra and Nagar Haveli) which had occupied lower rank than Punjab during 2001 crossed it in terms of literacy ranking during 2011(SAP 2010). Amazingly, it has happened despite the major intervention in elementary education sector in the form of SSA project in the state that by starting actually in 2002–03 covered almost the entire period of two censuses, i.e. 2001 and 2011. SSA in fact supplements the state efforts already in the field of elementary education in a project mode. And, there prevails a close connection between progress of schooling and literacy.

The gross enrolment in elementary education recorded variations on yearly basis during the period from 2001 to 2010 (Table 4.1).

In overall terms the total number of students enrolled varied between 28.47 and 30.86 lakh; with the lowest level during 2007 (i.e. 28.47 lakh students) but witnessed consistent rise during the subsequent three years, i.e. 2008, 2009 and 2010. Further, the gross enrolment of girls and boys recorded yearly sometimes varied by big margins also. But, the gross enrolment of both boys and girls improved substantially during 2010 over 2009. The gross enrolment of boys increased from 16.26 to 17.02 lakh over the period from 2001 to 2010. The gross enrolment of girls registered a decline during the first seven years (2001 to 2007). It was lowest during 2007 with level of 13.10 lakh but improved during the subsequent period to 13.84 lakh in 2010; but never attained its level of 2001 (i.e. 14.40 lakh).

*Table 4.1* Gross enrolment in elementary education in Punjab, 2001–2010 (in lakh)

| *Year* | *Boys* | *Girls* | *Total* |
|---|---|---|---|
| 2001 | 16.26 (53.03) | 14.40 (46.97) | 30.66 (100) |
| 2002 | 16.25 (52.74) | 14.56 (47.26) | 30.81 (100) |
| 2003 | 16.02 (53.08) | 14.16 (46.92) | 30.18 (100) |
| 2004 | 15.66 (53.19) | 13.78 (46.81) | 29.44 (100) |
| 2005 | 15.71 (53.51) | 13.65 (46.49) | 29.36 (100) |
| 2006 | 16.03 (53.61) | 13.87 (46.39) | 29.90 (100) |
| 2007 | 15.37 (53.99) | 13.10 (46.01) | 28.47 (100) |
| 2008 | 15.34 (53.84) | 13.15 (46.16) | 28.49 (100) |
| 2009 | 15.89 (54.77) | 13.12 (45.23) | 29.01 (100) |
| 2010 | 17.02 (55.15) | 13.84 (44.85) | 30.86 (100) |

*Source:* Gross enrolment figures from 2001 to 2007 are from Statistical Abstract of Punjab, ESO, Chandigarh (various issues) and from 2008 to 2010 from Economic Survey of Punjab, 2011–12.

*Note:* Figures in brackets indicate percentage shares.

*Table 4.2* Primary and upper primary gross and net enrolment ratios in Punjab

| | *Gross enrolment ratio* | | *Net enrolment ratio* | |
|---|---|---|---|---|
| *Year* | *Primary* | *Upper primary* | *Primary* | *Upper primary* |
| 2005–06 | N.A. | N.A. | 51.78 | 37.68 |
| 2006–07 | 81.33 | 69.03 | 55.49 | 44.02 |
| 2007–08 | 92.78 | 69.09 | 53.02 | 42.10 |
| 2008–09 | 76.19 | 72.85 | 59.69 | 49.64 |
| 2009–10 | 80.42 | 74.15 | 63.05 | 52.21 |
| 2010–11 | 112.22 | 100.88 | 89.41 | 71.76 |

*Source:* Figures from 2005–06 to 2007–08 from selected socio-economic statistics, 2011; and from 2008–09 to 2010–11 from DISE (2011–12), P. 36.

Thus during the decade (2001–2010) the relative proportion of girls and boys in gross enrolment changed to some extent. The proportion of boys in gross enrolment rose from 53.03 to 55.15 per cent from 2001 to 2010; but girls declined from 46.97 to 44.85 per cent.

Gross and net enrolment ratios (Table 4.2) during 2005–06 to 2010–11 also demonstrate a picture of gross under-achievement for the state. Both for primary and upper primary stages, the GER remained at lower level and crossed the mark of 100 per cent only during 2010–11. NER was found to be on substantially lower level. During 2005–06, the level was 51.78 and 37.68 per cent for primary and upper primary stage; attained the level of 89.41 and 71.76 per cent during 2010–11.

The dropout rates (Table 4.3) recorded yearly variations and overall remained at a higher level during the period from 2007–08 to 2012–13. The dropout rates were found to be higher in case of upper primary stage as compared to primary stage. Further, the proportion of out-of-school-age cohort students remained at a higher level both during primary and upper primary stages. During 2011–12, for primary and upper primary stage the proportion of over-age children was 9.36 and 13.62 per cent, respectively. And, the proportion of under-age children was 10.94 and 7.43 per cent. This persistence of dropout rates goes against the objectives of SSA which calls for removal of all types of gender gaps in education.

However, the situation becomes further complicated with the large number of out-of-school children (Table 4.4). Though there has been considerable decline in the number of out-of-school children, as per the January 2008 survey, still as many as 100,457 children were found to be out-of-school in the age-group between 6 and 14 years. Out of these, the

*Table 4.3* Dropout rates and proportion of over-age and under-age students in Punjab

| *Years* | *Primary* | | | *Upper primary* | | | *Share of over-age children (2011–12)* | *Share of under-age children (2011–12)* |
|---|---|---|---|---|---|---|---|---|
| | *Total* | *Boys* | *Girls* | *Total* | *Boys* | *Girls* | | |
| 2007–08 | 1.16 | 1.39 | 0.92 | 11.57 | 12.33 | 10.80 | Primary | Primary |
| 2008–09 | 8.50 | 8.84 | 8.16 | 9.58 | 10.83 | 8.32 | (9.36 per cent) | (10.94 per cent) |
| 2009–10 | 2.54 | 2.40 | 2.69 | 5.99 | 6.19 | 5.79 | | |
| 2010–11 | 2.25 | 1.85 | 2.65 | 0.57 | 0.54 | 0.61 | Upper primary | Upper primary |
| 2011–12 | 2.01 | 2.13 | 1.88 | 1.51 | 2.03 | 1.64 | (13.62 per cent) | (7.43 per cent) |
| 2012–13 | 1.65 | 1.75 | 1.56 | – | – | – | | |

*Source:* Figures for dropout rates are based on ESO (2012a: 91). Figures for over-age and under-age children are from DISE (2011–12: 29).

*Table 4.4* Out-of-school children in various age groups in Punjab, 2006 and 2008

| *Gender* | *Age group (6–14) years* | | | *Age group (6–8) years* |
|---|---|---|---|---|
| | *February–March 2006* | *January 2008* | *Decline (in no.)* | |
| Boys | 119,341 (52.42) | 53,565 (53.32) | 65,776 | 16,053 (53.49) |
| Girls | 108,304 (47.58) | 46,892 (46.68) | 61,412 | 13,959 (46.51) |
| Total | 227,645 (100) | 100,457 (100) | 127,188 | 30,012 (100) |

*Source:* SSA (2006–07: 68); SSA (2007–08:72).

*Note:* Figures in parentheses refer to the percentage share in the total.

proportion of boys (53.32 per cent) was more than girls (46.68 per cent). In age group 6–8 years, the total number of out-of-school children was 30,012. But, it is to be noted that as per SSA objectives, all children must have completed five years of primary schooling during 2007 by joining the education guarantee centres or alternative schools by 2003. Thus, SSA programme in the state was far behind the schedule as per January 2008 survey, for as many as 30,012 children were out-of-school. These students, if at all they have happened to join the schools in the subsequent period, would not only be over-age but also will be completing the primary stage of education quite late. But, a survey done during December 2012 again identified 30,939 out-of-school children in age group 6–14 years (SSA 2011–12: 22).

The state witnessed massive expansion of private sector in education. The proportion of students enrolled in private schools was considerable (Table 4.5). During 2011–12, in elementary education, 25.73 per cent of

*Table 4.5* Management-wise pattern of enrolment in elementary education in Punjab, 2011–12

| *Type of school* | *Primary (1–5)* | *Upper primary (6–8)* | *Elementary (1–8)* |
|---|---|---|---|
| Government | 1,360,923 (52.59) | 789,971 (56.37) | 2,150,894 (53.92) |
| Private | 651,024 (25.16) | 375,176 (26.77) | 1,026,200 (25.73) |
| Unrecognized | 550,746 (21.28) | 218,218 (15.57) | 768,964 (19.28) |
| Total | 2,562,693 (99.04) | 1,383,365 (98.71) | 3,946,058 (98.93) |

*Source:* Calculated from DISE (2011–12), p. 26.

*Note:* Figures not adding to hundred because of missing values as mentioned in DISE (2011–12).

*Table 4.6* Relationship between education budget, general budget and state income in Punjab

| *Time period (financial years)* | *Education budget (R.A.) (Rs. crores)* | *Education budget's share in state budgetary expenditure* | *Education budget's share in state income* | *Elementary education budget and its share in education budget* |
|---|---|---|---|---|
| 1978–81 (T.A.) | 108.65 | 23.82 | 2.65 | 39.69 (36.53) |
| 1999–02 (T.A.) | 1,983.18 | 17.19 | 2.97 | 603.43 (30.43) |
| 2005–08 (T.A.) | 2,381.07 | 11.28 | 2.09 | 537.14 (22.56) |
| 2008–11 (T.A.) | 3,651.45 | 12.71 | 2.05 | 809.99 (22.18) |

*Source:* Analysis of Budgeted Expenditure on Education, MHRD, New Delhi. Statistical Abstract of Punjab, ESO, Chandigarh.

*Notes*

1 Figures presented is triennium averages (T.A.) of concerned financial years. R.A. is for Revenue Account.

2 Figures in parentheses refer to the percentage share in total education budget.

3 All figures show actual expenditure levels except for 2010–11 which are revised estimates.

the students were enrolled in private schools. Amazingly, 19.28 per cent were enrolled in unrecognized schools. And, the share of government schools was 53.92 per cent. It means by and large half of total students were getting education in private schools both in case of primary and upper primary stage.

Punjab has been found to be spending less on education. Even a cursory look at the report card of Punjab pertaining to educational budget right now presents a disturbing picture (Table 4.6).

The share of education budget in general budget declined over the period. It was 23.82 per cent during TA (1978–81). But it came down to 17.19 per cent during TA (1999–02), to 11.28 per cent during TA (2005–08) with level of 12.71 per cent during TA (2008–11). As a proportion of state income, it was 2.65 per cent during TA (1978–81). But, it declined from 2.97 per cent during TA (1999–02), to 2.09 per cent during TA (2005–08) and to 2.05 per cent during TA (2008–11). The relative share of elementary education in overall educational budget declined from 36.69, to 30.43, to 22.56 and 22.18 per cent during the corresponding reported years. Further, the elementary education budget on average basis increased from Rs. 603.43 to Rs. 809.99 crores over the period from TA (1999–02) to TA (2005–08).

## Relative contribution of centre and state to SSA

The SSA Mission in Punjab was established by the state government in June 2000. It was formally launched on 24 July 2002. However, during the period from June 2000 to July 2002, data collection and family survey work were carried out for preparing the Annual Plan for the financial year 2002–03. The total cost of the project for a particular year is called Annual Work Plan and Budget (AWPB). The AWPB for the state of Punjab for the period of 11 years, i.e. 2002–03 to 2012–13, is given in Table 4.7. It is clear that the annual approved budget of SSA for the state of Punjab has increased from Rs. 14,213.99 lakh during 2002–03, to Rs. 23,278.14 lakh

*Table 4.7* Overall budget along with central and state share of SSA in Punjab (Rs. in lakh)

| *Year* | *Funding ratio (centre: state)* | *Annual work plan and budget approved* | *Central share* | *Punjab share* |
|---|---|---|---|---|
| 2002–03 | 75:25 | 14,213.99 | 10,660.49 | 3,553.50 |
| 2003–04 | 75:25 | 20,145.76 | 15,109.32 | 5,036.44 |
| 2004–05 | 75:25 | 20,078.31 | 15,058.73 | 5,019.58 |
| 2005–06 | 75:25 | 22,582.00 | 16,936.50 | 5,645.50 |
| 2006–07 | 75:25 | 23,278.14 | 17,458.61 | 5,819.54 |
| 2007–08 | 65:35 | 18,488.67 | 12,017.64 | 6,471.03 |
| 2008–09 | 65:35 | 26,510.47 | 17,231.81 | 9,278.66 |
| 2009–10 | 60:40 | 37,051.94 | 22,231.16 | 14,820.78 |
| 2010–11 | 65:35 | 68,895.38 | 44,782.00 | 24,113.38 |
| 2011–12 | 65:35 | 105,195.58 | 68,377.13 | 36,818.45 |
| 2012–13 | 65:35 | 106,653.09 | 69,324.51 | 37,328.58 |

*Source: SSA Authority Punjab*, Chandigarh.

*Note*: The funding pattern changed to 65:35 from 2010–11 to 2014–15 after the implementation of RTE Act from 1 April 2010 (ESO 2012 b: 211).

during 2006–07, to Rs. 36,911.80 lakh during 2009–10 and peaked to Rs. 106,653.09 lakh during 2012–13. Thus, the level of total budget (AWPB) approved under SSA for the state during 2012–13 was 7.50 times more than that of its level during 2002–03. The table also shows the respective shares of the central and state governments in the total budget of SSA. The respective budget of the GOI and GOP in the overall budget of SSA is decided on the basis of funding ratio. The share of GOI works out to be Rs. 10,660.49 lakh during 2002–03. It has increased to Rs. 69324.51 lakh during 2012–13. The share of GOP has increased from Rs. 3,553.50 to Rs. 37,328.58 lakh from 2002–03 to 2012–13.

The effectiveness of any project apart from many other things depends upon the amount of funds received and utilized. Table 4.8 shows the amount of fund received and utilized under the SSA by the state during the period from 2002–03 to 2009–10. The SSA in the state received from the GOI and GOP the total amount of funds equal to Rs. 11458.17 lakh during 2002–03. The amount received increased to Rs. 29,398.62 lakh during 2009–10. But, on the other side the amount utilized was Rs. 6,690.47 lakh during 2002–03, which increased to Rs. 22,925.97 lakh during 2009–10. There have been huge yearly variations so far as the ratio of funds utilized to funds received is concerned. Out of the eight years period for which data are reported for four years the utilization was more than hundred per cent. These years were: 2004–05, 2006–07, 2007–08 and 2008–09. In case of rest of the years the utilization was on a considerably lower side. The utilization was lowest during 2003–04.

*Table 4.8* Funds received and utilized from centre and Punjab (Rs. lakh)

| *Year* | *Funds received from* | | | *Fund utilized (total)* | *Share of funds utilized to received* |
|---|---|---|---|---|---|
| | GOI | GOP | *Total* | | |
| 2002–03 | 10,485.00 | 973.17 | 11,458.17 | 6,690.47 | 58.39 |
| 2003–04 | 6,476.00 | 3,083.00 | 9,559.00 | 4,449.83 | 46.55 |
| 2004–05 | 3,089.04 | 2,677.83 | 5,766.87 | 8,780.61 | 152.26 |
| 2005–06 | 14,683.89 | 4,905.58 | 19,589.47 | 11,857.44 | 60.53 |
| 2006–07 | 12,894.62 | 2,626.64 | 15,521.26 | 15,785.56 | 101.70 |
| 2007–08 | 10,493.88 | 4,468.27 | 14,962.15 | 15,313.47 | 102.35 |
| 2008–09 | 13,808.11 | 5,950.35 | 19,758.46 | 28,620.48 | 144.85 |
| 2009–10 | 20,044.00 | 9,354.62 | 29,398.62 | 22,925.97 | 77.98 |

*Source: SSA Authority Punjab*, Chandigarh.

*Note*: GOI stands for Government of India and GOP for Government of Punjab.

*Table 4.9* Indicators of utilization of SSA funds in Punjab

| *Year* | *Funds received as % of AWPB* | *Funds utilized as % of AWPB* | *Funds received as % of central share* | *Funds received as % of Punjab share* |
|---|---|---|---|---|
| 2002–03 | 80.61 | 47.07 | 98.35 | 27.39 |
| 2003–04 | 47.45 | 22.09 | 42.86 | 61.21 |
| 2004–05 | 28.72 | 43.73 | 20.51 | 53.35 |
| 2005–06 | 86.75 | 52.51 | 86.70 | 86.89 |
| 2006–07 | 66.68 | 67.81 | 73.86 | 45.13 |
| 2007–08 | 80.93 | 82.83 | 81.08 | 80.56 |
| 2008–09 | 74.53 | 107.96 | 80.13 | 64.13 |
| 2009–10 | 79.65 | 62.11 | 90.20 | 63.68 |

*Source: SSA Authority Punjab*, Chandigarh.

Another important dimension of SSA comes from analysis of fund flows on the basis of amounts budgeted, allocated and actually utilized (Table 4.9). First, the amount received was considerably less than that of approved amount of project under SSA budget, i.e. AWPB. There has been huge variation on this score from year to year. It was 80.61 per cent during 2002–03. It was as low as merely 28.72 per cent during 2004–05. It improved in the next year considerably and reached to 86.75 per cent during 2005–06.

It has attained the level of 79.65 per cent during 2009–10. Similarly, the funds actually utilized as proportion of AWPB constituted very small proportion in all the years but for 2008–09 when it crossed the mark of 100 per cent because of spill over of the preceding year. Further, the funds received as proportion of the central share was comparatively on the higher side most of the times than that of the state share. In case of GOI, the funds received as proportion of the stipulated share of the centre was extremely on the lower side during 2003–04 and 2004–05, respectively 42.86 and 20.51 per cent. But, for the rest of the years it was on higher side as high as 98.35 per cent during 2002–03. The GOI provided more than 80 per cent of its share during the previous three years, i.e. 2007–08, 2008–09 and 2009–10. But, the picture for the state contribution happens to be different. Amazingly, during the 2002–03, the state provided just 27.39 per cent of its stipulated share. The state has provided above 80 per cent of its share only during two years, i.e. 2005–06 and 2007–08. For the rest of the years, the state share was around 60 per cent. In this way, the fund actually utilized as proportion of the AWPB turned out to be grossly on the lower side which reduces the effectiveness and coverage of the project.

## State and district-wise expenditure

The SSA being broad-based in project mode programme involves spending on large number of items and activities (Table 4.10). Moreover, many newer activities were added over the period as per changed requirements as is clear from the breakup of expenditure for 2002–03 and 2011–12. During 2002–03, the total amount of expenditure on the SSA was Rs. 8,492.32

*Table 4.10* Activity-wise expenditure on SSA in Punjab, 2002–03 and 2011–12 (Rs. lakhs)

| *Item/activity* | *2002–03* | | *2011–12* | |
|---|---|---|---|---|
| | *Amount* | % | *Amount* | % |
| Teacher salary | – | | 22,950.54 | 30.13 |
| Teacher grant | 342.10 | 4.03 | 376.56 | 0.49 |
| Block resource centre | 26.08 | 0.31 | 3,892.59 | 5.11 |
| Cluster resource centre | 38.01 | 0.45 | 3,438.62 | 4.51 |
| Teacher training | 931.67 | 10.97 | 1,211.01 | 1.59 |
| Interventions for OOSC | – | – | 330.51 | 0.43 |
| Special training | – | – | 875.89 | 1.15 |
| Free textbooks | 487.66 | 5.74 | 2,001.11 | 2.63 |
| Uniforms | – | – | 4,800.59 | 6.30 |
| Interventions for CWSN (IED) | 6.81 | 0.08 | 3,432.64 | 4.51 |
| Civil works (including furniture) | 4,787.75 | 56.38 | 23,611.92 | 31.00 |
| Teaching learning equipment | – | – | 11.38 | 0.01 |
| Maintenance grant | 1,197.00 | 14.10 | 1,443.58 | 1.90 |
| School grant | 361.70 | 4.26 | 1,107.70 | 1.45 |
| Research and evaluation | 194.12 | 2.29 | 240.41 | 0.32 |
| Management and quality | 20.24 | 0.24 | 4,023.87 | 5.28 |
| Innovative activity | 31.00 | 0.37 | 600.11 | 0.79 |
| Community training | 68.19 | 0.80 | 808.18 | 1.06 |
| Residential schools for special category of children | – | – | 27.83 | 0.04 |
| State component | – | – | 776.02 | 1.02 |
| NPEGEL | – | – | 6.16 | 0.01 |
| Others including fixed assets | – | – | 57.36 | 0.08 |
| KGBV | – | – | 145.25 | 0.19 |
| Total | 8,492.33 | 100.00 | 76,169.85 | 100.00 |

*Source:* For 2002–03 data MHRD (2010: 21); for 2011–12 data SSA (2011–12:77).

lakh. The largest amount of expenditure (Rs. 4,787.75 lakh) (56.38 per cent) was incurred on civil works, followed by maintenance (i.e. 14.10 per cent) and teacher training (10.97 per cent). These three components accounted for 81.45 per cent of total expenditure of SSA during 2002–03. However, during 2011–12, again the major component of expenditure was civil works. The total expenditure on it was Rs. 23,611.92 lakh with share of 31 per cent. The component next in importance was teacher's salary with total expenditure of Rs. 22,950.54 lakh (30.13 per cent). The share of the other important components was as follows: uniforms (6.30 per cent), textbooks (2.63 per cent), maintenance (1.90 per cent), IED (4.51 per cent) and innovative activities (0.79 per cent).

The analysis of district-wise distribution of funds throws much light on the relative priority accorded to the various districts in the allocation of SSA funds. Table 4.11 shows the district-wise distribution of SSA funds from 2001–02 to 2010–11. It is to be noted that the number of districts increased during the study period. Three new districts were carved out of the existing ones. The districts of Barnala, Mohali and Tarn Taran were respectively carved out from Bathinda, Ropar and Amritsar. Thus, for the year 2007–08 and onwards, the distribution is shown for 20 districts and for the rest of years it was shown for 17 districts. The picture becomes very clear by excluding the expenditure incurred on State Project Office (SPO). During 2001–02, the highest proportion (8.44 per cent) of expenditure was incurred in the district of Gurdaspur and lowest in Nawan Shahar (3.98 per cent). The notice worthy fact which emerges is that the proportionate share of districts varies considerably on year to year basis. For example, the proportionate share of Gurdaspur declined to just 2.67 per cent during 2002–03 though it attracted huge share in the rest of the years. Moreover, no single district occupies the top position during each and every year. For various years, the highest proportionate share of different districts was as follows: 2001–02 (Gurdaspur); 2003–03 (Bathinda); 2003–04 (Hoshiarpur); 2004–05 (Firozpur); 2005–06 (Sangrur); 2006–07(Ludhiana); 2007–08 (Gurdaspur); 2008–09 (Gurdaspur); 2009–10 (Firozpur); 2010–11(Gurdaspur); 2011–12 (Firozpur). The five districts namely Amritsar, Firozpur, Hoshiarpur, Muktsar and Sangrur have improved their relative shares during 2011–12 over 2001–02.

The district-wise expenditure patterns have been analysed by relating it with other variables such as enrolment, per-student expenditure, out-of-school children, etc. (Table 4.12). The district-wise per student expenditures have been placed against the enrolment and out–of-school children share of the district for the single financial year, i.e. 2007–08. The perusal of data shows that the maximum amount of SSA expenditure was made in

*Table 4.11* District-wise distribution of SSA expenditure in Punjab (percentage), 2001–02 to 2011–12

| | *2001–02* | *2002–03* | *2003–04* | *2004–05* | *2005–06* | *2006–07* | *2007–08* | *2008–09* | *2009–10* | *2010–11* | *2011–12* |
|---|---|---|---|---|---|---|---|---|---|---|---|
| SPO | 6.98 | 17.33 | 0.59 | 2.15 | 1.90 | 2.55 | 1.17 | 1.89 | 1.63 | 1.33 | 1.30 |
| Amritsar | 5.80 | 8.65 | 6.37 | 9.17 | 9.53 | 5.71 | 11.75 | 10.85 | 7.48 | 7.68 | 7.87 |
| Barnala | N/A | N/A | N/A | N/A | N/A | N/A | 0.22 | 0.56 | 1.62 | 1.50 | 2.26 |
| Bathinda | 6.13 | 10.03 | 7.34 | 5.29 | 4.35 | 4.25 | 3.68 | 3.94 | 3.84 | 4.35 | 5.15 |
| Faridkot | 4.14 | 6.25 | 2.27 | 3.05 | 3.70 | 3.23 | 3.24 | 3.01 | 2.92 | 2.33 | 1.98 |
| Fatehgarh Sahib | 4.64 | 7.73 | 3.32 | 3.64 | 3.41 | 2.54 | 4.20 | 4.89 | 4.87 | 5.49 | 3.19 |
| Firozpur | 4.97 | 3.00 | 9.49 | 10.14 | 4.51 | 8.41 | 6.28 | 6.01 | 8.74 | 5.68 | 10.47 |
| Gurdaspur | 8.44 | 2.67 | 10.52 | 6.80 | 7.61 | 5.60 | 14.73 | 13.56 | 7.96 | 10.48 | 7.73 |
| Hoshiarpur | 7.78 | 3.78 | 13.61 | 6.66 | 5.35 | 8.71 | 6.89 | 6.25 | 6.76 | 8.00 | 10.12 |
| Jalandhar | 6.13 | 4.27 | 3.76 | 4.30 | 5.07 | 6.80 | 7.26 | 6.32 | 5.34 | 5.32 | 5.30 |
| Kapurthala | 4.39 | 0.44 | 4.59 | 3.70 | 5.48 | 4.49 | 3.37 | 4.01 | 5.13 | 3.79 | 3.09 |
| Ludhiana | 6.46 | 3.88 | 5.07 | 7.78 | 9.21 | 8.78 | 5.83 | 5.21 | 5.71 | 5.16 | 5.88 |
| Mansa | 4.67 | 7.65 | 3.64 | 3.29 | 6.33 | 5.07 | 3.56 | 3.89 | 4.06 | 3.76 | 3.66 |
| Moga | 4.64 | 8.36 | 5.25 | 3.73 | 3.13 | 5.47 | 3.42 | 3.59 | 3.87 | 4.06 | 3.40 |
| Mohali | N/A | N/A | N/A | N/A | N/A | N/A | 1.68 | 2.79 | 3.68 | 3.61 | 3.31 |
| Muktsar | 4.72 | 7.86 | 1.27 | 6.24 | 4.35 | 3.96 | 3.59 | 2.89 | 3.74 | 3.46 | 5.05 |
| Nawan Shahar | 3.98 | 2.37 | 5.63 | 2.97 | 3.26 | 5.18 | 2.67 | 3.66 | 3.18 | 3.46 | 2.36 |
| Patiala | 5.79 | 2.65 | 7.21 | 7.55 | 7.01 | 7.44 | 4.45 | 4.19 | 6.73 | 7.78 | 5.46 |
| Ropar | 5.63 | 2.67 | 4.15 | 7.79 | 5.82 | 4.21 | 5.02 | 5.26 | 5.56 | 6.02 | 3.42 |
| Sangrur | 4.71 | 0.40 | 5.94 | 5.73 | 9.98 | 7.61 | 5.55 | 4.67 | 4.08 | 2.98 | 5.20 |
| Tarn Taran | N/A | N/A | N/A | N/A | N/A | N/A | 1.43 | 2.56 | 3.08 | 3.75 | 3.81 |
| Total | 100 | 100 | 100 | 100 | 100 | 100 | 100 | 100 | 100 | 100 | 100 |

*Source*: *Annual Report*, Sarva Shiksha Abhiyan Authority Punjab, Chandigarh (various issues).

*Note*: N/A stands for not applicable.

*Table 4.12* District-wise SSA expenditure, enrolment and out-of-school children, 2007–08

| *District* | *SSA expr. (Rs. lakh)* | *Students enrolment (I-VIII)* | *Per-student expenditure (Rs.)* | *Enrolment share (%)* | *Expenditure share (%)* | *Out-of-school children (%)* | *Enrolment to population ratio* |
|---|---|---|---|---|---|---|---|
| Amritsar | 1,793.19 | 205,899 | 870.91 | 7.23 | 11.89 | 8.54 | 9.55 |
| Barnala | 33.98 | 55,573 | 61.15 | 1.95 | 0.23 | 1.69 | 10.55 |
| Bathinda | 561.74 | 167,160 | 336.05 | 5.87 | 3.73 | 7.02 | 14.13 |
| Faridkot | 494.48 | 76,523 | 646.18 | 2.69 | 3.28 | 3.82 | 13.89 |
| Fatehgarh Sahib | 640.63 | 59,903 | 1,069.45 | 2.10 | 4.25 | 1.06 | 11.13 |
| Firozpur | 957.78 | 242,213 | 395.43 | 8.51 | 6.35 | 12.62 | 13.87 |
| Gurdaspur | 2,246.50 | 238,855 | 940.53 | 8.39 | 14.90 | 4.37 | 11.35 |
| Hoshiarpur | 1,050.94 | 161,924 | 649.03 | 5.69 | 6.97 | 4.17 | 10.94 |
| Jalandhar | 1,107.41 | 244,482 | 452.96 | 8.59 | 7.34 | 6.20 | 12.46 |
| Kapurthala | 513.94 | 89,608 | 573.54 | 3.15 | 3.41 | 1.43 | 11.88 |
| Ludhiana | 889.19 | 312,068 | 284.93 | 10.96 | 5.90 | 8.20 | 10.29 |
| Mansa | 543.82 | 75,553 | 719.78 | 2.65 | 3.61 | 5.03 | 10.97 |
| Moga | 522.01 | 125,427 | 416.18 | 4.41 | 3.46 | 4.07 | 14.02 |
| Mohali | 255.62 | 59,924 | 426.57 | 2.10 | 1.70 | 1.64 | 8.58 |
| Muktsar | 547.99 | 112,573 | 486.79 | 3.95 | 3.63 | 6.17 | 14.48 |
| Nawan Shahar | 407.49 | 62,046 | 656.76 | 2.18 | 2.70 | 0.89 | 10.56 |
| Ropar | 766.24 | 71,004 | 1,079.15 | 2.49 | 5.08 | 7.02 | 11.29 |
| Patiala | 679.24 | 182,935 | 371.30 | 6.43 | 4.50 | 2.67 | 11.20 |
| Sangrur | 847.03 | 172,165 | 491.99 | 6.05 | 5.62 | 6.59 | 11.69 |
| Tarn Taran | 218.79 | 131,233 | 166.72 | 4.61 | 1.45 | 6.78 | 13.97 |
| Total | 15,078.00 | 2,847,068 | 529.60 | 100.00 | 100.00 | 100.00 | 11.69 |

*Source:* Annual Report, 2007–08, Sarva Shiksha Abhiyan Authority Punjab, Chandigarh. Statistical Abstract of Punjab, ESO, Chandigarh.

Gurdaspur district (Rs. 2,246.50 lakh, i.e. 14.90 per cent) and minimum in Barnala district (Rs. 33.98 lakh, i.e. 0.23 per cent). The student enrolment for elementary level of education was the maximum in Ludhiana district (312,068 students, i.e. 10.96 per cent) and the lowest in Barnala district (55,573 students, i.e. 1.95 per cent). Per student expenditure turned out to be highest in Ropar district (Rs. 1,079.15) and lowest in Barnala district (Rs. 61.15). But, out of the total number of out-of-school-children in the state, the highest proportion was in Firozpur district (i.e. 12.62 per cent) and the lowest in Kapurthala, i.e. 1.43 per cent. Here lies some sort of inequities in the distribution of SSA resources in the state.

The district with highest proportion of out-of-school-children (i.e. Firozpur) has shared not only the lower proportion of SSA resources (i.e. 6.35 per cent) but also the lower level of resources on per-student basis (i.e. Rs. 395.43). But the Gurdaspur district with comparatively lower proportion of out-of-school-children (i.e. 4.37 per cent) has secured the highest proportion of SSA resource (14.90 per cent). This district has got comparatively much higher level of resources on per-student basis also, i.e. Rs. 940.53. This in fact is the third highest level of resources after Ropar (Rs. 1,079.15) and Fatehgarh Sahib (Rs. 1,069.45). Similarly, the Muktsar and Tarn Taran districts had comparatively higher proportion of out-of-school-children and that of lower shares in SSA resources.

Pattern of flow of funds has been assessed by taking into account the distribution of the funds across various blocks in the district. Sangrur district has been selected purposively by taking into account the ratio of total elementary level enrolment to the respective population of the district. For the year 2007–08 (Table 4.12, last column), Sangrur district represents the state on the basis of such ratio as the value of such ratio for this district (11.69 per cent) was exactly equal to that of the overall ratio of the state, i.e. 11.69 per cent. The block-wise relevant data for all six blocks of Sangrur district are placed in Table 4.13 for two years, i.e. 2006–07 and 2007–08. It is clear that during these years pattern of distribution witnessed substantial change. During 2006–07, the highest proportion of funds was allocated to Malerkotla block (23.86 per cent), followed by Sunam block (17.72 per cent); Dhuri block (17.30 per cent); Bhawanigarh block (15.56 per cent); Sangrur block (14.40 per cent); Sherpur block (11.16 per cent). But, the proportionate shares changed drastically during 2007–08. The Malerkotla block which occupied the first rank during 2006–07 slipped to sixth rank in the subsequent year 2007–08 with share of 3.55 per cent. Rank of Sunam block rose to second with share of 38.48 per cent which was 17.72 per cent in the previous year.

*Table 4.13* Block-wise distribution of grants under SSA in Sangrur district (rural) (Rs.)

| *Block* | *2006–07* | *Rank* | *2007–08* | *Rank* |
|---|---|---|---|---|
| 1. Sangrur | 4,388,272 (14.40) | 5 | 3,104,600 (14.33) | 4 |
| 2. Malerkotla | 7,270,000 (23.86) | 1 | 770,000 (3.55) | 6 |
| 3. Dhuri | 5,270,000 (17.30) | 3 | 1,990,000 (9.18) | 5 |
| 4. Sunam | 5,399,348 (17.72) | 2 | 8,336,366 (38.48) | 1 |
| 5. Bhawanigarh | 4,740,800 (15.56) | 4 | 3,605,500 (16.64) | 3 |
| 6. Sherpur | 3,400,000 (11.16) | 6 | 3,860,000 (17.82) | 2 |
| Total | 30,468,420 (100) | | 21,666,466 (100) | |

*Source:* Gill *et al.* (2010), pp. 38–46.

*Notes*

1 Malerkotla refers to both of the Malerkotla-I and Malerkotla-II blocks.

2 Two Blocks namely Lehragaga and Andana had not received any grant during these two years.

3 Ranks are based on the proportionate shares in descending order.

## District-cum-component specific utilization

The under-utilization of SSA funds has drawn considerable amount of attention in the recent years. Under-utilization becomes more serious in the situation of under-allocation on one side and under-release of the committed funds on the other. In case of some components the funds utilized were either very low or nil. Further, the best results of any project could be realized only in the situation of releasing the budgeted funds on all the components and heads of spending. The under-expenditure on any one or more head of spending adversely affects the efficiency and performance of other sub-programmes because the things are dynamically integrated.

Audit Report (MHRD 2010) highlighted the various problems and hazards in the flow of SSA funds. Audit Report pointed out the problems in the manner as stated: In the first year of SSA (i.e. 2001–02), the government of Punjab received Rs. 5,517.08 lakh in three instalments (on 11 October 2001, 27 December 2001 and 22 January 2002). But, these funds remained with the Punjab government and were not released to the SSA Mission during that year. In addition, Rs. 1,839.03 lakh being the share of state government was also not released to them. In effect, therefore, year 2001–02 was 'Wash out Year' in terms of funds. The state government released these funds only in next year, i.e. 2002–03. Audit Report further held that the state government defaulted in two ways, viz. it did not pass on the Government of India funds to the state Mission in 2001–02 and did

*Table 4.14* Release of funds by the government of Punjab and India (Rs. in lakh)

| *Year* | *AWPB* | *GOI* | *Share* | *GOP* | *Shortfall* | *Release to* |
|---|---|---|---|---|---|---|
| 2002–03 | 14,213.99 | 5,517.08 (17.06.2002) | 973.17 (17.06.2002) | 1,839.03 | 865.86 | July |
| | | | | 1,622.67 | 1,622.67 | March |
| | | 4,868.00 (19.12.2002) | – | | | |
| Total | | 10,385.08 | 973.17 | 3,461.70 | 2,488.53 | |
| 2003–04 | 20,057.83 | 6,476.00 (25.09.2003) | 2,583.00 (25.08.2003) | 2,158.67 | *424.33 | Dec |
| | | | | | *500.00 | |
| | | | 500.00 (26.03.2004) | | | |
| Grand Total | | 16,861.08 | 4,056.17 | 5,620.37 | 1,564.20 | |

*Source:* MHRD (2010), p. 15.

*Note:* * Excess release.

not release their share. Even after these funds in respect of 2002–03 were released in June 2003, the state government did not fulfil their part of the obligation and deposited only Rs. 973.17 lakh (Table 4.14).

Yet, the state received an instalment of Rs. 4,868.00 lakh in December 2002 even though it had defaulted in providing matching funds to the Society. This time too state government's share against the instalment received from Government of India was not deposited during 2002–03. Overall short deposit of state government share was Rs. 2,488.53 lakh during 2002–03. The SSA Mission transferred funds of Rs. 6,321.50 lakh (out of the first instalment) to the various District Education Officers on 18 July 2002 and Rs. 5,036.60 lakh on 21 March 2003 (out of instalment including the previous balance). But, the overall short deposit of state government during both the years was Rs. 1,564.20 lakh.

An assessment of funds allocation and actual expenditure among the different components of SSA Mission has been restricted to three years (2009–10, 2010–11and 2011–12). The various components of spending have been clubbed under six broad headings. These are (1) Buildings: Civil Works; (2) Teacher Salary; (3) Other Variable Expenditure: Repair and Maintenance; (4) Equity and Efficiency: Education Guarantee Scheme (EGS); Alternative Innovative Education (AIE); Inclusive Education for Disabled (IED); Early Childhood Care and Education (ECCE); Education of SC/STs; Girls Education; (5) Quality: School Grants, Teaching Grants, Remedial/Learning Enhancement Schemes (RLES); Teacher Training;

Computer Aided Learning (CAL); Research, Evaluation, Monitoring and Supervision (REMS); and (6) Incentives: Textbooks and Work Books. It is to be noted that the analysis here is based exclusively on the above specified components and sub-components. The district-wise and above specified six components-wise data have been presented in terms of allocations, actual expenditure and rate of utilization for Triennium Average (TA) of three financial years, viz. 2009–10, 2010–11and 2011–12.

Table 4.15 provides actual allocation for all districts for six components, viz. (1) Buildings, (2) Teacher Salary, (3) Other Variable Expenditure, (4) Equity and Efficiency, (5) Quality and (6) Incentives for the TA (2010–12). It is clear that the total amount allocated was Rs. 56,224.50 lakh during TA (2010–12). Out of this amount, the various components received in the following manner: (1) Buildings (Rs. 23,797.10 lakh); (2) Teacher Salary (Rs. 18,398.83 lakh); (3) Other Variable Expenditure (Rs. 1,432.36 lakh); (4) Equity and Efficiency (Rs. 5,147.66 lakh); (5) Quality (Rs. 5,183.53 lakh); and (6) Incentives (Rs. 2,265.01 lakh). Their respective proportionate shares were as follows: (1) Buildings (42.33 per cent); (2) Teacher Salary (32.72 per cent); (3) Other Variable Expenditure (2.55 per cent); (4) Equity and Efficiency (9.16 per cent); (5) Quality (9.22 per cent); and (6) Incentives (4.03 per cent). Thus, the maximum allocations were made for Building and the lowest for Other Variable Expenditure.

Table 4.16 provides the share of these components in actual expenditures across districts. Their respective proportionate shares in the descending order were as follows: (1) Buildings (37.57 per cent); Teacher Salary (33.45 per cent); Quality (10.37 per cent); Equity and Efficiency (10.18 per cent); Incentives (4.64 per cent); and Other Variable Expenditure (3.79 per cent). Further, the component-specific inter-district behaviour essentially followed the overall pattern at the state level (Table 16). The two components namely buildings and teacher salary accounted for the largest proportion of expenditure for the districts. Moreover, in eight districts namely Amritsar, Barnala, Bathinda, Firozpur, Hoshiarpur, Mohali, Muktsar and Tarn Taran, buildings had consumed more than 40 per cent of the total expenditure.

Component-wise rate of utilization for the various districts reveals interesting scenario during TA (2010–12) (Table 4.17). For the state as a whole, overall level of utilization works out to be 67.30 per cent. Among districts, utilization was highest in Fatehgarh Sahib (84.45 per cent) and lowest in Gurdaspur (44.55 per cent). Further, utilization was below state average in case of five districts namely Firozpur, Gurdaspur, Moga, Patiala and Sangrur. Among the components, it was highest in case of Other Variable Expenditure (100.25 per cent) and lowest in case of Buildings (59.74 per cent). For

*Table 4.15* District-wise financial allocation under SSA in Punjab by various components, 2009–10 to 2011–12 (triennium average) (Rs. in lakhs)

| *District* | *Building* | *Teacher salary* | *Other variable expenditure* | *Equity and efficiency* | *Quality* | *Incentives* | *Total* |
|---|---|---|---|---|---|---|---|
| Amritsar | 1,438.76 | 1,358.49 | 93.58 | 415.81 | 373.06 | 163.25 | 3,842.94 |
| Barnala | 439.42 | 301.94 | 22.68 | 92.88 | 118.29 | 49.83 | 1,025.03 |
| Bathinda | 1,043.15 | 780.04 | 48.70 | 254.64 | 177.07 | 115.25 | 2,418.85 |
| Faridkot | 337.61 | 430.28 | 30.73 | 158.13 | 127.20 | 49.71 | 1,133.66 |
| Fatehgarh Sahib | 535.21 | 820.02 | 48.98 | 205.04 | 239.17 | 49.68 | 1,898.09 |
| Firozpur | 2,624.82 | 2,080.49 | 117.09 | 347.37 | 358.32 | 141.09 | 5,669.19 |
| Gurdaspur | 4,545.37 | 1,511.09 | 150.38 | 390.02 | 492.67 | 288.35 | 7,377.89 |
| Hoshiarpur | 2,674.17 | 1,103.72 | 126.55 | 256.39 | 440.71 | 156.25 | 4,757.80 |
| Jalandhar | 992.18 | 959.93 | 106.85 | 271.01 | 369.71 | 148.68 | 2,848.37 |
| Kapurthala | 867.12 | 727.34 | 58.18 | 119.42 | 205.01 | 71.60 | 2,048.68 |
| Ludhiana | 532.60 | 990.42 | 115.38 | 417.90 | 386.50 | 203.81 | 2,646.60 |
| Mansa | 700.17 | 875.29 | 36.95 | 128.93 | 155.38 | 77.51 | 1,974.23 |
| Moga | 627.33 | 1,014.89 | 45.85 | 175.10 | 192.74 | 84.65 | 2,140.56 |
| Mohali | 957.25 | 497.85 | 43.65 | 147.56 | 164.92 | 61.33 | 1,872.56 |
| Muktsar | 1,186.86 | 732.27 | 40.68 | 192.43 | 166.96 | 63.48 | 2,382.68 |
| Nawan Shahar | 431.16 | 556.62 | 48.84 | 111.31 | 164.22 | 54.67 | 1,366.82 |
| Patiala | 961.81 | 1,199.71 | 102.32 | 886.25 | 343.04 | 171.14 | 3,664.27 |
| Ropar | 856.40 | 971.97 | 58.49 | 134.38 | 214.38 | 85.10 | 2,320.73 |
| Sangrur | 1,199.64 | 918.11 | 76.80 | 236.03 | 282.06 | 140.47 | 2,853.12 |
| Tarn Taran | 846.06 | 568.37 | 59.68 | 207.04 | 212.12 | 89.17 | 1,982.44 |
| Punjab | 23,797.10 | 18,398.83 | 1,432.36 | 5,147.66 | 5,183.53 | 2,265.01 | 56,224.50 |
| Punjab, Per Cent | 42.33 | 32.72 | 2.55 | 9.16 | 9.22 | 4.03 | 100.00 |

*Source:* Calculated from the Annual Report 2009–10, 2010–11 and 2011–12 of Sarva Shiksha Abhiyan Authority Punjab, Chandigarh.

*Table 4.16* Share of various components in actual expenditure under SSA in Punjab, 2009–10 to 2011–12 (triennium average) (district-wise %)

| *District* | *Building* | *Teacher salary* | *Other variable expenditure* | *Equity and efficiency* | *Quality* | *Incentives* | *Total (Rs. lakhs)* |
|---|---|---|---|---|---|---|---|
| Amritsar | 40.39 | 32.16 | 2.84 | 11.93 | 8.69 | 3.99 | 2,970.61 |
| Barnala | 48.96 | 19.41 | 3.27 | 11.67 | 11.04 | 5.65 | 735.72 |
| Bathinda | 41.97 | 30.10 | 2.95 | 11.78 | 8.74 | 4.47 | 1,789.39 |
| Faridkot | 29.57 | 35.47 | 3.55 | 15.50 | 11.36 | 4.55 | 869.18 |
| Fatehgarh Sahib | 27.12 | 47.09 | 2.88 | 9.96 | 10.40 | 2.56 | 1,603.03 |
| Firozpur | 46.04 | 31.54 | 3.38 | 8.33 | 7.79 | 2.92 | 3,360.85 |
| Gurdaspur | 37.29 | 32.03 | 4.69 | 6.75 | 12.20 | 7.03 | 3,286.92 |
| Hoshiarpur | 48.07 | 28.49 | 3.58 | 6.73 | 9.66 | 3.48 | 3,397.40 |
| Jalandhar | 34.95 | 27.89 | 5.26 | 12.39 | 14.03 | 5.48 | 2,038.90 |
| Kapurthala | 37.75 | 35.44 | 3.99 | 7.86 | 10.84 | 4.12 | 1,414.60 |
| Ludhiana | 19.28 | 33.54 | 5.62 | 19.74 | 15.00 | 6.81 | 2,164.02 |
| Mansa | 39.53 | 36.63 | 2.81 | 8.04 | 8.48 | 4.51 | 1,445.88 |
| Moga | 34.69 | 37.31 | 3.40 | 10.42 | 9.31 | 4.87 | 1,411.77 |
| Mohali | 41.38 | 32.16 | 3.20 | 9.69 | 9.45 | 4.12 | 1,329.67 |
| Muktsar | 49.26 | 27.33 | 2.44 | 10.39 | 7.33 | 3.24 | 1,663.89 |
| Nawan Shahar | 30.57 | 39.76 | 4.39 | 9.50 | 11.32 | 4.47 | 1,089.00 |
| Patiala | 33.99 | 35.51 | 4.17 | 10.31 | 10.78 | 5.23 | 2,444.90 |
| Ropar | 31.37 | 46.50 | 3.20 | 6.59 | 8.44 | 3.89 | 1,757.62 |
| Sangrur | 26.20 | 37.09 | 5.08 | 11.92 | 13.00 | 6.70 | 1,667.96 |
| Tarn Taran | 40.08 | 28.92 | 4.33 | 10.63 | 10.98 | 5.07 | 1,400.33 |
| Punjab | 37.57 | 33.45 | 3.79 | 10.18 | 10.37 | 4.64 | 37,841.65 |

*Source:* Calculated from the Annual Report 2009–10, 2010–11 and 2011–12 of Sarva Shiksha Abhiyan Authority Punjab, Chandigarh.

*Table 4.17* District-wise rate of utilization of SSA funds in Punjab by various components, 2009–10 to 2011–12 (triennium average) (%)

| *District* | *Building* | *Teacher salary* | *Other variable expenditure* | *Equity and efficiency* | *Quality* | *Incentives* | *Total* |
|---|---|---|---|---|---|---|---|
| Amritsar | 83.39 | 70.33 | 90.16 | 85.22 | 69.21 | 72.59 | 77.30 |
| Barnala | 81.97 | 47.29 | 106.17 | 92.45 | 68.68 | 83.44 | 71.78 |
| Bathinda | 71.99 | 69.05 | 108.23 | 82.76 | 88.34 | 69.38 | 73.98 |
| Faridkot | 76.12 | 71.65 | 100.46 | 85.21 | 77.63 | 79.56 | 76.67 |
| Fatehgarh Sahib | 81.22 | 92.05 | 94.39 | 77.84 | 69.68 | 82.47 | 84.45 |
| Firozpur | 58.95 | 50.96 | 96.93 | 80.61 | 73.09 | 69.44 | 59.28 |
| Gurdaspur | 26.96 | 69.68 | 102.61 | 56.86 | 81.42 | 80.17 | 44.55 |
| Hoshiarpur | 61.07 | 87.70 | 96.00 | 89.13 | 74.44 | 75.72 | 71.41 |
| Jalandhar | 71.82 | 59.24 | 100.41 | 93.23 | 77.38 | 75.12 | 71.58 |
| Kapurthala | 61.59 | 68.92 | 97.04 | 93.14 | 74.77 | 81.38 | 69.05 |
| Ludhiana | 78.34 | 73.29 | 105.37 | 102.24 | 84.01 | 72.31 | 81.77 |
| Mansa | 81.62 | 60.51 | 110.01 | 90.21 | 78.88 | 84.19 | 73.24 |
| Moga | 78.06 | 51.90 | 104.62 | 84.05 | 68.19 | 81.28 | 65.95 |
| Mohali | 57.47 | 85.90 | 97.53 | 87.35 | 76.18 | 89.30 | 71.01 |
| Muktsar | 69.07 | 62.09 | 99.73 | 89.84 | 73.09 | 85.05 | 69.83 |
| Nawan Shahar | 77.21 | 77.79 | 97.83 | 92.92 | 75.04 | 89.01 | 79.67 |
| Patiala | 86.40 | 72.37 | 99.53 | 28.45 | 76.85 | 74.78 | 66.72 |
| Ropar | 64.38 | 84.09 | 96.26 | 86.22 | 69.20 | 80.34 | 75.74 |
| Sangrur | 36.43 | 67.39 | 110.41 | 84.24 | 76.90 | 79.52 | 58.46 |
| Tarn Taran | 66.34 | 71.24 | 101.52 | 71.87 | 72.50 | 79.58 | 70.64 |
| Punjab | 59.74 | 68.80 | 100.25 | 74.81 | 75.70 | 77.52 | 67.30 |

*Source*: Calculated from the Annual Report 2009–10, 2010–11 and 2011–12 of Sarva Shiksha Abhiyan Authority Punjab, Chandigarh.

the rest of the components the utilization was as follows: Teacher Salary (68.80 per cent); Equity and Efficiency (74.81per cent); Quality (75.70 per cent); and Incentives (77.52 per cent). In case of Buildings, the utilization varied between 36.43 per cent (Sangrur) and 86.40 per cent (Patiala). In case of Teacher Salary, the utilization varied between 47.29 per cent (Barnala) and 92.05 per cent (Fatehgarh Sahib). In case of Quality, the utilization varied between 68.19 per cent (Moga) and 88.34 per cent (Bathinda). In case of Equity and Efficiency, the utilization varied between 28.45 per cent (Patiala) and 102.24 per cent (Ludhiana). In case of Other Variable Expenditure, utilization varied between 90.16 per cent (Amritsar) and 110.41 per cent (Sangrur). And, in case of Incentives, utilization varied between 69.38 per cent (Bathinda) and 89.30 per cent (Mohali). *Thus, some districts and some components had brought down the overall level of proportion of funds allocated to that of expenditure.*

## Summing up

The foregoing analysis has highlighted the peculiar features of flow of funds provided by the central and state government for implementation of SSA project as a set of policy package in order to attain the pre-decided educational objectives in a time bound manner. The AWPB for the state of Punjab has increased by 7.50 times from Rs. 14,213.99 lakh during 2002–03 to Rs. 106,653.09 lakh during 2012–13. The ratio of funds utilized to funds received witnessed huge yearly variations. For four years (2004–05, 2006–07, 2007–08 and 2008–09) the utilization was more than 100 per cent. For rest of the four years (2002–03, 2003–04, 2005–06 and 2009–10), the utilization was considerably low. Further, the amount budgeted, allocated and actually utilized differs largely. The amounts received were found to be considerably lower than the approved budget. The funds actually utilized constituted a very small proportion of the AWPB for large number of years. Further, the funds received as proportion of the central share was comparatively on the higher side most of the times than that of the state share. The state has provided above 80 per cent of its share only during two years, i.e. 2005–06 and 2007–08 out of 10 years of study.

The SSA being broad-based in project mode programme involves spending on large number of items and activities. Many newer activities were added over the period as per changed requirements. During 2002–03, the largest proportion of expenditure (56.38 per cent) was incurred on the civil works followed by maintenance (i.e. 14.10 per cent) and teacher training (10.97 per cent). These three components accounted for 81.45 per cent of total expenditure of SSA during 2002–03. However, during 2011–12, again the major component of expenditure was found to be civil works with proportionate share of 31 per cent. The component next in importance was teacher salary (30.13 per cent); followed by uniforms (6.30 per cent); IED (4.51 per cent); textbooks (2.63 per cent); maintenance (1.90 per cent); and innovative activities (0.79 per cent). Inter-district analysis shows that the proportionate share of districts in total expenditure varied considerably on year-to-year basis. During 2001–02, the highest proportion (8.44 per cent) of total funds was allocated to the district of Gurdaspur and lowest to Nawan Shahar (3.98 per cent). No single district occupies the top position during each and every year. The five districts namely Amritsar, Firozpur, Hoshiarpur, Muktsar and Sangrur have improved their relative shares during 2011–12 over 2001–02.

The district-wise expenditure patterns point towards the existence of inequities in distribution of SSA resources when viewed in context of enrolment, per-student expenditure and out-of-school children. Per-student expenditure turned out to be highest in Ropar district and lowest in Barnala district. But, out of the total number of out-of-school-children in the state, the highest proportion was in Firozpur district and the lowest in Kapurthala. The district with highest proportion of out-of-school-children (i.e. Firozpur) has shared not only the lower proportion of SSA resources but also the lower level of resources on per-student basis. But the Gurdaspur district with comparatively lower proportion of out-of-school-children has secured the highest proportion of SSA resource. This district has got comparatively much higher level of resources on per-student basis also. Similarly, the Muktsar and Tarn Taran districts had comparatively higher proportion of out-of-school-children and that of lower shares in SSA resources. The pattern of flow of funds within the district shows considerable yearly variations. The block which occupied the first rank during one year slipped to last rank in the subsequent year.

The district-cum-component-specific analysis shows that out of the actual expenditure the various components stood in the following manner: Buildings (37.57 per cent); Teacher Salary (33.45 per cent); Quality (10.37 per cent); Equity and Efficiency (10.18 per cent); Incentives (4.64 per cent); and Other Variable Expenditure (3.79 per cent). Further, the component-specific inter-district behaviour essentially followed the overall pattern at the state level. The two components namely buildings and teacher salary accounted for the largest proportion of expenditure for the districts. Moreover, in eight districts namely Amritsar, Barnala, Bathinda, Firozpur, Hoshiarpur, Mohali, Muktsar and Tarn Taran the component called Buildings had consumed more than 40 per cent of the total expenditure of the concerned district.

For the state as a whole, the overall level of utilization works out to be 67.30 per cent during the TA (2010–12). Among the districts, the utilization was highest in Fatehgarh Sahib (84.45 per cent) and lowest in Gurdaspur (44.55 per cent). Further, utilization was below state average in case of five districts namely Firozpur, Gurdaspur, Moga, Patiala and Sangrur. Among the components, it was highest in case of Other Variable Expenditure (100.25 per cent) and lowest in case of Buildings (59.74 per cent). For the rest of the components the utilization was as follows: Teacher Salary (68.80 per cent); Equity and Efficiency (74.81 per cent); Quality (75.70 per cent); and Incentives (77.52 per cent). Thus, some districts and some components had brought down the overall level of proportion of funds allocated to that of expenditure.

The commencement of SSA in the state was not very well. In fact, the first year 2001–02 of SSA in the state was described as 'Wash out Year' in terms of funds (IPAI 2003: 15). The state government did not pass on the Government of India funds to the state Mission in 2001–02 and did not release their share also. The problem of under-utilization becomes more serious in the situation of under-allocation on one side and also underrelease of the committed funds. In case of some components the funds utilized were either very low or nil. Further, the best results of any project could be realized only in the situation of releasing the budgeted funds on all the components and heads of spending. The under-expenditure on any one or more heads of spending adversely affects the efficiency and performance of other sub-programmes because the things are dynamically integrated.

But, SSA could perform its designed role only in the situation of full implementation of the work plan and on it based budget. There are still huge gaps in the goals set by the SSA and their realization. Thus, instead of SSA intervention the state experienced strong fluctuations in enrolment level in elementary education. But normally it was expected that a well-designed programme such as SSA got translated into a stable and rising level of enrolment. The state must put more efforts to improve girls' enrolment as the state has already high female illiteracy particularly among those belonging to rural areas and weaker sections. The budgetary constraint at household levels for good majority of households, in situation of the emergence of private education on one side and hopeless delivered by state schools on other, may be compelling the parents to go for education decision making in a way which goes against girls' education in the given social milieu. The state has not achieved the desired level of enrolment ratios, dropout rates, enrolment of under- and over-age children, and out-of-school children, etc. The enrolment in private schools witnessed massive increase even after the working of SSA in government schools. It indicates that the SSA in itself is not sufficient to change the image of government schools in the perception of households as they continuously prefer the private schools. The SSA seems to have solved the problem of physical infrastructure to an extent but real problems of government schools remained unattended as they practically lie in the domain of state government such as providing of meritorious, regular and committed faculty, improvement of educational administration, monitoring and inspection, etc. The private school sector in the state is highly diverse, but a good majority does not follow any worthwhile academic standards and is of exploitative variety but essentially thrives on weakened government sector. The perpetuation of such a situation is not conducive for generation of quality human resources on large scale as special schemes make limited impact upon state schools and students have been opting for private schools in large numbers. It seems that the SSA impact can increase much more in the situation of generation of some sort of link between SSA grants and fulfilling of teaching and school head posts by states, which at present are lying vacant in the state. The state government has not provided enough financial support to education sector, as the share of education budget in general budget declined considerably over the years. The state has already been facing the problem of under-representation of rural students in professional and higher education (Ghuman *et al.* 2009).

Prevalence of such situation goes not only against the very spirit and purpose of the programme but also poses a serious threat to such a programme. Problems of under-utilization of SSA funds have been highlighted by the reports of the various expert, auditing and evaluation committees. It is clear that in the given situation of education and budgetary resources in the state, the SSA could prove a very useful policy instrument in improving the educational indicators both quantitatively and qualitatively. The financial and administrative intervention of the centre government with collaboration of the state government and other stakeholders has put a positive pressure on the system to improve the delivery mechanism. The SSA has in fact created a qualitatively different culture of social accountability and monitoring with the constitution of various committees and associations. The role of SSA lies also in the social sensitization and advocacy of the masses about the educational build-up in the society.

## References

DISE, 2011–12. *Elementary Education in India-Progress towards UEE*, National University of Educational Planning and Administration, New Delhi.

ESO, 2012a. *Gender Statistics of Punjab*, Economic and Statistical Organisation, Chandigarh, Punjab.

ESO, 2012b. *Economic Survey of Punjab*, Economic and Statistical Organisation, Chandigarh, Punjab.

Ghuman, R. S., Sukhwinder Singh and Jaswinder Singh Brar, 2009. *Professional Education in Punjab: Exclusion of Rural Students*, Punjabi University Publication Bureau, Patiala.

Gill, Sucha Singh, Inderjeet Singh, Lakhwinder Singh, Kesar Singh Bhangoo and Parmod Kumar Aggarwal, 2010. *District Human Development Report Sangrur*, Punjab State Planning Board, Chandigarh.

GOP, 2010. *Sarva Shiksha Abhiyan in Punjab: An Evaluative Study*, Department of Planning, Government of Punjab, Chandigarh.

HDR, 2004. Punjab Human Development Report, Concept, New Delhi.

IPAI, 2003. *Monitoring the Financial Aspects of SSA in Punjab*, Institute of Public Auditors of India, New Delhi.

MHRD, 2010. *SSA Punjab Report*, Department of Elementary Education, Ministry of Human Resources Development, prepared by IIPA, New Delhi (available at MHRD website); [downloaded on November 29, 2010].

PROBE, 1999. *Public Report on Basic Education in India*, Oxford University Press, New Delhi.

SAP, 2010. *Statistical Abstract of Punjab*, Economic and Statistical Organisation, Chandigarh, Punjab.

SSA, 2006–07. Annual Report, Sarva Shiksha Abhiyan Authority, Chandigarh, Punjab.

SSA, 2007–08. Annual Report, Sarva Shiksha Abhiyan Authority, Chandigarh, Punjab.

SSA, 2011–12. Annual Report, Sarva Shiksha Abhiyan Authority, Chandigarh, Punjab.

# 5

# ANALYSING FUND FLOWS AND EXPENDITURE UNDER SARVA SHIKSHA ABHIYAN IN HIMACHAL PRADESH

*P. Geetha Rani and Bansi L. Shukla*

## Background

Himachal Pradesh is well acclaimed for its educational development in a short span compared to Kerala. The momentum for education started in 1983 with literacy campaigns and a massive school building programme. Further, in 1997, the Government of Himachal Pradesh passed the Compulsory Education Act (Act No. 2 of 1998), much before the RTE Act of 2009 at national level. Even more significant has been the reduction in dropout ratio, very few out-of-school children, especially among girls and within that in SC/ST group. Almost every child in 6–14 age group, regardless of sex or caste, is enrolled in school. This is indeed the most significant success story of educational achievement in Himachal Pradesh during late 1990s (PROBE 1999; GoHP 2002; Dreze and Sen 2002; etc.). The state has committed high levels of investment in provisioning elementary education in sparsely inhabited areas such as Lahaul and Spiti where formal schools are functioning for extremely small numbers of children. Quite expectedly given the terrain, density of population and the pattern of habitations, the teacher–pupil ratio in the state is one of the best (1:16) in the country in 2009–10 (DISE: Himachal Pradesh 2010). For example, in districts like Lahaul and Spiti, on an average there are only four students per teacher. Achieving this has clearly been a high cost endeavour for the hilly state. On the other hand, this indicates the non-financial viability of such low PTR schools. Unit cost of provisioning of elementary education is quite high in a hilly state which has the highest per-student public expenditure on elementary education, around Rs. 21,177 in 2010–11 as against the national average of Rs. 9,766. Even before SSA, Himachal Pradesh had made impressive progress in elementary education. Now the concern is about ensuring quality and sustaining the achievements.

Given this backdrop, the main thrust of the chapter is to examine to what extent the state has addressed these issues under SSA both in terms of financing and achievement. Is SSA programme taken forward in achieving the quality of elementary education? If so, how SSA allocation, expenditures and fund flow pattern facilitated in improving the quality of education in the state? Accordingly, the rest of the chapter is organized as follows: second section briefs about the progress of elementary education in terms of the four SSA goals and an overview of financing elementary education. The third section examines resource allocation and its expenditure under SSA. Subsequent section examines fund flow pattern and its timing under SSA. The fifth section examines the quality concerns and the last section concludes.

## Progress of elementary education under SSA

Here, we briefly evaluate on four goals of SSA, viz., *all children in schools; bridging gender and social gaps; and all children to be retained in elementary education and quality education*. Net enrolment ratio is almost 100 per cent with no gender differential. Besides the dropout rates are marginal. Children not enrolled in schools though tiny compared to either Bihar or Uttar Pradesh has further reduced. For instance, the national survey of out-of-school children by an independent firm (SRRI of IMRB International) for MHRD found that Himachal Pradesh has only 4,942 children out-of-school in 2005.[1] There were only 2,811 out-of-school children in 2012 which is less than 1 per cent of total child population (Table 5.1).

Himachal Pradesh is implementing the Education Guarantee Scheme (EGS) at primary level in selected pockets to include out-of-school children. While EGS has enabled the state to expand coverage of several out-of-school children, it is recommended that a detailed analysis of the age and educational background of the remaining number of out-of-school children be undertaken to strategize according to the situation. EGS by itself may not be adequate for effective inclusion of the older never enrolled category of children. Two major issues reported about the out-of-school children pertain to children of migrant families as well as the dispersal of such children in very small numbers across habitation that makes it difficult to bring them together at one location. In the latter case, the state is finding it very difficult to track children of migratory families as these families have no

*Table 5.1* Out-of-school children and dropped out rates in Himachal Pradesh

| | *Out-of-school children* | *Dropout rates – Pry* | *Dropout rates – U. Pry* |
|---|---|---|---|
| 2003 | 7,498 | 2.15 | 1.93 |
| 2004 | – | 0.89 | 4.10 |
| 2005 | 4,301 | 0.90 | 1.33 |
| 2006 | 5,624 | 0.11 | 0.46 |
| 2007 | 4,075 | 0.01 | 0.01 |
| 2008 | 2,587 | 0.00 | 0.02 |
| 2009 | 2,854 | 0.33 | 0.32 |
| 2010 | 2,414 | 0.30 | 0.24 |
| 2011 | 2,943 | 0.003 | 0.023 |
| 2012 | 2,811 | 0 | 0 |

*Source:* Himachal Pradesh, DISE and Household Surveys, SSA Office, Shimla.

*Table 5.2* Dropout rates in selected districts during 2006 and 2012 (%)

| *Category* | *Chamba* | | *Lahaul-Spiti* | | *Sirmour* | | *State* | | |
|---|---|---|---|---|---|---|---|---|---|
| **2006** | Boys | Girls | Boys | Girls | Boys | Girls | Boys | Girls | Total |
| Primary | 0.47 | 0.72 | 0.33 | 0.00 | 0.22 | 0.22 | 0.10 | 0.12 | 0.11 |
| Upper primary | 1.64 | 3.97 | 1.44 | 0.32 | 0.98 | 1.49 | 0.34 | 0.66 | 0.49 |
| **2012** | | | | | | | | | |
| Primary | 0.02 | 1.00 | 3.35 | 0.74 | 0.00 | 0.00 | 0.00 | 0.04 | 0.00 |
| Upper primary | 0.00 | 0.00 | 3.20 | 5.45 | 0.00 | 0.00 | 0.00 | 0.00 | 0.00 |

*Source:* Household Survey (2006); Government of Himachal Pradesh; DISE Data 2012–13.

fixed pattern of migration. They are attached to contractors who move them to places where they get assignments making their movement very uncertain (GOI 3rd JRM 2006). District administrators have been asked to identify such children and enrol them in some formal or informal education. The state makes an effort to identify such children by location and plan for their education.

The dropout rate at the primary level is nil both at primary and upper primary levels during 2012 (Table 5.1). However, such aggregate trend does not hold good in districts like Chamba, Lahaul-Spiti and Sirmour, the dropout rates are relatively high at upper primary level (Table 5.2). It can be noted that girls dropout more often in all three districts compared to boys at upper primary level. Pratham also shows that the out-of-school children among 15–16 year old girls is considerably higher that it went up from 5.6 per cent in 2006 to 6.5 per cent in 2007 (ASER 2007). A study for 2006–07 in Nahan & Paonta block of Sirmour district has shown that the dropout rate is higher than the officially claimed rate and the proportion of out-of-school children is more than 2 per cent at primary level (as against official estimate of 0.22 per cent) in Sirmour district (Manuja and Tanwar 2007).

A cohort study by the state government in which children of all schools were tracked for seven years and it was found that cohort dropout rate is 2.04 per cent which also confirms that dropout rates are reduced to some extent. The State Project Office, SSA, is presently trying to develop in collaboration with Pratham a system of tracking the grade-wise progression of children. The available evidence clearly suggests that the first goal of SSA is that all children in the age group of 6–14 years should be in school is almost attained. It is equally important to note that goal 2 (bridging gender and social gaps) and goal 3 (all children retained in elementary education) are attained. That can be noticed from Table 5.2 that there is not much differential between dropout rates of boys and girls at primary level. At upper primary level, however, gender differential can be observed as among older girls in out-of-school children as well. Nonetheless, it is a smaller magnitude.

The role envisaged for a centralized state in the development model and part of the success lies in the long tradition of community participation of Himachal Pradesh's rural community. SSA has successfully built on this. Historically, although caste divisions were present, a subsistence economy ensured less economic differentiation. Interdependence within communities necessitated by physical environment and women's importance as a source of labour mediated both caste and gender divisions. Lesser polarization meant a lower incidence of elite capture and also a greater degree of access for all sections once the state began its active intervention in pursuit of development. Quality of leadership available in its formative years enhanced favourable conditions created by this social environment. Tremendous expansion in school system and innovative scholarship schemes[2] to retain girl students in school after primary classes provided access and impetus to build on favourable social conditions (Sanan 2004).

## Financing elementary education

Education subsidies, for example, can be justified if they improve living standards – improving cognitive skills, better health practices, preventing and curing disease, and so on (Demery 2000). Education is critical to enhancing the quality of this asset through improved productivity, employment and wages. Hence government investment in education is especially important for the poor and a critical component of the inclusive growth agenda of the Government of India in 11th and 12th five-year plans. Recognizing this well in advance, Himachal Pradesh ensures the highest priority to education. Data on functional classification of the Reserve Bank of India's publication 'State Finances: A Study of Budgets' shows the largest functional head is on education, followed by pensions, transport and communication and agriculture. The state was spending 7.08 per cent of GSDP on education in comparison to only 2.87 per cent by Punjab, 3.25 per cent by Kerala, 2.6 per cent by Haryana and 3.6 per cent at national level till the year 2000. The achievements of Himachal Pradesh in education have a great deal to do with government intervention; it has been substantial in elementary education for quite a long period of time. Kerala as well spent such higher allocations since 1970s through 1990s.

Government expenditure on education since 2001–02 reveal that the state was spending more than 2.5 per cent of GDP on elementary education. Total expenditure on general education was 5.24 per cent of GDP in 2001–02 which has come down to 4.68 per cent during 2009–10. State is spending around 20 per cent of the budget expenditure on education and around 10 per cent on elementary education (Table 5.3). Five-year plans

*Table 5.3* Public expenditure on education* in Himachal Pradesh (%)

| | *Expr. on education as % of GSDP* | *Expr. on elem. education as % of GSDP* | *Budget expr. as % of GSDP* | *Expr. on education as % of budget* | *Expr. on elem. education as % of budget* |
|---|---|---|---|---|---|
| 2001–02 | 5.16 | 2.84 | 26.69 | 19.35 | 10.62 |
| 2002–03 | 5.45 | 2.70 | 27.19 | 20.03 | 9.91 |
| 2003–04 | 5.02 | 2.54 | 26.97 | 18.62 | 9.44 |
| 2004–05 | 4.59 | 2.30 | 24.06 | 19.08 | 9.58 |
| 2005–06 | 4.66 | 2.28 | 23.84 | 19.54 | 9.57 |
| 2006–07 | 4.52 | 2.37 | 23.12 | 19.53 | 10.26 |
| 2007–08 | 4.72 | 2.79 | 22.25 | 21.23 | 12.54 |
| 2008–09 | 4.63 | 2.44 | 22.75 | 20.35 | 10.74 |
| 2009–10 | 4.68 | 2.34 | 23.14 | 20.21 | 10.10 |
| 2010–11(R) | 5.19 | 2.69 | 22.20 | 23.37 | 12.11 |
| 2011–12 (B) | 5.35 | 2.90 | 22.01 | 24.31 | 13.19 |

*Source:* Finance Accounts, Himachal Pradesh; Government of Himachal Pradesh.

*Notes:* *includes expenditures on education by other departments. B - Budget estimates; R - Revised estimates.

of Himachal Pradesh shows that during first six plans, most development expenditure was on expansion, i.e. opening new schools and provision for free and universal primary education. It was only during the seventh plan that the emphasis shifted to qualitative improvement and acceleration of the process of modernization, besides increasing access. During the Eighth plan, emphasis was on technical and vocational education in place of general education. During ninth plan, main focus was on both qualitative improvement and expansion of schools to meet the target of making primary education compulsory by 1997–98. Government embarked upon an expansion programme based on detailed mapping of the unserved habitations.

1. In the recent decade (2001–02 onwards), substantial amount of public expenditure is being incurred under SSA. Hence, a complete view of public expenditure on elementary education requires that both budgetary expenditures and those under SSA are viewed *in toto*. Around 90 per cent of the budget is spent on salaries of the teachers and staff and the rest around 10 per cent of the budget is spent on administration, monitoring, evaluation, teaching quality, incentives, infrastructure and decentralization. Infrastructure facilities, New Schools, teachers' trainings are provided under SSA while direct expenditure on students is shared between state and SSA. Expenditures on improving teaching quality and for decentralization of service of elementary education are being almost wholly incurred under SSA.

### *Expenditure on elementary education*

There has been gradual increase in expenditure of the Education Department ever since SSA started in the Pradesh. This increase ranges from 4 to 33 per cent but on the contrary the enrolment figures are declining from 3 to 5 per cent every year. As per the population projections by Registrar General of India, the population has now stabilized at replacement level and second reason is the shift of enrolment from government to private schools. While the share of enrolment has come down, the overall expenditure has gone up. With the increase in total expenditure and decrease in enrolment, per-student expenditure has increased significantly. It is to be noted that since the inception of SSA, the enrolment has been declining in Himachal Pradesh with a negative growth rate of 4 per cent. Per-student expenditure was Rs. 5,087 per annum in 2002–03, Rs. 25,809 per annum in 2011–12 with an annual average growth rate of 21.7 per cent. In addition to the expenditures on elementary education by the state government, the central transfers allocations through SSA. Per-student

*Table 5.4* Expenditure on elementary education, enrolment and per-student expenditures

| | *Expenditure on elementary education (Rs. in lakhs)* | *Enrolment in elementary* | *Per-student expenditure (in Rs.)* | *Per-student expenditures (SSA) (in Rs.)* |
|---|---|---|---|---|
| 2002–03 | 50,811 | 998,892 | 5,087 | 5,286 |
| 2003–04 | 52,853 | 971,323 | 5,441 | 6,093 |
| 2004–05 | 55,496 | 933,925 | 5,942 | 6,802 |
| 2005–06 | 60,433 | 897,402 | 6,734 | 7,834 |
| 2006–07 | 80,613 | 859,112 | 9,383 | 10,604 |
| 2007–08 | 95,265 | 839,602 | 11,346 | 12,650 |
| 2008–09 | 116,184 | 802,547 | 14,477 | 16,023 |
| 2009–10 | 134,471 | 767,872 | 17,512 | 19,418 |
| 2010–11 | 164,814 | 734,397 | 22,442 | 25,434 |
| 2011–12 | 176,347 | 683,267 | 25,809 | 28,567 |
| GR | 16.9 | −4.0 | 21.7 | 22.0 |

*Source:* Department of Elementary Education, Himachal Pradesh, and DISE.

expenditures increased with SSA expenditures from Rs. 5,286 to Rs. 28,567 during the same period with an annual average growth rate of 22 per cent (Table 5.4).

Such high per-child expenditure on account of small school size in Himachal Pradesh is due to its difficult topography. The fixed costs cannot be minimized. There is enhancement in teachers' salaries and other fixed cost every year but the enrolment is decreasing. The population growth is showing negative trends and also flow of children to the private schools is increasing due to the better economic conditions of the parents and better academic results of private schools. The per-child cost will keep on increasing and it will be difficult to sustain it for long. A welfare state has to keep a school functional even with fewer children although private school is within the same campus. However, the state needs to rethink about the financially unviable schools. The policy options could be to ensure reliable and good transport to nearby government schools or get the children admitted in the nearby private schools and bear the full expenditure of these children.

Among the several factors contributing to its successes on the human development front that one of these factors has been the consistently high public expenditure on human development (GoHP 2002). However, it is equally important to know that how this money is being spent in the case of the Department of Elementary Education, the Block Elementary Education Officers are the Drawing and Disbursing Officers (DDOs) who look after around 100 schools. After budgets are allotted to these departments, funds are further allocated to the DDOs directly by the head office in the month of April/May. The allocation letters are copied to the concerned treasury/sub-treasury. The main expenditure of the department is on salaries, material and supplies. Most of the budget for material and supplies is retained at head office and is utilized for making payments for purchase of textbooks for free distribution to students. The bills for these purchases are first verified by the district offices and then submitted to the head office for payment. There is a complaint on monitoring and regular inspection mechanism to verify whether books have reached the students for whom they were intended. However, distribution of textbook mechanism under SSA is different and payments are made from districts.

## Finances under SSA

SSA implementing society in the state is known as Himachal Pradesh Primary Education Society (HPPES). The organizing structure of SSA in Himachal Pradesh is similar to other states. However, the unique governance structures of SSA at Himachal Pradesh are the active involvement of State Institute of Educational Management and Training (SIEMAT) and District Institutes of Education and Training (DIETs) in the functioning of the scheme. Unlike in many other states, the SIEMAT is a key agency and an integral part of the State Project Office. It was established as part of the State Project Office under DPEP in 2000 and continues to be part of the SIS in the implementation. Its main responsibilities include: (i) Planning and administration; (ii) micro planning and institutional planning; and (iii) EGS, AIE and research. Its activities cover development of perspective and Annual Work Plans and Budget (AWPB); appraisal of districts' AWPB; working out strategies to reach out-of-school children; orientation and training of the state, district, block level planners, administrators, head of schools and functionaries of DIETs, BRCs; maintaining DISE; conducting education research and evaluation; providing professional and research support to the state and district-level institutions; implementation of innovative projects; documenting and dissemination of information (from state to national and international levels); and preparing agenda for the General Council and Executive Council Meetings for policy decisions. Yet another distinguished feature of the organizational set-up in Himachal Pradesh is that the DIET are District Project Offices with the Principal of the DIET as the District Project Officer and the faculties taking over the responsibility of different functional areas.

### *Outlays and releases under SSA*

Adequate funding, both in terms of amounts and timeliness, is the key to effective and successful implementation of the programme. Release of funds as compared to approved AWPB ranged from 50 to 80 per cent during initial years up to 2004–05 which has retarded the progress of the programme as compared to the physical and financial targets of AWPB. It has increased to almost 100 per cent from 2005–06 to 2009–10 except during 2006–07 (91 per cent). During the recent period the funds were not adequately available. Releases during initial years were less than PAB approvals and therefore mere 40 to 70 per cent expenditure were made against AWPB approvals although the expenditure against actual releases was between 65 and 97 per cent. After 2005–06, extent of funds release against approved outlays improved and therefore expenditure also increased by more than 80 per cent of approved outlays as well as funds were available (column 8, Table 5.5). Himachal Pradesh as a special category state has been a recipient of predominantly grant-based central support for its plans. Under SSA, the state is requesting for 90:10 funding pattern on the analogy of the North East States, which is presently 65:35 similar to other states.

Absorptive capacity is more than 90 per cent in construction of new upper primary schools and grant on free textbooks. On the contrary, out-of-school strategies show less than 50 per cent absorptive rates during all four years. Out-of-school children in Himachal Pradesh is less than 0.5 per cent but these are hardest to reach such as severely disabled children or migratory children of the floating population. There is also shortfall in innovation, research and R&E activities due to inadequate planning and timely availability of funds. During 2011–12, many items even civil works report less than 30 per cent absorptive capacity. Less expenditure on civil works is due to late receipt of PAB approval, funds and also the sanctions from the district authorities. In some cases there are also land disputes. Apart from civil works, NPEGEL (59 per cent) and KGBV (59 per cent) report very low absorptive rates (Table 5.6).

With near universal enrolment and declining enrolment trend, opening new schools (though for specific needs) is to be rationalized. Despite a per capita provision of schools better than that available in Kerala, there is no attempt to rationalize existing duplication even as more schools are announced each year (Sanan 2004). There is a need to expedite the PAB approvals, fund flow and sanctions at district level to increase utilization in

*Table 5.5* Funds releases from GOI against approved AWPB; budget outlays and expenditure under SSA in Himachal Pradesh

*(Rs. in lakhs)*

| *Year* | *AWPB* | *Opening balance* | *Releases by GOI (%)* | *Releases by state (%)* | *Total funds available** | *Expenditure* | *% of approved in WPB* | *% of expenditure in funds available* |
|---|---|---|---|---|---|---|---|---|
| | (2) | (3) | (4) | (5) | (6) | (7) | (8) | (9) |
| 2002–03 | 4,524 | 801 | 85 | 15 | 3,063 | 1,989 | 68 | 64.9 |
| 2003–04 | 11,004 | 1,074 | 75 | 25 | 7,522 | 6,332 | 68 | 84.2 |
| 2004–05 | 12,138 | 1,190 | 85 | 15 | 9,373 | 8,031 | 77 | 85.7 |
| 2005–06 | 12,301 | 1,342 | 75 | 25 | 12,595 | 9,871 | 102 | 78.4 |
| 2006–07 | 12,118 | 2,723 | 69 | 31 | 11,058 | 10,487 | 91 | 94.8 |
| 2007–08 | 12,198 | 571 | 75 | 25 | 12,322 | 10,947 | 101 | 88.8 |
| 2008–09 | 14,392 | 1,375 | 65 | 35 | 14,533 | 12,285 | 101 | 84.5 |
| 2009–10 | 16,641 | 2,249 | 65 | 35 | 16,595 | 14,722 | 100 | 88.7 |
| 2010–11 | 25,482 | 1,858 | 60 | 40 | 24,191 | 21,974 | 95 | 90.8 |
| 2011–12 | 30,262 | 2,217 | 68 | 32 | 25,547 | 18,843 | 84 | 73.8 |
| 2012–13 | 33,330 | 6,704 | 67 | 33 | 27,022 | 26,577 | 81 | 98.4 |
| GR** | 16.7 | 14.6 | 15.6 | 26.6 | 19.3 | 21.4 | – | – |

*Table 5.6* Intervention-wise absorptive rates in Himachal Pradesh during selected years

| *Components* | *2007–08* | *2008–09* | *2011–12* | *2012–13* | *Average* |
|---|---|---|---|---|---|
| New U. primary schools | 99.2 | 95.3 | 80.9 | 94.2 | 92.4 |
| Grants and free textbooks | 99.3 | 96.7 | 82.7 | 90.2 | 92.2 |
| Management cost | 99.7 | 85.6 | 84.2 | 83 | 88.1 |
| Cluster resource centre | 96.9 | 98.8 | 79.9 | 76.4 | 88.0 |
| State project office | 97.7 | 98.8 | 62.3 | 80.1 | 84.7 |
| Innovations | 84.2 | 55.5 | 83.4 | 106.7 | 82.5 |
| Block resource centre | 94.3 | 95 | 63.4 | 74.6 | 81.8 |
| Research and evaluation | 90.3 | 81 | 80.7 | 75.2 | 81.8 |
| Training | 84.4 | 78.9 | 73.2 | 74.9 | 77.9 |
| IED | 81.2 | 81.7 | 57.9 | 73.3 | 73.5 |
| NPEGEL | 81.7 | 68 | 70.5 | 67.8 | 72.0 |
| Major repairs (U Pry) | 87.3 | 175 | 0 | 0 | 65.6 |
| Civil works | 78.4 | 75.2 | 26.6 | 63.3 | 60.9 |
| KGBV | 52.3 | 35.8 | 75.6 | 72.9 | 59.2 |
| LEP | 0 | 100 | 63.1 | 4.1 | 55.7 |
| Out-of-school strategies | 53.2 | 39.7 | 43.7 | 42.6 | 44.8 |
| Total | 89.7 | 85.4 | 62.3 | 79.7 | 79.3 |

*Source:* Project Monitoring, Implementing and Supervision (PMIS) Reports; and Institute of Public Auditors of India (IPAI) Report, 2009, State Project Office, SSA, Himachal Pradesh.

civil works. One of the reasons for low absorption rates is that disbursement was sluggish on most interventions, affecting implementation.

Distribution of expenditures under SSA by various interventions in terms of civil works and other related activities, quality- and equity-related aspects would throw insights that in an educationally advanced state, expenditure would be in principle tilted towards quality-related activities, given its achievements. Pattern of distribution of expenditures suggest that even in a state where enrolments are declining to the tune of negative 4 per cent, yet civil works and new upper primary schools constitute the major chunk of the expenditures during the first as well as the second phases and also over the entire period accounting for 53 per cent (Table 5.7). The highest constituents are still on upper primary schools and civil works during the entire period of SSA. This indicates that there is no change in the norms of allocating SSA funds since the inception of the programme.

Quality-related components such as Block Resource Centre, Maintenance Grants, Toilets, Drinking Water, School Grants, Innovative

*Table 5.7* Distribution of expenditures by components under SSA, 2002–03 to 2012–13

| *Activity* | *Total exprs.* Phase I^* | *% of expenditure in total exp* | *Total exprs.* Phase II#* | *% of expenditure in total exp* | *Total expr** | *% of expenditure in total exp* |
|---|---|---|---|---|---|---|
| Civil works and school library | 12,568 | 26.4 | 17,405 | 18.4 | 29,973 | 21.1 |
| New U. primary school | 13,668 | 28.7 | 31,896 | 33.8 | 45,565 | 32.1 |
| Block resource centre | 964 | 2.0 | 4,700 | 5.0 | 5,664 | 4.0 |
| Maintenance grants | 3,900 | 8.2 | 4,849 | 5.1 | 8,748 | 6.2 |
| Toilets, drinking water | 1,913 | 4.0 | 4,013 | 4.2 | 5,926 | 4.2 |
| Interventions for girl children and free text, uniforms | 2,442 | 5.1 | 4,631 | 4.9 | 7,073 | 5.0 |
| School grants | 1,644 | 3.4 | 4,083 | 4.3 | 5,727 | 4.0 |
| Innovative activities | 1,322 | 2.8 | 4,321 | 4.6 | 5,644 | 4.0 |
| Teacher training | 1,568 | 3.3 | 3,161 | 3.3 | 4,729 | 3.3 |
| Teachers grants | 1,260 | 2.6 | 1,031 | 1.1 | 2,291 | 1.6 |
| Management and MIS | 1,280 | 2.7 | 2,830 | 3.0 | 4,110 | 2.9 |
| IED | 927 | 1.9 | 1,688 | 1.8 | 2,615 | 1.8 |
| TLE/LEP | 770 | 1.6 | 781 | 0.8 | 1,551 | 1.1 |
| Cluster resource centre | 802 | 1.7 | 4,206 | 4.5 | 5,008 | 3.5 |
| R&E/remedial teaching | 777 | 1.6 | 571 | 0.6 | 1,348 | 0.9 |
| State component and DPEP | 842 | 1.8 | 1,497 | 1.6 | 2,339 | 1.6 |
| NPEGEL | 267 | 0.6 | 187 | 0.2 | 454 | 0.3 |
| Community mobilization and training | 277 | 0.6 | 1,792 | 1.9 | 2,070 | 1.5 |
| Intervention for OSC | 280 | 0.6 | 263 | 0.3 | 543 | 0.4 |
| KGBV | 185 | 0.4 | 531 | 0.6 | 716 | 0.5 |
| Total | 47,657 | 100.0 | 94,437 | 100.0 | 142,093 | 100.0 |

*Source:* Based on data provided by State Project Office, SSA, Himachal Pradesh.

*Note:* ^ Phase I refers to 2002–03 to 2007–08; # Phase II refers to 2008–09 to 2012–13; * Rs. in lakhs.

Activities, Teacher Training, Teachers Grants, TLE, Cluster Resource Centre, Research & Evaluation constitute 36 per cent during the first phase and improved to 40 per cent during the second phase. Equity-related components such as Interventions for Girl Children, Intervention for Disabled Children, Interventions on Out-of-school children along with NPEGEL and KGBV contribute to less than 10 per cent of total expenditures under SSA. During first phase of SSA, equity-related entitlements constitute 8.6 per cent which decline to 7.7 per cent during the second phase (Table 5.7). One of the major reasons for such allocations is that allocations under SSA are based on uniform norms across states irrespective of the need. As has been pointed out in the chapter on Orissa, SSA allocations are not need based. This is one of the major problems in the design of the programme itself.

## Fund flow pattern under SSA

This section attempts to examine timing and pattern of release of funds from (i) Govt. of India (GoI) to State Implementing Societies (SIS) in Himachal Pradesh and (ii) State government of Himachal Pradesh to SIS. Budget Calendar in India runs from April to March. In principle, appraisal of the annual work plans and budget at the national capital to be done by 1st April by the Appraisal Mission and plans are to be approved by 15th April. The manual of 'Financial Management and Procurement' stipulated that the release of funds to SIS are to be carried out in two instalments in April and September every year (MHRD 2004b, 2009). Similarly, state governments are to transfer matching shares on approved outlay in such two instalments to SIS.

Not only adequate amount of money is transferred from centre to SIS but also equally important is at what time of the financial year, in how many tranches and how much money is transferred. As per the SSA guidelines in Chapter II, para 2.9.3, the releases from the centre will be in two instalments in April and September. But the two instalments were adhered to only in five years over the period 2003–04 to 2012–13. Number of instalments through which money was transferred from centre to SIS ranged between two and five times (Table 5.8).

Though there has been a guideline in SSA that more than 50 per cent of approved or sanctioned money to be released within second or third quarter of a financial year, nonetheless, it is always preferable to get a substantial share of sanctioned money getting released in the first two quarters so as to plan and implement the programme in an effective manner. But in practice, patterns of fund flow indicate that in three years more than

*Table 5.8* Amount and timing of release of funds in Himachal Pradesh, 2003–04 to 2012–13

| | *April–June* | *July–Sep* | *Oct–Dec* | *Jan–March* | *Total (Rs. in lakhs)* | *No. of instalments* |
|---|---|---|---|---|---|---|
| | *Quarter I* | *Quarter II* | *Quarter III* | *Quarter IV* | | |
| 2003–04 | 0.0 | 54.2 | 0.0 | 45.8 | 5,457 | 2 |
| 2004–05 | 16.3 | 42.1 | 0.5 | 41.2 | 6,144 | 4 |
| 2005–06 | 0.0 | 47.5 | 52.5 | 0.0 | 7,615 | 2 |
| 2006–07 | 0.0 | 51.6 | 0.0 | 48.4 | 6,251 | 4 |
| 2007–08 | 32.9 | 0.0 | 67.1 | 0.0 | 7,638 | 5 |
| 2008–09 | 24.3 | 25.7 | 50.0 | 0.0 | 7,851 | 2 |
| 2009–10 | 38.2 | 0.0 | 61.8 | 0.0 | 8,608 | 2 |
| 2010–11 | 0.0 | 0.0 | 47.6 | 52.4 | 13,787 | 2 |
| 2011–12 | 52.5 | 12.2 | 35.2 | 0.0 | 14,193 | 5 |
| 2012–13 | 36.1 | 29.6 | 0.0 | 34.3 | 10,737 | 3 |
| **Fund flow from Govt of Himachal Pradesh to SIS by quarters** | | | | | | |
| 2003–04 | 0.0 | 54.2 | 0.0 | 45.8 | 1,819 | 2 |
| 2004–05 | 0.0 | 16.1 | 41.6 | 42.4 | 2,073 | 4 |
| 2005–06 | 0.0 | 0.0 | 46.6 | 53.4 | 2,538 | 2 |
| 2006–07 | 0.0 | 51.6 | 0.0 | 48.4 | 2,084 | 2 |
| 2007–08 | 72.9 | 0.0 | 0.0 | 27.1 | 4,113 | 2 |
| 2008–09 | 0.0 | 22.3 | 21.8 | 55.8 | 4,605 | 6 |
| 2009–10 | 0.0 | 26.7 | 11.5 | 61.8 | 5,739 | 3 |
| 2010–11 | 0.0 | 5.4 | 21.9 | 34.6 | 8,546 | 5 |
| 2011–12 | 21.0 | 28.3 | 0.0 | 15.1 | 9,137 | 5 |
| 2012–13 | 0.0 | 51.2 | 19.4 | 18.6 | 9,581 | 5 |

*Source:* Institute of Public Auditors of India (IPAI) Report, 2009, State Project Office, SSA, Himachal Pradesh.

40 to 60 per cent of money released during either third or fourth quarter (Table 5.8 and Figure 5.1). Indeed, there are instances that bulk share of money getting released on 31st March, last day of the financial year from centre to states. And also there has been delay of more than 300 days in the first year of implementation which has been improved over time but still with a delay of 57–58 days during 2009–10 and 37–169 days of delay during 2012–13 (IPAI 2009).

Next, we compare the pattern and timing of fund flow from GoHP to SIS. In six years, a bulk share (60 to 90 per cent) of the money was released during either third or fourth quarter. Number of instalments were more

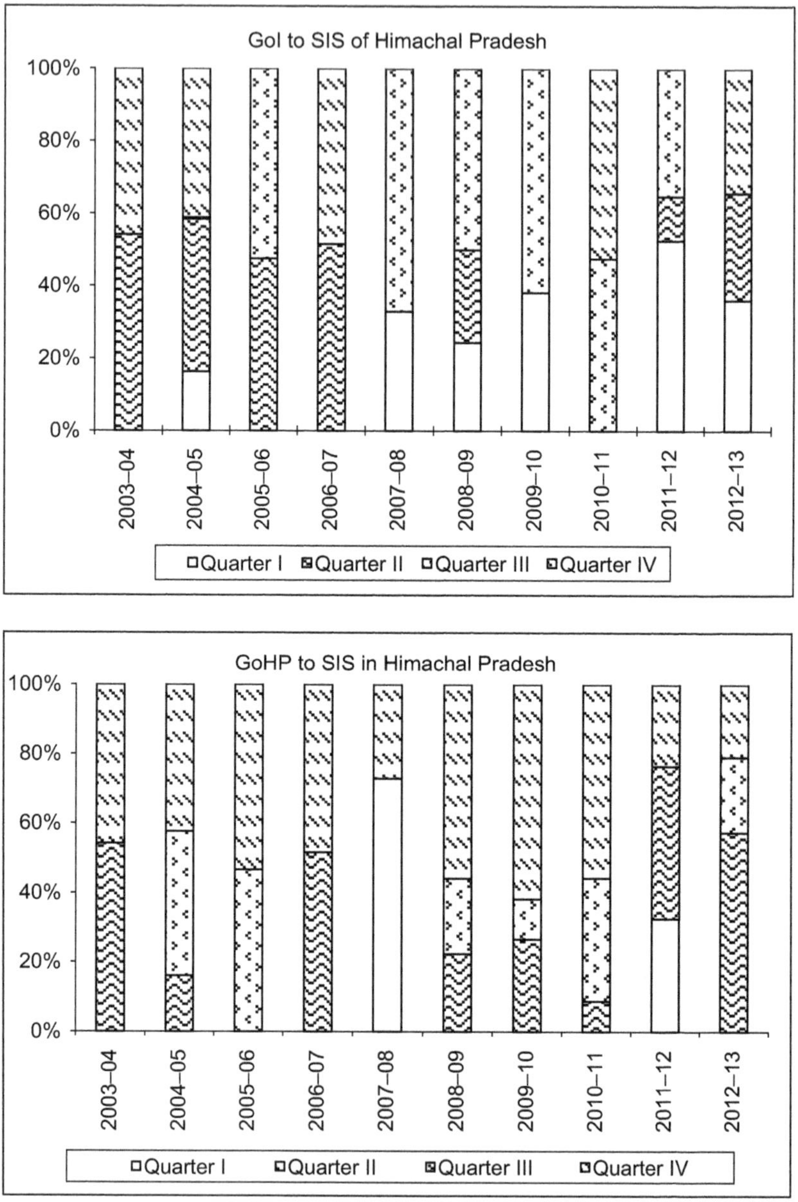


*Figure 5.1* Pattern of fund flow from GoI to SIS in Himachal Pradesh

*Source:* Institute of Public Auditors of India (IPAI) Report, 2009, State Project Office, SSA, Himachal Pradesh.

here ranging from two to six tranches which is a worse situation compared to the number of instalments from GoI to HPPES (Table 5.8). As per SSA guidelines in Chapter II, para 2.9.3, states that share is to be released within one month of the release of central share. Delay in release of central share further delays state share and still there was a delay of 9 to 394 days during 2003–04 to 2012–13 in the release of state share (IPAI 2009). Further it is noticed that the second instalment of the state share during last 5–6 years was released in March and therefore most funds remain unutilized. There have been gradual improvements in minimizing delays but there is ample scope for improvement for release of money in time and in few tranches for facilitating optimum utilization of resources (Table 5.8 and Figure 5.1).

### *Release of funds from districts to BRCs, CRCs and schools*

During initial years, the funds were sent from district to block level and then to schools via demand draft by post. This has caused further delays at BRC level. Now the funds are being sent to the schools directly from districts. It is proposed to improve fund flow by ensuring expeditious transfer of funds directly from the district to the school as followed in many other states via e-transfer. Transfer of funds from district to sub-districts and schools is not yet through e-transfers as the internet connectivity is yet to be established in a hilly state, characterized by smaller habitations with sparse population and tough topography. However, the districts Bilaspur and Hamirpur have switched over to the system of e-transfer almost completely and others are in the process (see Table 5.9).

Around 60 per cent transactions are being made through e-transfer which has reduced the time lag drastically. But that is not the case in many other districts. For instance, on an average, it took 36 days for funds to flow from one level to next lower level during 2006–07; 45 days during 2007–08; and 29 days during 2008–09 in district Sirmour. However, the scenario is much better in district Solan when compared to Sirmour that delay in release of funds ranged from a minimum of 4 to 84 days in Sirmour district; there was a delay of 8 to 30 days in Solan district (see Table 5.9).

It was further noticed that funds aggregating Rs. 250 lakh (2006–07: Rs. 150 lakh and 2007–08: Rs. 100 lakh) were released by HPPES to two districts of Sirmour and Solan (covered by IPAI study team) at the fag end of the financial years. The transfer was, however, affected in five instalments

*Table 5.9* Release of funds from districts to BRCs, CRCs and schools

| *Date of receipt* | *Amount (Rs. in lakh)* | *Date of release* | *Delay in days* | *Date of receipt* | *Amount (Rs. in lakh)* | *Date of release* | *Delay in days* |
|---|---|---|---|---|---|---|---|
| **2006–07** | **District Sirmour** | | | **2006–07** | **District Solan** | | |
| 22.06.06 | 50 | 27.08.06 | 50 | 18.07.06 | 150 | 30.08.06 | 28 |
| 18.07.06 | 150 | 28.08.06 | 25 | 23.09.06 | 100 | 30.09.06 | 7 |
| 25.09.06 | 100 | 12.12.06 | 64 | 15.01.07 | 150 | 25.01.07 | 10 |
| 16.11.06 | 9 | 12.12.06 | 12 | Total | 400 | – | 15 |
| 17.01.07 | 150 | 20.02.07 | 20 | **2007–08** | – | – | – |
| | | 20.03.07 | 48 | 01.06.07 | 200 | 29.06.07 | 14 |
| Total | 459 | – | 36.4* | 27.08.07 | 80 | 20.09.07 | 8 |
| **2007–08** | – | – | | 26.11.07 | 50 | 31.12.07 | 20 |
| 07.06.07 | 200 | 18.09.07 | 53 | 03.12.07 | 50 | 31.12.07 | 13 |
| 31.08.07 | 50 | 30.11.07 | 76 | 12.02.08 | 100 | 28.03.08 | 20 |
| 05.12.07 | 100 | 24.12.07 | 4 | Total | 480 | – | 18 |
| 06.12.07 | 6 | 21.03.08 | 84 | **2008–09** | – | – | – |
| 21.03.08 | 100 | 31.03.08 | 10 | 26.06.08 | 100 | 31.07.08 | 20 |
| Total | 456 | – | 45.4* | 06.09.08 | 10 | 20.09.08 | 14 |
| **2008–09** | – | – | – | 13.09.08 | 60 | 19.09.08 | 6 |
| 28.06.08 | 100 | 30.06.08 | 2 | 27.09.08 | 75 | 03.10.08 | 5 |
| 15.09.08 | 100 | 29.09.08 | 14 | 22.11.08 | 50 | 25.11.08 | 3 |
| 30.09.08 | 75 | 30.12.08 | 76 | Total | 295 | – | 4.7 |
| Total | 275 | – | 29.5* | | | | |

*Source:* Institute of Public Auditors of India (IPAI), 2009, State Project Office, SSA, Himachal Pradesh.

*Note:* * indicates average days of delay in a year.

each in 2006–07 and 2007–08 which is not in accordance with the provisions. The state transferred the funds to the district in September, but the schools receive them only in December. More specifically, teachers do not receive their TLM grants and schools do not receive their maintenance grants or funds for civil works until December, almost nine months after the beginning of the school year. As per cash book and ledger of BRC, Kandagahat in Solan district, there was an unspent balance of Rs. 25,327 under TLM (Table 5.10).

Further, in yet another block Nalagarh in Solan district, the unspent grants were found in a number of activities including maintenance grant,

*Table 5.10* Status of fund sanctioned and spent on TLM in BRCs, Kandagahat in Solan district

| *Year* | *Balance* | *TLM sanctioned* | *Expenditure* | *Unspent balance* |
|---|---|---|---|---|
| 2003–04 | Nil | 8,000 | 1,445 | 6,555 |
| 2004–05 | 6,555 | 4,000 | 1,015 | 9,540 |
| 2005–06 | 9,540 | 4,000 | 168 | 13,372 |
| 2006–07 | 13,372 | 4,000 | 45 | 17,327 |
| 2007–08 | 17,327 | 4,000 | – | 21,327 |
| 2008–09 | 21,327 | 4,000 | – | 25,327 |
| Total | | 28,000 | 2,673 | 25,327 |

*Source:* IPAI (2009).

*Table 5.11* Spillovers of unutilized grants: Nalagarh block in Solan district

| *Nature of grant* | *2006–07* | | *2007–08* | |
|---|---|---|---|---|
| | *Primary* | *Upper primary* | *Primary* | *Upper primary* |
| Maintenance grant | 95,872 | 38,110 | 72,753 | 42,544 |
| School grant | 45,486 | 25,693 | 28,621 | 26,687 |
| TLM | 35,025 | 24,500 | 44,100 | 19,000 |
| R&E | 7,030 | 3,590 | 4,432 | 2,200 |
| Community grant | 6,140 | 3,403 | 5,020 | 2,940 |
| CRC (TLM) | 31,121 | 7,900 | 31,853 | 6,148 |
| Total | 220,676 | 103,196 | 186,779 | 99,519 |

*Source:* IPAI (2009).

school grant, TLM, research & evaluation, community grant and CRC (TLM). It was noticed that there are unutilized grants at BRC, CRC and school level (Table 5.11).

Fifty schools were visited by the IPAI team on a sample basis in two districts. There is a need to get these grants utilized on a regular basis. Most of these grants remain unutilized as these are mostly released during last quarter of the year. One of the major reasons being identified for low absorptive capacity is found to be in adequate manpower at implementation level. However, the PAISA survey reports that 84 per cent schools received all three grants in 2011–12 and 52 per cent of schools received all three grants by November 2012 (PAISA 2012).

## Quest for quality

Though Himachal Pradesh has achieved successfully near universal enrolment and retention, quality is supposed to be the main thrust under SSA. But pass percentage and students passed with more than 60 per cent as per DISE from 2004 to 2009 in Grade 5 and 8 exhibit a dismal picture (Table 5.12). Girls are performing better in terms of results in almost all categories. At upper primary level, pass percentage with above 60 per cent marks is minimal for both boys and girls.

Besides performance levels, it is necessary to know learning achievements of children. The annual survey by Pratham is of help (Table 5.13),

*Table 5.12* Board examination pass rates by gender in Himachal Pradesh (%)

| *Indicator* | *2004* | *2005* | *2006* | *2007* | *2008* | *2009* |
|---|---|---|---|---|---|---|
| Pass % 5th class, boys | 95.63 | 96.55 | 96.43 | 96.42 | 95.68 | 97.39 |
| Girls | 96.02 | 97.21 | 96.91 | 96.83 | 96.94 | 97.83 |
| >60% 5th, boys | 54.79 | 54.13 | 45.57 | 48.81 | 46.65 | 57.42 |
| Girls | 58.41 | 57.88 | 50.71 | 52.54 | 51.28 | 60.39 |
| Pass % 8th class, boys | 78.6 | 78.68 | 79.75 | 70.57 | 73.91 | 72.63 |
| Girls | 78.66 | 78.62 | 80.15 | 71.46 | 75.9 | 71.34 |
| >60% 8th, boys | 18.9 | 20.56 | 14.32 | 15.5 | 18.18 | 29.6 |
| Girls | 21.45 | 22.25 | 16.72 | 15.41 | 22.08 | 33.66 |

*Source:* DISE, Himachal Pradesh.

*Note:* After the introduction of CCE such information is not available in DISE.

*Table 5.13* Learning attainment of literacy and numeracy skills, 2010

| *Standard* | *% of students who can read* | | *% of students who can* | |
|---|---|---|---|---|
| | *Std I text* | *Std II text* | *Subtract* | *Divide* |
| I | 6.8 | 4.7 | 6.0 | 1.9 |
| II | 16.2 | 17.1 | 23.5 | 4.1 |
| III | 35.6 | 31.0 | 46.9 | 13.5 |
| IV | 30.4 | 55.0 | 44.6 | 36.3 |
| V | 15.1 | 77.4 | 27.3 | 63.3 |
| VI | 7.1 | 89.4 | 17.3 | 75.5 |
| VII | 7.2 | 90.5 | 14.5 | 81.2 |
| VIII | 5.4 | 93.1 | 10.5 | 85.5 |
| Total | 15.7 | 58.3 | 24.3 | 46.0 |

*Source:* ASER (2011).

which shows that 55 per cent of 4th standard students can read text of standard II but only 36 per cent of them know arithmetic division. Almost 7 per cent of students of 8th standard cannot read text of standard II and more than 14 per cent of them cannot perform arithmetic division. Although in a comparison among states, Himachal Pradesh does reasonably well in terms of learning achievements (and the indicators are considerably better than its neighbouring states), there is a strong need for improving the quality of learning.

The aggregate utilization rates since inception of SSA do not seem to have any impact on achievement levels of children in class V to VIII (Figure 5.2).

We plotted aggregate utilization rates from 2001–02 to 2009–10 till December across districts over an average of percentage of children answering two questions correctly in menu, calendar, area and estimation. No clear relationship between utilization rates and achievement levels of children at upper primary level is discernible across districts. Utilization rates range between 70 and 80 per cent with widely varying achievement rates of 30 to 65 per cent. The state average is a utilization rate of 80 per cent with an achievement level of 53 per cent. Having tackled problems of access, enrolment and dropout, the expected next task normally that ought to follow is to ensure better quality of education. This is often a more difficult

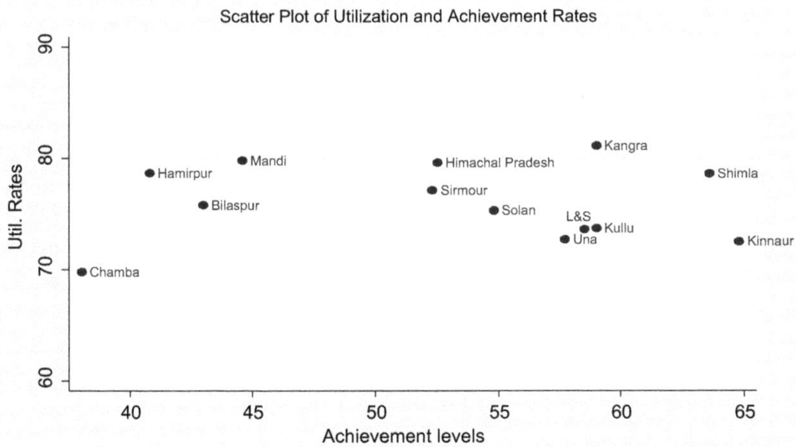


*Figure 5.2* Relationship between money spent on SSA and learning levels

*Source:* SPO, Shimla and ASER (2010).

objective to meet since just spending money does not ensure quality. It is clear that finances are only the necessary condition. The sufficient condition lies in effective teaching learning, which calls for better functioning of institutions.

## *Policy concerns*

Enrolment trends in government schools steadily decline both in rural and urban areas. Factors attributable to this downward trend include (i) replacement level of growth in relevant age group population like Kerala; (ii) enrolment shift from government to private schools. In response, state government has adopted a policy of merging schools that are presently serving lesser than 10 children where there is another school within 1.5 kilometres since 2011. It may be noted closing uneconomic schools started in Kerala during early 1990s. The criterion for closing down uneconomic schools stipulated by the Education Rules of Government of Kerala is that the minimum strength per standard in primary, middle and higher schools be 25. In Himachal Pradesh, GoI (2006) in one of its Joint Review Meetings (JRM) suggested that instead of surrendering such closed school buildings to the Department of Panchayat and Rural Development, the Department of Education can retain these buildings to facilitate community based educational activities in the form of computer centre, library, activity centre and even use them to replicate the concept of the model cluster school (JRM 2006).

Yet another serious concern is on teacher absenteeism which has a direct impingement on quality of education. World Bank report on Himachal Pradesh (World Bank 2007, 2009) points out that teacher absence is relatively high in the state by quoting Kremer *et al.* (2004). Even among those present, only about half the teachers were actually found to be involved in teaching. But, teacher absence is relatively low in the state going by the figures reported by Pratham. Teachers' attendance rates as per ASER report (2010) is around 90 per cent, which is one of the best in the country. Further, the school records of teacher and student attendance and through interactions with PTA and MTA members do not report absence to be a widespread problem. But the other finding is teachers being present but not teaching is a more serious issue which needs due attention. Here, the problem of accountability is a major concern not only in Himachal Pradesh but also in many other states.

The growth in number of private schools is also in part a reflection of falling standards in government schools. Till 1990s, private schools were a rarity in all but a handful of larger district towns. During 2002 as many as

*Table 5.14* Board examination results at primary and upper primary level

| *Management Type* | *% age of students passed at Class V* | | | | *% age of students passed at Class VIII* | | | |
|---|---|---|---|---|---|---|---|---|
| | *Boys* | *Girls* | *60% and above boys* | *60% and above girls* | *Boys* | *Girls* | *60% and above boys* | *60% and above girls* |
| Government | 96.5 | 96.9 | 47.4 | 52.5 | 79.9 | 80.3 | 18.4 | 21.2 |
| Private | 98.6 | 98.9 | 74.4 | 78.0 | 93.5 | 95.2 | 49.4 | 60.5 |

*Source:* Elementary Education in Himachal Pradesh by Shri B.L. Shukla.

1,273 private schools spanning all 12 districts are registered with state board of education apart from those registered with central boards of education. As argued by Sood (2003), private 'English medium' teaching shops, where teachers are paid less than a quarter the salaries paid to government teachers, are preferred by the latter for their own children. There is increasing attention to mounting shift of children to private schools and the issues of quality affecting elementary education in Himachal Pradesh (Sood 2003). One of the major reasons attributed to such shift being better examination results in private schools than government schools. Table 5.14 compares results in government schools with private schools in 2006–07.

Yet another concern is though, even if trained teachers are available, the state government employs para teachers, *vidya upashaks* and PTA teachers through Prathmik Sahayak Adhyapak/Primary Assistant Teacher (PAT) scheme, introduced in 2003. This was to achieve the task of UEE given the tough geographical conditions, financial constraints, reluctance of trained teachers to serve in remote areas, teacher's absenteeism, etc. In order to counter these problems effectively, such para teachers are recruited against regular vacancies, who are paid less than regular teacher salary. It may be noted that during 2007–08, there were 10,300 para teachers in the state, mostly teaching in primary schools (DISE 2008).

## Concluding remarks

Allegorically speaking, the hardware is already in place and only the software needs to be worked which is quality of education. The lessons held out by Himachal Pradesh are not so much in terms of what government should do as much as how it should go about it. Further as the enrolments show declining trends, the state needs to give more attention to the quality and consolidation of the existing facilities. Otherwise it will be difficult to sustain the higher cost in the long run. As argued, centralized delivery of basic services may have delivered positive results in an earlier phase, but accountable and effective government intervention at the present juncture requires strengthening the ability and capacity of local bodies to deliver them (Sanan 2004). There are several aspects of quality and one of them is local involvement. It is noted that the state has to work towards effective decentralization including the BRCs, CRCs and parent teacher committees. Local bodies along with delegated responsibilities must be delegated some powers including that of monitoring (Sood 2003).

With regard to approval budget, it is observed that District Elementary Education Plans are appraised at national level and it takes longer time (on an average two to three months) for finalizing the proceedings. There is a delay in finalizing and sending PAB proceedings to states. The proceedings need to be sent to states along with the first instalment of funds from GOI to speed up utilization at state level. There is still a gap of around two months in release of central share which is a matter of concern. In view of this, it would be appropriate to delegate the appraisal process to states. The state can be encouraged to build a strong resource group constituting visiting members from centre to facilitate the appraisal process.

In case of release of funds, it has been noticed that state shares are not being released in time and these are mostly released in March, therefore, funds remain unutilized. Hence, the state level release of funds also needs to speed up as that of releases from the centre in time. As per the norms, state share is required to be released within one month of release of central share for enhancing better utilization. State needs to step up contributing their counterpart funds and expedite fund flow to school to improve implementation and expenditure. Releases from state to districts should be monitored on monthly basis to ensure that funds are released in time.

With regard to the personnel, there is a need to fill the functional posts of coordinators, accounts personnel and engineers to speed up effective implementation and utilization of resources. Further, staff appointed under SSA should be non-transferable and contact/deputation should be coterminous with the project to ensure continuity. It is noticed that the officers at the key positions often serve with insufficient tenure. Further, there is a need for capacity building of VECs/teachers/BRCs/CRCs in accounts, maintenance and procurement. Most funds remain unutilized at these levels.

Relating to civil works, powers for sanctioning of civil works at district level is now with deputy commissioners who are busy in law and order and other important assignments and sanctions are unnecessarily delayed at that level. It will be better if school-wise sanctions after identification of gaps based on the DISE data are issued at the beginning of the year from State Project Office to avoid delays and spillovers. Since 2010–11, this process has been initiated. Equally important, state governments need to release the last instalment by October every year as per SSA norms to ensure that all grants and civil work instalments are released to schools well in time and these are utilized within the same financial year. Expenditure should be monitored regularly by the concerned intervention coordinator and bottlenecks, if any, may be taken care of at the appropriate level. Over all, intervention-wise planning and constant monitoring mechanism needs to be put in place to increase the absorptive rates of utilizations in interventions which lag behind. There is a need of a special drive for utilization of all unspent balances at school, CRC and BRC level.

Not only funding mechanism needs to be overhauled but also delivery mechanism of education, the system, institutions and teachers are to be made accountable for effective learning.

## Notes

1 This figure is 15 per cent higher than HP's own figure of 4,301. The difference is not big in absolute numbers and may be caused by a fluctuation of the migrant population. Labours from Bihar, Uttar Pradesh and Rajasthan migrate to Himachal Pradesh with their families as unskilled workers.

2 Poverty Stipend Scholarship, Girls Attendance Scholarship, Scholarship for Children of Army Personnel, Scholarship for the students belonging to IRDP families, Pre-metric scholarship for Scheduled Caste students, Lahaul and Spiti Pattern Scholarship and Scholarship for the Children of Army Personnel who are serving at the border areas are provided. Further, free textbooks are provided for OBC/IRDP students in non-tribal areas. Free textbooks and uniforms to SC students under SCP are being provided (Economic Survey, HP 2008–09).

## References


ASER, 2007. Annual Status of Education Report – Himachal Pradesh Rural, Pratham, New Delhi.

ASER, 2011. Annual Status of Education Report – Rural, Pratham, New Delhi.

Demery, Lionel, 2000. *Benefit Incidence: A Practioner's Guide*, The World Bank, Washington, DC.

Dreze, J. and A.K. Sen, 2002. *India: Development and Participation*, Oxford University Press, New Delhi.

GoHP, 2002. *Himachal Pradesh Human Development Report 2002*, Government of Himachal Pradesh, Shimla.

GoHP. Annual Work Plan & Budget, State Project Office & *Sarva Shiksha Abhiyan*, Himachal Pradesh, Shimla, various years.

GoI, 2006. Himachal Pradesh: State Report, Third Joint Review Mission, held during 13–20 January, Sarva Shiksha Abhiyan, India.

IAPI, 2009. Report on Monitoring of the Financial Management and Procurement Relating to *Sarva Shiksha Abhiyan* in Himachal Pradesh, Institute of Public Auditors of India, New Delhi.

JRM, 2006. Report of Fourth Joint Review Mission of Sarva Shiksha Abhiyan, Government of India, 17–27 July 2006, New Delhi.

Kremer, M., K. Muralidharan, N. Chaudhury, J. Hammers and F. H. Rogers, 2004. Teacher and Health Care Provider Absence: A Multi Country Study, mimeo. World Bank, Washington, DC.

Manuja, Binti and Preeti Tanwar, 2007. Enrolment trends in Government and Private Schools of Nahan and Paonta Blocks of Sirmour District: A Micro Study, submitted to District Project Office, Sarva Shiksha Abhiyan (SSA), Sirmour, mimeo.

MHRD, 2004. *Sarva Shiksha Abhiyan: A Programme for Universal Elementary Education; Manual on Financial Management and Procurement*, Department of Elementary Education and Literacy, Ministry of Human Resources Development, Government of India, New Delhi.

PAISA, 2012. Do Schools Get Their Money. Accountability Initiative, New Delhi.

PROBE 1999. *Public Report on Basic Education in India*, Oxford University Press, New Delhi.

Sanan, Deepak, 2004. 'Delivering Basic Public Services in Himachal Pradesh: Is the Success Sustainable?' *Economic and Political Weekly*, 39(9): 975–78.

Sood, Akshay, 2003. 'Himachal Pradesh: Critical Issues in Primary Education', *Economic and Political Weekly*, June 21.

World Bank 2007. *Himachal Pradesh: Accelerating Development and Sustaining Success in a Hill State*, Poverty Reduction and Economic Management, India Country Management Unit, South Asia Region.

World Bank 2009. India–Himachal Pradesh Public Financial Management Accountability Assessment, Report No. 48635-IN, June 2009, Financial Management Unit, South Asia Region.

6

# DO THE SSA FUNDS HIT THE TARGET?

## The case of Kerala

*M. Lathika and C.E. Ajit Kumar*

### Introduction

The case of the state of Kerala is celebrated as a model in a country where the general level of attainments in elementary education leaves much to be desired. Recent reports showed that about one-fifth of even the male population in the country as a whole is illiterate (2011), the median number of school years the males accomplished is less than five (2006) and the gender disparity is woefully high. Therefore the achievement of the goals of the Government of India (GoI)-assisted flagship programme called Sarva Siksha Abhiyan (SSA) like 'Universal Elementary Education (UEE)' by the year 2003 and attainment of eight years of schooling of children of 6–14 years by the year 2010 was generally considered as a case of stroll in the park for the state of Kerala. It was believed that with high and almost gender-neutral pre-SSA status in literacy (GOI 2011), median years of schooling (IIPS 2005; NFHS-Kerala 2005–06), non-attendance of a mere 2.4 per cent (GoK 2004 Educational Statistics; NSSO 66th round report), Kerala could achieve the SSA targets well in advance of the timeframe of the mission, and well ahead of other states in India – that too, with lesser costs.

Schooling is a regular and natural engagement of children in Kerala and the practice of education is diffused into all sections of the population, cutting across gender and region borders (Lathika and Kumar 2008). Yet, there are reports that the residual illiteracy and non-schooling are denser in certain pockets of the state and among the disadvantaged sections like the scheduled caste, scheduled tribes and economically weaker sections (SSA-Kerala report 2002–03; Kumar and Lathika 2007; GOI 2008a,b), and locating these children poses the real challenge for a project like SSA. The present study is an attempt to have a mid-term evaluation of SSA, with the specific objectives as:

a) To evaluate the educational status of Kerala at pre-SSA and mid-term periods, and to consolidate reliable estimates of the number of children un-reached by the current school educational system of the state.
b) To analyse the fund flow pattern and utilization levels of SSA in Kerala, in terms of the main objectives of the programme.
c) To ascertain whether the SSA project is taking the right course in the state in achieving its mission.

## Data and methodology

This study relies on secondary data made available by governmental agencies. However, to gain/validate information at the ground level, we have interviewed some chosen District Project Officers (DPO), Block Project Officers (BPO)/AEOs and school headmasters. The offices contacted personally were of the two south-most districts namely Thiruvananthapuram and Kollam which were purposively selected. The data collected have been compiled and tabulated in accordance with the demands of the objectives set for the study.

### *Constraints and limitations of secondary data*

However, we have certain constraints in using the educational statistics of Kerala, with respect to comparability of the data with all-India figures. In Kerala, the age at entry into schools is fixed as five years, while it is six years elsewhere in India. Moreover, eighth grade is a part of the high school section of the schools in Kerala (and fifth to seventh grades belong to the upper primary section.). Therefore, a student of age 14 years may, most possibly, be in the ninth grade (and hence out-of purview of SSA), rather than in the eighth grade as is normally the case with students of other states. This makes things complicated, especially when the expenditure up to the eighth standard is in question. The teachers who teach the eighth grade students are normally placed in the high school section, and hence the high school section might have derived some spillover benefits of the SSA funding. Though we have taken care in this regard during the analysis and discussion of the data, the confounding of certain results cannot be fully ruled out. In addition to this, the reliability of the estimates of out-of-school children, on the basis of the child census conducted as a pre-project activity of SSA, itself is doubtful, because wide variations and conflicting statements are made with regard to the out-of-school children and rate of enrolment by different state government and other agencies.

Moreover, the data on school enrolment and dropout in the 'Educational Statistics' – the only official source of enrolment data in Kerala – published by the state government agencies annually is to be taken with extreme caution as there could possibly be intentional over-reporting. The governmental policy of strictly adhering to a student–teacher ratio (exceeding which shall result in retrenchment of junior-most teachers of the subject in the school), and the practice of providing grant and other aids to schools in strict accordance with the student strength are real stimulants on the part of the school managers to resort to such practices of over-reporting of student attendance. With these backgrounds the authors have proceeded to make an evaluation of the SSA in Kerala.

The paper is divided into four sections. First section gives a brief account of the infrastructural facilities of schools and an evaluation of the educational performance of Kerala in the pre- and midterm-SSA periods. Second section makes an attempt to consolidate the estimates on the out-of-school children from the available literature, and to ascertain the fund use-efficiency for the SSA interventions aiming at UEE and zero dropout. It is reiterated that the second session only presents the estimates of out-of-school children in Kerala as reported by various governmental and other agencies. Though a number of studies have been made to this effect by many, still we lack a reliable and authentic record on a comprehensive quantification of the out-of-school children in Kerala. Fund flow pattern and utilization levels of SSA in terms of physical targets and financial achievements are addressed in the next section. Last part of the paper validates the conclusions drawn on the basis of secondary data with the field level observations made.

## Educational system and its performance

The infrastructural attainment of schools in Kerala is presented in Table 6.1. There are 12,044 schools in Kerala, and they are almost sufficiently distributed with an average area of coverage of about three square kilometres. Almost all the schools are having a pucca building, and with toilet and drinking-water facilities. The student–teacher ratio is fairly good with a tally of 25 students per teacher.

*Table 6.1* Infrastructural attainment of elementary schools in Kerala

| *Item* | *No. %* |
|---|---|
| No. of schools* | 12,644 |
| % of schools having**: Pucca building | 99.38 |
| Drinking-water facility | 96.11 |
| Toilet facility | 97.13 |
| Area covered by a school* | 3.07 $km^2$ |
| Female teachers as % of total* | 70.71 |
| Student–teacher ratio* | 25 |

*Source:* *SSA-Kerala Annual Report 2011–12; **NCERT. Educational Statistics 7th survey.

The state maintains an edge over the nation as a whole, in respect of the level of literacy, school-attendance rate, dropout rate and median years of schooling. As already mentioned, the number of children of 6–14 year age group remaining out-of-school is comparatively lower than that of the all India level. However, the school attendance rate of 6–14 year aged children was considerably short of 100 per cent, as NSSO (2011–12) data on school attendance rate in Kerala for that age-cohort stands at 97.6 per cent only. Note that the school attendance rate of 6–14 year aged children did not improve over the last seven active SSA-years in Kerala, while there occurred significant strides towards enrolment at the national level. One would naturally think that the state had developed apathy in recent years towards removing the residual non-enrolment. Data on school facilities pertain to mid-SSA period.

The dropout rate in the state, though appreciably lower than that of the all India tally, is still (2003–04) far above the zero level. All these suggest that the SSA could not make its presence strongly felt at least during the early years of SSA mission. But the issue that should cause greatest worry to Kerala is with regard to the quality of education. Kerala's performance in this regard in terms of the student achievement score (class V) for both Mathematics and Language was 35.9 and 35.0, respectively, while it was much higher (46.5 and 58.6, respectively) for India. The performance of the educational system in Kerala, in terms of the various parameters that are considered to be very relevant for a study like this, could be ascertained from Table 6.2.

*Table* 6.2 Educational performance of Kerala and India

| | *Kerala* | *India* | *Source* | *Year* |
|---|---|---|---|---|
| Literacy rate: male | 96.0 | 82.1 | Census India | 2011 |
| Literacy rate: female | 92.0 | 65.5 | | |
| | 97.6 | 87.1 | NSSO | 2009–10 |
| | 97.6 | 82.1 | NSSO | 2004–05 |
| School attendance rate % (5–14 years) Child | 97.2 | 78.6 | NFHS II | 1998–99 |
| Disparity index male and female | −1.74 | 6.7 | (computed by author) | |
| Disparity index urban and rural | 1.84 | 10.0 | | |
| Dropout rate (%): boys | 12.1 | 61 | MHRD 2006 | 2003–04 |
| Dropout rate (%): girls | 4.9 | 64.9 | | |
| Dropout rate (%): combined | 8.6 | 62.7 | | |
| *Median years of schooling* – male | 8 (8.1) | 4.9 (5.5) | NFHS 3 | 2005–06 |
| – female | 7.5 (7.6) | 1.9 (1.6) | NFHS 2 | 1998–99 |
| *Years of school* disparity index male and female | −1.74 | 6.7 | | |
| Disparity index U & R | 1.84 | 9.99 | (computed by authors) | |
| Student Achievement (class V): maths | 35.9 | 46.5 | NCERT 2003 | 2002 |
| Student Achievement (class V): language | 35 | 58.6 | | |

*Note:* Values given in parenthesis are median years of schooling correspond to 1998–99 Disparity index of Tilak, 1983.

## Tracing the out-of-school children and SSA strategies

The State Implementing Society of SSA, Primary Education Development Society Kerala (PEDSK), has claimed that they have, by far, attained the first two major goals of SSA by ensuring enrolment and retention of all children aged 5–14 years in schools, and they have brought the dropout rate to 0.5 (PEDSK 2007–08 and 2008–09). Surprisingly, they claimed in a later report (20011–12) that all the four goals of SSA were 'fully achieved by Kerala as early as 1990'. The approved outlay for SSA-Kerala for the period 2002–03 to 2011–12 amounted to Rs. 2,198.48 crore. The question naturally rises is if all the objectives of SSA were met more than a decade before the SSA was actually launched in the state, why the state ventured into the fray to fulfil the divine objectives of SSA and UEE by spending such a whopping sum. Things being so, the household survey carried out in Kerala as a pre-project activity during 2001 identified 16,800 children in the 6–14 year age group as out-of-school. Though statistics on enrolment and dropout are being regularly published by governmental agencies, an exclusive estimate on the total children out-of-school in Kerala has never been attempted till then.

On the other hand, we feel that the government is neither serious nor concerned about their new estimate of out-of-school children, as no initiative was taken by the government either to inform or to provide the list of such children they had identified from their locality, to the respective BPOs or DPOs. However, an interaction with some officers at these levels has disclosed that they were quite sure of the fact that there could be no child to be brought to schools from their areas. As thousands of schools are already declared un-economic schools and are earmarked for permanent closure, and many government and aided schools are reported to be struggling to keep the minimum student–teacher ratio required for retaining the teachers in service in the schools, the argument of these officers appears to carry some substance. As per census 2001, there were 5,531,381 children of 5–14 age group, and if the estimate of school attendance rate of 97.2 per cent (IIPS 2001) is granted for 2001 also, the enrolment gap could be worked out to be 132,753, which is much higher (roughly eight times higher) than the SSA 2001 estimate.

The SRI-IMRB 'Study Report on Out-of-school children' also estimated the total number of children out-of-school in Kerala in 2005. They had repeated the survey in 2009 also. Table 6.3 presents a compilation of the estimate in 2009, classified by various social groups. The report identified 23,242 (0.55 per cent of the total population of that age-cohort) children of 6–13 years to be brought to school in 2005. In their study in 2009, the number of out-of-school children had been reduced to 16,886 (0.37 per cent of the total), out of which more than three-fourths were boys. The striking message of these estimates is that education deprivation is rather a direct offshoot of their social deprivation. For instance, in 2005, the share in the total out-of-school children of the ST community which represented only 3.9 per cent of the population of that age-group, is 11.24 per cent, and 6.03 per cent of the these children are of SC community who formed only 2.8 per cent of the population. In 2009, though the number had been substantially declined, the concentration among the scheduled tribe class persisted. For instance, though the children of 6–13 years old who belonged to the scheduled tribe community was 4.43 per cent of the total children in the age-group, they comprised more than 36 per cent of the total out-of-school tribal children of the age. For a comparison the national picture is also depicted in the table. The table

*Table* 6.3 Children aged 6–13 and the incidence of their being out-of-school

| | *Population of children aged 6–13* | | *No. of out-of-school children aged 6–13* | | *Out-of-school children aged 6–13 (%)* | |
|---|---|---|---|---|---|---|
| | *Kerala* | *India* | *Kerala* | *India* | *Kerala* | *India* |
| All | 4,277,944 | 190,582,581 | 15,776 | 8,150,617 | 0.37 (0.55) | 4.28 |
| Muslim | 1,292,158 | 24,453,602 | 1,334 | 1,875,744 | 0.1 (0.48) | 7.67 |
| ST | 189,583 | 19,083,142 | 5,694 | 1,069,298 | 3.0 (4.83) | 5.6 |
| SC | 205,218 | 38,707,758 | 54 | 2,308,848 | 0.03 (1.73) | 5.96 |
| Others | 2,590,984 | 108,338,080 | 8,713 | 2,896,726 | 0.34 (0.27) | 2.67 |
| | % of total | | | | | |
| All | 100 | 100 | 100 | 100 | | |
| Muslim | 30.21 | 12.83 | 8.46 | 23.01 | | |
| ST | 4.43 | 10.01 | 36.09 | 13.12 | | |
| SC | 4.8 | 20.31 | 0.34 | 28.33 | | |
| Others | 60.57 | 56.85 | 55.23 | 35.54 | | |

*Source*: SRI-IMRB 'Study report on out-of-school children' 2005 and 2009.

*Note*: Values within parenthesis are the incidence in 2005.

shows that education deprivation was denser among some groups who are already considered to be socially disadvantaged (in 2005), and the trend did persist even after four years through the full operation of SSA (2009).

Moreover, on their visit randomly to some 25 schools in a district in the state (Palakkad), the SRI-IMRB team had observed that 345 students in 18 schools had dropped out. If the same rate is applied to all the 969 schools in the district, the number of dropped-out children would be more than 13,000 in that district alone (as on 2005), which challenges the claims of PEDSK regarding the attainment of UEE. The schools could take practically no measure to track the physical whereabouts of the students and motivate them to join back, once they start absenting themselves from school.

Another estimate of out-of-school children is attempted by the authors themselves. First, the total number of children in the 5–14 year age-group is worked out with the data on 5–14 age-group population ratio provided by SRS (2012) and NSSO 66th round (2009–10) applied on the census population figures (2011). The number of out-of-school children is estimated using the current school non-attendance rate (non-attendance rate = 100 – attendance rate) of 5–14 aged children reported by NSSO (report number 551). Though the estimates are made with the data from two government sources and correspond to periods distanced by more than one year, they are seen very close with a difference of just 1574. This exercise also points to two major conclusions that there are substantial number of children who still remain outside the formal elementary education system of the state and the number does not seem to appreciably decline with the progress of the SSA mission in the state. There exists great disparity between different estimates arrived at with different viewpoints of non-enrolment. Thus, the Government appears to have based the whole project on a thoroughly slippery ground (Table 6.4).

The state SSA report and the Educational Statistics of the Education Department bring out data on dropout. The dropout rate for class I to VIII in Kerala was reported (SSA Annual Report 2010–11; pp. 26) to be zero for 2006–07 and 2007–08. But the tendency to dropout emerged gradually again in 2010–11 with 0.27 per cent dropout for boys and 0.28 per cent for girls. These data indicate that dropout in Kerala are very negligible and the state is nearing to attain a zero level dropout. In this section, we made an attempt to have an estimate of dropout from grade-wise enrolment data of NUEPA district report cards of various issues. As district-wise figures are available, the estimate corresponding to all Kerala districts have also been presented. As the issue now in question is to ascertain whether the children could complete at least 5 grades by the year 2007, we seek to examine the case of enrolment in grade I in the year 2002–03. If all the children were retained, all these children would enrol to grade II in the year 2003–04, but for a few number of children who had happened to repeat. The tabulation is presented in Table 6.5.

Almost all the figures worked out for the districts, and for all the years, are negative. A negative figure indicates that some children who had not

*Table 6.4* Estimates of out-of-school children with data from government agencies

| *Estimate* | *Method* | *Male* | *Female* | *Total* |
|---|---|---|---|---|
| Population 5–14 years 2011 | SRS ratio (2012) projected on census population | 2,563,406 | 2,535,493 | 5,098,899 |
| | NSSO (2009–10) ratio on census population | 2,779,694 | 2,752,572 | 5,532,266 |
| No. of out-of-school children aged 5–14 | NSSO non-attendance rate (2009–10) on SRS population estimate for the age | 7,383 | 11,105 | 18,488 |
| | NSSO non-attendance rate (2009–10) on NSSO population estimate for the age | 8,006 | 12,056 | 20,062 |

*Source:* NSSO report No. 551 and SRS Report 2011 (chapter 2 – Population composition available at censusindia.gov.in/vital statistics/SRS-reports.html).

*Table* 6.5 Locating the children being dropped-out in elementary classes in Kerala, by districts: the case of 2002–03 admission (in grade I) cohorts

| *District* | *Enrolment in Grade I ($e_0$) ($i = 0$)* | *Number not enrolled in next grade* in grades ($e_{i-1} - e_i$)* | | | | | *No of drop-outs in Grade 6 – Grade 1 ($e_0 - e_5$)* |
|---|---|---|---|---|---|---|---|
| | | 2 ($i = 1$) | 3 ($i = 2$) | 4 ($i = 3$) | 5 ($i = 4$) | 6 ($i = 5$) | |
| | 2002–03 | 2003–04 | 2004–05 | 2005–06 | 2006–07 | 2007–08 | |
| Thiruvanthapuram | 37,927 | –1,007 | 16,831 | –6,101 | –12,396 | –2,086 | –415 |
| Kollam | 32,461 | 947 | –1721 | 1,394 | –4,089 | –2,135 | –3,306 |
| Alapuzha | 20,814 | –1,181 | 2,994 | 2,694 | –10,921 | –199 | –5,119 |
| Pathanamthitta | 12,926 | 643 | 1,215 | –1,208 | –839 | –1,035 | –643 |
| Kottayam | 22,662 | –1,120 | 535 | 40 | –3,462 | –2,233 | –3,968 |
| Idukki | 14,647 | 2,111 | –2,451 | –317 | –1,502 | –1,191 | –1,005 |
| Ernakulam | 30,504 | –5,498 | –823 | 657 | –3,352 | –1,254 | –6,956 |
| Thrissur | 46,490 | –454 | –2,780 | 283 | 1,042 | –2,297 | +4,367 |
| Palakkad | 41,699 | –753 | –1,916 | –1,522 | 796 | –8,779 | –2,614 |
| Malapuram | 70,703 | –6,786 | –471 | –5,927 | 4,960 | –12,303 | –3,246 |
| Kozhikode | 44,559 | –685 | 74 | 911 | –6,801 | –2,848 | –3,375 |
| Wayanad | 13,297 | 120 | –742 | –420 | –1,210 | –476 | –34 |
| Kannur | 21,158 | –13,320 | –2,829 | –814 | 293 | –2,923 | –14,197 |
| Kasaragod | 20,673 | 400 | 2,534 | –3,598 | –948 | 1,001 | 2,252 |
| Kerala | 430,520 | –26,583 | 10,450 | –13,928 | –38,429 | –38,758 | –38,259 |

*Source:* NUEPA. Elementary Education in India. District Report Cards. Various issues.

*Note:* *The repetition rate for 2007–08 is applied to all the years to arrive at an appropriate estimate of enrolment. $e_i$ is the enrolment corresponding to the ith grade.

been enrolled in a lower class in a year had been enrolled in the higher class in the next year, which clearly suggests that the enrolment in the previous year was not complete, questioning the claims of full retention and near-zero dropout of the PEDSK. Non-retention and dropout are still a reality in Kerala, and the second SSA goal of schooling all the children of 6–14 years at least for five years by the year 2007 is far from achieved.

If the SSA-Kerala were really serious about the first goal of SSA (complete enrolment), they would have been scrupulous about enquiring on the reasons why these children desisted from going to school, and also why they tended to let themselves dropout. SSA did not do such a survey. However, the NFH surveys and NSSO (2004–05, 2007–08 and 2009–10) examined the issue, and they have come out with various reasons and the proportion of non-attending-children who tend to desist from schooling due to each of these reasons. The proportions, as given in the NSSO reports, is compiled and presented in Table 6.6.

*Table* 6.6 Proportion (per 1,000) of never-enrolled persons (aged 5–29) and their distribution, by reason in 2009–10, 2007–08 and 2004–05

| *Reason* | | *Kerala* | | | *India* | | |
|---|---|---|---|---|---|---|---|
| | | *Male* | *Female* | *(Both)* | *Male* | *Female* | *(Both)* |
| School is far off | 2010 | 17 | 13 | 15 | 24 | 32 | 28 |
| | 2008 | 0 | 23 | 12 | 15 | 20 | 18 |
| | 2005 | 6 | 4 | 5 | 17 | 27 | 22 |
| To attend other domestic chores | 2010 | 20 | 34 | 201 | 41 | 404 | 229 |
| | 2008 | 0 | 0 | 0 | 7 | 28 | 20 |
| | 2005 | 29 | 336 | 189 | 25 | 300 | 167 |
| For helping in household enterprises | 2010 | 543 | 103 | 298 | 562 | 100 | 322 |
| | 2008 | 0 | 0 | 0 | 547 | 108 | 320 |
| | 2005 | 510 | 102 | 297 | 547 | 108 | 320 |
| Education not considered necessary | 2010 | 50 | 47 | 48 | 113 | 174 | 144 |
| | 2008 | 108 | 189 | 149 | 198 | 229 | 210 |
| | 2005 | 46 | 37 | 42 | 108 | 201 | 156 |
| (Others*) | 2010 | 370 | 491 | 438 | 261 | 289 | 276 |
| | 2008 | 882 | 716 | 798 | 357 | 710 | 538 |
| | 2005 | 408 | 521 | 467 | 303 | 365 | 335 |

*Source:* NSSO report 551 (round 66th – July 2009–June 2010); NSSO report 532. Education in India: 2007–08. Participation and Expenditure NSSO 64th round (July 2007–June 2008); NSSO report 517, status of education and vocational training in India 2004–05 (61st round) July 2004–June 2005.

*Note:* *NSSO 64th round elicited information on 11 more reasons of non-attendance. Many of those have been pooled.

Table 6.6 reveals that the reasons to desist from schooling do vary for boys and girls. In fact, the pattern of the proportion of non-schooling children is not very different for the state from the proportion of the nation as a whole. The main difference is that no child in Kerala reported non-attendance just because they had to help in the household enterprise during the 64th round of NSSO survey, though over half the boys and one-tenth of the girls in India reported this as the reason for their non-attending school during the NSSO 61st and 66th round. During the interim period, there occurred no great change in the fate of these children in the nation as a whole. In Kerala, many traditional household industries like coir, poultry, animal husbandry, etc. suffered great setbacks during the period resulting in a shirking off the employment potential, including child labour, in these industries. Moreover, NFHS II found that a lot many children (boys and girls) ceased attending school for they lost interest in their studies. But a large number of boys (and many girls, too) found the opportunity cost of attending school is higher, and they preferred, instead, to do activities that supplement the household income. But it is quite depressing that there occurred a spurt in the number of out-of-school children in Kerala who cited that they did not consider education necessary at all.

Though there was a substantial increase in the number of such children in India as a whole, (from 156 to 210) also, the spurt in Kerala (from 42 to 149), despite many interventions under SSA, is just alarming. In Kerala, Muslim girls tend to marry early. Marriage became a major hindrance for them in continuing their studies. In 1997–98, more than 11 per cent of the dropped-out girls discontinued their studies because of getting married. However, in their 2005–06 survey of NFHS, only 8.7 per cent is reported to have cited this reason. Table 6.7 demonstrates how much the state SSA was serious about arresting the incidence of dropout, by remedying the problems cited by the agencies.

This table is compiled from the information contained in recent SSA annual reports. It could be seen that the SIS has launched many initiatives to check the tendency to dropout.

## Did the mountain go to Mohammed?

It is, by far, amply evident that the estimate of the number of out-of-school children by the pre-project child census in Kerala was neither reliable nor was taken seriously by the implementing officers of SSA. The claims of PEDSK should be rather contested, and the existence of out-of-school 6–14 year old children in Kerala, even after 2007, could be but a stark reality. It is also true that it would be very difficult to locate the hidden cases of

*Table 6.7* SSA interventions aiming at dropouts in Kerala

| *Reasons* | *Remedies in SSA* | *Achievement* |
|---|---|---|
| School too far | The Kerala Education Rules stipulate that there should be at least an LP school within 1 km and a UP school within 3 km. | 454 AIE centres with 12,316 children. To enable this, school mapping exercise is in progress under the 'Mythri' programme. |
| Helping in house-hold enterprise | 'Learn & Earn' camps | 152 camps, 6718 girls in 2007–08. |
| Education not considered necessary | Parental awareness | Four-day 'sahavasa' (co-living) camps on life skills conducted in 2009–10. Mothers invited in these camps on the 4th day. 450 programmes involving 60,000 parents in 2007–08. |
| Domestic chores | Parental awareness | 450 programmes, 60,000 parents. |
| Costs too much | No fee for education in government and aided schools. 'Learn & Earn' camps. Free textbooks and other study material distributed | In 2009–10 itself, 128,071 teachers were given 20 days training. |
| Not interested in studies | Publication and free distribution of 'Little Scientist', 'Easy Maths', 'Meetti Hindi' | Extended to 100 panchayats in 2007–08. |
| Repeated failures | Home-based tuition | 2162 students. |
| Got married | Parental awareness, mothers meeting, community training, community mobilization programmes | Mothers invited to attend the 'sahavasa' camps. |

*Source:* SSA Annual Report 2007–8, 2009–10.

school deprivation. However, there could hardly be any possibility that the already prevailing social and economic deprivation, with which these estranged children are entangled, will ever allow them to continue their studies in schools, despite the costly interventions that SSA launched. But now the Constitution of India guarantees them compulsory elementary education, and it deems to be their right to get elementary level education. The huge funds already siphoned exclusively to bring these children to the mainstream education system in the state does not legitimately or morally justify their being out-of-school. If Mohammed does not come to the mountain, the mountain should go to him. The children should be located, their parents counselled, children motivated, brought to the nearby school and retained there till (s)he finishes his/her eighth grade – no matter the labour and costs it incurs.

However, in exceptionally rare cases, the un-enrolled or dropped-out children could go to alternate centres of education which SSA facilitates. Alternate and Innovative Education Centres, or, Multi-grade Learning Centres (AIECs or MGLCs) are thus temporary arrangements managed and run by a single teacher, meant for these 6–14 year old children who are brought and are taught the same elementary lessons (irrespective of their varied age and competencies). Table 6.8 presents the number of AIECs in Kerala, over the years, and the number of children classified by their social groups, enrolled in them. It could be seen that there was no substantial increase or decrease in either the number of centres or the number of children enrolled, though the ideal condition could be that the number of centres and children is successively reduced, and all the children, over the years, be brought to mainstream schools.

The most glaring aspect of this table is that a great majority of these children belong to either SC or ST communities. As per the pre-SSA status report, while 1.46 per cent of students dropped out during 1999–2000 the dropout for SC was 1.66 per cent and for ST it was 4.04 per cent (GoK, Educational Statistics 2000–01). Their domination keeps rather un-challenged over the years. This provides another reason to conclude that education deprivation is rather a glaring manifestation of their general social deprivation.

*Table* 6.8 Number of functional AIEC and children enrolled, by year

| *Period* | *No.* | *Children* | *SC* | *%* | *ST* | *%* |
|---|---|---|---|---|---|---|
| 2002–03 | 461 | 9624 | 3,860 | 40.1 | 4,792 | 49.8 |
| 2003–04 | 506 | 13,801 | 4,853 | 35.2 | 5,410 | 39.2 |
| 2004–05 | 481 | 13,406 | 4,310 | 32.1 | 5,760 | 43 |
| 2005–06 | 465 | 12,895 | 3,915 | 30.4 | 5,665 | 43.2 |
| 2006–07 | 496 | 16,438 | 4,365 | 26.7 | 6,732 | 41.2 |
| 2007–08 | 559 | 13,172 | 3,425 | 26 | 4,083 | 31 |
| 2008–09 | 559 | 19,298 | 3,520 | 18.2 | 4,275 | 22.2 |
| 2009–10 | 454 | 12,316 | 4,153 | 33.7 | 4,778 | 38.8 |
| 2010–11 | 446 | 11,455 | 3,931 | 34.3 | 4,856 | 43.4 |

*Source:* SSA Annual Report various issues.

## Fund flow and utilization levels of different SSA interventions

Table 6.9 gives the physical and financial achievement of these centres against the respective targets. Though they could meet the physical targets almost fully (especially in recent years), the financial achievement is far short of targets. Why the expenditure levels are too low is not clear. It may not, however, be that the AIECs became redundant due to complete enrolment, for, as we argued earlier, non-enrolment and dropout remain to be a stark reality in Kerala, even after many years of SSA operation.

Integrated Education for Disabled Children centres (IEDC) are meant for children with special needs (CWSN) who could not attend school due to their physical disability. Table 6.10 provides the number of IEDCs and the number of children enrolled in these centres. The physical and per-child financial achievement levels are also given in this table. As the case of AIECs, the financial achievement levels are also substantially short of the targets, though it is getting improved over the years. Of late (2010–12), the financial achievement level in respect of IEDC hovered around 80 per cent. SSA considers the number of actual beneficiaries as the physical achievement. However, as with the case of out-of-school children, a pre-project enumeration of disabled children of 6–14 years was made by conducting a 'house-to-house' survey. The survey identified 94,000 children as disabled. The education policy 1986 and modified policy 1992 places great emphasis on education of disabled children, as physical disability hinders

*Table* 6.9 Physical and financial achievements of AIECs against targets

| *Year* | *Physical* | | | *Financial (Rs. lakh)* | | |
|---|---|---|---|---|---|---|
| | *Target* | *Achievement* | *%* | *Target* | *Achievement* | *%* |
| 2002–03 | 12,774 | 11,527 | 90.2 | 134.7 | 1.56 | 1.2 |
| 2003–04 | 19,585 | 11,724 | 59.9 | 189.1 | 64.8 | 34.3 |
| 2004–05 | 13,801 | 13,801 | 100 | 414.0 | 197.4 | 46.2 |
| 2005–06 | 12,895 | 12,895 | 100 | 386.9 | 296.8 | 76.7 |
| 2006–07 | 16,438 | 15,400 | 93.7 | 511.1 | 270.6 | 52.9 |
| 2007–08 | 13,172 | 13,172 | 100 | 376.4 | 259.1 | 68.8 |
| 2008–09 | 19,298 | 19,298 | 100 | 276.6 | 228.7 | 82.7 |
| 2009–10 | 12,316 | 12,316 | 100 | 386.13 | 267.32 | 69.2 |
| 2010–11 | 11,455 | 10,622 | 92.7 | 1,400 | 1,197.9 | 85.9 |

*Source:* SSA Annual Report (various issues).

*Table 6.10* Physical and financial achievements for IEDC scheme for various years

| *Year* | *Physical (No.)* | | *Financial (Rs. lakh)* | | | | |
|---|---|---|---|---|---|---|---|
| | *Target* | *Achievement* | *Target* | *Achievement* | *Per-child target (Rs.)* | *Per-child achievement (Rs.)* | *% achieved per child* |
| 2002–03 | 88,636 | 53,512 | 1,063.6 | 7.35 | 1,200 | 14 | 1.17 |
| 2003–04 | 94,991 | 89,147 | 1,139.9 | 179.5 | 1,200 | 201 | 16.75 |
| 2004–05 | 89,147 | 87,154 | 414.0 | 462.4 | 464 | 531 | 114.44 |
| 2005–06 | 87,319 | 87,319 | 1,047.0 | 688.3 | 1,199 | 788 | 65.72 |
| 2006–07 | 132,705 | 126,120 | 1,586.3 | 901.8 | 1,195 | 715 | 59.83 |
| 2007–08 | 132,705 | 128,334 | 1,423.1 | 1,083.4 | 1,072 | 844 | 78.73 |
| 2008–09 | 134,570 | 127,607 | 1,112.4 | 929.8 | 827 | 729 | 88.15 |
| 2009–10 | 125,017 | 124,551 | 1,125.1 | 1,139.6 | 900 | 915 | 101.67 |
| 2010–11 | 122,157 | 120,167 | 2,809.6 | 2,297.4 | 2,300 | 1,912 | 83.13 |
| 2011–12 | 165,000 | 148,400 | 2,994.9 | 2,056.0 | 1,815 | 1,385 | 76.31 |

*Source:* SSA Annual Report Kerala (various issues).

seriously his/her school attendance. Unless the physical targets are fixed based on such an estimate, there is no point in fixing the target, nor in struggling to achieve the target. And if the physical targets are fixed not on actual enumeration and actual appraisal of degree of disability, the actual amount spent or the actual financial achievement may not legitimately indicate the performance efficiency of IEDC programmes.

Thus, AIECs and IEDCs are the only designated alternatives under SSA umbrella in the mainstream education system of the state, to address the issue of residual non-enrolment, or dropout; and hence spending on them would cater directly to meet the first two major objectives of SSA. The perspective plan for a 10-year period 2001–10 for the state as a whole projected an investment requirement of Rs. 1950 crores (SSA-Kerala Annual Report 2005–06). But, as already mentioned, the approved outlay for SSA-Kerala for the period 2002–03 to 2011–12 amounted to Rs. 2,198.48 crore. Spending at a massive scale would hence justify if the actual expenditure was towards AIECs and IEDCs, or things of that genre which targets directly the key SSA goals.

Table 6.11 depicts the amount spent on AIECs and IEDCs, over the years. These crucial interventions together accounted roughly for only 10 per cent of the total SSA annual expenditure for almost all the years. Initial years saw much less share. In 2008–09, both the interventions meant only less than 7 per cent of the total SSA expenditure. Thus, though there is enough evidence that a significant number of children of 6–14 years still remain out-of-school, and the mission mode project of SSA clearly

*Table 6.11* Allocation for AIECs and IEDCs as percentage of SSA total expenditure

| *Year* | *AIE* | *IED* | *Total* |
|---|---|---|---|
| 2003–04 | 6.63 | 2.23 | 8.85 |
| 2004–05 | 2.16 | 5.05 | 7.21 |
| 2005–06 | 2.38 | 6.33 | 9.71 |
| 2006–07 | 2.3 | 8.64 | 10.9 |
| 2007–08 | 1.88 | 7.87 | 9.75 |
| 2008–09 | 1.38 | 5.6 | 6.98 |
| 2009–10 | 1.39 | 5.91 | 7.3 |
| 2010–11 | 0.47 | 11.18 | 11.65 |
| 2011–12 | 0.02 | 8.23 | 8.25 |

*Source:* SSA Kerala reports various issues.

mandated that all of them should positively be enrolled either in a school or in alternate centres, as early in 2003, the government does not seem to be serious to take stock of the actual situation, or to locate the out-of-school children around, or even to allocate and spend enough fund for these centres. This appears to be a serious lapse on the part of SSA authorities. It is learnt that the experience with the non-formal education (NFE) scheme, which was introduced in 1979–80 and revised in 1987–88, has led to the creation of AIECs and MGLCs. They are meant for school abstainers like dropouts, working children and those who are unable to attend full-time schools, through programmes which provide flexible strategies for reaching children, including bridge courses, residential camps, dropin centres, summer camps, etc. But in actual practice, the curriculum and working of these centres in Kerala under the SSA umbrella are dubious and far from being qualified as either alternate or innovation centres.

## Education: a constitutional guarantee

India began its journey towards the achievement of free universal basic education more than six decades ago. 'Education For All' (EFA) is a constitutional obligation in India with the Indian constitution stating that 'the state shall endeavour to provide, within a period of ten years from the commencement of this constitution for free and compulsory education for all children until they complete the age of fourteen years'. A number of measures and programmes have been initiated by GoI during the last 60 years focusing on the goal of UEE. In 1986 the National Policy on Education (NPE) was launched which was a turning point towards achieving the goal of UEE. As part of the commitments made by the International Donor Community at the Jomtein Conference, a large multistate programme for EFA under the banner of District Primary Education Programme (DPEP) was initiated. The initiatives such as the Total Literacy Campaign (TLC) of the National Literacy Mission (NLM), the Supreme Court judgement declaring basic education as a fundamental right of every citizen; and at the international level, UNDP fixing basic education as a component of HDI have all transformed the status of UEE from merely an administrative measure of the state to one of a governmental mandate with legal obligation, societal responsibility and moral commitment.

SSA is supported by domestic resources, supplemented partially by external funding from the World Bank's International Development Association, United Kingdom's Department for International Development (DFID) and the European Commission (GOI 2009). Approximately 51 per cent of the Department of Elementary Education and Literacy budget is allocated for SSA (*Hindusthan Times* 2005; GOI 2005). However, the largest fund comes from the public through the education cess they pay. Thus providing education to all children is not only a constitutional obligation but is also an ethical responsibility of the government to provide the services for which they have collected funds from the public.

## Is AIEC/MGLC a valid excuse for violating education guarantee?

The government seems to be under the impression that, once an alternate system of education is set up, they have done what they are mandated to do to bring all children to school where regular school facility is not available. But the functioning of MGLCs was found to be far from perfect or not even satisfactory. The study conducted by the Indian Institute of Public Auditors appraised the functioning of these alternate centres as 'student enrolment, teaching in these centres and expenditure on this intervention was not as per the norms set by GoI' and they were found to be sceptical about the whole programme of these alternate centres. They have listed some major deficiencies observed in the functioning of these centres. Though a State Level Resource Group was constituted in 2003 to guide and monitor the activities of MGLCs, it was not reconstituted when its term came to an end in October 2004, thereby creating a void in guidance, supervision and monitoring the activities of these centres. Since the teaching in MGLCs is undertaken by educational volunteers or para-teachers who are not formally trained in teaching, and since the students of standards I to IV are engaged in the same division by a single teacher, normal procedure of teaching can neither be expected nor possible in MGLCs. Self-Learning Materials (SLM cards) are used in these centres instead of textbooks since a master textbook, covering everything for classes from I to IV, is yet to be designed. Strict directions are also given to revise these cards periodically along with the revision of books in regular schools, but, which seldom happened. These centres which are aimed at meeting the educational needs of the poorest and deprived students thus miserably failed in achieving the destined goal. The State Programme Officer – Kerala – has himself admitted that these centres had become 'schools without teaching'. Thus, these alternate centres of learning fail to transcend to the status of a true alternative for the disadvantaged class of people.

Apart from enrolment and retention up to 8th grade, the SSA mandates to achieve improvement in quality of education (goal 4). SSA interventions like providing textbooks and teaching/learning equipments, etc. free of cost, innovative activities, research and evaluation, remedial teaching, quality improvement programmes, training, and giving teacher grant,

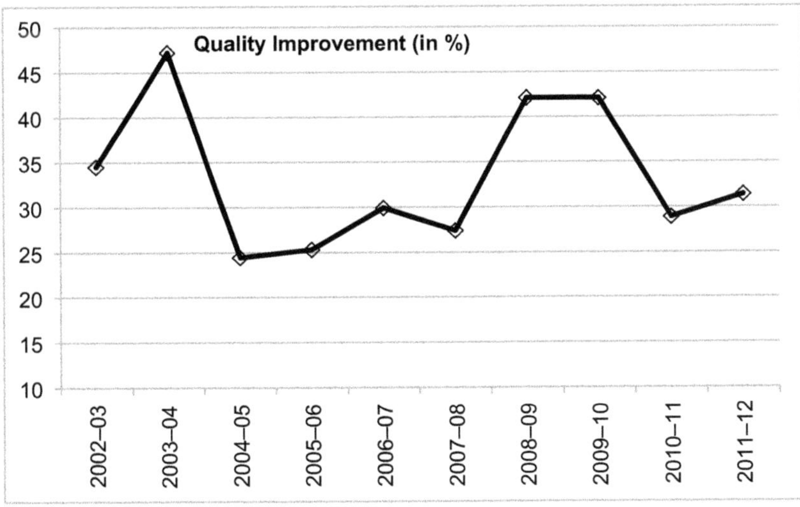


*Figure 6.1* Allocation (percentage of total expenditure) for quality improvement[1] in education

*Source:* SSA Kerala Reports various issues.

school grant, all cater to the achievement of this critical goal of SSA. The percentage of allocation over the years, out of the total expenditure, for these interventions aiming quality improvement, is given in Figure 6.1. These interventions incurred much higher share of expenditure than that of the interventions targeting goals 1, 2 and 3, namely, AIECs and IEDCs.

In many years, these quality enhancing interventions claimed more than a quarter of the total expenditure. In 2008–10, it incurred more than 42 per cent of the total SSA expenditure, but later it again dipped to around 30 per cent. All these suggest that the crucial interventions of AIECs, IEDCs and the nine quality enhancing interventions mentioned, that cater directly to the achievement of goals of SSA, namely UEE and quality enhancement of elementary education in time, incur an amount much less than 50 per cent of the total expenditure; and, of the two, the more crucial and mandatory objective of UEE incurred about 10 per cent of the total expenditure, all through these years.

## Observations from school visits

The authors have visited many schools in Thiruvananthapuram and Kollam districts so as to experience and understand the success/failures in the implementation and achievement levels of various SSA designed interventions.

Information collected at the school level illustrates certain key aspects/issues on SSA programme implementation. The school abstainers are mostly children of fishermen, agricultural labourers, workers of traditional unorganized sectors or the people of socially deprived sections like SC, ST or Muslim community. It seems that these children and their parents value the pursuits for food or other essentials of life more than school education. Moreover, most of these children being the first generation literates in their family, education is never a matter of serious concern to the family members, who are otherwise struggling to earn a living. In hilly regions, where people of ST community have settled in large numbers, children express their fear of wild animals on the way to school and back. Sudden floods and inappropriate transportation facility are major impediments to schooling, for which, unfortunately, none of the SSA interventions deemed to be a remedy. School abstention of children is rather a social malady and the arrest of it is a constitutional mandate. It is strongly felt that education deprivation is bound to the general – social, cultural and economic – deprivation of their family, and hence, a measure enabling them to tide over the deprivation of the whole family would only be an effective remedy. Coordinating the SSA interventions with other social welfare programmes might facilitate to stave off the problem. The economic deprivation could be managed well by the programmes like MGNREGS. If the parents (especially the mothers) are given job, through this programme or otherwise, very near to the schools of their children, it may help a great deal.

## What pulls the children to schools?

On an enquiry at the school (government or aided), it was discerned that for a considerable number of children in the school who perceive that the opportunity cost of attending school becomes greater than what they, or their parents, perceive to gain from school. Yet, the authorities could manage to lure them to these schools, by offering certain incentives, such as, mid-day meals, stipend (for SC/ST students), etc. Some school teachers even offer free transport facility and other study facilities to hesitant children, to lure them to their school and thereby avoid the chances of their getting retrenched for want of enough teacher–student ratio in the school. High rate of attendance is recorded on that day of the week in which full meal with egg is served. Another attraction for coming to school by the economically backward children, which their parents also whole-heartedly welcome, is the free supply of 5 kilogram of rice per student at times of a regional distress. In short, even at the thick of the SSA programme, which was implemented with the main goal of

UEE, the students are coming to school not solely due to the interventions of SSA.

## Conclusion

Kerala had perceptibly tackled the first generation problems in elementary education, like illiteracy, low school-enrolment, high gender disparity, etc. Hence, it was believed that the SSA goals could be very easily and very soon be achieved in the state. But, a detailed investigation at the state revealed that though the goals of SSA were well-articulated and sought to be implemented as a mission mode programme all over the country, Kerala had neither a reliable and well-intended estimate of the number of out-of-school children of 6–14 years, nor a well-chalked out plan for utilizing the huge funds that had flown in for the crucial interventions of SSA which targeted directly the attainment of UEE. A mid-term appraisal of SSA in the state suggested that there could be still many children around who are unable or un-concerned to attend school, and also the quality of the education that the children supposedly gained already is seriously in question.

## Note

1 Expenditure for the SSA interventions aiming quality, namely, free textbook, innovative activities, research and evaluation, teacher grant, remedial teaching, quality improvement programmes.

## References

GOI, 2005. Study on Monitoring the Financial Aspects relating to *Sarva Siksha Abhiyan in Kerala* conducted by Indian Institute of Public Auditors of India, sponsored by MHRD July.

GOI, 2008a. Educational Statistics 7th Survey 2007. NCERT, New Delhi.

GOI, 2008b. *Kerala Development Report*. Planning Commission, New Delhi.

GOI, 2009. Aide Memoire, SSA. 10th Joint Review Commission of SSA, 20–31 July 2009.

GOI, 2011. Family Welfare Statistics in India, Statistics Division, Ministry of Health and Family Welfare, Government of India.

GOK, 2004. *Educational Statistics since Independence*, Directorate of Public Instructions, Government of Kerala, Thiruvanathapuram.

*Hindusthan Times*, 2005. *Education Cess to Give Boost to Universalisation of Education*, New Delhi, 14 January.

IIPS International Institute of Population Sciences and ORC Macro, 2001. National Family Health Survey of India 1998–99, Kerala, Mumbai.

IIPS International Institute of Population Sciences, 2005. National Family Health Survey of India 2004–05, Kerala, Mumbai.

Kumar, Ajith C.E. and M. Lathika, 2007. 'Re-visiting Kerala's Performance on the Education Front'. *Review of Development and Change*, 12(2): 169–88.

Lathika, M. and C.E. Ajith Kumar, 2008. 'An Analysis of the Resource Use Efficiency of Education in Kerala'. *Journal of Educational Planning and Administration*, XXII(3): 295–308.

NSSO, 2006a. Report No. 516. Employment and Un-employment Situation among Social Groups in India 2004–05. New Delhi.

NSSO, 2006b. Report No. 517. Status of Education and Vocational Training in India 2004–05 (61st round), July 2004–June 2005, New Delhi.

NSSO, 2008. Report No. 532. Education in India: 2007–08. Participation and Expenditure (64th round), July 2007–June 2008, New Delhi.

NSSO, 2013. Status of Education and Vocational Training in India (66th round), July 2009–June 2010, New Delhi.

Primary Education Development Society of Kerala (various years). *Sarva Shiksha Abhiyan* Kerala, Annual Report.

Registrar General of India, 2012. SRS Report 2011 (chapter 2 – Population Composition), available at censusindia.gov.in/vital statistics/SRS-reports.html.

Social and Rural Research Institute (SRI), 2005. *All India Survey of Out-of-School Children in the Six to Thirteen Years Age-Group Population*.

SRS, 2012. SRS Statistical Report, 2012, Office of the Registrar General, India.

7

# BOTTLENECKS IN PROVISIONING FOR ELEMENTARY EDUCATION UNDER SARVA SHIKSHA ABHIYAN

## The case of Lalitpur and Rajnandgaon

*Praveen Jha and Pooja Parvati*

### Introduction

Uttar Pradesh is one of the least developed states in India with the lowest per capita income of Rs. 33,137 while the national average Rs. 67,839 in 2012–13 (Economic Survey, 2013–14). Only Bihar has lower per capita income than Uttar Pradesh. Uttar Pradesh is one of the most populous states, and there are no signs of reducing the rate of growth of population. For four decades from 1971 to 2011, rate of growth of population was persistently 2.5 per cent per annum, indicating its primitive stages of demographic transition. It has approximately 0.55 per cent Scheduled Tribe population, 20.7 per cent Scheduled Caste population as per 2011 census. While, the state Chhattisgarh was formed on 1 November 2000, the per capita income of the state is Rs. 50,691 during 2012–13, which occupies 24th position among 28 states and UTs (Economic Survey, 2013–14). Unlike Uttar Pradesh, rate of growth of population here is 1.8 per cent per annum during 1991 to 2011. But the composition of socially deprived population is 30.5 per cent Scheduled Tribe and 12.81 per cent Scheduled Caste population as per 2011 census.

The Planning Commission identified nine educationally backward states – Andhra Pradesh, Assam, Bihar, Jammu and Kashmir, Madhya Pradesh, Orissa, Rajasthan, Uttar Pradesh and West Bengal. These were identified way back in 1978 itself while preparing the sixth five-year plan.

Leaving Jammu and Kashmir, these states are known as BIMARU states. Among these nine states, the progress of elementary education in all Hindi-speaking states, except Uttarakhand, are doubly disadvantaged. The purpose here is to examine the improvement in certain key inputs, process and outcome indicators such as enrolment ratio, dropout rates and transition rates. SSA appears to have attained its goal in terms of GER at primary level. But the GER at upper primary level exhibits a huge gap and Uttar Pradesh reports a GER better than Bihar and Jharkhand. It is pathetic to note that the dropout at the primary and upper primary levels were alarmingly high in 2002–03 and still high in 2010–11. In terms of transition rate from primary to upper primary level, both Bihar and Uttar Pradesh occupy same levels, while Rajasthan outperforms (Table 7.1).

An important indicator at elementary level is percentage of schools established since 1994, which has shown the seriousness of state governments towards the target of achieving UEE by 2010. In Madhya Pradesh, Jharkhand and Uttar Pradesh the situation is quite similar that about 48 per cent of schools were established since 1994. While in Uttar Pradesh 25 per cent of schools were established after the initiation of SSA. However, in Jharkhand and Rajasthan the percentage of schools established after 2001 stands at 38.9 and 27.6 per cent, respectively (Table 7.1).

It is equally important to look at the government expenditure allocated towards education and more specifically to elementary education across these states. In all five states, the expenditure on education as a percentage of SDP has declined between the period 2002–03 and 2011–12. Though

*Table 7.1* Educational development indicators in selected states

| *States* | *GER (2002–03)* | | *Dropout (2002–03)* | | *GER (2010–11)* | | *Dropout (2010–11)* | | *Transition rate* (Pry to UP)* | *% of schools estd. since 1994** | *% of schools estd. since 2001** |
|---|---|---|---|---|---|---|---|---|---|---|---|
| | *Pry* | *UP* | *I–V* | *I–VIII* | *Pry* | *UP* | *I–V* | *I–VIII* | | | |
| Bihar | 74 | 25 | 62 | 48 | 128 | 65 | 35 | 58 | 76 | 28.3 | 23.3 |
| Chhattisgarh | 105 | 71 | — | — | 123 | 87 | 31 | 48 | 96 | 46.0 | 23.8 |
| Jharkhand | 75 | 31 | — | — | 147 | 81 | 28 | 45 | 76 | 48.3 | 38.9 |
| MP | 95 | 64 | 31 | 68 | 135 | 101 | 29 | 31 | 89 | 48.2 | 16.5 |
| Rajasthan | 97 | 56 | 57 | 23 | 110 | 82 | 51 | 53 | 90 | 54.6 | 27.6 |
| UP | 91 | 47 | 79 | 45 | 127 | 80 | 34 | 50 | 72 | 48.0 | 25.0 |

*Source:* Selected Educational Statistics, 2002–03; and School Educational Statistics 2010–11; * as on 30 September 2010, State Report Cards, 2011–12, NUEPA, New Delhi.

*Note:* UP – upper primary level.

expenditure on education as a percentage of SDP declined, the expenditure in state budget increased in all states except Madhya Pradesh. Share of expenditure on elementary education in total expenditure on education increased in all five states except Chhattisgarh. Bihar, however, retained its share of spending on elementary education in total expenditure on education. Yet another pattern is that extremely backward states in Bihar and Jharkhand allocate more than 60 per cent of expenditure on education towards elementary education. Chhattisgarh as well allocates more than 60 per cent though declined during 2011–12 (Table 7.2).

It clearly emerges from Tables 7.1 and 7.2 that both in terms of some of the key educational development and finance indicators, the performance of Chhattisgarh and Uttar Pradesh is far from satisfactory. In this light, the present chapter attempts to highlight some of the planning and institutional constraints with regard to fund transfers in SSA from the district to the level of schools, with illustrations from *Lalitpur*, one of the medium developed districts in Uttar Pradesh and *Rajnandgaon* (Chhattisgarh). The present chapter attempts to highlight some of the planning and institutional constraints with regard to fund transfers in SSA from the district to the level of schools.[1] The chapter is organized as follows: Following an examination of the trends with regard to public provisioning for elementary education in Chhattisgarh and Uttar Pradesh, the chapter presents an overview of spending in SSA, implementation challenges in SSA drawing from evidence gathered from two districts.

It is worthwhile to examine fund utilization issues at the level of districts as many of the development programmes/schemes funded by the central

*Table 7.2* Budget expenditure on education in selected states

| | *As a % of SDP* | | *As a % state budget* | | *% Expr on ele edu in total expr on ed.* | |
|---|---|---|---|---|---|---|
| | *2002–03* | *2011–12* | *2002–03* | *2011–12* | *2002–03* | *2011–12(B)* |
| Bihar | 4.58 | 4.08 | 17.1 | 21.85 | 60.9 | 60.87 |
| Chhattisgarh | 6.71 | 4.02 | 27.0 | 28.91 | 69.0 | 66.48 |
| Jharkhand | 3.90 | 3.07 | 13.9 | 19.81 | 69.8 | 72.20 |
| MP | 4.58 | 3.13 | 22.3 | 20.74 | 44.4 | 62.85 |
| Rajasthan | 4.78 | 2.68 | 20.4 | 22.85 | 57.3 | 58.60 |
| UP | 4.19 | 3.81 | 20.6 | 22.35 | 49.4 | 63.67 |

*Source:* Analysis of Budgeted Expenditure on Education, relevant issues.

*Note:* B – Budget estimate.

government have been designed taking the district as the main unit of planning and implementation. In some of these schemes such as in SSA, plans prepared in a decentralized process are required to be consolidated at districts. This implies that the needs for public expenditure are currently being identified and consolidated at the district level. Hence, examination of the process of fund utilization under these major schemes needs to be carried out primarily at the level of districts. As is well known, several states, especially the backward states, have been unable to utilize the full amount of funds available to them for plan expenditure (i.e. the funds meant for covering the entire costs, salaries of new staff hired as well as construction of buildings and procurements, under the programmes/schemes envisaged in the five-year plans). Hence, the present analysis focuses on the constraints faced at the district and sub-district level in utilization of funds available for plan expenditure in SSA.

The study relies on both the secondary and primary data. The secondary data relating to allocation and expenditures, fund flow are obtained from the Uttar Pradesh Education for All Project Board (UPEFAPB). The data on allocation and spending at district levels are obtained from the district project office at Lalitpur. The data on district and sub-district correspond to the period of four financial years, i.e. 2004–05 to 2007–08. The case study relies both on objective (quantitative) information and information relating to perceptions of concerned officials and grass root-level service providers such as Block Project Officer and school headmasters and teachers. The objectives of the chapter are as follows:

(i) to examine the approved budget outlays, funds released, total funds available and expenditure reported for the state and the sample district;
(ii) to explore the time-line of fund flow and fund utilization in the district;
(iii) to identify the major constraints in effective utilization of funds at the district, block and the ultimate delivery unit (the primary schools).

The primary data, at the district and sub-district and school levels, were collected through meetings and interviews carried out at relevant government offices in Lucknow, Lalitpur, in two blocks – (Barh and Jakhora), and in selected primary schools in the two blocks. Grass root-level service providers have been collected through meetings and interviews carried out at relevant government offices in Raipur, Chhattisgarh, in four blocks – two blocks in Rajnandgaon (Dongargaon and Chhuria), and in selected primary schools in the blocks. However, these meetings and interviews for capturing perceptions followed structured questionnaires.

Lalitpur is located in Bundelkhand region, the most backward region in Uttar Pradesh. Among the seven districts in the region, Banda, Hamirpur, Jhansi, Mahoba, Lalitpur, Chitrakoot and Jalaun, Lalitpur has lowest female literacy rate, i.e. 52.26 per cent as per 2011 census. However, as per the human development index, in 2005 Lalitpur stands with the rank of 49 out of 70 districts (GoUP 2008). As per 2011 census, the gap between male and female literacy rates was also higher than the state average. The decline in gender gap is quite substantial in both states but marginally improved in Lalitpur and Rajnandgaon. Rajnandgaon attained the highest literacy with 75.96 per cent and higher than national average (Table 7.3).

On the elementary education front, least enrolment ratio at upper primary was reported in Uttar Pradesh, followed by Chhattisgarh during 2011–12. However, Rajnandgaon performs better than Lalitpur (see Table 7.4).

*Table 7.3* Literacy rates in Lalitpur and Rajnandgaon

| *District* | *Literacy rates: 2001* | | *Literacy rates: 2011* | | *Gender gap* | |
|---|---|---|---|---|---|---|
| | *All* | *Female* | *All* | *Female* | *2001* | *2011* |
| Lalitpur | 49.3 | 26.0 | 64.95 | 52.26 | 25.1 | 24.15 |
| Uttar Pradesh | 56.3 | 51.1 | 69.72 | 59.26 | 27.3 | 19.98 |
| Rajnandgaon | 87.2 | 67.6 | 75.96 | 66.70 | 19.6 | 18.70 |
| Chhattisgarh | 77.4 | 51.9 | 70.28 | 59.58 | 25.5 | 20.99 |

*Source:* Census of India, 2001, 2011.

*Table 7.4* Gross enrolment ratio at primary and upper primary level in Lalitpur and Rajnandgaon

| *District/state* | | *2005–06* | *2007–08* | *2009–10* | *2011–12* |
|---|---|---|---|---|---|
| Lalitpur | Primary | 140.7 | 143.9 | 135.8 | 133.8 |
| | U. primary | – | 21.3 | 93.7 | 102.2 |
| Uttar Pradesh | Primary | 107.3 | 110.3 | 104.8 | 105.2 |
| | U. primary | 41.9 | 50.9 | 56.4 | 59.6 |
| Rajnandgaon | Primary | 113.0 | 121.6 | 122.0 | 120.0 |
| | U. primary | 81.1 | 90.4 | 96.5 | 104.7 |
| Chhattisgarh | Primary | 131.48 | 124.2 | 124.7 | 125.8 |
| | U. primary | 57.99 | 79.6 | 88.3 | 95.7 |

*Source:* District Report Cards, (DISE 2007, 2008, 2009); State Report Cards, (DISE 2007, 2008, 2009).

*Table 7.5* Availability of teachers, 2011–12 to 2013–14

| *Years* | *2011–12* | *2012–13* | *2013–14* |
|---|---|---|---|
| Average number of teachers per school (all schools) | | | |
| Chhattisgarh | 3.8 | 3.9 | 4.0 |
| Uttar Pradesh | 3.6 | 4.0 | 4.1 |
| All states | **4.7** | **5.1** | **5.3** |
| Average number of teachers per school (all government schools) | | | |
| Chhattisgarh | 3.4 | 3.3 | 3.4 |
| Uttar Pradesh | 3.3 | 3.4 | 3.3 |
| All states | **4.0** | **4.2** | **4.2** |

*Source:* DISE Flash Statistics 2013–14.

*Teacher availability*, a critical indicator for quality of education under SSA–RTE, remains a challenge. In both states, availability of teachers over the period of RTE implementation is less than the national average. With RTE in place, it is normal to expect improvement in the qualified teachers over the years, but the DISE data show dismal picture over the years (Table 7.5).

## Management structure of SSA: Uttar Pradesh and Chhattisgarh

Uttar Pradesh Education for All Project Board (UPEFAPB) was established on 17 May 1993 under Societies Registration Act 1860 as an autonomous and independent body for implementation of the Uttar Pradesh Education for All Project. The UPEFAPB consists of Parishad headed by Chief Minister as the President, Minister of Basic Education, Uttar Pradesh (UP) as the Vice President, the State Project Director (SPD) as the Ex-Officio Member-Secretary and in all having about 90 members comprising State Government officers, representatives of the Central Government and others. The Parishad provides overall policy guidelines and directions for implementation of the project activities and carries out the audited accounts and annual report of the Executive Committee. The UPEFAPB discharges these functions in relation to the activities under SSA for the entire state. The affairs of UPEFAPB are administered, subject to the rules and regulations and orders of the Parishad by an Executive Committee headed by Chief Secretary as Chairman, senior-most Secretary In-charge of SC/ST/OBC Welfare and School Education and other 27 officers as its members.

The State Project Office (SPO) is headed by a State Project Director (SPD) assisted by two Additional Project Directors and a number of professionals. The staff in the SPO continues to be borne on the strength of District Primary Education Programme (DPEP)-II and DPEP-III. The State Component Plan of UP for SSA, prepared for the first time in 2003–04 while for almost all other states, it began in 2002. It was sent to GOI for approval recommended that existing staff pattern/position in the SPO be accommodated in SSA when their duties and responsibilities under DPEP-II (30 June 2003) and DPEP-III (31 March 2006) are accomplished. At the district level the District Project Office (DPO) headed by District Basic Shiksha Adhikari (BSA), who is the principal executive to implement elementary education in the district, is responsible for planning/execution of SSA. The BSA is assisted by Deputy BSA and District Coordinators. To achieve the targets of SSA in a phased manner, District Education Project Committee was constituted in each district. District Magistrate as Chairman, Chief Development Officer as Vice-Chairman, BSA as Member Secretary are the office bearers among other 30 members of district officers and public representatives. Figure 7.1 illustrates the management structure of SSA in UP.

At Block level there are Assistant BSAs, Block Resource Centres (headed by BRC Coordinators) to provide support for activities such as teaching, training and planning process. Village Education Committee

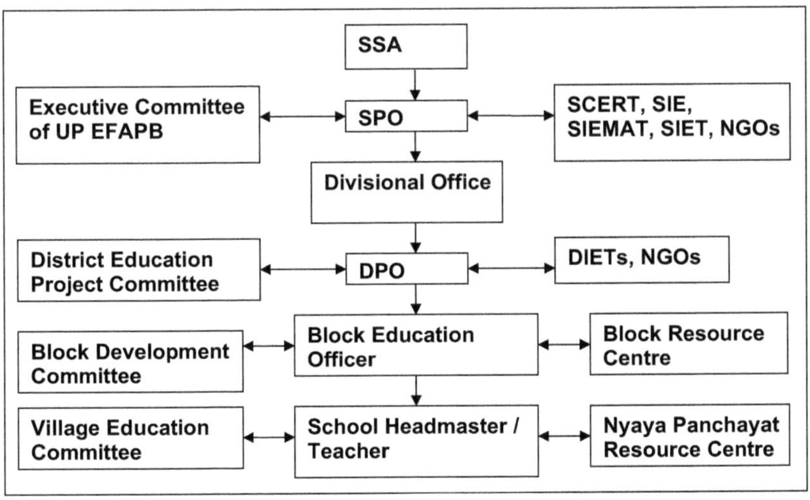


*Figure 7.1* Management structure of SSA in Uttar Pradesh

with Gram Pradhan as Chairman and Headmaster as Secretary is to prepare habitation/village level plan and execution of development works of the SSA. As per Rule 14 of Memorandum of Association (MOA), the meetings of the Parishad were to be held at least twice a year but no meeting was held with the result the annual accounts of SSA for the years 2003–04, 2004–05 and 2005–06 were submitted to GOI before getting clearance from Parishad (Report on Monitoring of the Financial Management and Procurement Relating to SSA in Uttar Pradesh, 2007). Besides, the project activities could not be reviewed/monitored by the highest statutory body at state level. The District Education Project Committee has to meet at an interval of two months in June, August, October, December, February and April of each year.

## Implementation apparatus of SSA: Chhattisgarh

To illustrate the implementation apparatus, we will discuss the structure and organization of SSA in Chhattisgarh (Figure 7.2). The state government of Chhattisgarh has established a registered society to receive, disburse and account for funds and to oversee project implementation. Rajiv

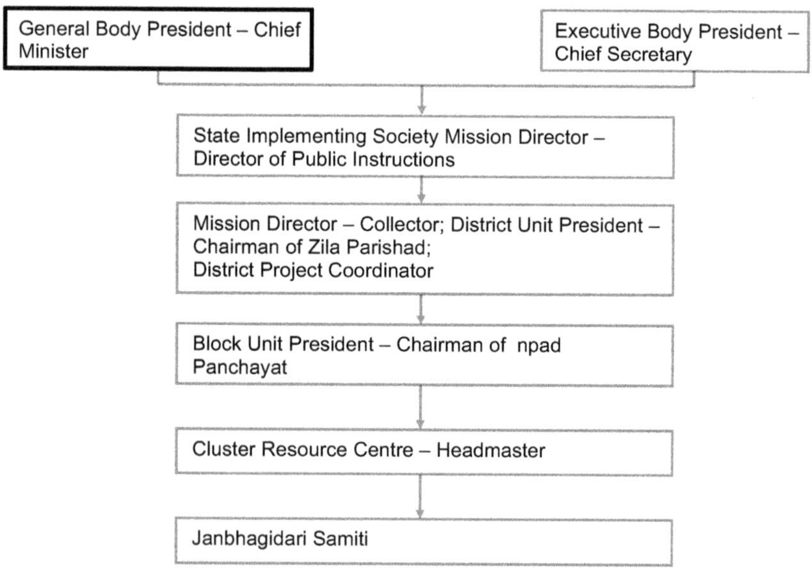


*Figure 7.2* Structure of SSA in Chhattisgarh

*Source:* State Project Office, Raipur.

Gandhi Shiksha Mission (RGSM), the society that implemented the District Primary Education Programme (DPEP), continues to support the implementation of SSA. The State Implementation Society (SIS) is set up with a core staff performing two types of functions: (i) managerial staff to perform supervisory function and (ii) execution staff who are directly involved with the project implementation process. The technical structure envisaged at the state level include State Council of Educational Research & Training (SCERT) and State Institute of Educational Management & Training (SIEMAT), with support from National institutes to assist districts to introduce improved classroom practices and in-service teacher training and orientation of educational administrators. The State Project Office (SPO) in Chhattisgarh, also known as the RGSM, compiles the Annual Work Plan and Budget (AWPB) for the state and submits the revised version of the plan to the Executive Committee of the state society. The state transmits the plan to the Project Approval Board (PAB), Government of India, for approval, which after meeting circulates its minutes with the revised AWPB to the state and districts. It is observed that the planning process is very elaborate and time consuming. There is no scope for any mid-year revision of the AWPB once it is approved.

In Chhattisgarh, it has been proposed to draft the plans in Hindi by the districts to have a better say of local experience in project formulation. But, several problems such as copying the format of other states, submission of the plan in English to the Government of India (GOI) were shared by officials at the RGSM. Constraints at the district level include rigid format for the plan leaving very little scope for the districts to modify their respective plans and thereby address the local needs. While the guidelines outline the need for transparency in all the decision-making processes, perceptions gathered from select officials in the RGSM point to the contrary.

## Bottlenecks in implementation

Having looked at the planning and institutional structure for SSA, we turn our attention to examining some of the implementation challenges that have plagued SSA since the scheme has been operational. These can be categorized as related to (i) under-utilization of funds, (ii) quality of fund utilization and (iii) institutional and budgetary processes that constrain fund utilization.

***(i) Fund utilization in SSA:*** With regard to fund utilization, although SSA is significantly better than spending under other schemes, concerns regarding adequacy of spending persist. At the national level, the extent of fund utilization under SSA as a proportion of total funds available

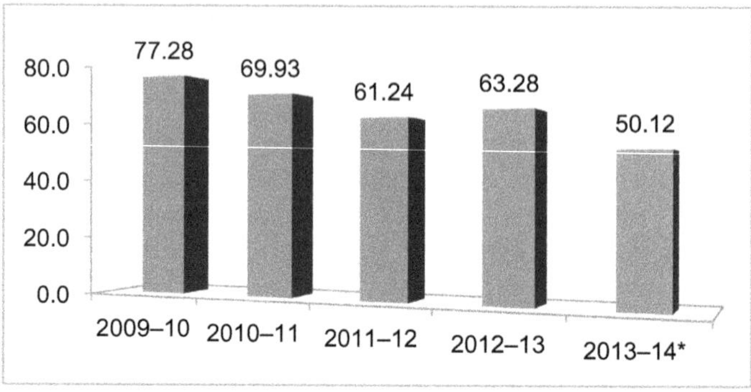


*Figure 7.3* Fund utilization in SSA at the national level, 2009–10 to 2013–14

*Source:* Compiled from Joint Review Mission Reports accessible at: http://www.ssa.nic.in/monitoring/joint-review-mission-ssa-1.

*Note:* Utilization figures for 2013–14 are up to November 2013. Figures include KGBV and NPEGEL allocations and expenditures.

(Figure 7.3) hovers at about 63 per cent (2012–13). It has also been observed that several states are unable to utilize funds adequately, they being: Bihar, Jharkhand, Madhya Pradesh, Orissa, Punjab, Uttaranchal and West Bengal.

It is useful to note here that unlike in the case of schemes such as National Health Mission (NHM), there is a tendency towards over-reporting in SSA. In SSA, even until 2009–10, disbursement of advances to the subsequent level of programme implementation was treated as expenditure. While some states like Himachal Pradesh, Rajasthan, Tamil Nadu, Chhattisgarh and Uttar Pradesh show noticeable increase in fund utilization levels, the break-down of the expenditure data reveals that this is largely attributable to two developments: recruitment of large number of para-teachers, and better utilization of funds in civil works while comparable utilization in other components is still not very high. Fund utilization concerns are not limited only to the national level; we find its manifestation at the sub-national levels as well, i.e. state, district and down to the school level. Tables 7.6 to 7.12 present evidence in this regard.

***(ii) Quality of fund utilization in SSA:*** To assess the quality of spending, we define some parameters of quality, such as skewed spending across financial quarters in a year, skewed spending across components and skewed spending on non-wage components. In the case of SSA, as in most other Centrally Sponsored Schemes (CSSs), most of the spending is towards the

*Table 7.6* Fund utilization in SSA in Chhattisgarh

| *Financial year* | *Approved budget (in Rs. million)* | *Available fund (in Rs. million)* | *Expenditure (in Rs. million)* | *Expenditure as % of available fund* | *Expenditure as % of approved budget* |
|---|---|---|---|---|---|
| 2001–02 | 78.0 | 0.0 | 0.0 | 0.0 | 0.0 |
| 2002–03 | 754.4 | 375.2 | 210.6 | 56.1 | 27.9 |
| 2003–04 | 2,183.0 | 1,180.8 | 755.9 | 64.0 | 34.6 |
| 2004–05 | 3,939.6 | 3,267.7 | 2,942.5 | 90.0 | 74.7 |
| 2005–06 | 5,506.8 | 4,356.9 | 4,274.7 | 98.1 | 77.6 |
| 2006–07 | 8,213.2 | 6,803.2 | 6,434.2 | 93.3 | 78.3 |
| 2007–08 | 7,644.3 | 4,784.4 | 4,129.4 | 86.3 | 54.0 |

*Source:* Data from 2001–02 to 2007–08 collected by CBGA from State Project Office, Rajiv Gandhi Shiksha Mission, Chhattisgarh, 2008. Data for 2012–13 compiled from Consolidated Audited Financial Statement for SSA in Chhattisgarh for 2012–13. Data on approved budget for Chhattisgarh accessed from Annexe C to G, from Minutes of 37th Quarterly Review Meeting of State Finance Controllers, March 2013.

*Table 7.7a* Fund utilization in SSA in Uttar Pradesh (Rs. in millions)

| *Year* | *Approved AWP&B* | *Unspent balance (spill over funds)* | *Funds released* | | | | | *Total funds available* |
|---|---|---|---|---|---|---|---|---|
| | | | *Funds released by GoI* | *Funds released by GoI* | *Total funds released* | | | |
| 2001–02 | 1,880.6 | 0.0 | 766.3 | 135.2 | 901.5 | 901.5 | 3583 | 39.74 |
| 2002–03 | 4,307.6 | 543.4 | 2,016.6 | 672.2 | 2,688.8 | 3,232.2 | 18,477 | 57.17 |
| 2003–04 | 10,588.4 | 1,384.3 | 3,336.3 | 1,112.1 | 4,448.4 | 5,832.7 | 47,427 | 81.31 |
| 2004–05 | 16,044.6 | 1,136.2 | 8,776.1 | 2,925.4 | 11,701.5 | 12,837.7 | 125,166 | 97.50 |
| 2005–06 | 26,418.9 | 475.6 | 18,279.9 | 6,093.3 | 24,373.2 | 24,848.8 | 223,374 | 89.89 |
| 2006–07 | 36,790.1 | 2,530.3 | 21,833.6 | 8,551.9 | 30,385.5 | 32,915.8 | 280,525 | 85.23 |
| 2007–08 | 34,415.2 | 2,525.3 | 20,475.8 | 11,413.9 | 31,889.7 | 34,415.1 | 293,509 | 85.28 |

*Notes*

1 AWP&B = Annual Work Plan & Budget.

2 Total Funds Available in the Financial Year = Unspent balance + Funds released in the year.

3 Figures for 2005–06 and 2006–07 include NPEGEL along with SSA figures. NPEGEL accounts for a small share of total expenditure under SSA. In 2006–07, the expenditure on NPEGEL accounted for less than 6 per cent of the total expenditure under SSA Framework in UP.

*Table 7.7b* Fund utilization in SSA in Uttar Pradesh (%)

| *Year* | *Expenditure as % of total funds released* | *Expenditure as % of total funds available* | *Expenditure as % of approved outlay* |
|---|---|---|---|
| 2001–02 | 39.7 | 39.7 | 19.1 |
| 2002–03 | 68.7 | 57.2 | 42.9 |
| 2003–04 | 106.6 | 81.3 | 44.8 |
| 2004–05 | 107.0 | 97.5 | 78.0 |
| 2005–06 | 91.6 | 89.9 | 84.6 |
| 2006–07 | 92.3 | 85.2 | 76.3 |
| 2007–08 | 92.0 | 85.2 | 89.3 |

*Source:* Office of Zila Basic Shiksha Adhikari, Sarva Shiksha Abhiyan, Lalitpur, 2008.

*Table 7.8* Fund utilization in SSA in Chhattisgarh

| | *2004–05* | *2005–06* | *2006–07* |
|---|---|---|---|
| Funds available (in Rs. million) | 91.1 | 190.4 | 281.9 |
| Total received (in Rs. million) | 90.0 | 184.1 | 280.4 |
| Total expenditure (in Rs. million) | 64.1 | 190.7 | 274.3 |
| Expenditure as a proportion of total funds available (%) | 70.33 | 100.13 | 97.29 |

*Source:* State Project Office, Rajiv Gandhi Shiksha Mission, Chhattisgarh, 2008.

*Table 7.9* Fund utilization in SSA in Uttar Pradesh

| **2004–05** | | | | | | |
|---|---|---|---|---|---|---|
| *Programme* | *Total funds available* | *DPO expenditure* | *Funds transferred to VEC/ BRC/ NPRC* | *Total expenditure* | *Expenditure at VEC/BRC/ NPRC as a % of funds available* | *Expenditure as a % of funds available* |
| DPO (SSA & NPEGEL) | 106,824,630 | 1,339,700 | 92,242,250 | 93,581,950 | 86.35 | 87.60 |
| DIET(SSA & NPEGEL) | 4,180,868 | 235,838 | 1,555,485 | 1,791,323 | 37.20 | 42.85 |
| Total | 111,005,498 | 1,575,538 | 93,797,735 | 95,373,273 | 84.50 | 85.92 |
| **2006–07** | | | | | | |
| DPO (SSA & NPEGEL) | 215,471 | 13,258 | 187,837 | 201,096 | 87.18 | 93.33 |
| DIET(SSA & NPEGEL) | 6,498 | 1,021 | 1,298 | 2,320 | 19.98 | 35.70 |
| Total | 221,970 | 14,280 | 189,135 | 203,416 | 85.21 | 91.64 |

*Source:* Office of Zila Basic Shiksha Adhikari, Sarva Shiksha Abhiyan, Lalitpur, 2008.

*Table 7.10* Fund utilization in SSA in Chhattisgarh: Case School 1

| | *2002–03* | *2003–04* | *2004–05* | *2005–06* |
|---|---|---|---|---|
| Total funds available (in Rs.) | 5,200 | 11,700 | 12,400 | 6,100 |
| Total expenditure (in Rs.) | 3,000 | 8,000 | 10,300 | 5,300 |
| Unspent balance (in Rs.) | 2,200 | 3,700 | 2,100 | 800 |
| Expenditure as a % of total funds received | 57.69 | 68.38 | 83.06 | 86.89 |

*Source:* Primary School Salhetola, Block Chhuria, District Rajnandgaon, 2008.

*Table 7.11* Fund utilization in SSA in Chhattisgarh: Case School 2

| | *2003–04* | *2004–05* | *2005–06* | *2006–07* | *2007–08* |
|---|---|---|---|---|---|
| Total funds available (in Rs.) | 11,580 | 17,894 | 11,944 | 11,328 | 9,355 |
| Total expenditure (in Rs.) | 5,451 | 16,950 | 8,260 | 10,983 | 8,041 |
| Unspent balance (in Rs.) | 7,894 | 944 | 3,684 | 355 | 1,314 |
| Expenditure as a % of total funds received | 47.07 | 94.72 | 69.15 | 96.95 | 85.95 |

*Source:* Primary School Khobha, Block Chhuria, District Rajnandgaon, 2008.

*Table 7.12* Pattern in fund flow from centre to state in Chhattisgarh

| *Financial year* | *Month of sanction (financial quarter)* | *Central share – month of receipt by SIS(financial quarter)* | *State share – month of receipt by SIS(financial quarter)* |
|---|---|---|---|
| 2004–05 | Jun (1st) | Jul (2nd) | Aug (2nd) |
| | Aug (2nd) | Sep (2nd) | Sep (2nd) |
| | Feb (4th) | Mar (4th) | Feb (4th) |
| | | | Mar (4th) |
| 2005–06 | Jun (1st) | Jul (2nd) | Aug (2nd) |
| | Oct (3rd) | Oct (3rd) | Dec (3rd) |
| | | Jan (4th) | Feb (4th) |
| | | Feb (4th) | Feb (4th) |
| 2006–07 | | Apr (1st) | May (2nd) |
| | | Jul (2nd) | Sep (2nd) |
| | | Dec (3rd) | |
| 2007–08 | May (1st) | Jun (1st) | Jul (2nd) |
| | | Sep (2nd) | |
| | | Dec (3rd) | |

*Source:* Collected by CBGA Team from State Project Office, Rajiv Gandhi Shiksha Mission, Chhattisgarh, 2008.

third and fourth financial quarters. Based on data analysis for four years, we find fund flow from centre to state continues to be skewed to the last two financial quarters (Table 7.12). Table 7.12 examines the periodicity of release of funds from the GOI and the state government to the SIS (RGSM) over 2004–05 to 2007–08. While the guidelines specify that the State share must be transferred to the SIS within a month of receipt of the share from the GOI, instances of delay in the state share have been found in Chhattisgarh.

A more detailed scrutiny of the proportion of funds flow as well as the number of instalments made at the state and district levels reflect divergence from the mandated guidelines (Tables 7.13 to 7.15). As in Table 7.13, the distribution of total disbursements is skewed with the major share of transfers happening at the very end of the year. The situation in 2006–07 is indicative of this phenomenon with just 0.98 per cent of the total as the first instalment while over 31 per cent was released only as the seventh instalment.

Not only is this a matter of concern that majority of the funds transferred are disbursed at the end of the year but also that there are so many instalments of fund flowing through one year, making the system work more in

*Table 7.13* Distribution of total disbursements in SSA in Chhattisgarh, 2004–07

| *Financial year* | *I* | *II* | *III* | *IV* | *V* | *VI* | *VII* | *VIII* |
|---|---|---|---|---|---|---|---|---|
| 2004–05 | 13.07 | 15.46 | 9.57 | 16.56 | 6.25 | 8.83 | 25.03 | 5.18 |
| 2005–06 | 5.37 | 3.13 | 37.46 | 12.23 | 0.59 | 14.92 | 25.67 | 0.59 |
| 2006–07 | 0.98 | 7.38 | 40.55 | 9.85 | 0.32 | 0.82 | 31.19 | 8.88 |
| 2007–08 | 38.6 | 32.57 | 4.94 | 23.88 | 0 | 0 | 0 | 0 |

*Source:* State Project Office, Rajiv Gandhi Shiksha Mission, Chhattisgarh, 2008.

*Table 7.14* Delay in receipt of funds under SSA in Uttar Pradesh

| *Year* | *No. of instalments* | | *% share of receipts in the 3rd quarter* | *% share of receipts in the 4th quarter* |
|---|---|---|---|---|
| | *Centre* | *State* | | |
| 2004–05 | 5 | 10 | 4.21 | 35.39 |
| 2005–06 | 6 | 11 | 30.69 | 16.47 |
| 2006–07 | 4 | 12 | 38.71 | 0 |

*Source:* UP EFAPB Office, Lucknow, 2008.

*Table 7.15* Share of expenditure across different quarters in Chhattisgarh

| *BEO/BRCC Dongargaon* | *2006–07* | *Expenditure share across quarters (%)* | *2007–08* | *Expenditure share across quarters (%)* |
|---|---|---|---|---|
| Quarter I | 974,882 | 23.77 | 1,008,800 | 16.92 |
| Quarter II | 857,307 | 20.90 | 1,097,761 | 18.41 |
| Quarter III | 263,600 | 6.43 | 3,113,288 | 52.22 |
| Quarter IV | 2,005,927 | 48.90 | 741,756 | 12.44 |
| Total | 4,101,716 | | 5,961,605 | |
| Total instalments | 19 | | 27 | |

*Source:* Basic *Shiksha Adhikari* Office, Block Dongargaon, District Rajnandgaon, 2008.

managing the fund flow rather than focus on quality of service delivery. As against the stipulated two instalments, there were eight instalments in 2004–05, seven in 2005–06, six in 2006–07 and five instalments in 2007–08. A course correction is observed only in 2007–08 when the first instalment is also the maximum with a total of four instalments for the year – a considerable achievement over the previous years.

The factors that lead to this are discussed in the next sub-section. Skewed spending across various components is another indicator of the quality of funds utilized. It is found that fund utilization is better for components that are more in the nature of disbursements, i.e. teachers' salary, school grants, maintenance grants and teacher grants while the expenditures are low for training and non-wage components such as monitoring and supervision, maintenance, etc. (Tables 7.16 to 7.18). Comparing Chhattisgarh and Uttar Pradesh in 2011–12, we find gross under-spending on crucial components such as BRCs, Community Mobilization, Innovative Activity, Electrification, Research & Evaluation and Community Training.

Spending on critical components that have a bearing on the quality of the scheme implementation has been on the decline (Table 7.17). TLE (dropped from 25 per cent in 2004–05 to less than 2 per cent in 2006–07) and Maintenance Grant (from 13 per cent in 2004–05 to 3 per cent in 2006–07) registered a sharp fall in the share of spending. Items such as CRC, Management Cost, School Grant, Teacher Grant and Teacher Training also show a decreasing trend in spending as a proportion of total spending under SSA in Rajnandgaon. It is also worthwhile to note that there has been no spending under SIEMAT and NPEGEL in the three years. Thus, it becomes clear that the spending priority under the scheme is

*Table 7.16* Component-wise spending in SSA in Chhattisgarh and Uttar Pradesh, 2011–12

| *Components* | *Chhattisgarh* | *Uttar Pradesh* |
|---|---|---|
| Teacher's salary | 44.38 | 41.75 |
| Teacher's grant | 98.72 | 92.75 |
| BRCs | 18.91 | 2.91 |
| CRCs | 36.65 | 37.86 |
| Teacher's training | 50.98 | 31.53 |
| Out of school children | 0 | 85.27 |
| Special training | 17.08 | 0 |
| Free textbooks | 45.66 | 16.76 |
| Two set of uniforms to children in govt. schools | 30.44 | 43.99 |
| Inclusive education | 20.56 | 45.61 |
| BRC (civil) | 17.63 | 73.43 |
| CRC (civil) | 6 | 0 |
| Total school | 54.55 | 32.01 |
| Additional classrooms | 27.3 | 77.52 |
| Toilets (no. of schools) | 27.21 | 100 |
| Drinking water (no. of schools) | 124.09 | 100 |
| Boundary wall | 5.51 | 77.73 |
| Separation wall | 0 | 0 |
| Electrification | 7.21 | 0 |
| Office-cum-store | 14.75 | 0 |
| Major repairs | 0.1 | 0 |
| Total civil works | 20.37 | 56.41 |
| Teaching learning equipment | 100 | 0.12 |
| Maintenance grant | 81.51 | 89.46 |
| School grant | 99.6 | 93.24 |
| Research & evaluation | 4.92 | 9.24 |
| Management cost & MIS SPO | 35.72 | 38.03 |
| Community mobilization | 13.36 | 0 |
| Learning enhancement | 22.41 | 0.65 |
| Innovative activity | 18 | 7.07 |
| Community training | 1.83 | 0.02 |
| Management & MIS district | 23.01 | 36.9 |
| Residential schools for specific category of children | 11.19 | 0 |
| Total outlay approved (SSA) | 31.26 | 43.85 |
| Total outlay approved (NPEGEL) | 17.49 | 64.78 |
| Total expenditure (SSA & NPEGEL) | *31.17* | *44.13* |

*Source:* Compiled from SSA website accessible at http://ssa.nic.in/page_portletlinks?foldername=financial-management.

*Table 7.17* Component-wise spending in SSA in Chhattisgarh, 2004–05 to 2006–07

| *Items* | *2004–05* | *%* | *2005–06* | *%* | *2006–07* | *%* |
|---|---|---|---|---|---|---|
| Teacher salary | 41.25 | 6.44 | 252.11 | 13.22 | 513.17 | 18.71 |
| BRC | 1.66 | 0.26 | 16.76 | 0.88 | 17.30 | 0.63 |
| CRC | 6.32 | 0.99 | 7.61 | 0.40 | 5.67 | 0.21 |
| Civil works | 169.12 | 26.39 | 887.14 | 46.52 | 1,680.84 | 61.28 |
| EGS/AIE | 0.00 | 0.00 | 0.71 | 0.04 | 2.32 | 0.08 |
| Free textbook | 19.90 | 3.10 | 270.09 | 14.16 | 169.19 | 6.17 |
| Innovation | 0.00 | 0.00 | 27.89 | 1.46 | 0.11 | 0.00 |
| IED | 0.09 | 0.01 | 1.49 | 0.08 | 8.80 | 0.32 |
| Maintenance grant | 87.21 | 13.61 | 107.23 | 5.62 | 88.76 | 3.24 |
| Management cost | 17.08 | 2.66 | 40.09 | 2.10 | 40.02 | 1.46 |
| Research & evaluation | 0.81 | 0.13 | 20.41 | 1.07 | 13.01 | 0.47 |
| School grant | 26.27 | 4.10 | 49.38 | 2.59 | 49.22 | 1.79 |
| Teacher grant | 27.72 | 4.32 | 30.09 | 1.58 | 24.87 | 0.91 |
| TLE | 163.60 | 25.53 | 93.90 | 4.92 | 50.02 | 1.82 |
| Teacher training | 20.16 | 3.15 | 85.83 | 4.50 | 72.65 | 2.65 |
| Community mobilization | 0.00 | 0.00 | 6.94 | 0.36 | 6.89 | 0.25 |
| BRC salary | 13.43 | 2.10 | – | – | – | – |
| CRC salary | 46.27 | 7.22 | – | – | – | – |
| Total | 640.94 | | 1,906.99 | | 2,742.90 | |

*Source:* State Project Office, Rajiv Gandhi Shiksha Mission, Chhattisgarh, 2008.

*Note:* Absolute figures are in Rs. million.

*Table 7.18a* Utilization of funds at village level in SSA in Lalitpur, Uttar Pradesh (in Rs. thousand)

| *Component* | *2005–06* | | | *2006–07* | | |
|---|---|---|---|---|---|---|
| | *Amount released to VEC* | *UC received* | *%* | *Amount released to VEC* | *UC received* | *%* |
| New school construction | 17,234 | 15,855 | 92.0 | 37,320 | 37,320 | 100.0 |
| Additional classroom | 54,810 | 54,810 | 100.0 | 87,500 | 86,800 | 99.2 |
| Electrification | 0 | 0 | 0.0 | 1,575 | 788 | 50.0 |

(*Continued*)

*Table 7.18a* (Continued)

| *Component* | *2005–06* | | | *2006–07* | | |
|---|---|---|---|---|---|---|
| | *Amount released to VEC* | *UC received* | *%* | *Amount released to VEC* | *UC received* | *%* |
| School development grant | 2,220 | 2,220 | 100.0 | 2,248 | 2,248 | 100.0 |
| TLM | 1,443 | 1,443 | 100.0 | 1,672 | 1,672 | 100.0 |
| TLE | 1,610 | 1,590 | 98.8 | 3,320 | 3,320 | 100.0 |
| BRC/NPRC/CRC | 458 | 458 | 100.0 | 442 | 442 | 100.0 |
| Maintenance grant | 4,146 | 4,146 | 100.0 | 5,194 | 5,194 | 100.0 |
| EGS/AIE | 2,188 | 2,188 | 100.0 | 397 | 325 | 81.8 |
| NBRC | 0 | 0 | 0.0 | 836 | 836 | 100.0 |
| ECCE | 834 | 834 | 100.0 | 785 | 735 | 93.6 |
| REMS | 0 | 0 | 0.0 | 436 | 358 | 82.0 |
| Shiksha Mitra Honorarium | 6,888 | 6,888 | 100.0 | 33,371 | 29,700 | 89.0 |
| SC/ST intervention | 0 | 0 | 0.0 | 323 | 323 | 100.0 |
| NPEGEL | 16,188 | 15,788 | 97.5 | 10,961 | 5,200 | 47.4 |
| Boundary wall | 4,026 | 3,981 | 98.9 | 0 | 0 | |
| VEC training | 53 | 53 | 100.0 | 0 | 0 | |
| Total | 112,096 | 110,252 | 98.4 | 186,380 | 175,260 | 94.0 |

*Source:* Office of Zila Basic Shiksha Adhikari, Sarva Shiksha Abhiyan, Lalitpur, 2008.

*Table 7.18b* Utilization of funds at village level in SSA in Lalitpur, Uttar Pradesh, 2007–08

| *Component* | *Amount released to VEC (in Rs. thousand)* | *UC received (in Rs. thousand)* | *% utilization* |
|---|---|---|---|
| New school construction (UPS) | 33,023 | 16,512 | 50 |
| ACR | 77,200 | 38,500 | 49.87 |
| Development grant | 2,526 | 1,263 | 50 |
| School repair | 5,790 | 2,896 | 50.01 |
| TLM | 1,863 | 1,863 | 100 |

| *Component* | *Amount released to VEC (in Rs. thousand)* | *UC received (in Rs. thousand)* | *% utilization* |
|---|---|---|---|
| TLE | 2,780 | 0 | 0 |
| Meeting/TA | 159 | 159 | 100 |
| Contingency | 209 | 209 | 100 |
| SC/ST intervention | 324 | 0 | 0 |
| ECCE | 1,536 | 768 | 50 |
| REMS | 533 | 267 | 50.09 |
| EGS | 1,882 | 941 | 50 |
| AIE | 1,821 | 911 | 50.02 |
| NBRC | 950 | 475 | 50 |
| DIET | 2,772 | 1,386 | 50 |
| Awards to school | 270 | 270 | 100 |
| Uniform/workbook for girls | 7,737 | 7,240 | 93.57 |
| Community mobilization | 538 | 538 | 100 |
| Library, sports | 1,080 | 1,080 | 100 |
| Total | 142,993 | 75,278 | 52.64 |

*Source:* Office of Zila Basic Shiksha Adhikari, Sarva Shiksha Abhiyan, Lalitpur, 2008.

skewed and attributable to poor planning and lack of coordination between the different implementing agencies.

***(iii) Institutional and budgetary factors constraining fund utilization:*** In order to facilitate drawing of recommendations for corrective measures, major factors can be clubbed under deficiencies in the process of decentralized planning in the schemes; bottlenecks in budgetary processes; and systemic weaknesses.

*(a) Deficiencies in planning:* In a district, owing to *multiple plans being formulated and implemented*, the true spirit of decentralized planning continues to be more of a concept. In 2008–09, there are more than 125 plan schemes implemented in Chhattisgarh while there were 336 plan schemes operational in Uttar Pradesh. Related to this is the problem of *low community involvement*. Since the Panchayat level functionaries are also responsible for overall implementation of other schemes at the district level, such as National Rural Employment Guarantee Scheme and Ambedkar Gram Yojana, a sense of ownership is absent among the staff with regard to SSA. *Delays involved in the planning process of the scheme* also derail the smooth

implementation of the scheme. Field observations reveal that the State Project Office was left with just five months to implement the entire year's plan in 2008 as the approval from the Project Approval Board took over six months to come through. Moreover, the district plans do not reflect the actual demands from the field as plans submitted in English are mostly cut–paste jobs (as shared by officials in the State Project Office).

*(b) Bottlenecks in budgetary processes:* Several hurdles relating to the existing budgetary processes in SSA impede effective fund utilization. Weak reporting of financial information by the financial management staff is a vital gap.[2] Instances of *irregularities in financial reporting* based on the Reports of Internal Audit and Accounts for Chhattisgarh and Rajnandgaon revealed the following gaps: delay in settlement of advances provided for procurement and other activities; reported mismatch with regard to Fixed Assets register maintenance and frequent physical verification of assets; transfer of funds under School Grant, Teacher Grant, Maintenance Grant and Teaching Learning Equipment (TLE) Grant to the account of BRC and CRC instead of the Mission instructions of transferring the money directly into the account of the schools.

Even at the school level (Primary School Bhiloni Lodha, Barh block, Lalitpur), no set guidelines are being followed for reporting as the UC also includes components of another scheme – Integrated Child Development Services (ICDS), i.e. Honoraria of Anganwadi Worker (AWW), Anganwadi Helper (AWH) and the Provisions for the Anganwadi Centre (AWC). Such irregularities are closely linked to issues of poor capacity. The *capacity of programme staff* to undertake the financial processes related to the scheme are woefully inadequate.

To add to this, the Programme Delivery and the Accounts staff are overburdened with *multiple reporting requirements*. This is compounded by staff shortage and untrained staff. Over-burdened accounts staff seems to be engaged most of the time in managing money in transit and ensuring that the reporting of the same gets done. It is thus not only counter-productive to the overall financial management processes by putting undue stress on the financial staff but also leads to immense delays in the scheme implementation and money lying unutilized for long periods. On the other hand, Programme Delivery staff, i.e. the teacher, also has multiple non-teaching responsibilities that keep them away from providing quality education.

Further, the problem related to *weak monitoring and supervision* also leads to ineffective implementation. The number of schools falling under the purview of one CRC is unwieldy and unmanageable. According to the norms, one CRC caters to about 10–12 schools. However, in Mohala block in Rajnandgaon, there were 10 clusters and 400 schools, making each CRC cater to about 40 schools, making it impossible to do any effective monitoring.

Moreover, *rigid norms and guidelines* in the scheme also lead to poor fund utilization and concomitantly poor outcomes. Stipulations under SSA such as need for provision of Completion Certificate by implementing agencies to the accounts division, failing which money would be treated as advance in the records compound the problem of utilization. In the case of the monitoring mechanism being unsound along with poor implementation at the grassroots level, it translates into poor fund utilization.

Lack of cooperation of the Gram Pradhan (President) in facilitating timely completion of activities such as disbursing uniforms, recruitment of Shiksha Mitra and proper use of money coming under the head of School Improvement Grant (SIG) have been cited as a case of *poor coordination.*[3] The common practice in most schools is to spend the money under School Improvement Grant (SIG) on painting the walls. Instances are aplenty where school buildings have not been completed owing to the Gram Pradhan not releasing the money (Didora village, Lalitpur).

Another vital concern relates to lack *of decentralization of financial powers*. The DPC although the authority at the district level to implement SSA has no financial powers to sanction funds. It is the District Magistrate (DM), also the District Mission Director (DMD) for SSA, who is the financial sanctioning authority. The DPC has a sanctioning authority on any amount under Rs. 25,000 (Rajnandgaon). This constrains day-to-day implementation as even for spending Rs. 700 a day beyond the specified Rs. 25,000, the DPC needs approval from the DM's office that is time-consuming, depending on the availability of the DM, other pressing matters and the chain of command followed at the DM's office to move the file for approval.

Key to the discussion on ineffective implementation and inadequate fund utilization is incidence of *delay in fund transfers* from one level of government to the other. Illustrations from the field on the time taken by funds to move from the SPO, Lucknow, to the DPO, Lalitpur, and further down to the VEC reveal that most of the money travels in the third and fourth quarters and remains parked for considerable time periods in the DPO despite having been officially disbursed. The SPO Lucknow released funds to the DPO Lalitpur in a total of *29 instalments* in 2007–08. Moving on, the DPO released this money in a total of *19 instalments*. This substantiates the, by now, well-known problem of over-burdened accounts staff who seem to be engaged most of the time in managing the money in transit and ensuring that the reporting of the same gets done. It is thus not only counter-productive to the overall financial management processes by putting undue stress on the financial staff but also leads to immense delays in the scheme implementation and money lying unutilized for long periods.

For instance, money for the BRC – Travel Allowance, Teaching Learning Material (TLM) and Contingency – was disbursed from the SPO in August 2007 (second quarter of the financial year) but was released by the Basic Shiksha Adhikari (BSA), DPO only by February 2008 (last quarter of the financial year). This apart, the money was parked at the SPO for *190 days* (Table A7.1 in Appendix). Given that the BRC serves as a professional support agency by providing decentralized training and teacher support activities, delay in receiving money disrupts implementation. Travelling to distant schools to provide continuous support to teachers and preparation of Teaching Learning Materials (TLM) are some of the critical activities that would be adversely affected.

Further, illustrations of money being spent merely for the sake of spending without rationalizing the objectives are also many, such as spending towards printing a Training Module on Gender Sensitization with the money coming in as late as on 29 March 2008, that too with the amount having been parked in the SPO for 32 days. Money for MIS Data Entry, Computer Education were disbursed by the SPO on 31 March 2008 and released by the DPO the very same day. With money coming in on the very last day of the financial year, it is clear that neither much of MIS data entry work nor any computer education would have been attempted at the district and the levels further down in 2007–08. At the school level also, delay in fund transfers are found.[4]

*(c) Systemic weaknesses:* Apart from the problems outlined, vital to the effective utilization of funds and proper implementation of any programme is a strong government apparatus to support and take forward any of these development initiatives. *Staff availability*, a critical indicator to assess the progress of a scheme, remains a challenge. This is true for both the Programme as well as the Accounts staff. Substantial vacancies in Programme and Finance Management staff at the district and state levels also lead to ineffective implementation. Lack of proper staff at all levels hampers various activities including implementation, planning, monitoring, reporting, training, etc. (see Tables 7.19a and 7.19b).

Related to the issue of staff shortage is the *poor capacity of available staff*. Absence of adequately trained personnel to implement the programme is also reflected in the low priority to this component in the scheme in terms of finances. Another aspect related to human resources is the *short tenure of the key implementing officials* of the programme. Findings from

*Table 7.19a* Availability of implementing officials (up to 30th Sep 2013)

| | *No. of districts/ CRCs* | *Sanctioned* | *In position* | *Vacant positions* |
|---|---|---|---|---|
| | State project officers (SPOs) | | | |
| Chhattisgarh | | 10 | 5 | 5 |
| Uttar Pradesh | | 29 | 17 | 12 |
| | District project officers (DPOs) | | | |
| Chhattisgarh | 27 | 81 | 61 | 20 |
| Uttar Pradesh | 75 | 150 | 89 | 61 |
| | Block resource centre coordinators (BRCCs) | | | |
| Chhattisgarh | 150 | 150 | 150 | 0 |
| Uttar Pradesh | 880 | 880 | 768 | 112 |

*Source:* Minutes of 39th Quarterly Review Meeting, Annexe J, accessible from: http://ssa.nic.in/financial-management/minutes-of-review-meeting-finance-controllers-of-sis/Minutes%20of%2039th%20Quarterly.

*Table 7.19b* Tenure of key officials in Lalitpur, Uttar Pradesh

| *Name of officials* | *Designation* | *Tenure* |
|---|---|---|
| Mr Adarsh Kumar Tripathi | BSA | 18.6.05–23.5.06 |
| Mr R K Verma | BSA | 23.5.06–17.6.06 |
| Mr Bhagwan Prasad Patel | BSA | 17.6.06–16.6.07 |
| Mr Naresh K. Verma | BSA | 16.6.07–02.7.08 |

*Source:* BSA Office, DPO, Lalitpur, 2008.

Lalitpur in Uttar Pradesh showed that the tenure of many important government officials was short with frequent transfers of key staff such as Basic *Shiksha Adhikari*, Block Development Officers and District Magistrates who have been in office for periods ranging from 15 to 20 days to two or four days.

Another critical aspect relating to systemic weaknesses is *poor infrastructure*. Lack of basic infrastructure is one of the important factors responsible for poor education indicators for both the states. Shortage of infrastructure leading to slow progress of the scheme remains a concern. Late start of civil works is another factor stalling scheme implementation. Field survey substantiates that children sit outside their school (Primary School Salhe Tola) in Chhuria block in Rajnandgaon that had only two classrooms for the 186 enrolled students.

## Concluding remarks

It becomes evident that despite considerable time having elapsed since the field investigation was conducted in the two states (and at the district and school levels), some of the challenges related to implementation persist.[5] While we find that some of the things have changed, for instance there is some improvement in fund flow due to improved systems and better banking arrangements with electronic mode of transfer of money from the state to the districts but the problem to resolve delayed and costly modes of transfer of funds to VEC (schools) remains.

Similarly, the number of levels/tranches through which funds are flowing has improved in most transfers from the centre to state (State Project Office) and from SPO to districts, but some states continue to be confronted by the concern to streamline this. Some specific improvements relate to trends in expenditure indicating that capacity to utilize funds have gone up, the Central Plan Scheme Monitoring System (CPSMS) registration has improved whereby more information can be accessed online in a timely and regular manner.

Having said this, we continue to observe manifestation of poor implementation by way of inadequate staffing, unreliable and untrained personnel (programmatic and financial), lack of coordination among different departments to implement specific interventions and so on that lead us to believe that despite some improvements, problems of effective implementation continue to rankle. These can only be addressed when there is sufficient capacity and scope for the state governments to plan these programmes in keeping with the state-specific contexts.

While it is still too early to comment on what would the implications of the central government's recent move to restructure the Planning Commission be on the working of these CSS, we would hope that some of our recommendations made in the past get reflected in this proposed change whereby the centre does away with some of the rigid conditionalities imposed on the states without the commensurate degree of flexibility inbuilt in the state's potential to mobilize revenue and implement these programmes in a locally relevant manner.

# APPENDIX

*Table A7.1* Funds in transit from state to district in SSA in Lalitpur, Uttar Pradesh

| *Component* | *Amount (in Rs.)* | *Date of disbursal from SPO* | *Date of release from BSA-DPO* | *Money in transit (no. of days)* |
|---|---|---|---|---|
| Salary | 500,000 | 2/6/2007 | 11/7/2007 | 39 |
| Maintenance grant (primary school) | 4,355,000 | 16/6/2007 | 11/7/2007 | 25 |
| Maintenance grant (U. primary school) | 1,980,000 | 16/6/2007 | 11/7/2007 | 25 |
| ECCE honorarium | 562,500 | 11/7/2007 | 24/8/2007 | 43 |
| Contingency & others | 40,000 | 25/7/2007 | 24/8/2007 | 30 |
| Shiksha Mitra Honorarium | 12,721,000 | 1/8/2007 | 24/8/2007 | 24 |
| Salary, travel allowance, contingency | 614,000 | 10/8/2007 | 31/8/2007 | 21 |
| TLM (primary school) | 1,124,500 | 18/8/2007 | 22/10/2007 | 64 |
| TLM (U. primary school) | 416,000 | 18/8/2007 | 22/10/2007 | 64 |
| BRC – travel allowance, TLM, contingency | 164,500 | 18/8/2007 | 28/2/2008 | **190** |
| NPRC – contingency | 289,100 | 18/8/2007 | 28/2/2008 | **190** |
| DPO – computer maintenance | 177,000 | 22/8/2007 | 28/2/2008 | **186** |

(*Continued*)

*Table A7.1* (Continued)

| *Component* | *Amount (in Rs.)* | *Date of disbursal from SPO* | *Date of release from BSA-DPO* | *Money in transit (no. of days)* |
|---|---|---|---|---|
| New primary school construction (1st instalment) | 1,746,000 | 23/8/2007 | 11/10/2007 | 48 |
| New U. primary school construction (1st instalment) | 14,580,000 | 23/8/2007 | 22/10/2007 | 60 |
| Additional classrooms (primary school) | 35,000,000 | 23/8/2007 | 22/10/2007 | 60 |
| Additional classrooms (U. primary school) | 3,500,000 | 23/8/2007 | 22/10/2007 | 60 |
| Integrated education for disabled | 526,800 | 1/9/2007 | 22/10/2007 | 51 |
| EGS/AIE | 2,639,250 | 10/9/2007 | 19/11/2007 | 69 |
| Overhead tank (primary school) | 1,584,000 | 8/9/2007 | 28/2/2008 | **168** |
| Overhead tank (U. primary school) | 2,460,000 | 8/9/2007 | 28/2/2008 | **168** |
| Research, evaluation, monitoring & supervision (REMS) | 20,000 | 8/9/2007 | 6/12/2007 | **148** |
| REMS (2nd instalment) | 150,500 | 22/10/2007 | 6/12/2007 | 46 |
| Residential bridge course | 3,705,800 | 24/9/2007 | 17/12/2007 | 83 |
| Shiksha Mitra Honorarium | 8,886,000 | 6/10/2007 | 19/11/2007 | 43 |
| School development grant | 2,410,000 | 6/10/2007 | 19/11/2007 | 43 |
| Free textbook | 9,007,000 | 3/11/2007 | 7/12/2007 | 34 |
| Shiksha Mitra Honorarium | 8,886,000 | 1/12/2007 | 18/12/2007 | 18 |
| New primary school construction (2nd instalment) | 1,746,000 | 1/12/2007 | 7/12/2007 | 7 |
| New U. primary school construction (2nd instalment) | 14,580,000 | 1/12/2007 | 7/12/2007 | 7 |
| Additional classrooms (primary school) | 35,000,000 | 1/12/2007 | 18/12/2007 | 18 |

| *Component* | *Amount (in Rs.)* | *Date of disbursal from SPO* | *Date of release from BSA-DPO* | *Money in transit (no. of days)* |
|---|---|---|---|---|
| Additional classrooms (U. primary school) | 3,500,000 | 1/12/2007 | 18/12/2007 | 18 |
| VEC training | 51,000 | 19/12/2007 | 24/1/2008 | 36 |
| Shiksha Mitra Honorarium | 8,886,000 | 11/1/2008 | 24/1/2008 | 14 |
| AIE honorarium | 560,000 | 11/1/2008 | 14/3/2008 | 64 |
| EGS honorarium | 600,000 | 11/1/2008 | 14/3/2008 | 64 |
| Salary | 1,169,500 | 11/1/2008 | 14/3/2008 | 64 |
| Travel allowance | 25,000 | 11/1/2008 | 14/3/2008 | 64 |
| Petrol, oil, lubricants (POL) | 100,000 | 11/1/2008 | 14/3/2008 | 64 |
| Vehicle hiring | 175,000 | 11/1/2008 | 14/3/2008 | 64 |
| Contingency & others | 200,000 | 11/1/2008 | 14/3/2008 | 64 |
| ECCE honorarium | 266,500 | 19/1/2008 | 14/3/2008 | 55 |
| Interim teachers honorarium | 416,000 | 19/1/2008 | 14/3/2008 | 55 |
| TLE | 2,780,000 | 23/2/2008 | 29/3/2008 | 36 |
| Girls education | 1,058,000 | 17/2/2008 | 29/3/2008 | 42 |
| Printing of training module (gender sensitization) | 9,148 | 27/2/2008 | 29/3/2008 | 32 |
| Equipment for resource centre (physiotherapy equipment for disabled children) | 87,500 | 28/2/2008 | 29/3/2008 | 31 |
| Shiksha Mitra Honorarium | 8,886,000 | 20/3/2008 | 29/3/2008 | 9 |
| Girls education | 380,000 | 26/3/2008 | 29/3/2008 | 3 |
| SC/ST intervention | 327,820 | 28/3/2008 | 29/3/2008 | 1 |
| JE/AE honorarium | 179,500 | 28/3/2008 | 31/3/2008 | 3 |
| MIS data entry | 30,000 | 31/3/2008 | 31/3/2008 | 0 |
| Computer education | 1,330,000 | 31/3/2008 | 31/3/2008 | 0 |
| Salary | 500,000 | 31/3/2008 | 31/3/2008 | 0 |

*Source:* Office of Zila Basic Shiksha Adhikari, Sarva Shiksha Abhiyan, Lalitpur, 2008.

## Notes

1 The chapter is based on analysis of secondary datasets compiled by government (DISE) and independent entities (Centre for Budget and Governance Accountability, Annual Survey of Education Report, Right to Education Forum and National Coalition for Education). On implementation constraints, the chapter draws primarily from evidence collected by CBGA from its 2008 study titled 'Constraints in Effective Utilisation of Funds in the Social Sector: A Study on Rajnandgaon (Chhattisgarh) and Lalitpur (Uttar Pradesh)' and significantly adds to the discussions through analysis of evidence from secondary government database. The authors wish to acknowledge Subrat Das, Jawed Alam Khan, GyanaRanjan Panda and Indranil who were also part of the CBGA Study. On education inputs, outputs and outcomes, apart from government data, the chapter relies on field assessments by ASER, RTE Forum and NCE studies.

2 Owing to poor capacity of the Management Information System (MIS) Unit in District Project Office, Lalitpur (there being only one ad-hoc MIS Data Entry Operator), the Statement of Expenditure (SoE) and the Ledger do not match. Another instance of poor record-keeping was found in Barh block in Lalitpur where the Assistant BRCC was unable to provide details of the trainings conducted and the materials purchased by the BRC.

3 Based on interview with Assistant BRCC, Block Barh, Lalitpur in 2008.

4 In 2007–08, money for all but one component came in the last two quarters, with the majority coming in the last (fourth) quarter of the financial year. While no money was received under the heads of Uniform, Cooking Gas, TLM and Maintenance, Honorarium for Shiksha Mitra had not come since January 2008 (as on August 2008). In a primary school surveyed in Chhuria block in Rajnandgaon, funds for School Grant, Maintenance Grant and Teacher Grant reached the school by December end.

5 39th Review Meeting of the State Finance Controllers, IPAI Review – based on Key Observations on Procurement, 28th–29th October 2013.

## References

Jha, Praveen and Pooja Parvati, 2014. '*Assessing Progress on Universal Elementary Education in India: A Note on Some Key Constraints*', Economic and Political Weekly, XlIX(16).

Joint Review Mission Reports, http://www.ssa.nic.in/monitoring/joint-review-mission-ssa-1.

MHRD, 2013. Analysis of Budgeted Expenditure on Education 2009–10 to 2011–12, Planning and Monitoring Unit, Department of Higher Education, Ministry of Human Resources and Development, GoI.

Minutes of 39th Quarterly Review Meeting, Annexe J, http://ssa.nic.in/financial-management/minutes-of-review-meeting-finance-controllers-of-sis/Minutes%20of%2039th%20Quarterly.

MOSPI, 2014. National Accounts Statistics, 2014, CSO.

RBI, 2012. *Handbook of Statistics on Indian Economy*, 2011–12, Reserve Bank of India, Mumbai, India.

39th Review Meeting of the State Finance Controllers, IPAI Review – Based on Key Observations on Procurement, 28–29 October 2013.

UNDP, 2013. Human Development Report 2013 – The Rise of the South: Human Progress in a Diverse World.

8

# PATTERN, TREND AND UTILISATION OF FUNDS UNDER SSA IN ODISHA

## Performance analysis of two sample districts

*Sailabala Debi and Surya N. Mishra*

### Introduction

The SSA, introduced in 2001–02 by the Government of India, aims at achieving the goal of universal elementary education (UEE) through mainstreaming all out-of-school (OoSC) children, bridging gender gap and social gap, universalising retention and improving overall quality of education in both primary and upper primary level. Despite significant achievements in almost all indicators of education, there are spatial/social/gender disparities in educational achievements all over India. Disparity is more pronounced in backward states/regions. The present study has attempted to examine both physical and financial achievements in elementary education in Odisha. Various programmes under SSA have been undertaken by the government and non-government agencies to achieve UEE within a stipulated time frame. In fact, substantial amount of funds have been allocated under SSA to achieve this goal. At the same time, it has also been observed that a substantial amount of total money allocated under SSA remains either unspent or un/underutilised. Now it is time to evaluate the programme in terms of performance of SSA based on expenditure made for various programmes in Odisha.

The chapter is divided into six sections. The first section describes the broad objectives and methods of analysis. In the second section, a brief outline of educational development of Odisha and general funding pattern for elementary education are presented. Third section presents the analysis of funding, utilisation and performance based on expenditure on different items under SSA. Some of the outcome indicators for primary education are discussed in this section. In fourth section, analysis of allocation and expenditure for sample districts is presented. The fifth section describes constraints of utilisation of funds in Odisha in general and in two sample districts in particular. The last section presents the conclusions and recommendations.

The broad *objectives* of the study are the following:

(i) to study the pattern and trend of financial performance based on expenditure under SSA;
(ii) to examine the linkage of financial resources with the physical target of SSA, particularly the quality component of education;
(iii) to evaluate the performance of SSA in two sample districts of Odisha;
(iv) to find out the constraints, if any, for full utilisation of funds under SSA.

### *Method of analysis*

In order to examine these objectives, this chapter concentrates on Odisha, which is an economically and educationally backward state with the demographic composition of about 40 per cent of its population being scheduled castes and scheduled tribes. After analysing the overall performance for the state as a whole, we have made an attempt to analyse the performance of SSA in two districts of the state. The district selection was made as per the allocation and expenditure under SSA (Table 8.12). Two districts were selected for the purpose on the basis of highest and lowest allocation and utilisation of funds. These districts are Ganjam, with the highest allocation, and Boudh, with the lowest allocation of funds.

The chapter is based on secondary data obtained mainly from Orissa Primary Education Programme Authority (OPEPA) office, Bhubaneswar, and Census Handbook and Statistical Abstract published by the Directorate of Statistics and Economics, Bhubaneswar. Various rounds of discussion with state and district officials were made to gather their opinions and observations on the reasons for non-utilisation of funds under SSA.

## Education in Odisha: a brief profile

Odisha is one of the educationally backward states associated with low levels of socioeconomic development. In this backdrop, it is necessary to examine the development of education so far and critically examine the

*Table 8.1* Literacy rate in Orissa over decades

| *Years* | *Male* | *Female* | *Total* | *GDI* |
|---|---|---|---|---|
| 1981 | 56.45 | 25.14 | 40.97 | 1.25 |
| 1991 | 63.09 | 34.68 | 49.09 | 0.82 |
| 2001 | 75.35 | 50.51 | 63.08 | 0.49 |
| 2011 | 82.40 | 64.36 | 73.45 | 0.28 |

*Source:* Census of India (2001 and 2011).

*Note:* GDI: gender disparity index = (male literacy/female literacy) – 1.

policies of the government for education. The selected indicators in this context are literacy, number of schools, enrolment, teachers and public expenditure on education. Despite a significant increase in the literacy rate in Odisha, there are significant regional and gender disparities in literacy rate. The gender disparity in literacy has declined over the years from 1.25 in 1981 to 0.28 in 2011 (Table 8.1).

The percentage of literacy has shown a significant improvement, but if we look at the female literacy we have moved forward by less than 7 per cent over the last five years or during the ongoing plan period. We are left with almost 36 per cent of female population yet to be mainstreamed.[1] Consider their situation in a global world, where they would not be able to write their names also. They will be subjected to multiple exploitations, such as informal labour, underpaid, harassed, etc., in various possible ways. We have not yet been able to achieve the target set in 10th plan or the vision document as well. The 11th plan does not have any specific focus to improve literacy situation, but National Literacy Mission (NLM), which was initiated in 1988 (7th plan), seems not to have achieved the desired target. It is necessary to improve the planning around achievement of 100 per cent literacy across gender and age group.

The perspective plan leading to actualsation of the Vision of Education for 2020 (*Vision 2020*) encompasses the following goals and milestones within the time frame prescribed for Odisha:

- GOAL-I: *Achieving a sustainable threshold level of 75 per cent literacy with at least 60 per cent female literacy by the end of the year 2005 and universal literacy by 2010.*

It is revealed that the goal of *Vision 2020* in respect of total literacy rate, *to achieve universal literacy by 2010*, was not achieved. But the target of sustainable threshold level of 75 per cent of literacy and female literacy rate of at least 60 per cent is achieved after six years, i.e. in 2011.

- GOAL-II: *All children, notwithstanding diversities and differences, should have equal and easy access to basic education of good quality comprising:*
  - Five years of Universal Primary Education (classes I to V) to be achieved by 2007
  - Eight years of UEE (classes I to VIII) by 2010
  - All children in school by 2003

Table 8.2 provides the information on enrolment in Odisha, which can explain the achievement in respect of goal-II of the vision document.

Table 8.2 clearly shows that the time scheduled for achieving each component of goal-II is over. The state is yet to achieve UEE (as reflected through NER), UPE and all children in school, which seems to be a remote chance even by 2015 unless all the OoSC are mainstreamed by the end of 2015. The state is striving hard to achieve all the targets in time for which the main constraint is its sociocultural diversities.

Some other indicators of education are placed in Table 8.3. It is found that the norm for the ratio of lower primary (LP) to upper primary (UP) (one UP per two LP schools) is also not achieved. The difference between male and female median years of schooling is quite large. Not much difference is found between genders as far as the OoSC are concerned. The higher dropout rate at upper primary level shows that the survival rate of children declines as they move to higher levels of education. The pupil–teacher ratio shows that the norm of PTR is fulfilled in the state.

*Table 8.2* Gross enrolment ratios (GER) and net enrolment ratios (NER)

| *Year* | *Children of 6–11 age group* | | *Children of 11–14 age group* | |
|---|---|---|---|---|
| | *GER* | *NER* | *GER* | *NER* |
| 2006–07 | 90.98 | 82.06 | 100.31 | 63.11 |
| 2007–08 | 96.66 | 84.23 | 104.95 | 76.62 |
| 2008–09 | 97.48 | 92.28 | 99.06 | 85.52 |
| 2009–10 | 98.04 | 92.88 | 104.11 | 85.68 |
| 2010–11 | 99.60 | 91.83 | 105.45 | 83.84 |
| 2011–12 | 99.69 | 93.27 | 104.93 | 90.85 |
| 2012–13 | 99.96 | 93.61 | 101.83 | 91.57 |

*Source:* OPEPA, Odisha.

*Table* 8.3 Achievement in different indicators of education in Odisha, 2011–12

| *Indicators* | *Rate/nos* | *Indicators* | *Rate/nos* |
|---|---|---|---|
| **Number of schools** | | **Dropout rate** | |
| Primary (govt + aided) | 36,096 | Primary | 5.37 |
| UP | 26,232 | Upper primary | 7.22 |
| Ratio of primary to UP (2:1) | 1.37:1 | **PTR** | 33 |
| **Median years of schooling (2008–09)** | | **Access** | |
| Male | 4.3 | Primary | 92 |
| Female | 1.6 | UP | 94 |
| **Out-of-school children in lakhs** | | **Retention rate** | |
| Boys | 1.36 | Primary (I–V) | 83.01 |
| Girls | 1.35 | Elementary (I–VIII) | 66.904 |

*Source*: OPEPA, Odisha.

*Table* 8.4 Percentage of expenditure on elementary education to total budget expenditure and SDP

| *Year* | *% of elementary exp to total budget* | *% of elementary exp to SDP* |
|---|---|---|
| 1985–86 | 8.7 | 1.3 |
| 1990–91 | 11.3 | 1.3 |
| 1995–96 | 10.8 | 1.9 |
| 2000–01 | 11.8 | 2.4 |
| 2006–07 | 6.9 | 1.3 |
| 2010–11 | 8.0 | 1.49 |
| 2011–12 | 7.4 | 1.47 |

*Source*: Various issues of Budget Document, Govt of Odisha.

The achievement of any goal depends on finance, which is one of the strong barriers in the state. The percentage of public expenditure on elementary education to SDP is much less than 2 per cent, except in the year 2000–01. *Most interestingly, the percentage share of expenditure on elementary education to total budget declined over the years (Table 8.4)*. This clearly indicates that the allocation of resources to education in general and to elementary education in particular has not been seriously taken up by the state. Table 8.4 presents the expenditure on elementary education and its share in state income (SDP).

Several research studies show that the expenditure on quality-related inputs like textbooks, scholarships, teacher training and other such items improves the children's participation in schools and reduces drop-out rate significantly. We have collected the information on expenditure on different items as it is provided in the budget. It is not the exact reflection of quality-related investments but roughly it gives some indication. Of the total expenditure, about 95 per cent is spent on salary and related expenditure for teachers and other non-teaching staffs. Very negligible proportion of the budget expenditure is spent on items related to quality improvement. Only 0.1 per cent is spent on scholarships, and development of textbooks receives less than 1 per cent (0.55 per cent). More importantly, almost all these expenditures related to quality items have declined significantly over the years (between 2006–07 and 2010–2011). If this trend continues, the goal of vision documents to provide quality education at the elementary level seems to be distant. Table 8.5 provides the information on different items of expenditure.

*Table 8.5* Function-wise percentage of expenditure on elementary education

| *Items* | *% of expenditure* | | *Increase(+)/ decrease(–)* |
|---|---|---|---|
| | *2006–07* | *2010–11* | |
| Direction, inspection and administration | 2.1 | 2.67 | 0.57 |
| Govt primary schools | 89.2 | 85.75 | –3.45 |
| Asst to non-govt primary schools | 0.3 | 2.63 | 2.33 |
| Non-formal education | 3.13 | – | – |
| Text books | 1.08 | 0.55 | –0.53 |
| Scholarships and incentives | 0.01 | 0.01 | 0 |
| Examinations | 0.03 | 0.01 | –0.02 |
| Special component plan for SC | 0.48 | 3.61 | 3.13 |
| Training | 1.05 | 0.8 | –0.25 |
| TSP (tribal sub-plan) | 2.27 | 3.46 | 1.19 |
| Other expenditure | 0.35 | 0.49 | 0.14 |
| Total | 100 | 100 | |

*Source:* Various issues of Budget Document, Government of Odisha.

## Pattern and trend of finances under SSA

The state has 30 administrative districts and 75 education districts. There are 314 Block Resource Centres (BRCs), 4,742 Cluster Resource Centres (CRCs), 6,234 panchayats and 51,349 villages. All the districts are covered under SSA. Before analysing the pattern and trend of financing system under SSA, the goals and achievements of SSA merit discussion.

### *Goals and achievements of SSA*

The achievements under SSA against its goals presented in Table 8.6 clearly indicate that the state is moving fast with all sincerity to achieve the desired goal stipulated under SSA. Despite significant achievements,

*Table* 8.6 Goals and achievements of SSA, Orissa

| *Goals* | *Achievements* |
|---|---|
| **All children in school, EGS, alternative schools, back to school camp by 2005** | Out-of-school children has come down from 1 million in 2002–03 to 72,000 in 2010–11 |
| | All eligible EGS centres were upgraded to regular schools and rest were closed |
| | NER has increased from 82.06 in 2006–07 to 91.83 in 2010–11 at primary and 63.11 to 83.84 at UP during the same period |
| **Bridging gender gaps: primary by 2007 and UP by 2010** | Gender gap at primary has come down from 12.21% in 2002–03 to 2.7% in 2008–09 and at UP 6.08% to 1.53% during the same period |
| **Universal retention by 2010** | Dropout declined from 18.05 in 2006–07 to 7.23 in 2010–11 at UP and 10.53 to 2.83 at primary during the same period |
| **Focus on elementary education of satisfactory quality with emphasis on education for life** | PTR has come down to 33 in 2010–11 |
| | Single-teacher school has come down to 7.9 in 2011–12 |
| | SCF has been prepared and syllabus revised |
| | QMT and ADEPT for quality improvement |
| | Extensive teacher training to untrained teachers |
| | Appointment of para teachers |
| | Mother tongue based education introduced in 537 schools |
| | Revised NT book introduced in Classes I and III |
| | Learning enhanced programme through various schemes used widely |

*Source:* OPEPA, Odisha.

the state is far away from achieving the goal. It is also a fact that most of the allocations for SSA are either not properly utilised or remained unspent, which is one of the important constraints of achieving the desired goal. This indicates that the fund is not a problem for achieving the goal, but there are some other reasons for not achieving the goal under SSA. An attempt is made here to examine this issue.

### *Allocation and expenditure under SSA in Odisha*

Table 8.7 clearly reveals that the norm on matching shares is not fulfilled either in the allocation or in respect of release of grants. Even though SSA was launched in 2001–02, it actually started operating in 2002–03. The expenditure as percentage to allocation increased from 15.6 per cent in 2002–03 to 65.3 per cent in 2012–13. The annual compound growth rate of expenditure (63 per cent) was more than two times of the growth rate of allocation (29 per cent) during this period. The funds allocated under SSA increased constantly from 2002–03 to 2007–08 but declined constantly from 2009–10 onwards. In the initial year, the unspent money was about 85 per cent and in 2012–13; it declined to 35 per cent, indicating significant utilisation of funds.

*Table 8.7* Details of allocation, release and expenditure under SSA in Odisha

| *Year* | *Approved outlay (Rs in 000s)* | *Share of allocation of funds (%)* | | *Actual share released (%)* | | | *% of exp. against approved outlay* | *% of exp. against available funds* |
|---|---|---|---|---|---|---|---|---|
| | | *Centre* | *State* | *Centre* | *State* | *Total* | | |
| 2002–03 | 1,630,776 | 75 | 25 | 32 | 3 | 35 | 15.59 | 43.60 |
| 2003–04 | 4,528,546 | 75 | 25 | 29 | 4 | 33 | 34.87 | 70.54 |
| 2004–05 | 5,759,875 | 75 | 25 | 35 | 15 | 50 | 43.73 | 72.59 |
| 2005–06 | 5,889,101 | 75 | 25 | 49 | 14 | 63 | 58.29 | 69.72 |
| 2006–07 | 8,778,543 | 75 | 25 | 47 | 17 | 64 | 67.69 | 82.57 |
| 2007–08 | 10,083,751 | 65 | 35 | 58 | 31 | 89 | 73.34 | 71.63 |
| 2008–09 | 9,734,331 | 65 | 35 | 47 | 26 | 73 | 78.92 | 76.62 |
| 2009–10 | 13,125,001 | 65 | 35 | 46 | 31 | 77 | 78.90 | 81.80 |
| 2010–11 | 18,507,800 | 65 | 35 | 40 | 19 | 59 | 47.85 | 58.63 |
| 2011–12 | 21,036,121 | 65 | 35 | 43 | 25 | 68 | 48.43 | 57.02 |
| 2012–13 | 26,809,612 | 65 | 35 | 39 | 26 | 65 | 65.27 | 95.22 |

*Source*: OPEPA, Odisha.

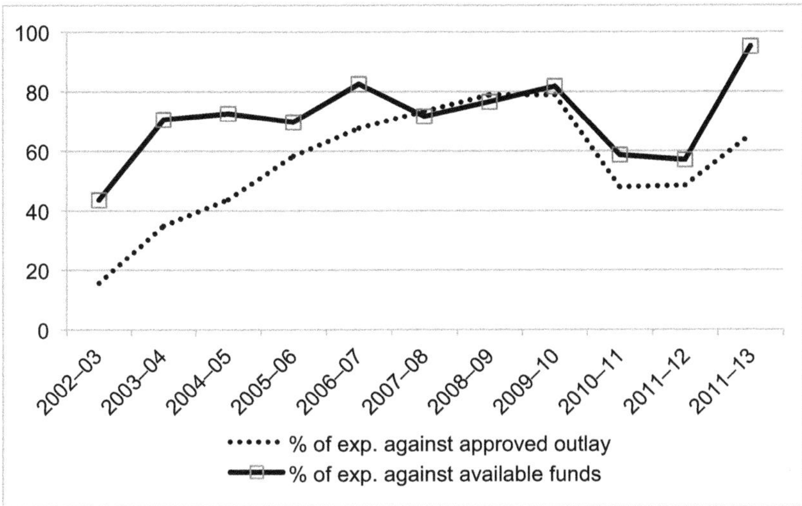


*Figure 8.1* Percentage of expenditure to be approved and available funds

Figure 8.1 shows the trend in percentage of expenditure under SSA in Odisha. It is interesting to note that all the money allocated was not released. The proportion of money released out of the allocation was 35 per cent in 2002–03 and it increased to 65 per cent in 2012–13. Not only the bulk of the total allocated money remained unspent, but also all the money that was actually released was also not spent. The expenditure as percentage to release of money was 43 per cent in 2002–03 and it significantly improved in 2012–13 as it was more than 95 per cent in this year. The reasons for not releasing the total allocated money and the unspent amount of the released grant need to be explored seriously.

### *Component-wise expenditure under SSA*

The overall allocation and expenditure may not reveal the share of each component under SSA which assumes more importance than overall allocation and expenditure. It provides a pointer to the policy makers for allocating the resources in the proper direction and on appropriate components. Table 8.8 presents the component-wise percentage of expenditure to allocation of resources under SSA. The allocated fund was the lowest for intervention for OoSC children. It may be noted that the proportion of expenditure on intervention to OoSC has declined suddenly

*Table* 8.8 Component-wise percentage of expenditure to allocation of resources under SSA

| | 2002–03 | 2003–04 | 2004–05 | 2005–06 | 2006–07 | 2007–08 | 2008–09 | 2010–11 |
|---|---|---|---|---|---|---|---|---|
| Block resource centre | 0.00 | 7.24 | 6.43 | 42.17 | 46.06 | 51.66 | 35.52 | 20.00 |
| Cluster resource centre | 0.00 | 4.69 | 2.46 | 57.77 | 83.49 | 51.64 | 75.43 | 40.00 |
| Civil works | 0.08 | 37.45 | 45.91 | 68.40 | 84.17 | 79.94 | 81.67 | 86.00 |
| Interventions for out-of-school children | 0.00 | 18.17 | 36.22 | 39.90 | 33.09 | 45.30 | 13.76 | 37.00 |
| Free text books | 29.58 | 37.78 | 55.88 | 71.07 | 65.07 | 92.84 | 52.47 | 100.00 |
| Innovative activities | 1.86 | 10.97 | 35.53 | 96.20 | 77.38 | 90.17 | 86.11 | 88.00 |
| Interventions for disabled children | 0.00 | 15.05 | 22.49 | 51.09 | 53.79 | 91.13 | 86.45 | 78.00 |
| Maintenance grant | 93.82 | 88.42 | 77.21 | 90.79 | 97.49 | 82.44 | 84.72 | 100.00 |
| Management and MIS | 5.07 | 19.31 | 25.18 | 48.92 | 46.50 | 52.85 | 53.28 | 75.00 |
| Research and evaluation | 14.18 | 64.25 | 47.27 | 46.25 | 49.05 | 54.84 | 59.04 | 75.00 |
| School grants | 87.31 | 62.19 | 81.28 | 89.16 | 98.75 | 85.70 | 89.66 | 100.00 |
| Teacher grants | 55.36 | 63.13 | 90.82 | 93.26 | 77.15 | 82.74 | 92.92 | 100.00 |
| Teaching learning equipment | 0.00 | 7.71 | 31.28 | 59.66 | 26.10 | 70.06 | 57.24 | 58.00 |
| Teacher training | 0.39 | 10.41 | 21.25 | 24.43 | 25.69 | 49.74 | 61.58 | 67.00 |
| Community training | 0.36 | 35.36 | 33.11 | 54.31 | 39.47 | 52.11 | 91.26 | 69.00 |
| Teachers' salary | 0.00 | 76.05 | 76.69 | 42.59 | 55.41 | 74.75 | 93.54 | 64.00 |
| **Total** | 15.59 | 34.87 | 43.73 | 58.29 | 67.75 | 73.34 | 78.92 | 78.00 |

*Source*: OPEPA, Odisha.

from 45.3 per cent in 2007–08 to 37 per cent in 2010–11, which is a cause of concern. Even the expenditure for the intervention of disabled children has declined constantly from 2007–08 onwards.

### *Performance-based expenditure under SSA*

Since SSA aims at improving the quality of education, the performance of SSA can also be judged in terms of the expenditure on quality-related items via-a-vis other items. Component-wise expenditure shows that the expenditure on quality-related items was 56 per cent in 2003–04 and it declined to 21.38 per cent in 2010–11. The quality-related items include the expenditure on text books, innovative activities, research and evaluation (R&E), teaching learning equipment (TLE), school grants, teacher grant, teacher training and community training. In recent years, the highest proportion of expenditure was made on civil works followed by teachers' salaries. These two together consume about three-fourth of the total expenditure and the rest was on other items. The proportion of expenditure to total expenditure on OoSC declined from 10.5 per cent in 2003–04 to 0.54 per cent in 2010–11. This may not be adequate to mainstream the OoSC within the time schedule. The resources available for intervention of disabled children are also found to be quite inadequate. Table 8.9 presents the expenditure on quality component under SSA.

As stated above, the proportion of quality-related expenditure has constantly declined over the years and this is clearly shown in Figure 8.2.

### *Outcome/performance of primary education in Odisha*

The outcome indicators at primary level indicate the performance at this level. We have taken the performance of students as per ASER study in rural Odisha at two points of time. The decline in expenditure on quality-related components is also reflected in its outcome, as seen from Table 8.10. If one examines the achievements in respect of some important quality indicators, it is surprising to find that after the introduction of SSA since 2001 most of the quality indicators show depressing picture. This again confirms the linkage between the decline in the expenditure on quality-related components and its resultant outcome. It is found that in all the indictors the performance shows constant decline. The programme of SSA is specifically aimed at improving quality at primary level, which seems not to have achieved in the rural Odisha even after a decade. All the indicators in Table 8.10 show a decline in 2010–11 instead of improvement after five years.

*Table 8.9* Expenditure on quality-related items under SSA (%)

| *Components* | *2002–03* | *200–04* | *2004–05* | *2005–06* | *2006–07* | *2007–08* | *2008–09* | *2010–11* |
|---|---|---|---|---|---|---|---|---|
| Quality-related items* | 55.8 | 18.92 | 19.35 | 19.95 | 9.42 | 9.42 | 15.34 | 21.38 |
| Civil works | 0.2 | 39.89 | 40.28 | 39.21 | 57.24 | 57.24 | 44.01 | 41.85 |
| BRC | 0 | 0.13 | 0.26 | 1.06 | 0.49 | 0.49 | 0.23 | 0.25 |
| CRC | 0 | 0.3 | 0.47 | 7.09 | 3.61 | 3.61 | 0.38 | 0.90 |
| Interventions for out of school children | 0 | 10.53 | 9.07 | 6.46 | 4.34 | 4.34 | 0.51 | 0.54 |
| Interventions for disabled children | 0 | 1.38 | 1.11 | 2.01 | 1.39 | 1.39 | 1.42 | 1.97 |
| Maintenance grant | 43.3 | 12.63 | 8.92 | 6.05 | 3.11 | 3.11 | 4.43 | 3.09 |
| Management and MIS | 0.65 | 1.98 | 2.73 | 3.27 | 3.94 | 3.94 | 3.61 | 4.15 |
| Teachers' salary | 0 | 14.23 | 17.8 | 14.91 | 16.47 | 16.47 | 30.07 | 25.88 |
| Total | 100 | 100 | 100 | 100 | 100 | 100 | 100 | 100 |

*Source:* OPEPA, Odisha.

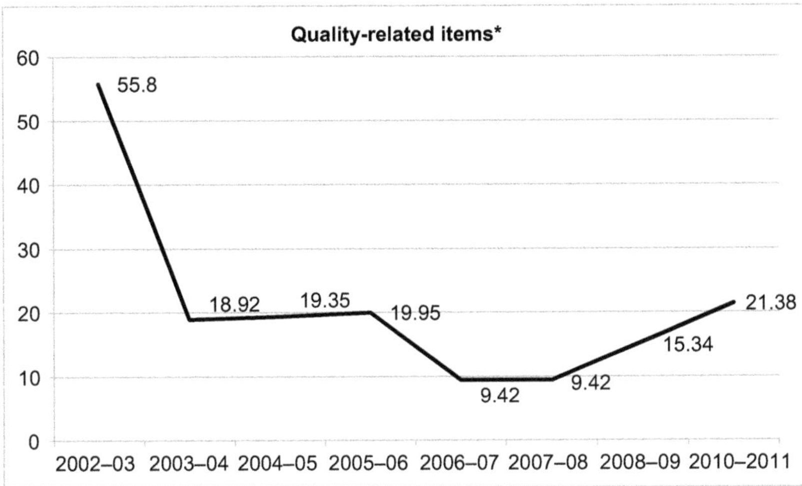


*Figure 8.2* Percentage of expenditure on quality-related items

*Table 8.10* Performance of students at primary level in some of the quality-related components in rural Odisha

| *Indicators of quality* | *2006–07* | *2010–11* |
|---|---|---|
| % children (Std I–II) who can read letters or more | 78.1 | 76.1 |
| % children (Std I–II) who can recognise numbers 1–9 or more | 76 | 71.9 |
| % children (Std III–V) who can read Std I text or more | 69.4 | 61.4 |
| % children (Std III–V) who can do subtraction or more | 57.4 | 52.1 |
| % of untrained teachers (SS + regular + para + others) | – | 8.37 |
| % teachers present (average primary schools) | 91.1 | 89.1 |
| % teachers present (average UP schools) | 87.2 | 83.8 |
| % schools with no teachers (primary) present | 0.4 | 1.3 |

*Source:* ASER study (2011).

### *Gap in achieving universalisation of elementary education*

Since SSA aimed at achieving the UEE, we examined it through NER at the upper primary level (Table 8.11). When Net enrolment ratio is 100, then one can say that the UEE is achieved. No doubt the state is moving towards achieving UEE very fast, but there are many less developed districts in the state which are far away from achieving the goal of UEE.

*Table 8.11* Gap in achieving UEE and outcome index in Odisha

| *Year* | *NER* | *Gap in UEE* | *Outcome index* |
|---|---|---|---|
| 2006–07 | 63.1 | 36.9 | 0.326 |
| 2007–08 | 76.6 | 23.4 | 0.463 |
| 2008–09 | 85.5 | 14.5 | 0.505 |
| 2009–10 | 85.7 | 14.3 | 0.495 |
| 2010–11 | 83.8 | 16.2 | 0.662 |
| 2011–12 | 90.9 | 9.2 | 0.557 |
| 2012–13 | 91.6 | 8.4 | 0.670 |
| 2013–14 | 91.0 | 9.0 | 0.677 |

*Source:* OPEPA, Bhubaneswar, Flash Statistics, DISE, NUEPA, Various Issues.

The outcome index reflects the performance in primary education in the state. For this, we have considered the outcome index estimated by NUEPA from time to time. It includes: the average number of instructional days; average working hours for teacher; percentage change in enrolment in government schools over the previous year; gross enrolment ratio (GER) of SC, ST and Muslim children; dropout rate; transition rate from primary to upper primary level. Table 8.11 presents the outcome index at upper primary level for various years. It is noticed that the value of index has not shown uniformity in its pattern. In the year 2012–13, the rank of the state in respect of outcome index is 15 at the all-India level. In 2013–14, the outcome index has shown improvement by seven points, but the rank of the state at the national level has come down by 10 points. The outcome indicators clearly present the performance of primary education, and the declining rank of state at the national level raised serious doubts about the quality of primary education.

## Analysis of expenditure in two sample districts under SSA

The district of Boudh is educationally less developed than that of Ganjam. The literacy rate in Boudh is 57.7 per cent as against 60.7 per cent in Ganjam. The Proportion of SC and ST population in Boudh is 34 per cent while the same in Ganjam is about 22 per cent. Both the primary and upper primary schools are much higher in Ganjam than in Boudh. Not only the incidence of dropout is higher in Boudh as compared to Ganjam but GER is also lower in Boudh than Ganjam. However, the district of Boudh is relatively less developed in respect of education than Ganjam.

We have selected these two districts for analysing the SSA funds. The district selection was made on the basis of highest and lowest allocation of resources under SSA. The two districts selected for the purpose are Ganjam (highest allocation) and Boudh (lowest allocation). But the expenditure as percentage to allocation is much higher in Boudh than that in Ganjam. *It is worth noting that the utilisation pattern in a backward district, i.e. Boudh seems to be much better than that in the context of educationally better-off district, i.e. Ganjam.*

### *Frequency of grant released from the state to district*

It is generally said that one of the reasons for unspent money under SSA is delay and irregularity of the release of grants to the districts. Table 8.12 presents the details of release of grants by the state to the districts at different points of time. It is generally believed that the release of grant is made at the beginning of the financial year in order to make the expenditure in a planned manner. But contrary to this belief, it is found that the first grant released by the state to the districts is at the end of May and that too only 7.12 per cent of the total grant. The highest proportion of the grant is

*Table 8.12* Frequency of grant released from the state to district

| *Boudh* | | | *Ganjam* | | |
|---|---|---|---|---|---|
| *Date of release* | *Amount release** | *Percentage to total* | *Date of release* | *Amount release** | *Percentage to total* |
| 23 May 2009 | 10,400 | 7.12 | 23 May 2009 | 53,300 | 7.46 |
| 11 June 2009 | 22,100 | 15.13 | 11 June 2009 | 113,000 | 15.81 |
| 27 August 2009 | 11,800 | 8.08 | 07 August 2009 | 60,400 | 8.45 |
| 16 October 2009 | 11,800 | 8.08 | 20 November 2009 | 327,000 | 45.72 |
| 20 November 2009 | 57,300 | 39.24 | 05 January 2010 | 1,000 | 0.14 |
| 05 January 2010 | 1,000 | 0.14 | 09 February 2010 | 128,000 | 17.89 |
| 09 February 2010 | 19,900 | 13.63 | 31 March 2010 | 33,310 | 4.66 |
| 31 March 2010 | 12,720 | 8.71 | Total | 715,000 | 100 |
| Total | 146,030 | 100 | | | |

*Source:* OPEPA, Odisha.

*Note:* *Rs in thousands.

released in the month of November followed by February. This actually distorts the plan of expenditure not only at the district level but to implement the plan finally at the school level. Table 8.12 presents the frequency of the grant released by the state authorities to the district level. The pattern is similar for both the sample districts.

### *Allocation and expenditure under SSA in Boudh and Ganjam*

In absolute terms, both the allocation and expenditure in Boudh are always found to be much lower than those in Ganjam. But the proportion of expenditure to allocation over the years reveals that there is not much difference between the two districts. The proportion of expenditure to allocation has increased constantly in Ganjam during 2002–03 to 2010–11 showing uniform pattern while the same shows lot of variation in Boudh during the same period. The coefficient of variation in allocation over the years in Boudh was as high as more than 75 per cent, while the same was 54 per cent in Ganjam during the same period. In respect of utilisation of funds, the variation in Ganjam was 74 per cent as against 96 per cent in Boudh. Table 8.13 provides the allocation and expenditure under SSA for Boudh and Ganjam.

*Table 8.13* Year-wise allocation and expenditure under SSA in Boudh and Ganjam (Rs in 000s)

| | *Boudh* | | | *Ganjam* | | |
|---|---|---|---|---|---|---|
| | *Allocation* | *Expenditure* | *% of exp. in allocation* | *Allocation* | *Expenditure* | *% of exp. in allocation* |
| 2002–03 | 4,304 | 995 | 23.12 | 187,469 | 3,501 | 18.68 |
| 2003–04 | 44,146 | 18,549 | 42.02 | 372,327 | 114,321 | 30.70 |
| 2004–05 | 199,033 | 23,584 | 11.85 | 513,218 | 178,651 | 34.81 |
| 2005–06 | 54,725 | 31,178 | 56.97 | 422,644 | 241,312 | 57.10 |
| 2006–07 | 106,392 | 76,921 | 72.30 | 650,828 | 473,364 | 72.73 |
| 2007–08 | 67,112 | 4,333 | 64.56 | 1,084,313 | 791,659 | 73.01 |
| 2010–11 | 254,927 | 201,105 | 78.96 | 1,334,403 | 1,004,889 | 75.31 |
| **CV* (%)** | 75.54 | 96.06 | | 53.76 | 74.07 | |

*Source:* OPEPA, Odisha.

*Note:* *Coefficient of variation.

### *Component-wise expenditure in Boudh and Ganjam*

It was found that despite the level of allocation being the highest in Ganjam district and lowest in Boudh, there is not much difference in achievement level between the two districts. This indicates that the less developed district of Boudh has channelised its resources in the proper direction to achieve the desired objective of the SSA. Civil works and salary take away three-fourth of the total expenditure in both the districts. The intervention for mainstreaming the OoSC children has shown to be nil, whereas there are 2,289 and 21,422 OoSC children, respectively, in Boudh and Ganjam. This is really a matter of concern.

### *Performance-based expenditure under SSA in Boudh and Ganjam*

In respect of quality components, it was observed that the total expenditure was about 9 per cent in 2006–07 and it was doubled (raised to 18 per cent) in 2008–09 and it declined in 2010–11 in Boudh district, while Ganjam shows increased expenditure in quality-related items. This pattern clearly shows that the concerns of quality improvement in less developed regions (Boudh) are not taken up seriously as desired in SSA objectives (Table 8.14).

Figure 8.3 shows the percentage of expenditure on quality-related items in Boudh and Ganjam. Table 8.14 shows the expenditure on quality-related items in Ganjam and Boudh. The most important observation that can be drawn from the table is that the expenditure for OoSC and disabled children was nil in recent years. Unless these children are mainstreamed, the objective of UEE will remain as unfinished agenda.

#### *What is the status of sample districts in respect of outcome of primary education?*

At the state level we have seen that UEE is yet to be achieved. It is very interesting to note that the less developed districts are performing better than the educationally developed districts. In Boudh, universalisation has been almost achieved, while Ganjam is far away from this goal. The outcome index reflects the quality of primary education as discussed earlier for the state. In respect of the outcome index, there is significant improvement in the less developed district (Boudh), while the improvement is slow in the developed district (Ganjam) between the two time periods (Table 8.15).

*Table 8.14* Component-wise expenditure (percentage to total expenditure) of Boudh and Ganjam

| *Items of expenditure* | *Boudh* | | | | *Ganjam* | | | |
|---|---|---|---|---|---|---|---|---|
| | *2006–07* | *2007–08* | *2008–09* | *2010–11* | *2006–07* | *2007–08* | *2008–09* | *2010–11* |
| BRC | 0 | 0 | 0 | 0.16 | 1.06 | 0.82 | 0.39 | 0.27 |
| CRC | 0 | 0 | 0 | 0.75 | 6.99 | 4.32 | 0.49 | 0.98 |
| Civil works | 71.45 | 28.54 | 26.85 | 43.85 | 58.16 | 62.37 | 38.98 | 51.96 |
| Intervention for out-of-school children | 0.15 | 0.00 | 0 | 0.16 | 1.73 | 1.57 | 0.00 | 0.00 |
| Free text books | 1.06 | 3.41 | 2.89 | 3.92 | 3.46 | 2.84 | 4.85 | 11.53 |
| Innovative activities | 3.69 | 1.67 | 8.20 | 5.45 | 1.15 | 0.78 | 1.89 | 1.21 |
| Intervention for disabled children | 1.34 | 3.87 | 2.25 | 0.00 | 0.74 | 1.23 | 1.12 | 0.00 |
| Maintenance grant | 1.10 | 2.35 | 2.50 | 3.44 | 3.20 | 1.97 | 4.68 | 3.01 |
| Management and MIS | 1.68 | 1.02 | 4.77 | 6.54 | 3.14 | 0.96 | 1.68 | 4.74 |
| Research and evaluation | 0.16 | 0.17 | 0.01 | 0.60 | 0.83 | 0.19 | 0.41 | 0.60 |
| School grant | 0.51 | 0.94 | 2.38 | 3.07 | 1.33 | 0.86 | 3.83 | 3.01 |
| Teachers grant | 0.61 | 0.58 | 0.41 | 0.66 | 1.07 | 0.73 | 0.80 | 0.87 |
| TLE | 1.76 | 3.37 | 1.21 | 0.46 | 0.06 | 0.14 | 0.51 | 0.26 |
| Teachers training | 0.83 | 2.28 | 2.39 | 1.53 | 0.76 | 0.90 | 3.70 | 1.24 |
| Community training | 0.02 | 0.55 | 0.31 | 0.93 | 0.11 | 0.05 | 0.33 | 0.52 |
| Teachers salary | 15.64 | 51.24 | 45.83 | 28.48 | 16.21 | 20.27 | 36.42 | 31.33 |
| TOTAL | 100 | 100 | 100 | 100 | 100 | 100 | 100 | 100 |
| **Quality-related items*** | **8.64** | **12.98** | **17.80** | **16.62** | **8.76** | **6.49** | **16.31** | **19.24** |

*Source*: OPEPA, Odisha.

*Note*: *Free text books, innovative activities, school grant, teacher grant, TLE, teacher training, community training.

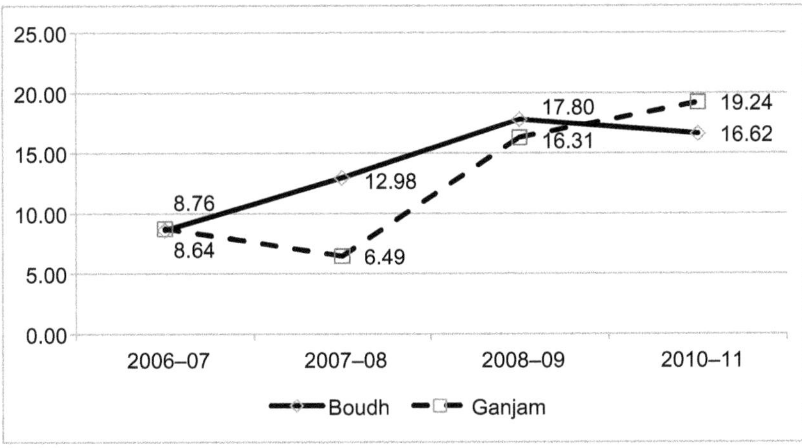


*Figure 8.3* The pattern of expenditure in Boudh and Ganjam

*Table 8.15* Gap in achieving UEE and outcome index in Ganjam and Boudh

| *Year* | *Boudh* | | | *Ganjam* | | |
|---|---|---|---|---|---|---|
| | *NER at UP* | *Gap in UEE* | *Outcome index* | *NER at UP* | *Gap in UEE* | *Outcome index* |
| 2006–07 | 60.9 | 39.1 | – | 58.4 | 41.6 | – |
| 2007–08 | 84.9 | 15.1 | 0.463 | 84.7 | 15.3 | 0.525 |
| 2009–10 | 94.6 | 5.4 | 0.703 | 90.0 | 10.0 | 0.656 |
| 2010–11 | 99.8 | 0.2 | 0.240* | 77.0 | 23.0 | 0.131* |

*Source:* OPEPA, Bhubaneswar.

*Note:* *Improvements.

## Constraints/barriers of utilisation of funds under SSA

On the basis of the analysis of the data, we tried to find out the main *constraints* of utilisation of funds allocated under SSA. Some of the constraints were also found out on discussion with the officials at the state level as well as at the district level of the selected districts.

- The allocation of funds is planned as per the specified *norm*, while the expenditure is made as per the *need*. This mismatch results in bulk of unspent money.

- The release of funds is usually delayed, which is one of the important barriers for utilisation of the fund.
- Frequent transfer of head of the office, i.e. SPD and DPC, appointment of contractual staff and non-filling of the teaching posts for quite a long time create problems for implementing the programme.
- Generally, it is found that the constitution of VEC is not made in time, which is a stumbling block for carrying out the expenditure. Sometimes it is found that even if the fund is released, it cannot be utilised unless VEC is constituted. Further, lack of coordination between collector and DPC at the district level and headmaster and VEC chairman at the sub-district level creates formidable problems in utilisation of funds.
- Land litigation is usually a problem which delays the civil works. Also, lack of proper supervision of civil works is a general problem.
- Effect of quality intervention in the long run is not properly realised by the implementing authorities, which perhaps is the reason for not increasing allocation on quality components.
- In Ganjam district, the DPC post was lying vacant for quite a long period of time for which the utilisation of funds was not being made in time. When DPC joined, the civil work was taken up first, because (i) it consumes more money, (ii) the unspent money is not lapsed and (iii) the utilisation of more funds of the total allocated funds can be shown.
- Boudh district faced the problem of political intervention in implementing the programme many times. This either delays the implementation or the money remains unutilised/unspent.

## Conclusions and recommendations

- The expenditure of SSA for Odisha has increased constantly. Component-wise expenditure shows that the expenditure on quality-related items was 56 per cent in 2002–03 and it declined to 21 per cent in 2010–11. The highest proportion of expenditure was made on civil works followed by teachers' salaries. These two together consume about three-fourth of the total expenditure and the rest was on other items. The proportion of expenditure to total expenditure on OoSC declined from 10.5 per cent in 2003–04 to nil 2010–11, which is a matter of concern. Also, the proportion of expenditures to total outlay on OoSC is the lowest (less than 14 per cent) among all the components. There is gap between the published statistics of number of OoSC children and the actual number as reflected through NER. The state is yet to achieve UEE. The quality at primary level is found to be deteriorated in rural areas.

- Coming to district level performance, it was found that despite the level of allocation being the highest in Ganjam district and lowest in Boudh, there is significant difference in achievement level between the districts. The less developed district is nearing to UEE, while Ganjam is away from this goal. This indicates that the less developed district of Boudh has channelised its resources in the proper direction to achieve the desired objective of the SSA. In respect of outcome indicators, Boudh has shown better improvement than Ganjam. This shows that less developed region (Boudh) is in line with SSA objectives. More interestingly, it was found that the expenditure on OoSC is nil from 2008–09 onwards in both the districts, while there are quite a large number of OoSC in both the districts.

On the basis of the analysis and the constraints listed above, the following *recommendations* are made to overcome/reduce the constraints for non-utilisation of the funds under SSA:

- There is constant improvement in the utilisation pattern as it has increased from 15 per cent in the initial year of SSA to 78 per cent, and the state has to keep this momentum in order to achieve the full utilisation of funds under SSA.
- The frequency in release of grant needs to be reduced to maximum three installments.
- State has improved its *efficiency* but now needs to evaluate its *effectiveness*. There is a need for continuous evaluation of the allocation and expenditure of funds under SSA and constant monitoring needs to be done from time to time to find out the reasons for non-utilisation of funds, particularly for quality-related items.
- Frequent transfer of state and district level officials and appointment of permanent teachers need to be taken up seriously by the state.
- The expenditure on quality components – particularly the expenditure on OoSC – needs to be increased in order to mainstream all the OoSC in time to achieve UEE.
- Proper coordination between different authorities from the apex level to the grass root level is most needed, and the political intervention into the implementation of the plan under SSA – particularly in the backward districts – should be avoided.

The planning should be *need-based* rather than *norm-based* for the achievement of the goal of SSA in time. Appropriate measures need to be taken up by the state to ensure that the performance not only needs to be better but needs to be consistent.

## Note

1 Literacy Facts at a Glance, National Literacy Mission Authority (2001), Government of India.

## References

*Census of India*, Government of India, 2001 and 2011.

Debi, Sailabala, 2001. 'Financing Elementary Education: Reviewing the Experiences of Odisha', *Journal of Educational Planning and Administration*, 15(3): 355–68.

*Economic Survey*. *2009–11*. Planning and Co-ordination Department, Government of Odisha, Bhubaneswar.

Government of India, 2001. 'Literacy Facts at a Glance', *National Literacy Mission Authority*.

Government of Odisha, 2003. 'Vision. 2020'.

National Family Health Survey (NFHS). 1992–93, 1998–99 and 2005–06. International Institute of Population Studies, Mumbai.

Odisha Primary Education Authority (OPEPA), www.opepa.in (accessed on 28 March 2009 and 20 April 2011, 4 December 2014).

*Statistical Abstract of Odisha*, 2012. Directorate of Statistics and Economics, Govt of Odisha, Bhubaneswar.

Tilak, J.B.G., 2002. 'Education in Orissa: A Review of Progress, Problems and Perspectives for Future on School Education', *Back ground paper for Human Development Report, UNDP, Odisha.*

# 9

# REVIEW OF SSA FUND FLOW PATTERN

## Case studies from Mumbai and Raigad in Maharashtra

*Madhu Paranjape*

### Introduction

Maharashtra is widely acclaimed as the most progressive state and the *per capita* income at current prices is estimated at Rs 95,339 (provisional estimate) in 2011–12, as against Rs 83,395 during the previous year and fourfold increase since 2001. The per capita income is higher than the per capita National Income and the state maintained the fourth rank after Goa, Delhi and Haryana (Government of Maharashtra 2013). Maharashtra is the second largest state in India after Uttar Pradesh as far as population is concerned as per 2011 census. On the education front, historically, the social reform movements in Maharashtra have played a significant role in bringing education to the disadvantaged sections of the population, namely girls in general and children from lower castes in particular. 'An egalitarian thrust led to multifaceted innovations and interventions in education including starting of hostels for children of all castes, reservations for *dalits*, and schools for girls' (Government of Maharashtra 2002). The movements led by thinkers and social reformers like Mahatma Jyotiba Phule, Shahu Maharaj, Gopal Ganesh Agarkar, Maharishi Karve in the nineteenth century and Babasaheb Ambedkar in the twentieth century influenced the post-independence status of education as well as its spread in Maharashtra. Karmveer Bhaurao Patil, founder of Rayat Education Society, played a pioneering role in educating people from backward castes and poor masses. Indeed, as early as in 1918, a bill called Bombay Primary Education Act was introduced in the legislature providing for compulsory education of children between the ages 6 and11 years in six towns of Bombay. However, it did not succeed due to insufficient funds and poor response of the people (Prabhu and Kamdar 2001).

As per 2011 Census, Maharashtra stands sixth with literacy rate at 82.9 per cent. But this is a slip from its fourth rank in 2001. Kerala has maintained its top position with literacy rate at 93.9 per cent. Unlike Kerala, there are enormous intra-state disparities, gender and rural and urban and social group differentials, which reflect adversely on many developmental achievements. Paranjape (2007) concludes that the distribution of education is extremely skewed, particularly in the rural regions and specially among the socially backward sections. This gets reflected in the Educational Development Index (EDI)[1] that in 2008–09 Maharashtra ranked 15 with an EDI value of 0.70 (NUEPA 2009). In 2011–12 even with an EDI of 0.72, Maharashtra's rank slipped to 17 (NUEPA 2012).

Sarva Shiksha Abhiyan (SSA), a centrally sponsored scheme, was launched in January 2001 with the primary objective of universalization of elementary education for all children in the age group of 6–14 years by 2010. SSA is designed to subsume all other major educational interventions by the government, and all existing schemes of elementary education of the central government are to converge with SSA from April 2002. In Maharashtra, the programme was introduced from January 2002. It also aims to bridge all social, gender, and regional gaps with active participation of the community. Bringing all children into school and expanding enrolment to all children in the eligible age group has been one of the major objectives of SSA. Though resource allocation towards SSA has been on the rise over the years, the concern is under-utilization of released funds and/or large amounts lying unspent. A noteworthy fact is that such underutilization is found with an inadequacy in the amount of funds released with reference to approved annual work plan and budget (AWP&B). For instance, during 2001–05 in Maharashtra, as against an approved outlay of Rs 21,560 million, only Rs 9,110 million was available. This results in a paradoxical situation that resources required are more but unutilized with lesser allocation than budgeted.

Given this backdrop, the present chapter attempts to examine fund flow pattern in two sample districts, economically and educationally developed Mumbai, and on both the accounts, backward Raigad in the Konkan region of Maharashtra, also known as Mumbai division. The main objectives of the chapter are:

(i) to examine the available resources allocated in the approved AWP&B;
(ii) to look at the extent of out-of-school children (OSC) yet to be covered.

The rest of the chapter is organised as follows: The second section presents a brief account on status of elementary education in Maharashtra followed by an overview of the two sample districts. The third section examines the pattern of allocation and expenditure under SSA in Maharashtra and the sample districts. This section also highlights the view from the field. The fourth section examines the extent of OSC covered. The last section brings out the findings.

## Elementary education in Maharashtra: a brief account

Elementary education in Maharshtra (from class I–VII) consists of primary (class I–IV) and upper primary (class V–VII), which is different from the national structure and in many other states as recommended by the National Policy on Education 1986. The proportion of children both at primary and upper primary level is almost ensured to be enrolled in schools. It is to be noted that the proportion of under- and over-aged children are not very high compared to many other states as the age-specific enrolment ratios reveal. But, at the same time, National Sample Survey (NSS) data from 64th round shows that 6–8 per cent of children in age group 6–14 years are not attending school. If the population projection for the year 2006 (Registrar General of India 2006) is considered, number of children in the age group 6–10 years was about 10.25 million and that in the age group 11–13 years was 8.34 million. Applying the proportion of OSC by the 64th NSS round, it is seen that as of 2007–08, in Maharashtra more than 1.2 million children in the age group 6–13 years were not attending school. Not much progress has taken place since then as NSS data from 66th round (Government of India 2013) reveals that even during 2009–10, in Maharashtra, 5.3 per cent children in the age group 5–14 years were not attending school. With estimated population of 20.1 million children in this age group, the stark reality is that an estimated 1.07 million children remain out of school towards the conclusion of a decade of SSA.

Ministry of Human Resources Development (MHRD) estimated that in Maharashtra there are 207,345 (1.27 per cent) OSC. However, experts maintain that gross enrolment ratio cannot give a true picture about OSC. Hence, information can be captured only through household surveys or sample surveys.

Besides the non-enrolled children, dropped out children would amount to huge numbers. Though dropout rates have been improved at state level, still there is a long way to attain in terms of the socially deprived sections both at primary and at a higher degree at upper primary level (Table 9.1). Sustaining the enrolled children in the education

*Table 9.1* Gross enrolment ratios and dropout rates for primary and upper primary class group in Maharashtra

| | *Gross enrolment ratio* | | | | *Dropout rates* | | | |
|---|---|---|---|---|---|---|---|---|
| | *Primary* | | *Upper primary* | | *Primary* | | *Upper primary* | |
| | *All* | *Girls* | *All* | *Girls* | *All* | *ST* | *All* | *ST* |
| 1990–91 | 124 | 117 | 79.7 | 67.1 | 31.71 | – | 52.85 | – |
| 2000–01 | 101.9 | 99.7 | 90.6 | 85.8 | 17.26 | – | 37.41 | – |
| 2005–06 | 112.3 | 111.3 | 100.6 | 101.5 | 12.33 | 28.21 | 20.75 | 48.16 |
| 2006–07 | 113.6 | 110.9 | 101.5 | 102.1 | 11.07 | 21.02 | 20.35 | 48.62 |
| 2007–08* | 107 (94) | 104 (93) | 91 (92) | 94 (92) | 10.15 | 18.91 | 18.56 | 44.02 |

*Source:* Human Development Report Maharashtra (2002); Data book for DCH 2010 at http:/planningcommision.gov.in; Selected Educational Statistics.

*Note:* Figures in parenthesis give age-specific ratios for 6–10 and 11–13 years; *64th NSS round.

system requires many more efforts by the state, most enabling of which is adequate financial support.

In Maharashtra, 90 per cent of primary schools are run by Zilla Parishads or municipalities. At the same time, more than 90 per cent of secondary schools are privately run (Government of Maharashtra 2002). While 60 per cent of enrolment in classes I–IV is in government managed schools, in classes V–VII the same drops to 27 per cent (NUEPA 2012). Further, as per 64th round of National Sample Survey Organization (NSSO), 74 per cent of students in classes I–VII get free education and another 3 per cent get concessions in tuition fees. The same survey has also revealed that average annual expenditure per student is Rs 1,751 for classes I–IV and Rs 2,346 for classes V–VII (Government of Maharashtra 2009).

As observed from Table 9.2, the proportion of budgeted expenditure on education (by all departments) in Maharashtra, during 1990–91 to 2007–08, has fluctuated around 24 per cent, peaking to 28 per cent in 2000–01, again dipping to the average and then rising again. It is further observed that the rise and decline has been mainly in the proportion of expenditure by the Education Department, while the proportion of expenditure on education by other departments has consistently maintained the level of 3–4 per cent. The average share of elementary education in the total expenditure on education has been about 46 per cent, which is below the average 51 per cent of all states. At the all-India level, Elementary

*Table* 9.2 Trends in financing of education in Maharashtra

| *Year* | *% of state budget* | *% of NSDP on education* | *Elementary* | *Secondary* | *Higher* | *Technical* |
|---|---|---|---|---|---|---|
| 1990–91 | 23 | – | 40.4 | 39.8 | 12.6 | 4.2 |
| 1995–96 | 24 | 2.90 | 44.7 | 39.8 | 9.2 | 4.3 |
| 2000–01 | 28 | 4.55 | 49.2 | 34.2 | 12.1 | 3.7 |
| 2005–06 | 24 | 3.38 | 45.2 | 39.3 | 10.4 | 4.3 |
| 2006–07 | 23 | 3.33 | 45.6 | 38.7 | 11.0 | 3.9 |
| 2007–08 | 25.1 | 2.77 | 45.4 | 40.4 | 9.85 | 3.5 |
| 2008–09 | 24.5 | 2.82 | 46.4 | 39.2 | 9.72 | 3.7 |
| 2009–10 | 27.5 | 2.45 | 46.9 | 41.5 | 7.7 | 3.5 |
| 2010–11(R) | 28.9 | 2.88 | 46.4 | 39.8 | 10.0 | 3.2 |
| 2011–12(B) | 28.6 | 2.78 | 45.0 | 42.2 | 9.0 | 3.2 |

*Source:* Based on Analysis of Budgeted Expenditures on Education (MHRD 2008, 2013).

Education accounted for 50.2 per cent of the total expenditure on education in 2009–10, followed by Secondary Education, which was 31.3 per cent. The share of University and Higher Education and Technical Education was 11.9 per cent and. 4.9 per cent, respectively.

Since mid-1980s, social sector expenditures have been less than 6 per cent of state income. Table 9.2 reveals that the proportion of state income spent on Education Department has consistently declined since 2000–01 when it had peaked to 4 per cent. Proportions of allocation for Elementary Education were also highest in 2000–01 and 2001–02 at 2 per cent of Net State Domestic Product (NSDP), thereafter declining steadily. The proportion spent by Maharashtra has always been below national average which also has declined from 3.9 per cent in 1990s to 3.26 per cent in the year 2004–05. After that it again started increasing but at a very slow rate.

At all-India level during 2011–12, only 3.36 per cent of GDP was provided in the budgets of the Education Departments. When the provision for education for all departments including Education Departments is taken into account, this percentage works out to be 4.17 per cent (MHRD 2013), while the same in Maharashtra was 2.78 per cent. In 2011–12, allocation for elementary education was 1.77 per cent of GDP.

Table 9.3 gives average schooling (classes I–VII) for 1999–2000 and dropout rates (per 100) for 1998–99 of districts with literacy rates above 86 per cent among the 35 districts.

*Table* 9.3 Educational development in select districts in Maharashtra

| *District* | *2011* | *1999–2000* | *1998–99* | *2006–07*$ | | | |
|---|---|---|---|---|---|---|---|
| | *Literacy rates* | *Mean years* | *Dropout rates* | *Primary* | | *Upper primary* | |
| | | *In years* | *7th Std* | *NER*[2] | *Cohort dropout* | *NER* | *Cohort dropout* |
| Mumbai | 90.3 | 5.85 | 19 | 86.3 | 4.6 | 95.5 | 15.7 |
| Nagpur | 89.5 | 6.29 | 19 | 99.0 | 2.9 | 99.5 | 2.0 |
| Amravati | 88.2 | 5.59 | 35 | 99.9 | 10.3 | 88.4 | 9.4 |
| Akola | 87.6 | 5.36 | 34 | 99.2 | 14.3 | 99.5 | 7.8 |
| Thane | 86.2 | 5.46 | 34 | 99.8 | 9.3 | 98.3 | 16.2 |
| Pune | 87.2 | 5.74 | 30 | 99.4 | 0.2 | 99.5 | 0.1 |
| Sindhudurg | 86.5 | 6.36 | 15 | 99.7 | 5.7 | 99.0 | 8.8 |
| Wardha | 87.2 | 6.26 | 31 | 97.1 | 1.1 | 99.8 | 2.8 |
| Raigad** | 83.9 | 5.31 | 43 | 99.8 | 26.9 | 99.9 | 2.9 |
| Maharashtra | 82.9 | 4.97* | 31 | 98.0 | 9.7 | 97.5 | 10.1 |

*Source*: Human Development Report Maharashtra (2002).

*Notes*

* In 2011, this figure is 5.12 years.

** Raigad is included as it is part of our case study.

$ Sen *et al*. (2010).

With the exception of Sindhudurg, it is evident that high literacy rates and higher average years of schooling in Elementary Education (classes I–VII) do not necessarily lead to lower dropout rates at subsequent levels of education. In fact, the dipping of ranks of Raigad at both the literacy levels and dropout rates is very stark. The dropout rates at the primary level in 2006–07 as well is far from satisfactory. But at the upper primary level it is marginal. It suggests that if the children are retained at the primary cycle, their continuation at the upper primary is quite feasible. But looking at the net enrolment ratio (NER), Mumbai has the least NER at the primary and Amravati has the least at the upper primary level. As noted earlier, the inter-district disparity in Maharashtra even in terms of universal enrolment still remains. In order to further explore the inter-district disparity, the main thrust of the chapter is to examine the fund flow pattern in allocation and expenditure under SSA in the economically developed Mumbai and the economically and educationally backward district Raigad. Interestingly, both belong to the Konkan region of Maharashtra.

### *Salient features of the sample districts*

Mumbai has a population of 12.4 million with a literacy rate of 90 per cent (2011 Census). This most populated metropolitan city in the country is divided administratively into two districts: Mumbai and Mumbai Suburban. At the same time, in terms of school education, all primary schools in the two districts are under the jurisdiction of the Brihan Mumbai Municipal Corporation (BMC) and the upper primary schools are under the jurisdiction of the Deputy Director of School education. The focus of this chapter is on the SSA work in the jurisdiction of BMC. The approved AWP&B for this region was Rs 278.4 million in 2008–09 and Rs 328.8 million in 2009–10. The district has 12 Urban Resource Centres (URCs), 177 Cluster Resource Centres (CRCs) and 1,186 primary schools. For the present study, one URC and one primary school were selected randomly for field visit.

Raigad has a total population of 2.21 million and literacy rate is 77 per cent. This is a district with rural features. The urban population is only 24 per cent. Scheduled tribes (ST) form 12 per cent of the population. The approved AWP&B for this district was Rs 336.1 million in 2008–09 and Rs 359.2 million in 2009–10. Raigad has 15 Block Resource Centres (BRCs), 239 CRCs and 844 Village Education Committees (VECs). The Zilla Parishad office is located at Alibag. One VEC was selected randomly for field visit.

Although Mumbai and Raigad are in the same region and at a distance less than 60 km, they are highly disparate in their socioeconomic features (see Tables 9.4 to 9.6).

*Table 9.4* Key demographic features in Mumbai and Raigad

| *District* | *Population (in thousands)* | *% of urban population* | | *Literacy* | | *Percent of SC/ ST population* |
|---|---|---|---|---|---|---|
| | *2011* | *2011* | *2001* | *2011* | *2001* | *2001* |
| Mumbai | 12,478 | 100 | 100 | 90.0 | 87.1 | 5.6 |
| Raigad | 2,635 | 36.9 | 24.2 | 83.9 | 77.3 | 14.6 |
| Maharashtra | 112,373 | 45.2 | 42.4 | 82.9 | 77.3 | 19.1 |

*Source:* (i) Census tables, 1991, 2001, (ii) Government of Maharashtra 2001, (iii) Various reports of Economic Survey of Maharashtra.

*Table* 9.5 Work participation rates and main workers in Mumbai and Raigad (%)

| *District region* | *WPR* | | *Main workers* | | *Net per capita income (Rs)* |
|---|---|---|---|---|---|
| | *2001* | *1991* | *2001* | *1991* | *2010–11* |
| Mumbai | 38 | 35 | 35.9 | 34.6 | 133,426 |
| Raigad rural | 45 | 46 | 31.8 | 41.6 | |
| Urban | 34.1 | 33 | 30.4 | 30.4 | 103,197 |
| Maharashtra | 43.5 | 43 | 36.9 | 39.3 | 83,395 |

*Source:* (i) Census tables, 1991, 2001; (ii) Socioeconomic review of districts, 2000–01, Government of Maharashtra; (iii) Various reports of Economic Survey of Maharashtra.

*Table* 9.6 Enrolments in elementary standards, 2010–11

| *District* | | *Enrolment* | *NER* | *Cohort dropout** | *Gender parity index 2007–08 to 2010–11* | |
|---|---|---|---|---|---|---|
| Mumbai | Primary | 774,474 | 72.7 | 6.5 | 0.91 | 0.92 |
| | Upper primary | 639,791 | NA | 6.8 | | |
| Raigad | Primary | 192,698 | 89.3 | 26.9 | 0.92 | 0.91 |
| | Upper primary | 141,145 | 73.7 | 2.86 | | |
| Maharashtra | Primary | 10,384,478 | 88.3 | 9.7 | 0.89 | 0.89 |
| | Upper primary | 5,697,291 | 69.8 | 10.05 | | |

*Source:* (i) Sen *et al.* (2010); (ii) http://dise.in/Downloads/Publications/Publications 2011–12/DRC 2011–12.pdf; (iii) Various issues of Elementary Education in India: District Report Cards, NUEPA.

*Note:* *As on 30th September 2007.

Work participation rate (WPR) for Maharashtra has remained almost unchanged during 1991–2001. Since 1991 there has been an increase in the WPR in Mumbai and urban areas of Raigad. The rural WPR in Raigad has actually declined. The WPR includes both main workers and marginal workers. Figures in Table 9.5 reveal that the ratio of main workers has marginally increased in Mumbai but sharply declined in the rural areas of Raigad. Data shows that the tertiary sector is predominant in Mumbai, with share of more than 60 per cent of main workers. This is in complete contrast with the predominance of primary sector in Raigad, with more than 50 per cent of main workers. It is pertinent to note that GSDP for primary sector has recorded negative growth in 2000–01, 2004–05 and 2008–09 (Government of Maharashtra 2010). Given such disparity of economic conditions, in particular economic stagnation in Raigad and with reference to Tables 9.4–9.5, it is not surprising that though Raigad has impressive literacy rates, gender parity index and mean years of schooling, its dropout rates at the primary level are much higher.

### *Data*

Maharashtra Prathmik Shikshan Parishad (MPSP), a registered state level autonomous body, was constituted to implement programmes related to primary education, particularly the District Primary Education Programme in the state. This body is responsible for the SSA scheme. For the analysis on allocation and expenditure under SSA at the state level (State Project Office or MPSP) and at district level, secondary data are collected from the District Project Office of the two districts, besides the primary data collected at the block and school level. Other secondary data sources used in the chapter are from Census of India, Analysis of Budgeted Expenditure on Education, DISE data, Economic Survey of India, Economic Survey of Maharashtra, etc.

## Pattern of allocation and expenditure under SSA in Maharashtra

The approved outlay of the AWP&B has been on the rise in Maharashtra similar to that of any other state except for the year 2007–08. But the amount released varied in a range of 38.6 per cent in 2003–04 to 79.7 per cent in 2006–07. It is interesting to note the directly proportional relationship between the highest amount of approved outlay and the highest share of total amount of money released. But overall, 59.9 per cent of the approved outlay has been released during 2002–08 (see Table 9.7). Yet another pattern to be noted from Table 9.7 is that the matching shares between the centre and states are never adhered to in any of the years. During the 10th plan period (2002–03 to 2006–07), the matching share between centre and states was 74:26 and during the first year of the 11th plan was 86:14. Further, it exhibits no uniform pattern, but in the last few years share of the centre has fallen below 70 per cent.

With regard to the pattern of allocation vis-à-vis expenditures, there has been substantial improvement in the percentage of expenditures in the

*Table* 9.7 Approved outlay and amount released under SSA in Maharashtra (Rs in lakhs)

| *Year* | *Approved outlay* | *Amount released* | | *Total released* | *Matching share %* | | *% Released in approved outlay* |
|---|---|---|---|---|---|---|---|
| | | *GoI* | *GoM* | | *GoI* | *GoM* | |
| 2001–02 | 1,044,892 | 0 | 0 | 0 | | | |
| 2002–03 | 43,122 | 15,390 | 1,990 | 17,380 | 89 | 11 | 40.3 |
| 2003–04 | 76,477 | 20,527 | 8,963 | 29,490 | 70 | 30 | 38.6 |
| 2004–05 | 86,306 | 36,017 | 8,349 | 44,366 | 81 | 19 | 51.4 |
| 2005–06 | 87,651 | 50,235 | 14,520 | 64,755 | 78 | 22 | 73.9 |
| 2006–07 | 101,551 | 52,268 | 28,639 | 80,907 | 65 | 35 | 79.7 |
| 2007–08 | 89,523 | 45,730 | 7,450 | 53,180 | 86 | 14 | 59.4 |
| **Total** | **484,630** | **220,168** | **69,911** | **290,079** | **76** | **24** | **59.9** |
| 2010–11 | 210,847 | 85,537 | 46,058 | 131,595 | 65 | 35 | 62.4 |
| 2011–12 | 293,499 | 102,963 | 41,209 | 144,172 | 71 | 29 | 49.1 |
| 2013–14@ | 141,694 | 33,660 | 22,044 | 55,704 | 60 | 40 | 39.3 |

*Source:* (i) Maharashtra Prathmik Shikshan Parishad (MPSP), Mumbai; (ii) Various financial statements available at ssa.nic.in.

*Note:* @, As of September 2013.

total amount released. It is above 90 per cent on an average of all the years. However, as noted earlier, as the gap between approved outlay and amount released was large, the expenditure as a per cent of approved outlay range between 22 and 77 per cent with a very low average of 18 per cent during 2002–08 (Table 9.8).

From Table 9.9, it is observed that until 2006, utilization of grants has been low when seen as proportion of AWP&B. However, this has mainly been a problem of inadequate release of funds rather than of under-utilization. This is borne out by the fact that fund utilization as proportion of grants available was always above 80 per cent. The year 2007 marked a clear improvement, both in terms of fund release and fund utilization. But this progress did not sustain in subsequent years. In 2011–12, proportion of approved outlay released was below 50 per cent and so was the proportion of funds utilized against approved outlay.

The Performance Audit Report 15 of 2006 (CAG 2006) on SSA has faulted Maharashtra as one of the 11 states for irregular diversion of funds to schemes/activities beyond scope of SSA. Some of the lacunae

*Table* 9.8 Pattern of expenditures under SSA in Maharashtra (Rs in lakhs)

| *Year* | *Expenditure* | *% of expenditure in released* | *% of expenditure against approved outlay* |
|---|---|---|---|
| 2002–03 | 9,671 | 55.6 | 22.4 |
| 2003–04 | 33,364 | 113.1 | 43.6 |
| 2004–05 | 38,960 | 87.8 | 45.1 |
| 2005–06 | 60,459 | 93.4 | 69.0 |
| 2006–07 | 78,360 | 96.9 | 77.2 |
| 2007–08 | 54,010 | 101.6 | 60.3 |
| 2010–11 | 137,872 | 95.9 | 65.4 |
| 2011–12 | 119,305 | 82.8 | 40.6 |
| 2013–14@ | 46,416 | 81.5 | 32.8 |

*Source:* (i) Maharashtra Prathmik Shikshan Parishad (MPSP), Mumbai; (ii) Various financial statements available at ssa.nic.in.

*Note:* @ As of September 2013.

*Table* 9.9 Allocation and expenditure under SSA in Maharashtra (Rs in lakhs)

| | *2004–05* | *2005–06* | *2006–07* | *2007–08* | *2008–09* | *2009–10* |
|---|---|---|---|---|---|---|
| Open Bal* | 4.4 | 11.3 | 14 | 27.6 | 12.4 | 19.6 |
| Actual Rel* | 51.4 | 73.9 | 79.7 | 74.6 | 94.9 | 50.3 |
| Expen* | 44.4 | 69 | 78.2 | 94.2 | 93.6 | 57.5 |
| Expen** | 79.5 | 81 | 83.5 | 92.1 | 87.2 | 82.3 |
| Closg Bal* | 11.5 | 16.2 | 15.5 | 8.1 | 13.7 | 12.3 |
| AWP&B | 86,305.7 | 87,651.4 | 101,550.6 | 87,916.1 | 109,234.7 | 119,386.5 |

*Source:* MPSP, Mumbai.

*Notes:* * As % of AWP&B; ** as per cent of grants available.

highlighted in the implementation of the scheme during 2002–05 were the following:

a) During 2003–05, government did not open new primary schools. However, in most of the villages, Vastishala (alternate schools) were opened.

b) As of November 2005, 0.11 million children continued to remain 'out of school', out of 1.58 million identified in March 2002.
c) Despite availability of funds, only 37 per cent of civil works (construction of class rooms, toilets and provision of drinking water facilities) taken up could be completed as of March 2005, mainly due to land problem.
d) Out of 76,407 primary and upper primary schools, 6,480 were single-teacher schools.
e) Supply of textbooks to 0.81 million children was delayed up to six months, affecting the quality of education.
f) In eight districts, 0.11 million disabled children were identified. However, 858 disabled children were provided aid and appliances out of 5,521 selected for this purpose.
g) The Governing Council and the Executive Committee did not monitor the implementation of SSA regularly. The Council never met during 2002–05.

## SSA fund flow pattern: two case studies

In the case of Mumbai, from Figure 9.1, we can see that for Mumbai the proportion of allocated funds actually released has been much lower than the overall state figures. The maximum that was released was

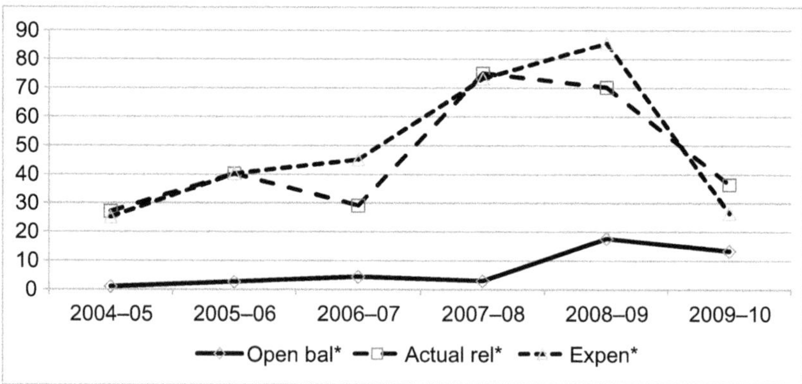


*Figure 9.1* Allocation and expenditure under SSA in BMC

*Note:* *As per cent of AWP&B. Anomaly in the figures of 2006–07 could not be reconciled with the data.

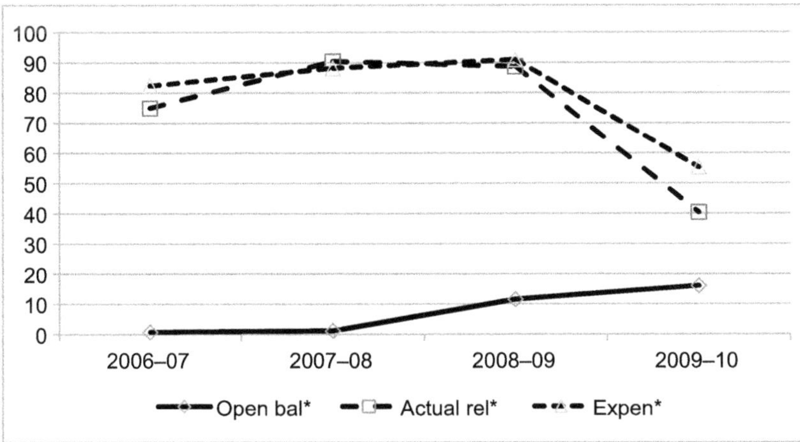


*Figure 9.2* Allocation and expenditure under SSA in Raigad

*Note:* *As per cent of AWP&B.

81 per cent of AWP in 2008–09. However, as per information given by BMC, in April 2009 nearly 10 per cent of the AWP had to be refunded bringing down the grant released to 70 per cent of AWP. In contrast, the performance of Mumbai in terms of utilization rates is better than the overall state performance. More than 90 per cent of the released grants are utilized.

With regard to Raigad, as observed from Figure 9.2, the proportion of allocated funds under AWP&B made available in case of Raigad was below 80 per cent in 2006–07. This situation was similar to that of the state as a whole. However, in 2007–08, unlike Mumbai and rest of Maharashtra, Raigad received 90 per cent of allocated funds. Like Mumbai, Raigad too has high utilization rates.

For the year 2009–10, there was a dip in the proportion of funds released and funds utilized. This is because the data pertains to end of January, 2010. This is also a significant pointer to the fact that *less than 50 per cent of the allocated grants reach the districts by the time major part of the academic as well as financial year is over*. As a result of better utilization rates in Mumbai and Raigad, opening balances, as shown in Figures 9.1 and 9.2, are much lower than in Maharastra, as reported in Table 9.9.

*Table 9.10* Expenditures and flow of funds in Raigad and Mumbai (Rs in lakhs)

| | *Raigad district* | | *Mumbai (BMC)* | | *Maharashtra* | |
|---|---|---|---|---|---|---|
| | *2008–09* | *2009–10* | *2008–09* | *2009–10* | *2008–09* | *2009–10* |
| | (*up to* 31.03.09) | (*up to* 31.01.10) | (*up to* 31.03.09) | (*up to* 31.01.10) | (*up to* 31.03.09) | (*up to* 28.02.10) |
| AWP&B | 3,360.61 | 3,592.08 | 2,790.79 | 3,288.60 | 109,234.70 | 119,386.10 |
| Funds available | 3,367.00 | 2,025.00 | 2,453.50 | 1,640.00 | 117,215.10 | 83,422.50 |
| Expenditure | 3,056.74 | 1,979.70 | 2,388.87 | 869.20 | 102,253.50 | 68,676.85 |
| Funds as % of AWP | 100.19 | 56.37 | 87.91 | 49.87 | 107.31 | 69.88 |
| Exp. as % of AWP | 90.96 | 55.11 | 85.60 | 26.43 | 93.61 | 57.52 |
| Exp. as % of funds | 90.79 | 97.76 | 97.37 | 53.00 | 87.24 | 82.32 |

Flow of grants as % of annual work plan (AWP&B)

| *Month* | *From MPSP* | | *From MPSP* | | *From Central and State Govts* | |
|---|---|---|---|---|---|---|
| | *2008–09* | *2009–10* | *2008–09* | *2009–10* | *2008–09*@ | *2009–10* |
| June–Aug | 11.9 | 13.9 | 12.5 | 15.2 | 10.5 | 15.1 |
| Sept–Oct | 16.4 | 5.6 | 17.9 | – | 24.4 | 10.1 |
| Nov–Dec | 16.4 | 20.9 | 14.3 | 21.3 | 42.3 | 25.1 |
| Jan–Feb | 19.6 | – | 14.7 | – | – | – |
| March | 24.4 | – | 21.5 | – | 17.5 | – |
| Total | 88.7 | 40.4 | 81.0 | 36.5 | 94.7 | 50.3 |

*Note*: Percentages are calculated from data provided by respective offices.
@,obtained from data available in Annual Audit Report for the year ended 31 March 2009.

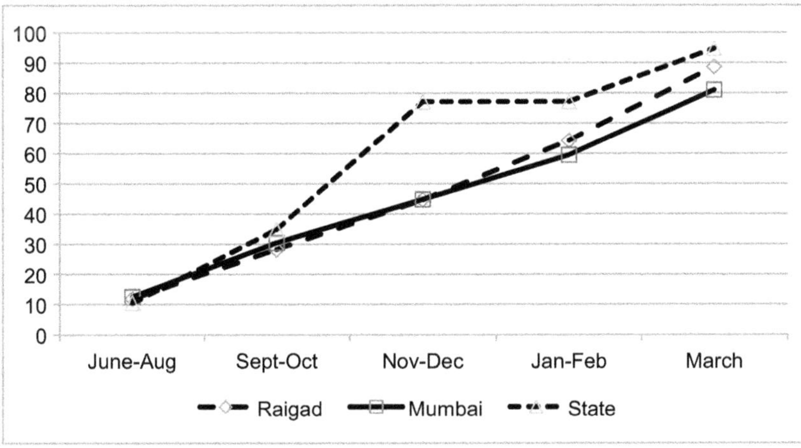


*Figure* 9.3 Fund flows, 2008–09

## Pattern of expenditures and flow of funds

Table 9.10 gives absolute figures of the funds available as well as the flow of grants. The funds available include the grants released and the unspent balance of the previous year together with the interest earned. In absolute terms, it is seen that Mumbai had a lower budget than Raigad. Relatively also, Mumbai received less grants, as seen in Figure 1. The factors for this situation are explored in sub-section 'View from the field: some highlights'. Further, Table 10 and Figure 3 highlight the slow release of funds. During 2008–09, by December, the districts had received less than 50 per cent of the AWP&B.

### *Some observations*

Once funds are received at state level, some features of their disbursal as revealed during the visits to Maharashtra MPSP office in Mumbai, Zilla Parishad office in Alibag and the sample URC and VEC are as follows:

(i) Estimates of BRCs for the next academic year are submitted to District Education Officers before end of January.
(ii) The first instalment is allocated to BRCs for school grant, teacher grant and maintenance grant in the month of July.
(iii) The BRCs then distribute funds to CRCs and VECs.
(iv) The VEC and URC that were visited informed that funds become available only by September.

This slow release of funds affects intervention-wise expenditures as seen in Table 9.11.

- It is evident that uniformly for both years, the interventions which get funds from first instalment onwards show near total utilization (note that for 2009–10, utilization of 100 per cent cannot be expected even for these interventions, since Table 9.12 reveals release of 50 per cent grants by end of February 2010).
- Interventions for OSC, inclusive education, research and evaluation and girls' education show poor and inconsistent utilization.

## View from the field: some highlights

In this sub-section, we highlight some observations from visits to a VEC and a URC.

- Some issues of VECs – experience at Uchede village, Pen Taluka, Raigad
    - The requirement of at least three quotations for every item that requires minimum expenditure of Rs1,000 delays even minor repairs.
    - Very often meetings of VEC do not take place for lack of quorum. This delays sanction for expenses leading to delayed expenditure or unutilized grants.
    - Children have to sit on the floor as there is no provision for benches/desks in the grants.
    - The practice of granting permission for establishment of private English medium schools in the vicinity of Zilla Parishad schools is resulting in fall in enrolment at these schools.
- Some issues in Mumbai: experience from BMC and URC in Mumbai
    - The enrolment in BMC schools is declining. As a result, no new schools are sanctioned in the last four years.
    - Senior BMC teachers are deputed as coordinators and their vacancies are filled by para-teachers.
    - For expenditures to be made by CRCs, sanction of the concerned Municipal Councillor is necessary. The Councillors do not attend meetings regularly despite several reminders and this delays expenditure.
    - The funds disbursed by URC to CRCs remain unutilized for want of sanction.

*Table 9.11* Comparative intervention-wise expenditures in Raigad and Mumbai (expenditures as percentage of AWP&B)

| | *Intervention* | *Raigad district* | | *Mumbai (BMC)* | | *Maharashtra* | |
|---|---|---|---|---|---|---|---|
| | | 2008–09 (*up to* 31.03.09) | 2009–10 (*up to* 31.01.10) | 2008–09 (*up to* 31.03.09) | 2009–10 (*up to* 31.01.10) | 2008–09 (*up to* 31.03.09) | 2009–10 (*up to* 28.02.10) |
| 1 | New schools | – | – | – | – | – | – |
| 2 | New teachers salary | 94.1 | 92.3 | – | – | 100.0@ | 69.6@ |
| 3 | Teacher grant | 100.0 | 100.0 | 91.2 | 100 | 100.0 | 90.5 |
| 4 | BRC | 100.0 | 75.6 | 82.6 | 35.6 | 99.6 | 53.3 |
| 5 | CRC | 100.0 | 100.0 | 98.5 | 100 | 91.8 | 93.5 |
| 6 | Teachers training | 100.0 | 82.5 | 86.6 | 48.33 | 90.0 | 75.0 |
| 7 | OSC | *16.3* | 40.2 | *46.2#* | *39.1* | 98.1 | 48.0 |
| 8 | Remedial | – | 98.2 | – | 100 | – | 72.7 |
| 9 | Free text books | 100.0 | 5.5 | 91.6 | 2.2 | 99.8 | 46.6 |
| 10 | IED | 100.0 | 37.4 | 92.3 | 12.8 | 98.4 | 45.1 |
| 11 | Civil works | 92.1 | 47.6 | 100 | 0 | 95.5 | 61.4 |
| 12 | TLE | 100.0 | 94.6 | – | – | 98.7 | 76.0 |
| 13 | Maintenance | 100.0 | 100.0 | 98.3 | 96.8 | 100.0 | 93.9 |
| 14 | School grant | 100.0 | 100.0 | 98.7 | 99.1 | 99.7 | 94.7 |
| 15 | Research and evaluation | 100.0 | 21.7 | 98.7 | 18.6 | 100.0 | 52.4 |
| 16 | Management and quality | 100.0 | 62.3 | 99.9 | 29.7 | 82.1 | 66.5 |
| 17 | Innovative activity | 100.0 | 2.3 | 99.1 | 1.4 | 66.5 | 56.5 |
| 18 | Community training | 100.0 | 100.0 | 100 | 100 | 100.0 | 55.6 |
| 19 | NPEGEL+KGBV | – | – | 99.4 | 42.4 | 96.4 | 38.5 |

*Notes*

# inconsistent utilization.

1 Results obtained from expenditure reports provided by Raigad ZP office, Alibag, BMC office and MPSP office, Mumbai.

2 @ Includes teachers' salary (recurring).

*Table 9.12* Funds flow and expenditure in a URC# under BMC

| *Month* | *2008–09* | *2009–10* |
|---|---|---|
| July–Aug | 38.9 | 71.9 |
| Sept–Oct | 28.4 | 6.7 |
| Nov–Dec | 9.6 | 5.3 |
| Jan–Feb | 16.3 | 15.2 |
| March | 6.7 | 0.8 |
| Expenditure as % of funds | 96.45 | 85.7 |
| Total funds received | 41.73 lakhs | 37.42 lakhs |

*Note:* #URC No.1- Kasturba Gandhi Cross Rd 2 Municipal School, Borivali (East), Mumbai. Figures are percentages of total funds received.

- URC1 had to refund to BMC cumulative interest on unutilized grants for the period 2005–10, amounting to Rs 2.3 lakhs.
- During 2009–10, URC1 had to also refund Rs 1.06 lakhs from teacher grant, school grant and maintenance grant due to merger of eight schools on account of fall in enrolment.

In Table 9.12, we can observe the manner in which funds are received by an URC/BRC

## Meeting the target on out-of-school children

Targeting 'out-of-school' children is a major challenge in many states, including Maharashtra. With a view to identify OSC, the state conducted household level surveys in 2006 and 2008. During 2006, about 0.17 million children and during 2008, about 0.14 million children were found to be affected due to migration (Government of Maharashtra 2009). The Performance Audit Report 15 has highlighted the non-fulfilment of the target of achieving the declared primary goal of SSA, namely to enrol every out-of-school child in the age group 6–14 years either in a school or in an alternative education facility by 2003 (later modified to 2005). According to survey conducted in March 2002, out of 17.5 million child population in the age group of 6–14 years in the state, 1.58 million children (9 per cent) were identified to be out of school in March 2001. Out of these children, 1.44 million children were covered in regular and alternate schools and as of November 2005, 0.11 million children remained out of school (CAG 2006). However, as per the data from MPSP, OSC reduced from 1,578,863 in 2002–03 to 56,080 in 2009–10.

Given the fact that estimating and identifying the OSC is fraught with many difficulties, the few observations at the sample districts are in order.

(a) Mumbai

- The identified OSC are admitted to classes that are conducted by NGOs under Mahatma Phule Education Guarantee Scheme (MPEGS).
- The survey to identify OSC was conducted by the NGOs in 2006. But, this was not a door-to-door survey.
- The last door-to-door survey by BMC was in 2001 and next one in 2010.
- In 2009, BMC had identified 20,000 OSC and at present 1,100 MPEGS classes are conducted.
- Due to floating population in the slums, it is difficult to get estimates of OSC. There is a possibility of underestimation or even double counting of some OSC.
- The ad hoc implementation of the scheme is apparent by the fact that BMC does not provide space for MPEGS classes. So makeshift arrangements are made in temples, volunteers' homes, etc.

(b) Raigad

- In Raigad district, the numbers of OSC who had benefited from SSA were 6,190 and 2,116 in 2008–09 and 2009–10, respectively.
- Now, reportedly only 333 OSC remain to be covered. However, the officials confessed that the estimates are very often faulty, since identification exercise is not conducted scientifically.
- Many OSC are migrant seasonal workers. Once they return, the children are to be admitted in their hometowns.
- Many children of migrant population dropout and have to be readmitted.

## Findings

In the context of Constitutional Directive on universalization of elementary education, the above sections highlight that Maharashtra presents a picture of shortfall between the lofty ideals and gigantic efforts of the social reformers, thinkers, philanthropists and educationists on the one hand and the contemporary status of elementary education on the other hand.

Maharashtra stands tall, second to Kerala, in terms of literacy rates, including those for females. In contrast, it lags behind many other states in overall educational development. Distribution of education across regions, social groups and gender remains extremely uneven. It is claimed that as of November 2005, only 0.11 million children remained out of school from among the 1.58 million children identified in 2001. But the fact overlooked is that the persistent dropouts each year are adding to the number of OSC and this truth is revealed by the 64th round of NSS that *in 2007–08 about 1.2 million children were out of school, putting a question mark on the efficacy of SSA.*

The third section reveals that there is an improvement in the overall utilization of funds released under SSA thereby satisfying much of the several requirements, including those for quality education. Yet, there are several bureaucratic hurdles in timely release of grants. This drawback is preventing effective planning and execution of activities related to aspects of equity and access. The *ad hoc* manner of identifying OSC, the informal arrangements made to run classes under MPEGS and over-dependence on para-teachers instead of regularly appointed staff are the stumbling block towards fulfilment of the primary goal of SSA – which is to get every child in school.

The findings of this micro-level inquiry serve the limited purpose of identifying the drawbacks that impact the flow of funds and prevent effective implementation of SSA, in terms of fulfilling its primary objective of universalization of elementary education. There is a need to explore in a more detailed macro-level socioeconomic study whether the significantly large presence of OSC is reflection of contradictions between aspects of equity and access and the present education policy of both the central and state governments.

## Notes

1 EDI is a composite index covering four groups of indicators, representing access, infrastructure, teachers and outcome.
2 NER (net enrolment ratio) is defined as number of persons of specified age group attending corresponding level of classes to the estimated population in that age group.

## References

CAG. 2006. *Audit Report (Civil) for the year ended 31 March 2006*, available at http://www.cag.gov.in/html/reports/civil/2006_15_peraud/highlights.pdf (accessed on 10 October 2013).

Government of India. 2013. *Status of Education and Vocational Training in India. NSS 66th Round, Report No. 551*. National Sample Survey Organization, Ministry of Statistics and Programme Implementation, New Delhi.

Government of Maharashtra. 2001. *Socio-Economic Review of Districts 2000–01*. Directorate of Economics and Statistics, Planning Department, Mumbai.

Government of Maharashtra. 2002. *Human Development Report Maharashtra 2002*. Government of Maharashtra, Mumbai.

Government of Maharashtra. 2009. *A Report on 'Participation and Expenditure on Education', 64th NSS round*. Directorate of Economics and Statistics, Planning Department, Mumbai.

Government of Maharashtra. 2010. *Economic Survey of Maharashtra 2009–10*. Directorate of Economics and Statistics, Planning Department, Mumbai.

Government of Maharashtra. 2013. *Economic Survey of Maharashtra 2012–13*. Directorate of Economics and Statistics, Planning Department, Mumbai.

MHRD. 2008. *Analysis of Budgeted Expenditure on Education 2005–06 to 2007–08*. Ministry of Human Resources Development, Government of India, New Delhi.

MHRD. 2013. *Analysis of Budgeted Expenditure on Education 2009–10 to 2011–12*. Ministry of Human Resources Development, Government of India, New Delhi.

NUEPA. 2009. *Elementary Education in India: District Report Cards 2007–08*, National University of Educational Planning and Administration, New Delhi.

NUEPA. 2012. *Elementary Education in India: Progress towards UEE*, National University of Educational Planning and Administration, New Delhi.

Paranjape, M.S. 2007. 'Uneven Distribution of Education in Maharashtra – Rural-Urban, Gender and Caste Inequalities', *Economic and Political Weekly*, 42(03): 213–216.

Planning Commission. 2010. 'Databook for DCH 2010', Government of India, available at http://planningcommision.gov.in (accessed on 08 December 2013).

Prabhu, Seeta and Kamdar, Sangeeta. 2001. 'Educational Attainment in Kerala and Maharashtra: Comparative Perspective', *Perspectives in Education*, Vol. 17, Special Issue, 2001.

Registrar General of India. 2006. *Projected population (5–18 year) up to 2016*, Office of Registrar General and Census Commissioner, Government of India, available at http://www.educationforallinindia.com/projected-population-upto-2016-by-RGI.htm (accessed on 15 January 2011).

Sen, Tapas K. *et al*. 2010. *Matching Human Development across Maharashtra with Its Economic Development*, mimeo. National Institute of Public Finance and Policy, New Delhi.

# 10

# FUND-FLOW PATTERN UNDER SARVA SHIKSHA ABHIYAN IN WEST BENGAL

## A case study of Bankura district

*Archita Pramanik*

*'If a man empties his purse into his head, no man can take it away from him. An investment in knowledge always pays the best interest.'*

Benjamin Franklin

### Introduction

Education leads to the formation of a stable and democratic society by contributing to the society's human capital (Schultz 1961) formation. Fostering human resource development is one of the main goals of every nation. Education and especially primary education becomes the backbone of growth for any country. Along with the enhancement of human capital, education also leads to generation of positive externalities which have spill-over effects for the society as a whole (McMohan 2004). The social rate of return from education is always higher than the private rate of return, but individual often hesitates to invest the maximum possible amount in education because of the risk factors related to it (Becker 1965). Hence, it is expected that special attention would be provided by the government for the betterment of this sector through proper funding and infrastructure development. The most explicit action will be to provide a child with basic minimum education.

In a country like India, where it is mandatory to provide free and compulsory education to the children between the age group of 6–14 years, the public provisioning of education is very essential. Compulsory education for all children of 6–14 years was a Constitutional target in India mandated to be achieved within 10 years from its commencement

(1950). However, since the Directive Principles of the Constitution are not enforceable by law, it took many more decades and much more indignant public action for the education to finally become basic right of the children. Many national policies were formulated since independence. But the launch of Sarva Shiksha Abhiyan (SSA) in a mission mode in 2001–02 all over the country increased the pace towards achieving universal elementary education (UEE). Along with the aim of achieving universal enrolment, retention, etc., the SSA also tries to address the fiscal constraint faced by the states in increasing their expenditure on elementary education (Mukherjee and Aiyar 2010).

As a result, the elementary education scenario witnessed considerable transformations over the years, such as numerical expansion of elementary schools in the country, narrowing of gender gap, an increase in percentage of enrolled children belonging to scheduled castes and tribes, etc. Even though the programme has been successful to a large extent, some serious problems still remain, which made the growth of education sluggish in the country. The level of dropouts in general and in particular of children belonging to disadvantaged and weaker sections has remained high, along with low levels of attendance and poor level of learning achievement (Sinha and Reddy 2011). In addition to the existence of some rigidity in the implementation process, it has also been observed that over the times the extent of financial resources provided for this kind of education in the country has remained insufficient.

The target of spending 6 per cent of GDP on education has never been achieved in the country till today. But it must be noted that despite recognising the contribution of education to economic growth and development, the pattern of allocation of resources to education in India is still far from satisfactory (Tilak 1989). The coverage of the centrally sponsored scheme (CSS) (through which central government contributes resources to the state education sector) has varied over time, and they have maintained no uniformity in distribution over different states. Along with regional imbalance, budgetary imbalance arising out of resource sharing mechanism, fiscal crisis, government's approach towards fiscal reform, etc. have altogether led to under-investment in the field of elementary education in India.

The National Policy on Education and its accompanying Programme of Action, issued in 1956, emphasised on the importance of decentralisation of planning and management at all levels as well as greater community participation. It sought to improve education planning and management structures but it also had its limits, leading to unsatisfactory results.

## Objectives of the study

So far, it becomes clear that the condition of elementary education in India is not impressive. The states in India are resource constrained with varying fiscal health and in such a situation providing matching grants for SSA becomes difficult for the states. Because of this imbalance between the centre and the state, several CSS might have faced problems, and their implementation might not have been efficient, leading to an unsatisfactory result in the elementary education structure.

The study therefore intends to evaluate the success of SSA in an educationally backward state like West Bengal. The success of the programme is determined based on the fulfilment of the objectives of SSA. The questions raised in this study tries to throw light on the efficiency in utilisation of the funds provided for the purpose, equality in distribution of the funds and the nature of distribution. It also questions the quality of students, whether it has improved or not after implementation of SSA. Another aim of SSA is to bridge the social gaps in education. To what extent this objective has been fulfilled and how far the community participation has assisted in achieving these goals are the other areas which have been addressed in this study. In a way, it has been tried to access whether the problem lies in implementation or in the utilization of funds in SSA.

## Methodology

Since the study includes analysis of the financing pattern in SSA by the state and the centre, quantitative method has been chosen here to carry out the research. Correlation has been used to understand the pattern of funds allocation and the efficiency of funds utilisation in the state by the Government of India (GOI) as well as the state itself.

Again, to understand the community participation in elementary education, qualitative method is used. A case study of two schools in Bankura district of West Bengal has been done to bring out the underlying picture of the local level governance in elementary education. Interviews have been conducted with the headmasters and teachers and few students of the two schools surveyed in the district of Bankura. Face-to-face interviews have been conducted with the finance officer of the district project office and also with the additional state project director of the state project office.

The study is based almost solely on the data from the secondary sources, mainly the reports of SSA from state project office, financial statement of district project office, District Information System for Education (DISE) reports and other economic reports from different governmental sources like Ministry of Human Resource and Development, Finance Commission Report, State and Centre Budget, West Bengal State education Department, Reserve Bank of India, National Sample Survey Organisation (NSSO), etc.

## West Bengal's economy

West Bengal is an unusual and, indeed, unique state in the country. It is the only state in India to have been ruled continuously (since 1977) by a Left Front government for over a quarter of a century. This government in turn has been motivated by a vision of political, economic and social change that has been different from that observed among most other state governments or the central government (West Bengal Human Development Report 2004). Regardless of such political stability, the economic indicators of the state do not show much of an improvement. In terms of per capita state domestic product (SDP), West Bengal had been the richest state in India in 1960, but by the end of the last millennium, the SDP (per capita) rank of the state declined to nine. Its per capita income (NSDP) in current prices in 2004–05 was the lowest among the middle-income states – Tamil Nadu, Kerala, Karnataka and Andhra Pradesh having overtaken West Bengal. It has been found that the growth rate of total revenue receipts did not remain constant throughout with growth rates fluctuating between 8 and 20 per cent.

The growth rate of tax revenue experienced major fluctuations over the last decade, and it was remarkably high (around 20 per cent) in the pre-crisis period. There was a sharp decline in 2008–09, and thereafter growth rate of tax revenue increased steadily to around 23 per cent in 2010–11. Non-tax revenue growth also experienced similar fluctuations with absolute level actually falling below that of the previous period (Roychowdhury 2011). With fluctuating growth of tax and non-tax revenue, the state confronted with gross fiscal deficit and revenue deficit growth rates of 18 per cent between 2005–06 and 2010–11. Decline in the agricultural productivity and diminishing share in industrial production in the state can be the reasons behind the depressing economic condition of the state.

Like the economic scenario, the social development of the state is also of great concern. The Human Development Index (HDI) score of the state is 0.305, which places the state in the 10th position among 17 major states of India. The high degree of occupational dependence on agriculture, especially in terms of agricultural labour, and its rapidly declining income share is an indication of a higher incidence of poverty in the countryside. There is a large rural–urban gap in infant mortality rate, and the gap has not come down since the mid-sixties along with wide prevalence of anaemia among women. The community health care management initiative is not strong enough to address issues related to community's health awareness (West Bengal Development Report 2010).

The HDI of West Bengal has also revealed that the extent of relative deprivation at the district level is much more as compared to the overall Indian situation. The relationship between urbanisation and human development is much stronger in the high-income group in West Bengal compared to that in the low-income category (Bhattacharya 1998). In rural West Bengal, only 32 per cent of the households have access to electricity. In terms of access to safe drinking water, the scenario is somewhat better. The current statistics shows that the literacy rate in West Bengal has improved over time but there remains variation in inter-district literacy rate within the state. The enrolment rate has also increased in the state of West Bengal, but the mean years of schooling in West Bengal is only four years, which places it just above Bihar, which ranks last in this regard among the major states of India. This is because the school dropout rate at primary level is phenomenally high in West Bengal. The rural inequality in West Bengal is low; but then, the spending power per capita is also low in the state. Rural Punjab or rural Kerala is much more prosperous than rural West Bengal (Khasnabis 2009).

## Educational scenario of the state

West Bengal is the most densely populated state in the country, and because of various historical, sociological and economic reasons provision of elementary education has been very challenging. The literacy rate in West Bengal is higher than the national average. But the rate of growth of literacy in the state was lower than that at the all-India level during the 50th and 55th NSS Rounds (West Bengal Development Report 2010). The educational progress and the spread of education are highly uneven in the state in terms of gender, religion, locations and districts. In terms of literacy of the SC, ST and the Muslim population, the state shows existence of gaps.

Some of the districts have a much lower literacy rate than the state and national average, and are also below the average of some educationally poor states of the country. These backward districts rank at the bottom of the Human Development list, hosting the majority of the agricultural labourers of the state with severely disadvantaged health facilities, infrastructure, employment, etc. Districts with a higher concentration of Adivasis, Muslims and Dalits tend to have lower literacy rates. The correlation between a high concentration of backward communities and a lower rate of literacy is quite strong in the state (Rana 2010). The enrolment of children from educationally disadvantaged communities, i.e. SC, ST and Muslim, in primary education has been more or less equal to the national level, but the same has decreased for upper primary level. Husain and Chatterjee (2009) have reflected that the primary education completion rate of Muslims is lower than that of not only the Hindu upper castes, but also of Hindu backward castes in both rural and urban West Bengal.

The quality of education in the state has also not kept pace with time. The Annual Status of education Report 2012 (ASER 2013) shows 41 per cent of the children from all schools in class four cannot read text book of class two. Study by Pratichi research team in 2003 also showed children of classes three and four could not even write their names properly. Complaints were also found against teachers like 'they don't teach', 'they don't come to school', 'they come late', 'they sleep in classes, 'they make the children pick the grey hair of teachers', and so on. The poor quality of teaching (including teacher absenteeism) combined with other socio-economic problems (such as the involvement of children in sibling care, economic activities, etc.) has contributed to a high level of absenteeism among the children. The presence of private tuition has also been a matter of concern in the state. Although the government of West Bengal has banned private tuition by school teachers, it needs to be noted that private tuition at the primary level is provided by those who are not subject to the ban. According to ASER 2012, 72 per cent of the children in government schools and 69 per cent children in private schools attend private tuitions.

To some extent, the low level of funding in the elementary education by the state can be blamed as a reason for the degrading quality of education in the state. The budgeted expenditure on education and training in West Bengal has declined proportionately over time. Although it is higher than the central government figures, many of the states such as Assam, Bihar, Chhattisgarh, Kerala, Maharashtra, Rajasthan, Tripura, Uttarakhand and Uttar Pradesh have allocated, out of the state budget, a higher proportion on education and training in revenue account than in West Bengal. In the decade of 1970s, the highest amount of expenditure out of total expenditure on education (revenue account) used to be incurred on elementary education. However, from the early 1980s, secondary education gradually replaced elementary education in terms of budgetary allocation (West Bengal Human Development Report 2004).

Nevertheless, increased budgetary expenditure is no solution to improve the quality of education. 'Some specific thought must be given to how any resources affect the incentives of people in the schools. One cannot expect to improve student achievement and outcomes simply by putting more resources in to the existing schools' (Hanushek 2013: 136). Perhaps, more important matter of concern is the question of efficient utilisation as well as rationalisation that crops up mainly when one finds inter-school differences in outcome indicators.

While the physical infrastructure of schools has visibly improved under District Primary Education Programme (DPEP), the distribution of teachers across schools is far from optimum. Although, by and large, the training programmes have been successful in sensitising the teachers about the need for learning modern pedagogical tools, they have not been effective in orienting the teachers towards the need for closing inter-group disparities and weakening the close association between the student's innate social characteristics and his/her learning achievement (Chakraborty *et al.* 2005). Therefore, it can be inferred that the low quality of education, disparity in gender, caste, religion, increasing prevalence of private tuition, etc. in the state can be the outcome of decreasing share of state's budget on elementary education, inefficient utilisation of the funds and negligence of the government in monitoring the elementary education sector.

To make any scheme successful in a particular state, it is important to have state's full support and commitment. The financial assistance for the programme is provided by the centre as well as the state following the matching grants criteria. At the beginning of the programme, the centre to state ratio of finance was 85:15, then it changed to 75:25, and the current ratio is 65:35. The obligation of providing for new investments was more on centre than on states so far. But the changed pattern of funding resulted in inequality in terms of flow of funds in the states of the country. It is found that some states like Jharkhand, Karnataka, Mizoram, Orissa, Gujarat, Haryana, Tripura, etc. received more than 75 per cent of GOI share during the 10th Plan period at the cost of other states that got less than stipulated amount (Geetha Rani 2007).

The larger the states' own education budget, the larger the resources it receives from the centre, due to the matching grants criteria. Poor states with smaller outlays for education receive less from the centre, and inequalities are thereby aggravated. The allocations by the Finance Commission, which aims at maintenance of the education system, are probably guided by a 'rewarding' motive. Also, while implementing the schemes, the states are hardly allowed to amend the rules or guidelines for expenditure. Therefore, in this case, it is not impossible that states implement them without any sense of ownership of the schemes (Jha *et al.* 2008). At a macro perspective, it has been found that the share of centre in SSA for the state of West Bengal has hardly attained the prescribed level.

## Financial allocation to SSA in West Bengal

Currently, the share between centre and the states in allocation of funds to SSA is in the ratio of 65:35. Has the criteria on matching grants been followed in practical terms? Table 10.1 shows the result. The central government initially tried to provide the state with matching grants. But the ratio changed with time. At first the ratio was 80:20, then it became 75:25, and then finally 50:50. The table shows that centre's share hardly reached 75 per cent except for the first year. The centre to state's ratio also shows that centre's share diminished along with time. The state has not been able to provide sufficient amount for the SSA according to the matching grant criterion, and so the centre has also not contributed the same.

The reasons put forward by several studies are low tax collection by the central government as well the state's slow growth in own tax revenue collection (Roychowdhury 2012), coupled with slow growth of education cess (special tax levied by the central government to finance basic education in the country) collection (Mukherjee and Sikdar 2012) and high deficit of the state and the centre (Bagchi 2006 and Dasgupta 2012).

*Table 10.1* Centre and state's share in SSA in West Bengal

| *Year* | *Centre's grant as a % of total* | *State's grant as a % of total* | *Centre:State share* | *Other sources as a % of total* |
|---|---|---|---|---|
| 2001–02 | 81.5 | 14.4 | 5.7 | 04.2 |
| 2002–03 | 68.2 | 22.3 | 3.1 | 09.6 |
| 2003–04 | 53.4 | 17.8 | 3.0 | 28.9 |
| 2004–05 | 59.3 | 17.9 | 3.3 | 22.9 |
| 2005–06 | 51.9 | 20.9 | 2.5 | 27.4 |
| 2006–07 | 65.2 | 21.1 | 3.1 | 13.7 |
| 2007–08 | 61.7 | 33.3 | 1.9 | 05.1 |
| 2008–09 | 44.1 | 23.8 | 1.9 | 32.2 |
| 2009–10 | 54.7 | 33.0 | 1.7 | 12.4 |
| 2010–11 | 52.6 | 28.4 | 1.8 | 21.5 |
| 2011–12 | 49.8 | 27.3 | 1.8 | 26.1 |

*Source*: MHRD and own calculation.

## Inter-district study

Analysis of the flow of funds shows that the process of delivery of the funds from the centre to the states, from the states to the districts and from districts to the schools involves various government implementing bodies. To determine the efficiency in utilisation of the funds at the micro level, it is necessary to understand how smoothly the decentralisation process works at the district level and how far it has been successful in achieving UEE in West Bengal. In economic terms, the concept of efficiency can easily be defined as the relationship between inputs and outputs, whereby economic efficiency is increased by an increase in units of output per unit of input. This can occur by holding output constant and decreasing input or by deriving greater production from the same level of input. But education does not have a well-defined production function, and so it does not have a well-defined single indicator of output. For the typical profit-maximising firm, it is possible to put money values on the inputs of the production process and, in turn, assess its efficiency. Therefore, a firm achieves maximum efficiency when the price of the inputs used to make the commodity is equal to the marginal cost of production of the commodity. In education, this is not feasible since many of the outputs are unquantifiable in terms of market prices. As a result, in education combination of several parameters like teachers, buildings, class size, curriculum, student–teacher ratio, etc. are used as proxy for the inputs. Table 10.2 shows a district-wise account of various parameters on the efficiency of education system in West Bengal.

The child population of the districts, the out-of-school children, the child density per school, the student–teacher ratio and percentage of schools with girls' toilet facility in the districts are taken as the parameters in the table. The child population of each district has been taken to show the total number of children between the age group 5 and 14 years in each district. The out-of-school children show the number of children in the district not attending school. This shows how successful SSA has been in bringing universal attainment rate. Child density shows the ratio of children in the district to the total number of schools in the districts. Student–teacher ratio along with high teacher quality is a significant indicator in ascertaining the educational structure (Hanushek 2003). The ideal student–teacher ratio according to Right to Education (RTE) norms is 35, i.e. for every 35 students there has to be one teacher. Finally, the percentage of schools with girls' toilet facility has been taken as an indicator because the existence of girls' toilet facility instead of common toilets helps in bringing more number of girl children to schools. In India, studies have shown that girls do not prefer to go to school because there are no separate

*Table 10.2* District-wise education parameters

| *Districts* | *Child population (age 5–14), 2008–09* | *Out-of-school children 2008–09* | *Student–teacher ratio* | | *Child density per school 2008–09* | *Percentage of schools with girls' toilet facility* | |
|---|---|---|---|---|---|---|---|
| | | | *2002–03* | *2008–09* | | *2002–03* | *2008–09* |
| Bankura | 580,054 | 10,336 | 35 | 34 | 168 | 4 | 38.5 |
| Barddhhaman | 1,288,729 | 19,713 | 44 | 43 | 322 | 13.2 | 82.3 |
| Birbhum | 616,313 | 11,364 | 47 | 38 | 260 | 4.1 | 13.1 |
| DGHC | 210,459 | 5,320 | 35 | 22 | 272 | 11 | 12.1 |
| Dakshin Dinajpur | 307,414 | 7,992 | 46 | 42 | 263 | 2.9 | 27.7 |
| Howrah | 696,189 | 15,702 | 50 | 42 | 330 | 8 | 33.1 |
| Hugli | 775,714 | 6,564 | 52 | 39 | 259 | 10.6 | 43.2 |
| Jalpaiguri | 696,234 | 24,419 | 66 | 48 | 342 | 3.7 | 32.6 |
| Koch Bihar | 563,360 | 5,780 | 54 | 52 | 309 | 31.7 | 29.6 |
| Kolkata | 937,097 | 10,646 | 43 | 33 | 660 | 21.2 | 31.7 |
| Malda | 765,203 | 9,036 | 61 | 58 | 406 | 2.7 | 10.1 |
| Murshidabad | 1,282,039 | 36,228 | 70 | 47 | 405 | 7.9 | 32.8 |
| Nadia | 870,845 | 2,510 | 59 | 33 | 335 | 6.9 | 45.9 |
| N 24 Parganas | 1,826,977 | 18,941 | 58 | 48 | 505 | 17 | 44.5 |
| Pashchim Medinipur | 1,017,478 | 8,535 | 41 | 30 | 218 | 2.7 | 12.1 |
| Purba Medinipur | 866,379 | 4,966 | 49 | 38 | 273 | 2.5 | 10.1 |
| Purulia | 518,663 | 28,401 | 44 | 49 | 174 | 1.8 | 57.4 |
| Siliguri | 265,994 | 9,207 | 59 | 78 | 670 | 6.6 | 61.7 |
| S 24 Parganas | 1,413,459 | 16,961 | 73 | 52 | 385 | 7 | 30 |
| Uttar Dinajpur | 636,840 | 30,005 | NA | 45 | 445 | | 47.8 |

*Source:* DISE District Report Cards.

toilets for them (Rana *et al.* 2003). So, girls' toilet facility has been taken as one of the parameters to understand if it has led to an increase in enrolment in the schools.

On comparison of the child population between the age group of 5 and 14 years with the total enrolment of students, the results show that even after the implementation of SSA in 2001–02, there still remains huge enrolment gaps in the districts of West Bengal (Table 10.2).

The high student–teacher ratio which existed during the initial years of SSA has to some extent reduced in the districts. But the reduction is unequal, as some districts like Malda, Siliguri and South 24 Parganas still show high student–teacher ratio. In Siliguri the ratio increased from 59 to 78, though there was an increase in the number of schools between 2002–03 and 2008–09. It can be said that increasing number of schools cannot single-handedly solve the problem of access to schools. Indeed, there has been an increase in the number of schools with girls' toilet facility in the districts, which shows that funds provided for the construction of separate toilets have been utilised to some extent, but still enrolment gap has not been bridged.

In case of inter-district allocation of funds, it can be shown whether the funds allocated was in proportion to the number of schools, number of teachers, student–teacher ratio, enrolment rate, etc. Table 10.3 shows

*Table 10.3* Ratio of funds approved by GOI to the districts of West Bengal

| *Districts* | *2004–05* | *2005–06* | *2006–07* | *2007–08* | *2008–09* | *2009–10* | *2010–11* | *2011–12* | *Total* |
|---|---|---|---|---|---|---|---|---|---|
| Bankura | 3.5 | 5.3 | 5 | 5.7 | 4.5 | 3.8 | 4.4 | 4.5 | 36.7 |
| Bardhaman | 9.6 | 12.8 | 1 | 4.7 | 6.7 | 6.1 | 6.3 | 6 | 53.2 |
| Birbhum | 3.6 | 5 | 4.5 | 3.6 | 3.7 | 3.3 | 4.5 | 4.1 | 32.3 |
| Cooch Bihar | 3.2 | 5.2 | 4.3 | 4.4 | 3.2 | 3.3 | 3.5 | 4.3 | 31.4 |
| Dakshin Dinajpur | 2.1 | 1.6 | 2.2 | 3.9 | 2.8 | 2.5 | 2.8 | 3.1 | 21 |
| Darjeeling | 1.7 | 2 | 1.5 | 1.6 | 1.4 | 1.2 | 1.3 | 1.1 | 11.8 |
| Hoogly | 5.9 | 5.5 | 5.8 | 3.6 | 4.2 | 4.1 | 3.7 | 4.1 | 36.9 |
| Howrah | 5.8 | 5.1 | 5.1 | 4.7 | 3.1 | 3.1 | 3.4 | 4 | 34.3 |
| Jalpaiguri | 3.8 | 2.7 | 4.5 | 6 | 6.1 | 6.2 | 5.2 | 6 | 40.5 |
| Kolkata | 3.8 | 3.6 | 2.2 | 2 | 1.8 | 1.8 | 1.5 | 1.9 | 18.6 |
| Malda | 3.6 | 3.4 | 4.9 | 5.3 | 5.7 | 5.7 | 5.5 | 6 | 40.1 |
| Murshidabad | 6.6 | 8.9 | 10.1 | 10.4 | 8.6 | 9.2 | 10.8 | 11.5 | 76.1 |
| Nadia | 6.9 | 6.3 | 9.1 | 7.4 | 5.3 | 5.5 | 5.5 | 5 | 51 |
| N 24 Parganas | 9.1 | 6 | 7.4 | 8.9 | 8.8 | 6.9 | 7.4 | 8.8 | 63.3 |
| Pashchim Medinipur | 8.5 | 8.2 | 6.8 | 5.2 | 8.1 | 7.3 | 8 | 7.2 | 59.3 |
| Purba Medinipur | 7.2 | 6.9 | 7.2 | 4.3 | 6.5 | 10.4 | 5.8 | 5.8 | 54.1 |
| Purulia | 2.7 | 1.7 | 2.7 | 4.6 | 4.4 | 4 | 4.7 | 4 | 28.8 |
| Siliguri | 1.9 | 2 | 1.6 | 1 | 1.3 | 1.2 | 1.4 | 1.8 | 12.2 |
| S 24 Paraganas | 7.6 | 8.7 | 9.1 | 8.4 | 8.2 | 8.7 | 9.5 | 5.9 | 66.1 |
| Uttar Dinajpur | 3 | 2.6 | 5.1 | 4.3 | 5.6 | 5.8 | 4.7 | 4.9 | 36 |

*Source*: SSA Report West Bengal.

the ratio of funds allotted by the GOI to the districts of West Bengal. It is the ratio of total amount approved by the government to each district to the total amount approved every year.

The funds have not been allocated equally among the different districts of the state. This may be because of difference in the demands for grants as well as difference in the sizes of the districts. The maximum amount was approved to Murshidabad district, followed by South 24 Parganas and North 24 Parganas. Murshidabad has the highest percentage of out-of-school children among all the districts. But in terms of child population and school-going children, North 24 Parganas has the highest percentage followed by South 24 Parganas. In a way it can be said that, in order to increase enrolment Murshidabad has been allotted more funds compared to other districts. North and South 24 Parganas have been allotted funds according to the size of the child population, number of government schools, etc. But if a comparison is made between the districts receiving high funds in terms of number of schools, total enrolment and number of teachers, then a different picture is drawn. The number of schools increased in all the three districts between 2002–03 and 2011–12 according to the DISE data, but enrolment increased only in Murshidabad. The other two districts show fall in enrolment even with increased number of schools and teachers. On the other hand, Siliguri is one of the districts where the student–teacher ratio increased to 78 in 2008–09 with increase in the number of schools, but is among one of the districts receiving least percentage of funds.

To find out whether the funds were allotted strictly in accordance with the educational parameters, which determine the educational outcomes, a correlation between the funds approved and several education parameters has been done. Here, a cumulative sum of the total funds approved by the GOI to the different districts of the state from 2004–05 to 2011–12 has been considered, and the parameters chosen are number of students, number of teachers, number of schools, enrolment percentage and student–teacher ratio. These parameters indicate whether the funds provided have been effective in increasing enrolment, number of teachers and number of schools and decreasing the student–teacher ratio.

The correlation between the funds approved and the number of schools is significant at 0.01 levels. The correlation between the funds approved and the number of teachers is also significant. But the other parameters are not statistically significant. This implies that the number of students, enrolment ratio and the student–teacher ratio is not significantly correlated with the amount of fund approved. A negative correlation is even found for the category of student–teacher ratio. Therefore, it can be said that the number of students and enrolment have not been efficient and the student–teacher ratio is not at all correlated to the funds; increase or decrease in funds has not influenced the said ratio.

Also, the allocated funds remain unspent or are spent ineffectively in some areas, while other regions are kept starved of essential support. For example, Murshidabad, which has the highest percentage of out-of-school children, has got the highest amount from the centre. The enrolment has also increased in the district from 730,791 in 2002–03 to 736,785 in 2011–12. However, it cannot be said that the rate of enrolment growth is statistically significant.

What is worse is that this paradox of surfeit and shortage of resources, in a climate of the overall lack of resources, reveals a perverse pattern. Schools in marginal areas that are in greater need of support and supplies (often serving Adivasi, Muslim and Dalit children) remain more resource-starved than those in relatively more privileged locations. Table 10.4 shows the percentage of SC, ST and Muslim population in each district and their enrolment rate in 2011–12.

Murshidabad district of West Bengal has the highest percentage of Muslim population, i.e. 64 per cent of the population in the district are Muslims. In accordance to that, the Muslim enrolment in the district is 66 per cent and only 49 per cent of the Muslim girls are enrolled in schools. Whereas in case of SC and ST population of the district, 13 per cent of the SCs and only 1 per cent STs were enrolled in schools in 2002–03, which came down to 12.5 per cent in 2011–12 for the SCs. Fifty per cent of the population in Cooch Bihar are SCs, followed by Jalpaiguri (36 per cent), South 24 Pargans (32 per cent) and Bankura (31 per cent). If fund allocation is compared with this, then it is observed that Cooch Bihar got 31 per cent of the total funds allotted, which is far less than districts with lower SC population like Nadia, Malda and North 24 Parganas which have SC population less than 5 per cent. The enrolment rate of SCs in Cooch Bihar also declined from 54 per cent in 2002–03 to 47.6 per cent in 2011–12. Same is the case of Jalpaiguri, where it reduced from 45 per cent to 40 per cent between 2002–03 and 2011–12. In case of ST population, Jalpaiguri has the highest percentage of 18.87 per cent followed by Puruliya (18.27 per cent), Dakshin Dinajpur (16.7 per cent) and Pashchim Medinipur (14.27 per cent).

Here also same situation exists. Dakshin Dinajpur and Puruliya received 21 per cent and 28 per cent of the funds approved, respectively, which is very less as compared with districts getting higher percentage of funds with lower ST population. This reflects a clear policy bias in favour of better endowed schools operating in better locations and catering to children from

*Table 10.4* SC, ST and Muslim population in each district and their enrolment

| *Districts* | *Total population* | *% ST population* | *% SC population* | *% Muslim population* | *% ST enrolment 2011–12* | *% SC enrolment 2011–12* | *% Muslim enrolment 2011–12* |
|---|---|---|---|---|---|---|---|
| Darjeeling | 1,609,172 | 12.69 | 16.09 | 5.31 | 32.6 | 11 | 1.2 |
| Jalpaiguri | 3,401,173 | 18.87 | 36.71 | 10.78 | 23.5 | 40.1 | 14.1 |
| Cooch Bihar | 2,479,155 | 0.57 | 50.11 | 24.24 | 0.82 | 47.6 | 36 |
| Uttar Dinajpur | 2,441,794 | 5.11 | 27.71 | 47.36 | 6.2 | 27.4 | 54.1 |
| Dakshin Dinajpur | 1,503,178 | 16.12 | 28.78 | 24.01 | 19.3 | 31.8 | 25.8 |
| Malda | 3,290,468 | 6.9 | 16.84 | 52.05 | 6.6 | 22.4 | 55.1 |
| Murshidabad | 5,866,569 | 1.29 | 12 | 63.67 | 1.6 | 12.5 | 66 |
| Birbhum | 3,015,422 | 6.74 | 29.51 | 35.08 | 8.8 | 31.5 | 41.7 |
| Barddhaman | 6,895,514 | 6.41 | 26.98 | 19.78 | 9.4 | 36.7 | 20.6 |
| Nadia | 4,604,827 | 2.47 | 29.66 | 25.41 | 3.7 | 30.6 | 32.4 |
| North 24 Parganas | 8,934,286 | 2.23 | 20.6 | 24.22 | 3.6 | 22.7 | 32.8 |
| Hugli | 5,041,976 | 4.21 | 23.58 | 15.41 | 5.8 | 32.3 | 17.5 |
| Bankura | 3,192,695 | 10.36 | 31.24 | 7.51 | 12 | 40 | 8.7 |
| Puruliya | 2,536,516 | 18.27 | 18.29 | 7.12 | 20.2 | 22.2 | 8.5 |
| Purba Medinipur | 4,417,377 | 0.6 | 17.98 | 11.32 | 0.79 | 18.1 | 16.8 |
| Paschim Medinipur | 5,193,411 | 14.87 | 0.45 | 11.32 | 19 | 24.5 | 13.1 |
| Howrah | 4,273,099 | 0.45 | 15.42 | 24.44 | 0.36 | 19 | 35.1 |
| Kolakata | 4,572,876 | 0.21 | 6.01 | 20.27 | 0.33 | 6.5 | 20.3 |
| South 24 Parganas | 6,906,689 | 1.23 | 32.12 | 33.34 | 1.6 | 30.9 | 42.8 |

*Source:* West Bengal Backward Classes Welfare Department and DISE data.

comparatively better-off families. On the other hand, children in depressed regions go to schools having much less resources. Poor public provision in terms of school infrastructure, the number of teachers, regularity of school inspections, and the supply of mid-day meal provisions, in the areas with lower levels of development is a major concern for equity in public spending as observed through analysis of both primary and secondary data. In particular, large variations exist in the stock of teachers across schools, and there is shortage of teachers in most of them (Majumdar and Rana 2012).

## Component-wise allocation of funds

If a comparison is made between the funds provided under different components of SSA, then it can be argued that the component-wise grants have increased for the state as a whole but the funds have not been fully utilised except for some. Table 10.5 shows the comparison of funds allotted under several components of SSA in 2005–06 and 2011–12 to West Bengal.

The maximum expenditures that have been undertaken fall under the categories of maintenance, teachers grant, free text books and school grants. Lowest expenditures have been carried out under the heads of teaching learning equipment, teacher's training, research and evolution, innovative activities and community training. In case of civil works, it is found that 83 per cent of the allocated funds were utilised in 2005–06 which came down to 50 per cent in 2011–12. Civil works is one of the major interventions under SSA for which one-third of the total fund is earmarked for construction of new school buildings, additional classrooms, and provision of drinking water and toilet facilities.

For increasing the accessibility of the eligible learners at the elementary level, the assessment of existing classroom vis-à-vis the provision of safe drinking water and toilet facility are the essential components under civil works. But this category shows a declining trend in expenditure from 2005–06 to 2011–12, which can be a reason behind the existing gap in enrolment of students in the state. The government also provides grants for innovative activities which include innovative activities for girl's education, early childhood care and education, interventions for children belonging to SC/ST community and computer education for upper primary level, which includes training for students as well as for teachers. But the expenditure against this category also shows a diminishing trend. Similarly, the community training grants are also left unutilised. Expenditure in community training is important since the village education committees (VECs) and the ward education committees (WECs) are vital for the development

*Table 10.5* Funds allocated and spent on different components of SSA in West Bengal (Rs in lakhs)

| *Components* | *Allocation 2005–06* | *Expenditure 2005–06* | *(Exp/ allo) %* | *Allocation 2011–12* | *Expenditure 2011–12* | *(Exp/ allo) %* |
|---|---|---|---|---|---|---|
| Teachers salary | 35,139 | 4,611 | 13.12 | 225,081 | 89,860 | 39.92 |
| Textbook | 5,539 | 4,191 | 75.66 | 12,147 | 10,492 | 86.37 |
| TLE | 1,727 | 564 | 32.68 | 4,614 | 103 | 2.23 |
| BRC (other than civil works) | 478 | 383 | 80.1 | 1,706 | 819 | 47.99 |
| CRC (other than civil works) | 1,063 | 213 | 20.06 | 2,158 | 809 | 37.50 |
| Maintenance | 2,023 | 1,607 | 79.44 | 5,494 | 4,979 | 90.64 |
| IED | 1,282 | 774 | 60.33 | 8,102 | 3,836 | 47.34 |
| School grant | 1,138 | 1,135 | 99.73 | 4,230 | 3,978 | 94.05 |
| Teacher grant | 1,648 | 1,060 | 64.34 | 1,851 | 1,594 | 86.13 |
| Civil works | 29,189 | 24,311 | 83.29 | 167,034 | 84,310 | 50.47 |
| EGS/AIE | 14,261 | 5,595 | 39.23 | NA | NA | NA |
| Teacher's training | 5,808 | 489 | 8.42 | 12,084 | 2,455 | 20.32 |
| Community training | 166 | 157 | 94.55 | 3,777 | 1,616 | 42.78 |
| Innovative activities | 793 | 488 | 61.52 | 2,000 | 454 | 22.70 |
| a. REMS (dist.) | 434 | 317 | 72.94 | 1,194 | 247 | 20.71 |
| b. REMS (state) | 30 | 0 | 0 | NA | NA | NA |
| Total (REMS) | 465 | 317 | 68.16 | NA | NA | NA |
| Management cost (dist.) | 3,533 | 2,026 | 57.36 | 11,381 | 4,172 | 36.66 |
| Management cost (state) | 260 | 167 | 64.17 | 4,777 | 1,099 | 23.01 |
| Total (mgt.) | 3,793 | 2,193 | 57.83 | 16,158 | 5,271 | 32.62 |
| SIEMAT | 300 | 0 | 0 | NA | NA | NA |
| Total | 104,811 | 48,088 | 45.88 | 483,787 | 210,823 | 43.58 |
| NPEGEL | 1,134 | 741 | 65.37 | 858 | 133 | 15.50 |

*Source:* SSA Report, MHRD data, India Stat, own calculation.

of the education system as the work of maintenance, monitoring of civil works, etc. are allotted to them. Lower amount of expenditure in these essential heads shows that the funds have not been essentially utilised in the state.

## The case of Bankura district

To appropriate a better picture of the state's primary education situation, the Bankura district is used as a case study. Bankura is a district of West Bengal included in the 'Rarh' region on the western part of the state. It is one of the backward districts of the state and also receives special funds from the Ministry of Panchayati Raj as Backward Regions Grant Funds. It is one among the districts with high SC population. In terms of education, the district's literacy rate is 70 per cent, which is below the state average. Also, the 2011 census data show a gap of 20 per cent in male (81 per cent) and female (60 per cent) literacy rates. Ministry of Human Resource Development in connection with SSA has identified 11 of the 22 blocks of the district as educationally backward blocks. In elementary education in particular, only 40 per cent of the SC children are enrolled in primary schools. The student–teacher ratio is around 36 per cent for the district. The district report has shown that a total of 1,380 teachers are needed to maintain the RTE specified ratio of 1:30. Proposal for increasing the teachers' posts has not yet been sanctioned by the concerned authority. Also, proposals are yet to be confirmed regarding maintenance of student–classroom ratio of 1:35 which right now is around 1:39.

The funds' utilization pattern of the district shows that during the year 2005–06, only half of the amount approved under teaching learning material (TLM) and only one-third of the amount provided for girl children, SC, ST and minorities was utilised. Maximum amount utilised in that year was under the heads school grant, teachers grant and civil works. None of the approved funds under teaching learning equipments was used during the year. A comparison of the expenditure pattern between the years 2005–06 and 2011–12 shows that funds spent for girls' education, SC, ST and minorities increased to a substantial level, whereas expenditure under teachers grant and school grants decreased along with low spending on community mobilisation. The expenditure under TLM for the district has showed a dissatisfactory result as it has remained low throughout the time period. The funds for maintenance and civil works have more or less been utilised in the district throughout the time period.

In this kind of a situation, when two of the government primary schools were visited in the district, it came out that the infrastructure of the schools was not up to the mark. The schools were not under the educationally backward blocks. One of them was in the Bankura town and the other was in the outskirts, merely 10 km from the town. Personal interviews with the teachers and students were undertaken to understand their level of participation and their viewpoints regarding the current financial structure of SSA. The study reflected that the maintenance grants and the grants for civil works were not enough for the schools to undertake new classroom construction. One of the schools had only one classroom with four classes taking place together. The headmasters were of the opinion that the funds do not reach them on time and this leads to delay in the construction process.

There was serious need for TLM in one of the schools as it did not even have benches and tables. The number of students in the schools was also not much and some kind of social gap existed there. The SC students faced discrimination from the upper castes, as the students from upper caste families were not sent to the government primary schools. The headmasters also complained about the non-receipt of any funds for sports and boundary walls. The activities of the local communities were dormant as they did not involve themselves in any constructive activity for the schools. The lack of expenditure for community mobilisation was one of the reasons for this. Also, because of more political power of the local political parties, the participation of the parents lacked enthusiasm. The headmasters were the only active working bodies in the school as well as in the VECs and WECs. Another interesting observation was the prevalence of private tuition among the students. Even if the students belonged to low-income families, almost all of them take private tuition. Existence of private tuition among the students of these two schools partly supports the ASER 2012. Overall, the schools were not able to show a picture-perfect scenario of education system of the district.

## Conclusion

The study thereby concludes that the state of West Bengal faces educational inequality even after achieving a literacy rate which is higher than the national average. Achieving mere literacy rate does not imply equality and efficiency in education system. The state suffers from ineffective utilisation of funds among districts with large enrolment gaps still existing in all the districts. Resource shortage of the state coupled with high deficit and low revenue generating agriculture and industrial sector has made the state incapable of spending matching grants in SSA. Even though centre's share in providing grants for SSA was high during the initial periods of SSA, the share has declined during the later years.

Not only resource crunch, the state also suffers from the inability to utilise the funds properly on time. The study has shown the existence of unspent funds under the categories of civil works, free text books, TLM, community mobilisation, and innovative activities, which comprise the major elements in SSA. As a result, the state has fallen prey to the hands of high number of out-of-school children, social gap, lack of initiatives among the community members, low infrastructure of the schools, untimely receipt of funds, etc. Even though the funds provided have been utilised in building new schools, toilets, and drinking water facilities, these have not helped in achieving complete enrolment in schools. It has been detected that districts with higher SC and ST population have not received adequate funds, and therefore the enrolment of children from the minority communities has not improved much. Not only there exists a gap in enrolment, but the quality of the education system is also a major question here. Employment of new teachers and decline in student–teacher ratio in almost all districts have not helped the state reach the RTE specified student–teacher ratio. The number of students attending private tuition has not decreased. The high percentage of students attending private tuitions in the state puts a question mark on the teacher quality vis-à-vis the education system.

Same has been the case of Bankura district which shows low female literacy rate, poor quality of infrastructure, untimely receipt of funds, etc. The district with 50 per cent of the blocks identified as educationally backward blocks and one among the highest SC populated districts could utilise only one-third of the money provided for girls, SC, ST and Muslim children in 2005–06, which later improved a bit. Where the district is in need for more teachers to maintain the student–teacher ratio and the student–classroom ratio, the teachers grant and the school grants have declined. Existence of private tuition is also very prominent in the district even among the children from the lower income group families.

The state therefore needs to focus more on optimum utilisation of funds rather than demand for more funds from the centre. The areas where there is more need of funds for minority and backward communities should be identified and funds must be utilised properly in those areas. The monitoring of the funds by the local communities is a very important aspect of SSA, so the utilisation of funds for community participation must be potent. The state also lacks proper supervision by the education officers in the district schools. To make the SSA successful in the state, the need of the hour is to undertake stricter supervision, optimum utilization of funds in all the components of SSA and strong involvement of local communities.

## References

ASER. 2013. *Annual Status of Education Report 2012*, Pratham, New Delhi. Available at www.pratham.org.

Bagchi, K. A. 1998. 'Studies on the Economy of West Bengal since Independence'. *Economic and Political Weekly*, 33(47/48): 2973–8.

Bagchi, A. 2006. 'India's Fiscal Management Post-Liberalisation: Impact on the Social Sector and Federal Fiscal Relations'. *Economic and Political Weekly*, 41(39).

Becker, Gary S. 1965. *Human Capital: A Theoretical and Empirical Analysis with Special Reference to education*. New York: National Bureau of Education Research.

Bhattacharya, B. 1998. 'Urbanization and Human Development in West Bengal: A District Level Study and Comparison with Inter-State Variation'. *Economic and Political Weekly*, 33 (47/48): 3027–32.

Chakraborty, A., Bagchi, B., Das, K., Bandyopadhyay, D., and Upadhyay, S. 2005. *An Assessment of In-Service Teachers' Training Programmeme in Five Districts of West Bengal*. (Sponsored by the State Project Office, West Bengal District Primary Education Programme.) Kolkata: Institute of Development Studies.

Dasgupta, Z. 2012. 'Development Expenditures of the States in the Post-Liberalisation Period'. *Economic and Political Weekly*, xlvii(34).

Geetha Rani, P. 2007. 'Every Child in School: The Challenges of Attending and Financing Education For All in India' in *Education For All: Global Promises, National Challenges*. International Perspectives on Education and Society, 8: 201–56.

Hanushek, A., Erik. 2003. 'The Failure of Input Based Schooling Policies'. *The Economic Journal* 113, F64-F98, Royal Economic Society. Blackwell Publishing.

Hanushek, A., Erik. 2013. 'Financing Schools', in John Hattie and Erik M. Anderman (eds), *International Guide to Student Achievement*, pp. 134–6. New York: Routledge.

Husain, Z., and Chatterjee, A. 2009. 'Primary Completion Rates across Socio-Religious Communities in West Bengal'. *Economic and Political Weekly*, 44 (15): 59–67.

Jha, P., Das, S., Mohanty, S. S., and Jha, N. K. 2008. *Public Provisioning of elementary education in India*. India: Sage Publications.

Khasnabis, R. (2009). 'The Economy of West Bengal'. *Economic and Political Weekly*, 43(52): 103–15.

Kumar, A.C.E., and Lathika, M. 2012. 'Sacred Goals and Injudicious Spending: A Mid-Term Appraisal of Sarva Shiksha Abhiyan (SSA), Kerala'. *Journal of Educational Planning and Administration*, XXVI(3): 445–64.

Majumdar, M., and Rana, K. 2012. 'In Defence of Public Expenditure: Voices from West Bengal'. *Economic and Political Weekly*, XLVII(40).

McMohan, W. W. 2004. 'The Social and External Benefits of Education', in Geraint Johnes and Jill Johnes (eds), *International Handbook on the Economics of Education*. Northampton, MA: Edward Elgar.

Mukherjee, N. A., and Aiyar, Y. 2010. 'Fund Flows and Expenditure in SSA: A Case Study of Nalanda District, Bihar', in National Seminar on financing of Elementary

Education in States: Fund Flow Pattern and Utilisation of Resources under Sarva Shiksha Abhiyan, NEUPA, New Delhi.

Mukherjee, N. A., and Sikdar, S. 2013. 'Public Expenditure on Education in India by the Union Government and the Roadmap for the Future' in *India Infrastructure Report: Private sector in education*, IDFC Foundation, Routledge, New Delhi.

Rana, K. 2010. *Social Exclusion in and through Elementary Education: The Case of West Bengal.* Pratichi Occassional Paper No 1. Pratichi (India) Trust in association with UNICEF Kolkata.

Rana, K., Das, S., Sengupta, A., and Rafique, A. 2003. 'State of Primary Education in West Bengal'. *Economic and Political Weekly*, 38(22): 2159–64.

Roychowdhury, P. 2011. 'West Bengal Public Finances: An Analytical Perspective'. Working Paper No. 7. Centre for Training and Research in Public Finance and Policy, Centre for Studies in Social Sciences, Calcutta.

Schultz, T. W. 1961. 'Investment in Human Capital'. *The American Economic Review*, 51 (1).

Sinha, S., and Reddy, A. N., 2011. 'School dropouts or 'pushouts'? Overcoming barriers for the Right to Education' in Govinda, R. (eds), *Who goes to school? Exploring exclusion in Indian education*. New Delhi: Oxford University Press.

SSA Manual on Management and Procurement. 2004. Department of Elementary Education and Literacy, Ministry of Human resource development, Government of India.

SSA Annual Report West Bengal. 2008–09. West Bengal Education Department.

Tilak, J. B. J. 1989. 'Centre State Relations in Financing Education in India'. *Comparative Education Review*, 33 (4).

West Bengal Development Report. 2010. Planning Commission, Government of India.

West Bengal Human Development Report. 2004. Development and Planning Department, Government of West Bengal.

# 11

# FUND FLOWS AND EXPENDITURE IN SARVA SHIKSHA ABHIYAN

## A case study of Nalanda district, Bihar

*Avani Kapur and Anit N. Mukherjee*

### Introduction

India's drive towards achieving universal elementary education has picked up pace after the Sarva Shiksha Abhiyan (SSA) came into force in 2001. It is financed through a national 'education cess' levied on all federal taxes and supplemented by budgetary allocations, both by the centre as well as the states. Before SSA came into existence, elementary education was mainly in the domain of states. Budgetary allocations varied from state to state depending on fiscal capacity, teacher recruitment policy and importance attached to social sectors such as education in overall state government policy. This was manifested in wide variations in enrolment, attendance and completion rates across states. Lack of access to and poor quality of school infrastructure was an important factor in poor outputs and outcomes (PROBE Team 1999; Dreze and Kingdon 2001).Coupled with differences in administrative efficiency, reflected in teacher absenteeism, India was some distance away from achieving Millenium Development Goals (MDG) on universal primary education (Kremer *et al.* 2005).

One of the goals of SSA, therefore, is to address the fiscal constraint faced by the states to increase their expenditure on elementary education. The SSA norms and guidelines provide the link between the broad macro objective and actual implementation on the ground. In 2009, the Right to Free and Compulsory Education Act (RTE) came into force. SSA was envisaged as the programmatic vehicle for delivering this fundamental right. The law envisages a decentralized delivery framework. Sections 21 (1) and 21 (2) of RTE mandate the creation of School Management Committees (SMCs) tasked with making annual School Development Plans (SDPs) and monitoring finances and activities at school level. This emphasis on decentralization was anchored in the recognition that delivering a right to education requires a focus on the local – the school and the individual learning needs of children. To quote from the revised framework of the SSA, 'the need for the creation of capacity within the education system and the school for addressing the diversified learning needs of different groups of children who are now in the school system' (Ministry of Human Resource Development 2011a).

Consequently, while the programme design of SSA incorporates elements of decentralization such as the creation of SMCs, requirement of micro-planning through SDPs, and monitoring of school functioning by the local community; the norms for unit costs used for budgeting are set at the national and at times state level with limited flexibility at the lower levels of authority. This creates tension between financial centralization and operational decentralization, ultimately leading to problems in fund flows and implementation bottlenecks.

The purpose of this study is to address the issue of complementarity and conflict between the dual goals of increased financial allocation based on a set of national norms and increased local participation in implementation and monitoring. Specifically, we focus on processes – planning, allocation of funds and programme implementation – rather than on actual outcomes. We illustrate the procedural challenges using a case study of a district in one of India's most economically backward states, Bihar. We analyse two specific modes of financial transfers under SSA: (a) the school grants which are annual grants that come to all schools and (b) infrastructure grants which are provided through Annual Work Plans on a normative basis. The specific school grants that we analyse are School Development Grant (SDG), School Maintenance Grant (SMG) and the Teaching Learning Material Grant (TLM) which covers all schools in the country. At the state and district level, the amount of the grants and the mode of fund transfer is homogenous, which offers us the opportunity to isolate the process-related factors for the purposes of our study. Further, as the launch of the RTE was accompanied by a push towards infrastructure creation, we also looked at infrastructure grants (classroom, boundary walls, girls' toilet, etc.) coming to schools.

In brief, our results indicate that: (a) the fund flow bottlenecks lead to less than optimal utilization of school grants, (b) the centralized norms lead to a system of grants that are tied to specific items, whereas the requirement on the ground is better served by giving untied grants with *de facto* expenditure powers to the school authorities and (c) the lack of capacity and local-level factors have resulted in significant delays in civil work construction and large sums of unspent money lying with the school or district administration. The results are indicative of potential handicaps in a large class of public spending programmes in the social sector which have a similar devolution structure as the SSA.

The scheme of the study is as follows. Second section provides a background to the debate on decentralized public spending programmes and discusses the literature on targeting efficiency and local capture. Third section explains the structure of the financial planning and devolution of SSA grants in India, and explores the problems in the processes leading to weaknesses in actual implementation. Fourth section uses survey data collected in Nalanda district in Bihar to illustrate the problem of mismatch between central norms and school needs. The last section concludes with some recommendations for future policy.

## Background

There is an extensive and growing literature on the decentralization debate in development policy. The theoretical (macro) strand deals with the issues of fiscal federalism and inter-governmental transfers (Tiebout 1956; Musgrave 1969; Oates 1972; Rao and Singh 2005). The consensus is that if people 'vote with their feet', a federal structure leads to greater level of responsiveness of sub-national governments in the delivery of public goods and services. However, productivity of public infrastructure expenditure across regions may also determine the optimal level of decentralization. Within a range of parameter values for local capacity, full centralization may dominate partial decentralization, although both of them are inferior to full decentralization as a steady-state solution (Arcalean *et al.* 2007). In our analysis, we try to address the issue of the degree of decentralization in scheme design and link it to the process-related constraints that affect the efficiency of expenditure vis-à-vis allocations for SSA by different states, districts, blocks and service delivery units.

A more recent strand of literature explores the process of decentralization from an implementation (micro) perspective (Besley and Coate 1999). In developing countries, the existing socioeconomic inequalities may be reinforced with a decentralized framework of implementation of public spending programmes. These 'local capture' theories indicate that decentralization may not always lead to intended results due to the dominant local groups cornering the largest benefit deriving from their greater allocative power over devolved resources (Bardhan and Mookherjee 2000). This is especially true if the expenditure power is combined with powers of identification of beneficiaries in public spending programmes targeted at the poor. This renders public expenditure 'excludable', leading to socially sub-optimal solution (Galasso and Ravallion 2005; Bardhan and Mookherjee 2006a,b). In such a case, central mandates in the form of service delivery norms can play an important role (Kochar *et al.* 2009).

In case of non-excludable local public goods, the extent of elite capture may be less, since it is in everyone's best interest to have a functioning school or health centre in the area under their jurisdiction. The issue may be more about allocations, processes and monitoring involving local stakeholders such as SMCs or village health and sanitation committees. All these are mandated by central guidelines which are followed in implementing a scheme such as SSA. However, this arrangement *per se* leads to a situation of partial decentralization which the theoretical literature has shown to be sub-optimal. There may be a trade-off between targeting efficiency and the extent of control that the local authority has in planning, allocation and utilization of resources. The local community group and service provider has better access to information vis-à-vis actual needs, than a central planner who imposes rigidity in the process to achieve higher social welfare objectives. How well a national scheme functions may depend on how this balance is achieved.

On the outcome side, evidence from education decentralization reform in Latin America has shown that participation in reform (*de jure* autonomy) does not necessarily lead to more decision-making at the local school level (*de facto* autonomy). Moreover, schools exercising greater autonomy in administrative decisions such as teacher staffing, salaries and incentives appear to be more effective in raising student performance (King and Ozler 2005).

However, few previous studies have looked in detail at the *process* of decision-making – what are the roles and responsibilities of community groups, the quantum of funds controlled by the schools, the actual transfer of the grants to enable expenditure and the items that are demarcated for the 'tied grant' as per centrally mandated norms. This study is an attempt to understand these process factors that finally lead to sub-optimal efficiency in expenditure at the final service delivery point.

## Planning, allocation and expenditure of SSA grants in India

Expenditure in social sectors has undergone significant changes in the last decade. The central government has been instrumental in the increase in allocations for education, health, urban and rural development. These are subjects included in the domain of the states at the time of drawing up of the Constitution. In 1976, most of them were transferred to the concurrent list, thereby giving the central government a greater say in sectors such as elementary education, public health and rural employment. However, the most significant changes have happened in the last decade, facilitated by financial support to national level missions[1] such as the Sarva Shiksha Abhiyan (SSA), National Mid-day Meal Scheme (MDM), National Rural Health Mission (NRHM), Mahatma Gandhi National Rural Employment Guarantee Scheme (MGNREGS), Pradhan Mantri Gram Sadak Yojana (PMGSY) and other Bharat Nirman schemes (Figure 11.1).

This is part of the wider restructuring in the nature of India's fiscal federalism framework which devolves funds from the central to the state governments as per the recommendations of successive Finance Commissions. For the first time, the 12th Finance Commission provided for limited 'equalization' grants for two sectors – education and health to eight states which were deemed to be lagging behind in social indicators due to their low revenue capacity (Table 11.1).

In terms of the absolute amount of the transfers, nearly 70 per cent went to two states – Bihar and Uttar Pradesh. These funds are transferred from the central pool of resources to the state exchequer and therefore are accounted for in the state budget.

With the launch of the RTE, the total quantum of funds increased significantly. The 13th Finance Commission awarded a total of Rs 24,068 crores for elementary education to be divided amongst states for the period of 2010–15. Of this, Bihar and Uttar Pradesh together were allocated 38 per cent of the total transfers (Table 11.2).

### *Finances under SSA*

For the central government, SSA is the primary vehicle for delivering elementary education. Launched in 2001, as a Centrally Sponsored Scheme (CSS), the scheme is funded primarily by the centre while implementation rests with the state governments. Fund flow patterns for SSA have been changing over the years. During the 10th Five Year Plan (2002–07),

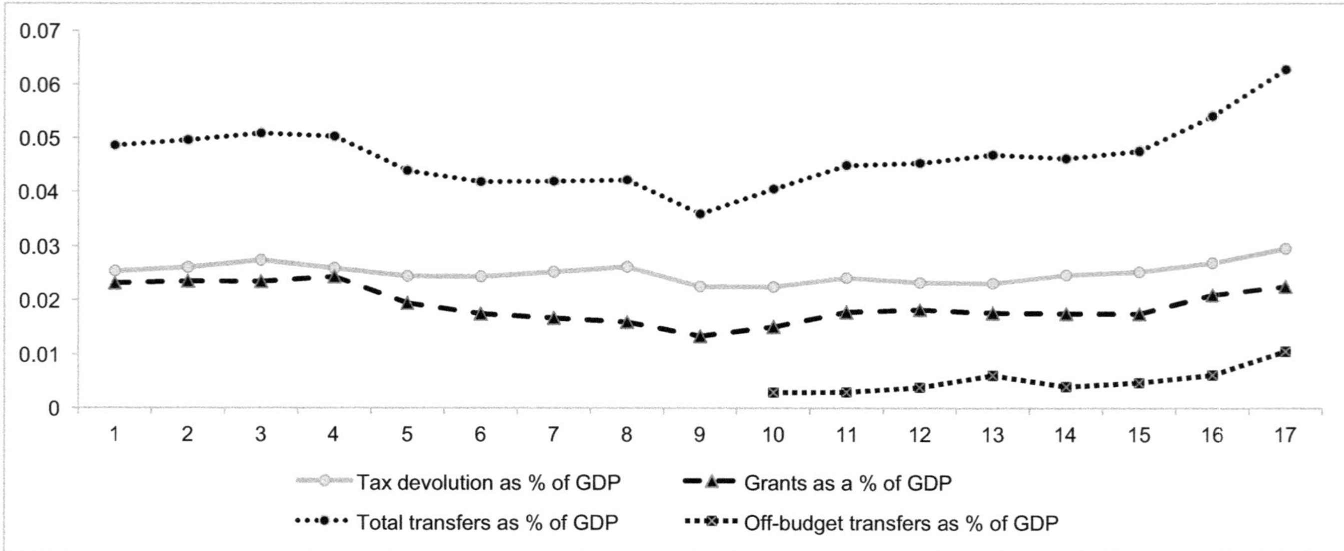


*Figure 11.1* Transfer to states, 1990–91 to 2006–07

*Source*: Chakraborty *et al.* 2010.

*Table 11.1* Grants-in-aid for education sector

| *State* | *2005–06* | *2006–07* | *2007–08* | *2008–09* | *2009–10* | *2005–10* |
|---|---|---|---|---|---|---|
| Assam | 183.20 | 200.60 | 219.66 | 240.53 | 263.38 | **1,107.37** |
| Bihar | 443.99 | 486.17 | 532.36 | 582.93 | 638.31 | **2,683.76** |
| Jharkhand | 107.82 | 118.06 | 129.28 | 141.56 | 155.01 | **651.73** |
| Madhya Pradesh | 76.03 | 83.25 | 91.16 | 99.82 | 109.30 | **459.56** |
| Orissa | 53.49 | 58.57 | 64.13 | 70.22 | 76.89 | **323.30** |
| Rajasthan | 20.00 | 20.00 | 20.00 | 20.00 | 20.00 | **100.00** |
| Uttar Pradesh | 736.87 | 806.87 | 883.52 | 967.45 | 1,059.36 | **4,454.07** |
| West Bengal | 64.83 | 70.99 | 77.73 | 85.11 | 93.20 | **391.86** |
| **Total states** | **1,686.23** | **1,844.51** | **2,017.84** | **2,207.62** | **2,415.45** | **10,171.65** |

*Source:* Finance Commission of India, 2004.

*Table 11.2* Grants-in-aid (in crores of rupees) to states for elementary education, 13th Finance Commission

| *State* | *2010–11* | *2011–12* | *2012–13* | *2013–14* | *2014–15* | *Total* |
|---|---|---|---|---|---|---|
| Andhra Pradesh | 170 | 179 | 188 | 198 | 207 | **942** |
| Arunachal Pradesh | 4 | 4 | 5 | 5 | 6 | **24** |
| Assam | 31 | 40 | 49 | 59 | 59 | **238** |
| Bihar | 585 | 699 | 818 | 946 | 970 | **4,018** |
| Chhattisgarh | 136 | 154 | 173 | 194 | 200 | **857** |
| Goa | 2 | 2 | 2 | 2 | 3 | **11** |
| Gujarat | 72 | 85 | 98 | 113 | 115 | **483** |
| Haryana | 40 | 43 | 46 | 49 | 51 | **229** |
| Himachal Pradesh | 20 | 21 | 23 | 24 | 25 | **113** |
| Jammu and Kashmir | 80 | 85 | 90 | 95 | 99 | **449** |
| Jharkhand | 223 | 266 | 311 | 359 | 369 | **1,528** |
| Karnataka | 104 | 119 | 135 | 152 | 157 | **667** |
| Kerala | 25 | 27 | 28 | 29 | 31 | **140** |
| Madhya Pradesh | 320 | 384 | 452 | 523 | 537 | **2,216** |
| Maharashtra | 131 | 140 | 149 | 159 | 165 | **744** |
| Manipur | 3 | 3 | 3 | 3 | 3 | **15** |
| Meghalaya | 9 | 10 | 10 | 11 | 12 | **52** |
| Mizoram | 1 | 1 | 1 | 1 | 1 | **5** |
| Nagaland | 1 | 1 | 1 | 2 | 2 | **7** |
| Orissa | 170 | 187 | 204 | 223 | 232 | **1,016** |
| Punjab | 36 | 41 | 45 | 50 | 52 | **224** |

(*Continued*)

*Table 11.2* (Continued)

| *State* | *2010–11* | *2011–12* | *2012–13* | *2013–14* | *2014–15* | *Total* |
|---|---|---|---|---|---|---|
| Rajasthan | 287 | 320 | 356 | 394 | 409 | **1,766** |
| Sikkim | 1 | 1 | 1 | 1 | 1 | **5** |
| Tamil Nadu | 111 | 126 | 141 | 158 | 164 | **700** |
| Tripura | 4 | 4 | 5 | 5 | 5 | **23** |
| Uttar Pradesh | 723 | 871 | 1,027 | 1,192 | 1,227 | **5,040** |
| Uttarakhand | 31 | 35 | 40 | 45 | 46 | **197** |
| West Bengal | 355 | 416 | 480 | 548 | 560 | **2,359** |
| **All states** | **3,675** | **4,264** | **4,881** | **5,540** | **5,708** | **24,068** |

*Source:* Finance Commission of India, 2009.

the centre was responsible for providing 75 per cent of the total approved SSA allocations. For the financial year 2009–10, the sharing formula stood at 60:40. With the launch of the RTE, the share of centre and state governments was placed at 65:35 from 2010–11 onwards (see Figure 11.2). Till 2014–15, these funds were credited directly to a parallel autonomous body responsible for implementation of the scheme at the state level, known as the State Implementation Society (SIS). These were accounted as 'off-budget transfers'. From financial year 2014–15, the centre's share will be routed through the state treasury, which will then transfer the funds to SSA society along with the state's own share.

### *Institutional architecture for SSA*

As mentioned earlier, SSA envisaged a new institutional arrangement that partly bypass the sub-national government administration and seek to involve the local community in planning, monitoring and implementation. The details of the organizational structure are given below.

#### *Central level*

The Ministry of Human Resource Development (MHRD) and within it the Department of School Education and Literacy (DoSEL) is the key policy body for designing, funding and monitoring SSA. Its specific responsibilities include: setting norms and standards, providing resources to states, approving state plans for SSA, developing capacity through training of human resource personnel, providing academic support to state governments, disseminating good practices across states and monitoring outputs and outcomes.

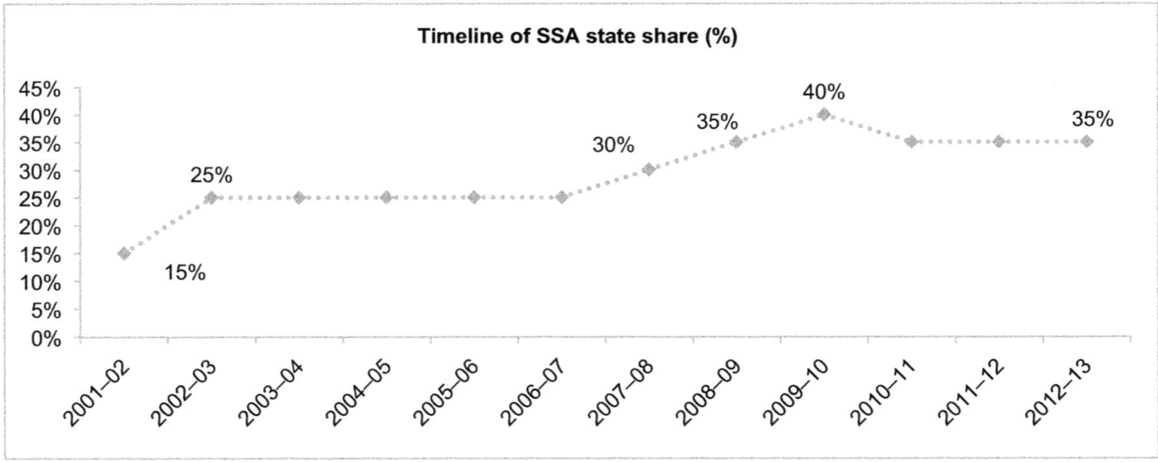


*Figure 11.2* Timeline of SSA state share (%)

*Source:* Ministry of Human Resource Development, 2011a.

### *State level*

SSA activities at the state level are financed and managed by SISs that have been set up in parallel to the education department of the state. The SIS is responsible for state level planning of the programme, disbursement of funds to the district, providing academic support, including teacher training, and monitoring implementation of SSA. In contrast, the state education department (running in parallel) is mainly responsible for disbursement of teacher salaries; state schemes such as scholarships, uniforms, etc. and administrative costs for the delivery of education.

### *District level*

The district is the key administrative unit for the delivery of social sector programmes. The institutional arrangements at the district mirror the parallel structures present at the state level. State line department programmes are implemented and monitored by the District Education Officer (DEO). SSA activities, on the other hand, are the responsibility of the District Project Officer/Coordinator (DPO/DPC) who is in charge of the District Implementation Unit (DIU) under SSA. As a consequence of the decentralized framework of educational delivery under SSA, a key role of the DIU is the preparation of district level plans. These plans are envisaged as an aggregation of SDPs based on school needs. In most states, the DIU is also the conduit through which funds flow from the SIS to schools based on central norms and guidelines.

### *Block and cluster*

The block, headed by the Block Development Officer (BDO), is the smallest administrative unit. As with the district, the block has two official positions – the Block Education Officer (BEO) of the state education department and an SSA-specific Block Resource Centre Coordinator (BRCC). The BRCC is the main body responsible for monitoring schools and providing academic support. To manage the day-to-day implementation, SSA created one more layer of administration below the block called a cluster. A cluster caters to between five and 15 villages (depending on size and population), headed by Cluster Resource Centre Facilitator/Coordinator responsible for providing academic support to schools.

### *Village and school level*

A strong component of the SSA structure is its focus on decentralized planning and delivery of education. At the school level, SMCs comprising parents, teachers and local government representatives are the main body responsible for making annual plans, monitoring school functioning and utilization of funds received under SSA.

### *Planning, budgeting and fund flow process under SSA*

Tracking resource flows for SSA requires an understanding of the planning, allocation, release and final expenditure sequence.

The process of implementation of SSA requires that: (a) Annual Work Plan and Budgets (AWP&Bs) are drawn up, (b) approvals are obtained from the respective ministry (MHRD in this case), (c) instalments are released to implementing agencies and (d) expenditures are incurred. A typical (annual) cycle is depicted in Figure 11.3.

As per the guidelines of SSA, the AWP&Bs are supposed to start from the creation of a SDP, prepared by SMCs, so that the specific needs of each school can be addressed within the scope of the SSA guidelines and norms. These should ideally be assessed at the cluster level, then sent to the block and onto the DPO. Finally, district plans are to be consolidated into one state AWP&B, which is then approved by MHRD at the centre.

After the plan is approved by the MHRD, the first instalment of the funds is released to the SSA autonomous body or SIS by the centre. The state government also releases its share to the SSA pool available with the SIS. Information on state releases and actual expenditure is recorded as a grant-in-aid item under the DoSEL. This can be obtained from the budget documents of each state. (See Figure 11.4 for a diagrammatic representation of SSA fund flows.)

The release of the second instalment of the approved funds from the centre is contingent upon the state government providing its share as per the formula, and expenditure of at least 50 per cent of the money transferred to the SIS by the centre and state government combined. Once received by the SIS, these funds are released to the respective districts, specifically the DPO/DPC who in turn sends it onwards to SMC bank accounts.

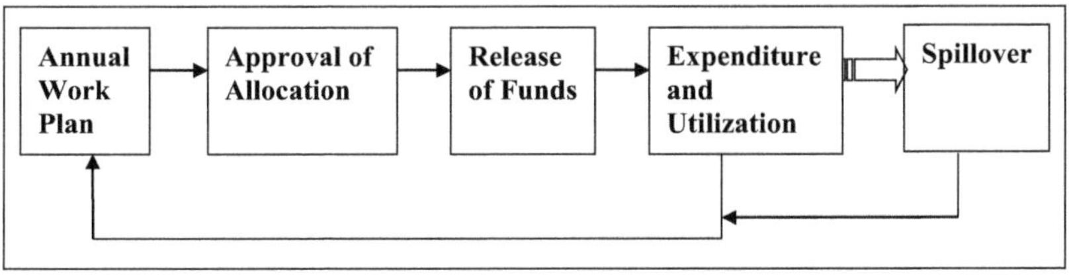


*Figure 11.3* Annual planning, allocation and expenditure workflow

*Source:* MHRD, 2011a.

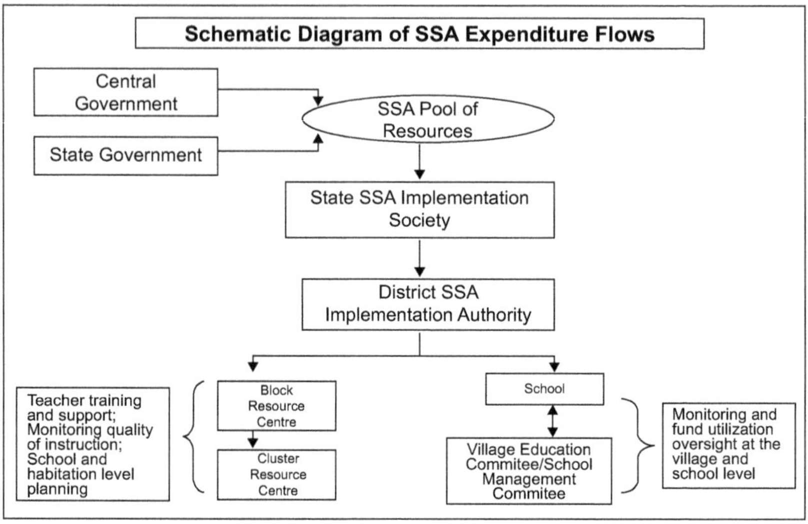


*Figure 11.4* Schematic diagram for fund flow under SSA

*Source:* Adapted from MHRD, 2011a.

At every stage, however, there are information and execution bottlenecks that hinder the implementation of the programme. Some of these are outlined below:

### *Mismatch between centre and state priorities*

The AWP&Bs are approved after negotiations between the centre and state governments with the final decision taken by SSA's Project Approval Board (PAB) at the central level. This is done to ensure standardization of education delivery and supervise implementation by states. Consequently, however, this often results in a tension between central government priorities and state perceived needs resulting in a mismatch between allocations proposed by states and those approved by the centre. For instance, in 2010 Bihar increased its own state budget for activities related to children's entitlements[2] by a significant 78 per cent. Perhaps as a consequence, Bihar proposed a low allocation for entitlements (uniforms, transport and textbooks) under SSA. However, given the central government's own prioritization of entitlements, Bihar's entitlement budget under SSA was enhanced by over 200 per cent. Similarly, in 2013–14, the central government's infrastructure priorities were reflected in a cut in budgets for Teaching Learning

*Table 11.3* Approved SSA allocations as a proportion of proposed plans (%)

| | *2009–10* | *2010–11* | *2011–12* | *2012–13* | *2013–14* |
|---|---|---|---|---|---|
| Bihar | 86 | 74 | 92 | 57 | 47 |
| Andhra Pradesh | 75 | 110 | 99 | 81 | 37 |
| Maharashtra | 85 | 123 | 83 | 63 | 63 |
| Himachal Pradesh | 89 | 106 | 72 | 81 | 42 |
| Rajasthan | 109 | 115 | 100 | 95 | 67 |
| Madhya Pradesh | NA | 96 | 76 | 77 | 43 |

*Source:* Calculated from SSA Portal. www.ssa.nic.in.

Material (TLM) and quality-related items such as the Learning Enhancement Programme (LEP).

The difference between proposed and approved allocations for six states is given in Table 11.3. A lower proportion of approval compared to proposed implies a cut in state AWP&Bs, while higher proportions (i.e. over 100 per cent) indicate approvals of more funds by the centre than initially proposed by the state. It is evident that the difference is not uniform across states and over the period under consideration. However, the divergence has increased from 2011–12 to 2012–13, pointing to a mismatch in central and state priorities post-RTE and a reduced absorptive capacity in the context of increased resource allocation to achieve RTE norms. Performance in 2013–14 deteriorated considerably, which may have been due to cutbacks in plan expenditure across the board to achieve fiscal targets. Therefore, imposition of a hard budget constraint has considerable adverse consequences vis-à-vis fund allocation for RTE.

### *Significant gap between allocations and releases*

The planning process is conducted without complete information on actual financial performance of the programme within the AWP&B cycle and the total resource availability under the programme. This provision in the SSA guidelines is supposed to ensure speedy implementation of the AWP&B. However, it often results in a lower quantum of funds released compared to allocations. For instance, the AWP&Bs may not be approved until the first quarter starts, which involves transfer of ad-hoc amount to the states to meet current expenditure. These releases are then 'adjusted' during the second instalment after taking into account states utilization record of the previous year. Moreover, plans are approved without taking into account the hard budget constraint or the actual funds available by the Ministry, resulting in a mismatch between releases and approved allocations. For example, in 2012–13, the Ministry approved AWP&Bs worth Rs 69,937 crores. However, the central budget allocation for SSA was only Rs 25,555 crores.

### *Delays in the release of Funds*

As mentioned, both centre and state governments contribute to SSA funds. However, release and expenditure for implementing the plan is dependent on sanctions obtained at multiple levels. Since most states do not release their share to the SIS till the centre has released its share, delays in the release of the first instalment from the centre to the SIS often results in delays of funds by the state and consequently to the District Project Offices. (See Figure 11.5 and Table 11.4 for more details.)

It is important to note that at times these 'releases' to the districts may not be the actual release of funds as some expenditure is booked by the state governments in the name of the district. For instance, most of the expenditure incurred on printing materials such as textbooks or other training materials as well as buying computers under Computer Aided Learning (CAL) and in some cases even transfer of teacher salaries is centralized at the state level.[3] The case of Madhya Pradesh is an interesting one. Panchayats in Madhya Pradesh have a lot more control on school financing and funds for all infrastructure activities are routed through the panchayat account. As such, of the 90 per cent 'released to Sagar' in

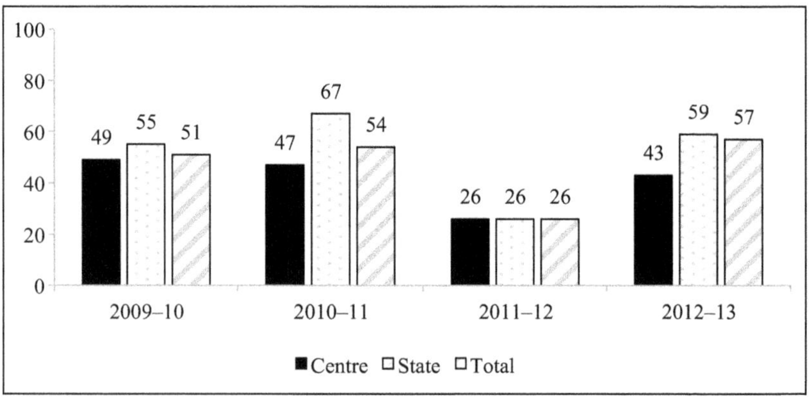


*Figure 11.5* Quantum of funds released to SIS in Bihar (%)

*Table 11.4* Timing of funds released to SIS in Bihar, 2012–13 (%)

| | GOI | GOB | *Total including 13th FC grants* |
|---|---|---|---|
| Apr–12 | 0 | 0 | 0 |
| May–12 | 29 | 7 | 17 |
| Jun–12 | 29 | 20 | 21 |
| Jul–12 | 80 | 20 | 47 |
| Aug–12 | 80 | 39 | 63 |
| Sep–12 | 80 | 39 | 63 |
| Oct–12 | 80 | 62 | 71 |
| Nov–12 | 80 | 95 | 89 |
| Dec–12 | 99 | 95 | 98 |
| Jan–13 | 99 | 95 | 98 |
| Feb–13 | 99 | 100 | 99 |
| Mar–13 | 100 | 100 | 100 |

*Source:* Documents obtained from SSA office, Bihar.

*Note:* Proportions are out of total released and thus add up to 100 per cent. GOI – Government of India; GOB – Government of Bihar; FC – Finanace Commission.

2009–10, a significant 66 per cent was actually spent by the state in the name of the district.

This raises some important questions regarding the autonomy of the district. The significant degree of 'expenditure' undertaken by the states themselves leave little flexibility for districts to (a) plan – as the funds released to them are substantially lower than was allocated and (b) incur expenditure in accordance with their specific needs.

Finally, once received by the district, funds are transferred to bank accounts of SMCs. Till recently, the transfer of funds from the district to the SMC was done via cheque – which would take time to prepare, disburse and clear, resulting in further delays. Today however, most states have shifted to a core banking network and funds are transferred electronically. Despite this change, there is still often a time lag between when funds are transferred and when they reach the school bank account. Informal interviews with district officials suggest that there are two main reasons for this. First, the banking sector is extremely stretched and lacks capacity particularly in rural areas. Given that these funds are not viewed as 'priority' in comparison to say MGNREGA wages, release of funds tends to be delayed by the bank. Moreover, lack of information with headmasters regarding transfer of funds results in no pressure placed on the banking sector to prioritize these funds. Finally, even the sanctioning of funds within the government system often entails a long paper trail, and there can be delays between the sanctioning of the letter and the actual release of funds. Schools cope with these delays in various ways. Headmasters may either use leftover funds from previous years or rely on community contributions or at times even use their own money to purchase essential items and 'adjust' books accordingly once money is received. While such practices enable schools to function in the interim, they do result in serious accountability problems.

There have been attempts in some states (for instance, Madhya Pradesh) to centralize disbursement by transferring funds directly from the SIS to the SMC bank accounts. However, these too have had their share of setbacks due to lack of nationalized banks in remote areas and the inability to collate and update bank account details of the SMCs in a centralized manner.

## Understanding school grants

In our approach, school grants provide the link between the dichotomy between norms and implementation in project design. The SSA guidelines stipulate the type and the amount of grants that are devolved to schools; Table 11.5 provides the schematic diagram for all types of SSA grants going to schools at the time of the survey. There is a distinction between primary (Std I–V) and upper primary (Std VI–VIII), and whether the school has three classrooms or more. The unit cost of building a classroom, boundary wall or toilet is as per the State Schedule of Rates which varies considerably between states and across years. Apart from the grants mentioned, there are separate grants for toilets, boundary walls, computers, kitchen sheds and ramps for the physically challenged children. The SSA does not provide a corpus at the school level to hire teachers.

Therefore, if we consider that there are no single-teacher schools, the minimum amount of grants that will be transferred to a school is Rs 11,000 per year. As per SSA norms, every school receives three grants – School Development Grant (SDG), School Maintenance Grant (SMG) and Teaching Learning Material Grant (TLM).[4] The other two – civil works repair and furniture – are essentially demand-based, and will depend on whether they are sanctioned as part of the approved AWP&B for the district.

The main question to be asked, therefore, is whether the design and implementation of the scheme is efficient or not? For the purpose of simplicity, efficiency has been defined here narrowly to mean: (a) the timeline between plan approval and funds reaching the service provider; (b) whether *all* the normative grants actually reach the service provider; and (c) whether the central mandates and norms correspond to the actual

*Table 11.5* Devolution of school grants under SSA

| *Grant amount per school* | *Purpose of utilization* |
|---|---|
| **School Development Grant (SDG)** | |
| Rs5,000 per year per primary school<br>Rs7,000 per year per upper primary school<br>Rs12,000 per year if the school is primary+upper primary (Std I–VIII) | This grant can be used for buying school and office equipment such as blackboard, sitting mats, chalk, duster, registers and other essential supplies |
| Note: Primary and upper primary schools are treated as separate schools even if they are in the same premises | The grant amount varies by type of school, i.e. whether it is primary, upper primary or elementary |
| **School Maintenance Grant (SMG)** | |
| Rs 5,000–7,500 per year if the school has up to three classrooms<br>Rs7,500–10,000 per year if the school has more than three classrooms | This grant can be used for whitewashing, beautification, repair of toilets, hand pump, playground, school building, etc. |
| Note: Primary and upper primary schools are treated as separate schools even if they are in the same premises | The grant amount depends on the number of classrooms in the school and excludes headmaster and office rooms |
| **Teaching-Learning Material Grant (TLM)** | |
| Rs500 per teacher per year in primary and upper primary schools | This grant can be used at the discretion of teachers to buy charts, posters and other teaching aids |

*Source*: MHRD, 2011a.

needs faced by the schools. New evidence from countrywide surveys conducted over the last two years suggest that around 85 per cent of schools receive their normative grants, but over half the schools get them in the second half of the financial year. Moreover, taking India as a whole, less than 60 per cent of schools received all three grants – SDG, SMG and TLM in 2008–09. While this increased to 74 per cent in financial year 2011–12, it still implies that over 25 per cent of schools do not get all the normative grants that should reach them under SSA (Accountability Initiative 2009; Accountability Initiative 2012b).

In the next section, we explore this question further by analysing data from a survey of schools in Nalanda district of the north Indian state of Bihar. Our analysis points to the fact that on both counts, the SSA fails to meet the standards of efficiency that we have defined above.

## Norms, fund flows and expenditure: evidence from Nalanda, Bihar

This section is based on a set of two surveys conducted in Nalanda, Bihar. The surveys were a part of an extensive two-round district study conducted by the Accountability Initiative. About 142 to 148 schools were selected randomly from rural areas in each of the eight PAISA districts across six states, including Nalanda.[5] The sampling frame was the list of schools given in DISE 2009–10. Schools without either primary (Std I–IV/V) or upper primary sections (Std V/VI–VII/VIII) were excluded, as were private unaided schools. Schools were sampled from each block of a district on the basis of the share of schools in that block as a fraction of total schools in the district. The sampled schools were surveyed twice – first during May to August 2011, and then during July–September 2013.

The survey questionnaire collected information about student enrolment and attendance, teacher appointment and attendance, status of school infrastructure (such as toilets and classrooms) as on the date of survey. Information about infrastructure activities carried out, as well as details about the grants received were collected for the two financial years, 2009–10 and 2010–11 in the first round, and 2011–12 and 2012–13 in the second round.[6] Data at the school level was collected from passbooks and cashbooks at the school level and thus could not be manipulated. Further, the data obtained from the surveys was tracked back through the SSA administration to map out the timing of release of funds by the districts (Figure 11.6).

### *Findings from flow of school grants*

The data from the surveys point to a mismatch between allocation for school grants and their releases by the district and significant time lags in the receipt and expenditure of grants at the school level. First, not all the money allocated for school grants was released. In Nalanda district in 2009–10, while 99 per cent of the funds allocated for TLM were released and 97 per cent for SDG, only 57 per cent of funds allocated for SMG were released. There have, however, been some improvements in 2012–13. All the TLM funds allocated were released in 2012–13, and 96 per cent of funds for SDG and 89 per cent for SMG were released.

Second is with respect to timing. In 2009–10, all the funds for SDG and SMG were released by July and for TLM it was released by August. However, schools reported receiving the funds mainly by October – two to three months after the release. Similarly in 2012, while most funds were released by the district by July-August and only one per cent was released in March

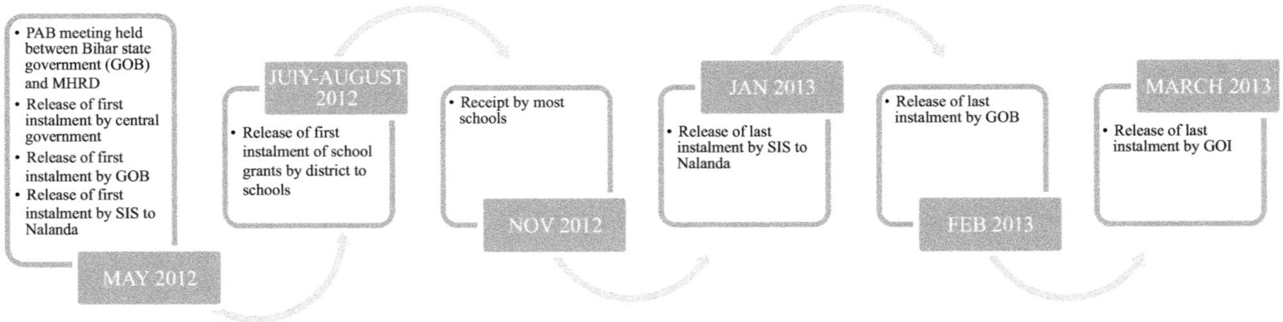


*Figure 11.6* Timeline for fund flow in Nalanda, 2012–13

*Source:* Official Records of SSA District Administration, Nalanda.

(the last month of the financial year), most schools reported receiving the funds only in November.

Third, the delay in receipt has consequences for withdrawal and expenditure. For instance, while the bulk of the schools reported receiving the grants by December in 2011–12 and November in 2012–13, less than 80 per cent of the schools were able to spend the money in the same financial year in 2011–12. The situation was similar in 2012–13, with the exception of SDG where 84 per cent of the schools had withdrawn the money. This means that a number of schools withdrew funds after the end of the financial year (see Figure 11.7a and 11.7b).

It is important to note here that the data collected information on withdrawal of funds rather than actual expenditure, as it was collected through bank passbooks. Given that the withdrawal itself was significantly delayed, actual expenditure was probably even later.

The tardiness in fund flows has two important consequences. First, it means that there are no resources available to address actual needs and

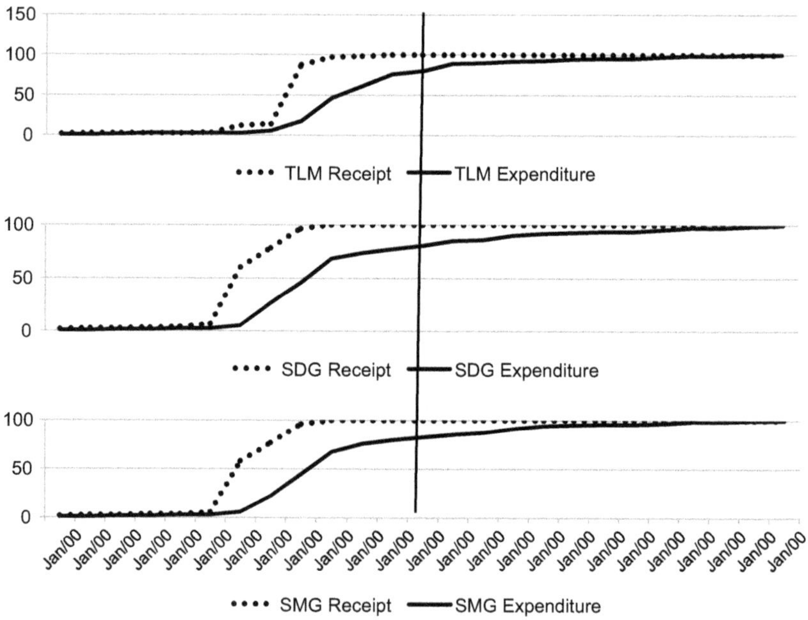


*Figure 11.7a* Percentage of schools reporting receipt and expenditure of school grants, 2011–12

*Source:* PAISA DRC Survey 2013

*Note:* Data are for Nalanda district.

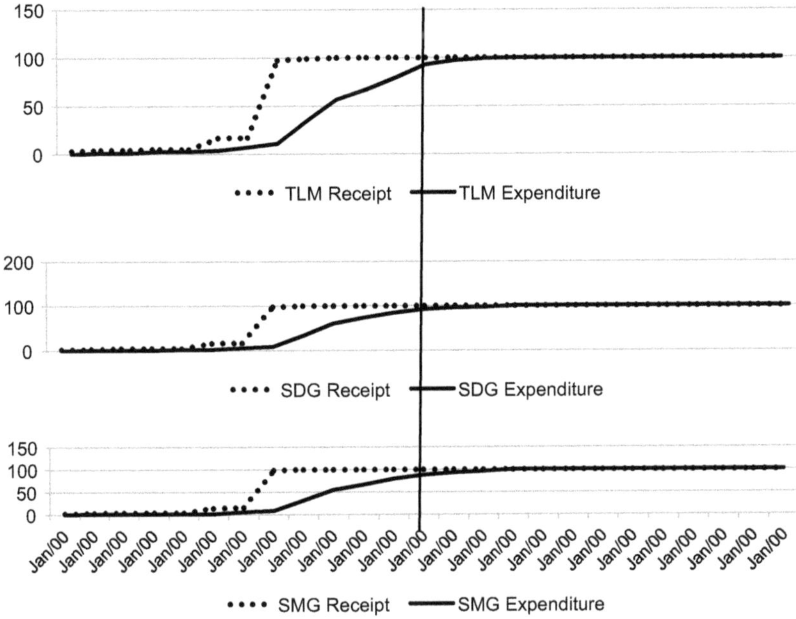


*Figure 11.7b* Percentage of schools reporting receipt and expenditure of school grants, 2012–13

*Source*: PAISA DRC Survey 2013.

*Note*: Data are for Nalanda district.

also leads to bunching of expenditure towards the end of the school year rather than in the beginning. One example that was cited related to fixing a leak in the roof of the school building. Since funds arrived late, children had to sit in one room during the monsoon season which led to overcrowding. Even after the rainy season, the room could not be used for holding classes due to the fact that the blackboard became unusable because of the dampness. When funds arrived in November, it was used to renovate the playground rather than carry out the repair.[7] Second, the inability to spend funds in the same financial year can have consequences on the receipt of funds in the next year (Figure 11.8).

For instance, as Table 11.6 shows, there is a significant difference in the proportion of schools that report receiving the grants – TLM is the highest and SMG is the lowest. This is surprising since these three grants are meant to be available to all schools annually under SSA. However, the block and district administration can withhold the disbursal of the grants if the school

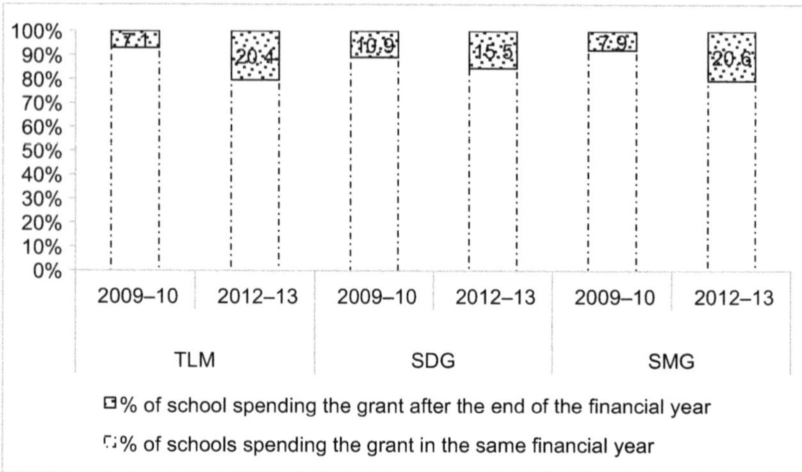


*Figure 11.8* Summary of grants spent by schools (by type)
*Source:* PAISA DRC Survey 2013.

*Table 11.6* Summary of grants reported received by schools (by type)

| | *TLM* | *SDG* | *SMG* |
|---|---|---|---|
| % schools receiving grant in both years (2009–10 and 2010–11) | 76.42 | 67.48 | 65.85 |
| % schools not receiving a grant in both years (2011–12 and 2012–13) | 86.18 | 82.17 | 75.38 |

*Source:* PAISA DRC Survey 2011 and 2013.

and the community group (in Bihar the SMC is called the Vidyalaya Shiksha Samiti or VSS) have not submitted the necessary documents showing utilization of the grants in the previous year.

In 2009–10, a small study was done in 100 schools in Nalanda which included questions on reasons for not being able to spend the school grants. Among reasons cited for not being able to spend the grants, 'lack of time' was the most common, followed by 'administrative/VSS problems' and 'difficulty in withdrawing grant money from bank accounts' (Figure 11.9).[8] The normative grants provided to schools under SSA falls in the category of 'tied' grants, i.e. grants which have to be used for a specific purpose. For example, TLM grants have to be used for teaching aids in class, SDG is

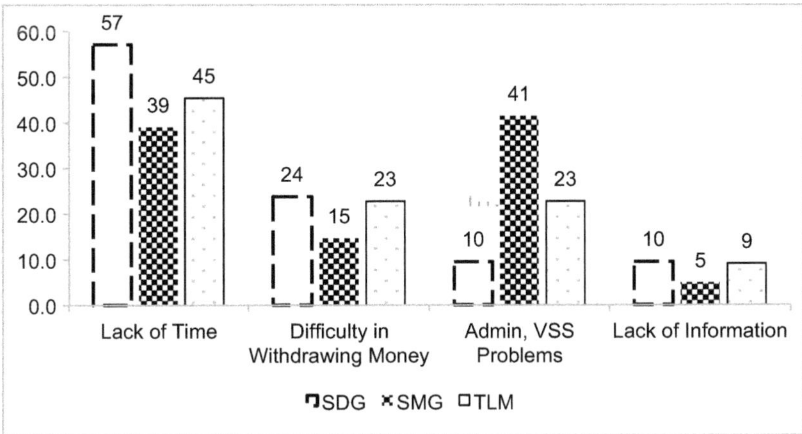


*Figure 11.9* Reasons for not spending SSA grants

*Source*: Field Survey 2009–10.

provided specifically to procure items such as chalk, duster, blackboards and other articles used in the classrooms, while SMG is to undertake painting of school buildings and other small maintenance work in the school compound. This leaves very little scope for spending on items such as story books, furniture, recreational activities, etc.

The problem with norm-based 'tied grants' is precisely the fact that schools are constrained to provide inputs specified in the guidelines, while the requirement may be very different. Since the same norms apply to all states and districts in the country, the assumption that all schools need the same inputs for better infrastructure and quality of education is often not applicable. Moreover, the SSA norms for school grants are not fixed on a per-child basis – thereby putting schools with high enrolment at a disadvantage.[9]

### *Findings from fund flows of infrastructure grants*

The second big item under which funds are given to schools is physical infrastructure. With the launch of the RTE, and the resultant infrastructure norms, most schools have received significant funds for classrooms, boundary walls, girls' toilet and other toilet facilities. The 2013 PAISA DRC survey had asked questions regarding demand for infrastructure activity, funds received for activities and the gap in the withdrawal of funds and completion of the activity. Given that Bihar has a high student–classroom ratio (79 in 2011 as opposed to the average of 30 in India) and has a significant shortfall in RTE indicators, unsurprisingly there was demand for and receipt of funds for civil works.

However, flow of funds for civil works and the actual withdrawal and construction activities indicate significant bottlenecks. Analysis of District Monthly Reports for Nalanda indicate that while 55 per cent of the funds allocated for civil works were released by the district in 2009–10, the number fell to only 22 per cent in 2012–13 (Figure 11.10).

*Table 11.7* RTE shortfall in Nalanda

| *Shortfall in schools (%)* | *2011* | *2013* |
|---|---|---|
| Usable hand pump/tap | 25 | 17 |
| Complete boundary wall | 55 | 69 |
| Playground | 59 | 70 |
| Girls' toilet | 65 | 44 |
| Boys' toilet | 72 | 49 |
| Library books | 23 | 33 |
| Library room/shelf | 96 | 95 |
| Usable blackboards | 23 | 43 |
| Teaching material (besides textbooks) | 12 | 8 |

*Source:* PAISA District Surveys 2011 and 2013.

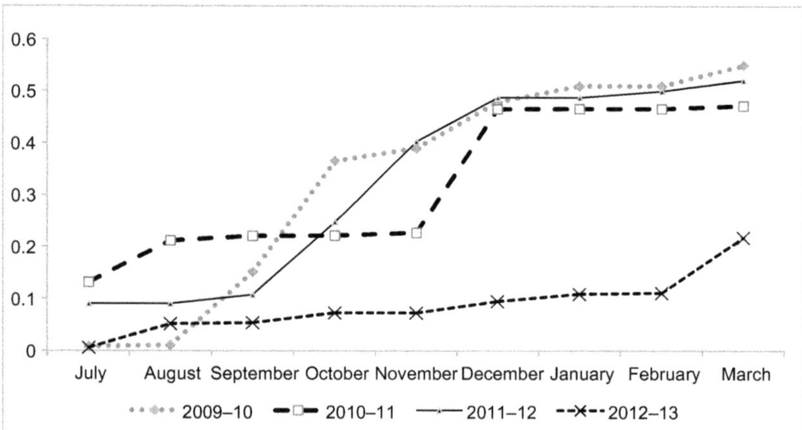


*Figure 11.10* Timing of release of civil work funds by the district (funds released as a % of allocations)

*Source:* Montly Progress Reports collected from the district.

To map out this process at the ground level, PAISA District Survey 2013 tried to trace the receipt, withdrawal and implementation of construction activities in schools. Respondents were also asked about needs and whether they had demanded for specific infrastructure items in order to see if funds were in relation to school needs. The survey found that 56 per cent of schools in Nalanda reported receiving money for additional classrooms and 23 per cent for headmaster rooms. When respondents were asked whether they had demanded for specific infrastructure funds (many in fact had not but of those that did), the requests were highest for classrooms followed by drinking water and headmaster room. However, more schools received grants for headmaster room rather than drinking water. Interestingly, the probability of receiving funds for additional classroom increased by 11 percentage points if the school requested for it – indicating a mismatch between school needs and funds received (Table 11.8).

The survey found significant delays in receipt and withdrawal of funds. For instance, 25 per cent of schools took six months or more between receipt and withdrawal of funds for additional classroom (ACR) and 38 per cent of schools took over six months to get the constructions started after receiving the funds. Moreover, there was a median gap of three months between receipt of funds and start of construction. While the norms suggest that classroom construction should be completed within 3–6 months, in Nalanda, on average it takes 15 months to finish construction. In fact, 50 per cent of schools took more than a year to build a separate classroom. These delays exist across many districts of India (see Table 11.9).

Reasons behind this gap suggest that these are a consequence of gaps in planning and decision-making. Local level problems on the ground, together with the mismatch between school needs, fund flows and school

*Table 11.8* Construction activities: Nalanda (%)

| *Activity* | *% of receiving grant in 2011–12 or 2012–13* | *% schools requesting for (of those who requested)* |
|---|---|---|
| Classroom | 56 | 9.6 |
| HM room | 23 | 5.8 |
| Ramp | 13 | 0.7 |
| Separate girls' toilet | 12 | 4.3 |
| Drinking water facility | 9 | 5.8 |
| New toilet | 9 | 5.2 |
| Major repairs | 2 | 4.5 |

*Source*: PAISA District Studies 2013.

*Table 11.9* Time taken for construction activities across districts (in months)

| *District* | *Activity* | *Fund receipt and start of activity* | *Start and completion of activity* |
|---|---|---|---|
| Medak | Classroom | 1 | 12 |
| Nalanda | Classroom | 3 | 15 |
| Purnea | Classroom | 4 | 11 |
| Satara | Classroom | 2 | 10 |
| Purnea | Separate toilet for girls | 6 | 1 |
| Kangra | Separate toilet for girls | 3 | 3 |
| Sagar | Separate toilet for girls | 1 | 2 |
| Jaipur | Separate toilet for girls | 1 | 1 |
| Udaipur | Separate toilet for girls | 1 | 2 |
| Kangra | Boundary wall | 4 | 2 |
| Jaipur | Boundary wall | 5 | 2 |
| Udaipur | Boundary wall | 4 | 4 |

*Source:* PAISA District Studies 2013.

capacity to spend, result in a lot of unspent money and delays in construction. The arrival of money in school bank account without requisite information on how to spend it results in delays in withdrawal of funds. In addition, civil work construction in particular is a long process which entails getting funds sanctioned, in some cases acquiring land, getting technical and administrative sanctions, procurement and tendering processes, completion certificates, etc. Further, schools also face local level problems such as negotiating labour rates, monsoon season, lack of roads to transfer materials, etc. Consequently, completing construction can take anywhere between two months to over a year.

It is no surprise then that most states across India were unable to meet the target of completing RTE norms by 2013. The case study of Nalanda points to the failures in planning – when annual budgetary and planning cycles follow one year (in fact nine months as the plan starts getting made by December as previously stated), but actual activities take over a year and a half.

## Governance and monitoring systems

The situation is further aggravated by a weak and overstretched governance architecture which is unable to respond to bottlenecks on the ground. For instance, the surveys asked questions on the first point of contact for schools on problems related to grants, infrastructure or teachers. In Nalanda, the block was identified as the main point of contact for all the three problems.

Despite this, 13 per cent of schools reported never being visited by a block official. Of those schools that were visited by block officials, there was on average a five-month gap since the block official had officially[10] monitored the schools.[11] Further, as stated earlier, lack of nationalized banks in the district and location of the banks contribute to further delays. For instance, in Nalanda in 2013, only 23 per cent of schools had accounts in nationalized banks while the remaining 77 per cent had accounts in grameen or cooperative banks. In terms of distance, 45 per cent of schools had banks at a distance of over 5 km (Accountability Initiative 2014).

## Summary and conclusions

Through a case study of SSA fund flows in Nalanda district in Bihar, this study discussed the recent policy stance in India for a greater role of the central government in financing of social sector programmes – especially education and health. As far as implementation is concerned, new institutional arrangements have been set up that partly bypass the sub-national government administration and seek to involve the local community. The problem with the planning and allocation guidelines is that they have a set of norms that are applicable for all states. This leads money being tied to specific items of expenditure, leaving little scope for micro-planning. We have shown that there is often a mismatch between what the service providers (in our case, the schools) require and what comes to them as tied grants. Moreover, there are coordination and implementation problems that lead to a loss in targeting the actual needs of the school. This is further exacerbated by capacity and capability constraints at the lower levels and not enough effort has been undertaken to address this constraints.

On the input side, therefore, there is a need to reform the existing norms and ensure that funds are allocated for the purpose they are actually needed. While the RTE framework emphasizes the need for localized delivery to address diverse needs of schools and children, our description indicates that the current model 'partial decentralization' has served not only to undermine the powers of the SMC but also to undermine the very objective of the RTE. Our description of the case study indicates that there are social welfare gains to be had moving from the current 'partial decentralization' to 'full decentralization', where schools exercise much greater influence over funds, functions and functionaries. More specifically, three key reforms emerge from this study.

### *Providing untied block grants to SMCs*

As we have seen in this study, from the process point of view, providing a portion of grants as untied grants for school inputs can solve coordination and targeting problems to a large extent. While the district could identify broad areas of expenditure taking into account school needs, schools should be given flexibility to spend on activities prioritized by them. In 2011, the MHRD's Joint Review Mission itself had recommended that the government move away from the current 'one-size fits all' approach to a system that 'reflect(s) the student strength for all schools, a scale or "slab" system could be devised which would provide larger school grants for larger schools' (MHRD 2011b).

### *Capacity building for planning*

Weak capacity at the local level to plan and spend funds effectively is often cited as the main constraint to greater financial and functional decentralization and devolution. While SMCs in their current form may well not have the required capacity, in the current dual structure there is little incentive for them to participate in the planning process in the absence of autonomy and power. Concerted efforts will thus need to be made by all levels of government to train and mobilize SMCs and facilitate them in making SDPs.

### *Tracking expenditures through real-time management information systems*

A key process-related inefficiency that was identified was the presence of bottlenecks in the release and expenditure of funds at all levels and incomplete information on the quantum and timing of fund flows. A real-time management information system (MIS) is thus critical in enabling transparency and accountability. This can go a long way in ensuring that both district and SMCs have access to data on timing of fund flows, thereby leading to greater predictability of fund flows and informed planning. Further, it can help higher levels of government in identifying bottlenecks in real time.

### *Acknowledgements*

This chapter is based on data collected by Accountability Initiative under the PAISA District Studies, 2011 and 2013. The authors thank the entire Accountability Team including the partners and volunteers who participated in the survey without whom this chapter would not have been possible. A special mention and thanks must be made to Ambrish Dongre and Vibhu Tewary who provided the results from the survey data analysis and to Yamini Aiyar for her comments and guidance.

## Notes

1 These are also known as Centrally Sponsored Schemes which are a specific purpose grant, funded directly by the central ministries/departments and implemented by states or their agencies. This assistance tends to be in areas that are

predominantly or have traditionally been state subjects, where the Centre wishes to motivate states to take up programmes and provides additional funding.

2 Entitlements refer to schemes for uniforms, textbooks, scholarships or cycles.

3 In government parlance, this is known as SPO booking.

4 In 2013–14 and 2014–15, the Central government has not sanctioned the TLM grant. However, at the time of this study, TLM was still received by the schools.

5 Sample size was calculated under the assumption that (a) 90 per cent schools would receive the school grants, (b) margin of error is 5 per cent and confidence level is 95 per cent and (c) non-response rate is 10 per cent.

6 Every effort was made to visit the same school in the second round as well. In instances where the schools were shut down due to reduced enrolment, they were replaced with randomly selected schools in the same block.

7 Nadiouna Upper Primary School, Rajgir Block, Nalanda.

8 VSS: Vidyalaya Shiksha Samiti – community group to oversee school functioning and civil works.

9 In fact, in 2011, the MHRD's 11th Joint Review Mission (MHRD's monitoring committee for SSA) had recommended that the government move away from the current system, which they described as a 'one size fits all' method of determining grant allocations to a system that 'reflect(s) the student strength of the school rather than providing the same grant for all schools, a scale or "slab" system could be devised which would provide larger school grants for larger schools'. However, it has not been adopted till date.

10 Surveyors were asked to check the 'monitoring book' available at school level which is supposed to have the date of visit and signature of the person who visited.

11 Muralidharan *et al.* 2013 had found a negative correlation between school inspections and teacher absenteeism. In fact, they found that increasing the probability of a school having been inspected in the past three months from 0 to 1 is correlated with a 7 percentage point reduction in teacher's absence (or 30 per cent of the observed absence rates). The finding held true for both cross-section and panel estimates, bivariate as well as multiple regressions and with and without state/district fixed effects.

## References


Accountability Initiative. 2009. *PAISA Report: Do Schools Get Their Money 2009*. New Delhi: Accountability Initiative.

Accountability Initiative. 2010. *PAISA Report: Do Schools Get Their Money 2010*. New Delhi: Accountability Initiative.

Accountability Initiative. 2012a. *PAISA District Studies 2011*. New Delhi: Accountability Initiative.

Accountability Initiative. 2012b. *PAISA Report: Do Schools Get Their Money 2012*. New Delhi: Accountability Initiative.

Accountability Initiative. 2014. *PAISA District Studies 2013 (forthcoming)*. New Delhi: Accountability Initiative.

Arcalean, Calin, Gerhard Glomm, and Jens Suedekum. 2007. "Public Budget Composition, Fiscal (De)Centralization and Welfare." *IZA Discussion Papers 2626*. Germany: Institute for the Study of Labour (IZA).

Bardhan, Pranab, and Dilip Mookherjee. 2000. "Capture and Governance at Local and National Level." *American Economic Review* 90(2): 135–9.

Bardhan, Pranab, and Dilip Mookherjee. 2006a. "Decentralization and Accountability in Infrastructure Delivery in Developing Countries." *Economic Journal* 116(508): 101–27.

Bardhan, Pranab, and Dilip Mookherjee. 2006b. "Pro-poor Targeting and Accountability of Local Governments in West Bengal." *Journal of development Economics* 79: 303–27.

Besley, Timothy, and Stephen Coate. 1999. "Centralized versus Decentralized Provision of Local Public Good." 7084. National Bureau of Economic Research (NBER).

Chakraborty, Pinaki, Anit N Mukherjee, and H K Amarnath. 2010. "Incidence of Central Government Expenditure at the State Level." *Working Paper No. 66*. New Delhi: National Institute of Public Finance and Policy.

Dreze, Jean, and Geeta Gandhi Kingdon. 2001a. "School Participation in Rural India." *Review of Development Economics* 5(1): 1–24.

Dreze, Jean, and Geeta Gandhi Kingdon. 2001b. "School Participation in Rural India." *Review of Development Economics* 5(1): 1–24.

Finance Commission of India. 2004. "Report of the Twelfth Finance Commission (2005–2010)." New Delhi.

Finance Commission of India. 2009. "Report of the Thirteenth Finance Commission (2010–2015)." New Delhi.

Galasso, Emanuela, and Martin Ravallion. 2005. "Decentralized Targeting of Anti-Poverty Programme." *Journal of Public Economics* 89(4): 705–27.

King, Elizabeth, and Berk Ozler. 2005. "Whats Decentralization Got to Do with Learning." *Interfaces with Advanced Economic Analysis Discussion Paper No. 054*. Kyoto University.

Kochar, Anjini, Kesar Singh, and Sukhwinder Singh. 2009. "Targeting Public Goods to the Poor in a Segregated Economy." *Journal of Public Economics* 93: 917–30.

Kremer, Michael, Karthik Muralidharan, Nazmul Choudhury, Hasley F Rogers, and Jeffrey Hammer. 2005. "Teacher Absenteeism in India: A Snapshot." *Journal of European Economic Association* 3(2–3): 658–67.

Ministry of Human Resource Development (MHRD). 2011a. "Sarva Shiksha Abhiyan: Framework of Implementation." New Delhi: Ministry of Human Resource Development.

Ministry of Human Resource Development (MHRD). 2011b. "11th Joint Review Mission." New Delhi.

Muralidharan, Karthik, Jishnu Das, Alaka Holla, and Aakash Mohpal. 2014. "The Fiscal Cost of Weak Governance: Evidence from Teacher Absence in India." *NBER Working Paper No. 20299*. July.

Musgrave, Richard. 1969. "Theories of Fiscal Federalism." *Public Finance* 24(4): 521–32.

Oates, Wallace E. 1972. *Fiscal Federalism*. New York: Academic Press.

PROBE Team. 1999. *Public Report On Baseic Education in India*. New Delhi: Oxford University Press.

Rao, M Govinda, and Nirvikar Singh. 2005. *Political Economy of Fiscal Federalism in India*. New Delhi: Oxford University Press.

Tiebout, Charles. 1956. "Pure Theory of Public Expenditures." *Journal of Political Economy* 64: 416–24.

# 12

# IMPLEMENTING RIGHT TO EDUCATION IN UTTARAKHAND

## The missing links

*Siba S.Mohanty and Nilachala Acharya*

### Introduction

Uttarakhand, as a state of the Indian Union, formed in the year 1999. Since its inception, Uttarakhand has remained one of the fastest growing state economies in the country. The growth of Gross State Domestic Product (GSDP) has been well above the national Gross Domestic Product (GDP) average in most of the years since 2000. The per capita GSDP in the state that was lower than the national average at the time of state formation grew from 19,457 INR in 2001 to 52,125 INR in 2011–12 compared to an increase from 20,943 INR to 37,851 INR for the country as a whole during the same period. The share of agriculture in the GSDP has declined from around 26 per cent to 11 per cent during this period compared to a decline from 22 per cent to 16 per cent for the country as a whole. While the share of industries has declined at the national level from around 27 per cent to 25 per cent, in the case of Uttarakhand, it has increased from 23 per cent to 34 per cent during the same period (Mohanty 2012: 3). To be precise, the transition to a non-agricultural economy in Uttarakhand has been rather rapid compared to the country as a whole. Being a state economy with a high rise in per capita income and rapid pace of urbanization, Uttarakhand could presumably have brought in a lot of dynamism in the popular aspirations related to educational and social outcomes in the state.

It is noteworthy to mention here that some of the prominent drives behind demand for a new state were probably an urge for self-governance and a perceived marginalisation when the state was a part of the erstwhile Uttar Pradesh (Mohanty *et al.* 2014: 364; Mohanty and Chaturvedi 2012: 23). Such sense of deprivation and marginalisation might have emerged from prolonged apathy of the state and national governments towards basic developmental outcomes in the hilly regions of the state. On many counts, including some educational indicators, the then region representing present Uttarakhand was lagging way behind other parts of the state of Uttar Pradesh. With the emergence of Uttarakhand state, as a separate entity, it was hoped that some attention would be given towards improvements in educational outcomes as well as other indicators of human development in the predominantly hilly state. In fact, out of 13 districts of the state, only 4 districts – Haridwar, Uddham Singh Nagar, Nainitaal and Dehradun – are partially non-hill districts and the other 9 districts are in hilly terrains. A time (closing years of the last millennium) when at a national level, the policy makers were preparing the country towards an agenda of universalisation of education, the state of Uttarakhand was struggling for the recognition of its hill development aspirations. The beginning of the new millennium made some remarkable breakthrough towards the national agenda in the form of launching of Sarva Siksha Abhiyan (SSA) with targets to be achieved within specific timeframes. Education as a fundamental constitutional right came at a much later stage; but SSA probably was beginning of the process of capacity creation towards announcement of a formal constitutional right. In order to discuss the progress made in Uttarakhand towards achievement of the objectives of the Right to Education (RTE), it is imperative that we also discuss the ground realities in Uttarakhand when the state was formed.

The Right to Education Act, adopted on 1st April 2010, made India achieve a distinctive recognition of being one of the few countries where free and compulsory education is a constitutional guarantee. This breakthrough Act encompasses several elements of inclusion and universalisation, making it a unique legislation towards a just Indian society. While the provisions of the Act are still under debate by the policy analysts of different orientations, the scope of the present chapter is confined to the implementation of the Right of Children to Free and Compulsory Education Act in the state of Uttarakhand and an analysis of the progress towards its stated objectives. The chapter is broadly classified into four parts. In the first part, we have briefly presented a historical account of educational development in Uttarakhand and the way the broad elements and objectives of the RTE Act fits in the state context. In the second section, we have presented an analysis of the progress towards achieving the objectives of RTE. The third section highlights one of the major developmental contradictions in Uttarakhand state, namely the hill-plain divide in education. In the last section, some issues regarding the quality of education are highlighted through an analysis of some primary inputs collected through a fieldwork[1] in the Vikash Nagar Block of Dehradun district.

## *An historical account of the educational development in Uttarakhand*

By the year 2002–03, Uttarakhand had around one school at the elementary level for 100 children in the age group 6–14 years compared to a school for 234 children in the country as a whole. These figures, based on the data on number of schools (Mehta 2003, 2009, 2013) imparting elementary education in India and the age-wise population (GOI 2001, 2011), show an improvement in the infrastructural base to approximately a school for 89 children in Uttarakhand and 179 children for the country as a whole[2] in the year 2009–10. On the face of it, the situation of Uttarakhand seems much better than the national scenario in both the years. But given the geographical peculiarities of the state and location of population in a scattered and sparse manner, such figures may not reveal much than the fact that the progress towards making the infrastructure base of education was less visible in Uttarakhand than in the country between 2002 and 2010–11. One such instance could be the number of schools in Uttarakhand, which grew only by 28 per cent during this phase compared to a 54 per cent increase in the total number of schools in the country.

The progress of some other indicators during this phase also deserves attention. The number of privately managed schools in Uttarakhand as a proportion of total schools had increased from around 12 per cent in 2002–03 to more than 22 per cent in 2010–11, compared to an increase from 12 per cent to 19 per cent in the country (Table 12.1).

There is no dearth of analysis that shows the problems associated with increasing private responsibility in educational provisioning. Just to mention one such instance of increasing private-run schools in the state, it is found that the number of private schools has increased by almost 126 per cent over the period in the state (Mehta 2003, 2009, 2013–14). While some see this as a compromise with the established norms of governance in provisioning for education (Kalama *et al.* 2011), some others view this as a problem of non-compliance to the basic philosophy of adequacy, equity and distributive justice (Brighouse 2000; Brighouse 2004).

*Table 12.1* Progress in school-related indicators in Uttarakhand and India, 2002–10

| *Indicators* | *2002–03* | | *2009–10* | |
|---|---|---|---|---|
| | *Uttarakhand* | *India* | *Uttarakhand* | *India* |
| Private schools as % of total schools | 12.33 | 11.7 | 21.69 | 19.49 |
| Primary schools without building (%) | 2.57 | 6.34 | 3.6 | 13.7 |
| Primary schools without classrooms (%) | 14.5 | 11.7 | 2.4 | 4.12 |
| Schools without boundary wall (%) | 32.9 | 34.2 | 22 | 47 |
| Schools with 0 or 1 teacher (%) | 23 | 20.5 | 12.55 | 9.33 |
| Schools without drinking water facility (%) | 39.3 | 27.8 | 11.7 | 8.2 |
| Schools without a girl's toilet (%) | 69.7 | 78.8 | 23 | 25 |

*Source:* Mehta (2003, 2009, 2013–14).

Infrastructure facility too plays an important role in enduring socially acceptable minimum standards of education in any country. There is enough literature to suggest a strong link between school infrastructure and educational outcome as well as well-being of pupils (Jha *et al.* 2008; Cuyvers *et al.* 2011). At the time of state formation, among all schools providing elementary education in Uttarakhand, 32 per cent schools did not have boundary walls, 2.6 per cent primary and 9.6 per cent upper primary schools were without any buildings, 14.5 per cent primary and more than 20 per cent upper primary schools were without any classrooms, around 23 per cent primary schools were running with a single or without any teacher, around 39 per cent schools were without drinking water facility and around 70 per cent schools were without any girls toilet facility. On many counts, the situation was worse in Uttarakhand than the Indian scenario. Information presented in Table 12.1 portrays a comparative picture of the situation and progress in Uttarakhand and India between 2002 and 2010. Our purpose here is not to make a comparison with the national average but to highlight the amount of gap that existed in the education system in India (including Uttarakhand) even after close to seven decades of *political* freedom.

Given this backdrop, we have attempted in this chapter to study the RTE in the state context of Uttarakhand. As is well-known, the RTE has a few stated components. These include: (a) an element of universalisation in the provisioning of free and compulsory education; (b) an element of attainment towards achieving a minimum acceptable standard of quality education; (c) an element of free education in the form of lessening the burden of parents from payments like school fees, textbooks, mid-day meal, uniforms, transportation, etc., at least in the phase of elementary education; (d) an element of responsibility for inclusion of children in their appropriate age group levels of education and holding the school responsible for their performance so that remedial measures are proactively taken for such inclusion; and (e) an element of punishment for non-conformity to RTE rules (GOI 2010). Accordingly, the Government of Uttarakhand also adopted Uttarakhand Right of Children to Free and Compulsory Education Rules, 2011 on 31st October 2011. While the spirit of the Central Act was maintained, some further changes were made in the Act to make it suitable for the context of Uttarakhand (GOUK 2011). The underlying rules of the Uttarakhand Act are listed below:

(a) Special training of children through interventions by the Block Education Officer (BEO) and School Management Committees (SMCs) for inclusion of over-age children.
(b) A differential standard of pupil classroom/school ratio for rural and urban areas with provision of review of progress in every three years.
(c) Free transportation or boarding facilities for children without neighbourhood schools and living in difficult terrains.

Through a notification dated 2nd July 2013, the Government of Uttarakhand further amended the existing rules under RTE apart from changing some nomenclature of officials under the governance of RTE. To cite a few such prominent changes, the notification included children of manual scavenger's family and all children with severe disability as defined in clause (o) of section 2 of the National Trust for Welfare of Persons with Autism, Cerebral Palsy, Mental Retardation and Multiple disabilities Act 1999 under the purview of RTE Uttarakhand. It removed the time limit of three months for self-declaration of conformity to the Act by schools run by non-government agencies. The Uttarakhand Act made it mandatory for the Chief Education Officer to cross check, verify and certify the correctness of such self-declaration by the privately managed schools. The sub-rule 10 of rule 20 of the principal Act was also amended by increasing the tenure of the elected members from one year to three years. In rule 33 of the Act, the Uttarakhand notification gave a liberty to the Chief Education Officer to notify the sanctioned strength of the teachers within a time frame of three years instead of three months as mentioned in the original rules. The State Act also freed the schools run by minority institutions from preparing annual plans and reporting structures under the Act

(GOUK 2013). So, while the Uttarakhand Act was made more inclusive and context-specific in some sense by considering some state-specific realities, it also diluted the spirit of the Act by providing liberties to authorities to delay the implementation of some critical rules under the Act. It is in this broad backdrop, we shall discuss the dynamics of implementation of the Act in the state.

In the forthcoming sections, we have made a situation analysis of Uttarakhand after two years of implementation of the RTE in the state on the basis of secondary information available from the Ministry of Human Resource Development, Government of India and Sarva Sikshya Abhiyan. As noted earlier, we have also used some analysis of the quality of provisions in the state on the basis of primary data collected by Pratham Education Foundation (PEF) in the Vikash Nagar Block of Dehradun district during 2012 and 2013. Our analysis broadly covers the key objectives of the Act for maintaining quality of education and the effectiveness of the governance system operating in provisioning of education.

## Progress on achieving the stated objectives of RTE in Uttarakhand

Notwithstanding the norms of governance laid down under RTE that came at a later stage, SSA had been conceived as a vehicle for universalisation of education in India since 2001. Under SSA, an Annual Work Plan and Budget (AWP&B) is prepared at different levels of SSA governance, approved by the Project Approval Board (PAB), and depending on the stated norms for responsibility sharing by the Union Government, State Government and grants-in-aid contributions from the Finance Commission; funds are made available for the implementation of the programme. Since a decade-long implementation of SSA was expected to provide a necessary ground for the implementation of RTE, it may be pertinent to have a look at the progress made under SSA in Uttarakhand.

Figure 12.1 provides a glimpse of progress of SSA in Uttarakhand and is prepared based on the data given in the annual work plan and budgets for various years. Some interesting issues of concern emerge from Figure 12.1. First, barring a couple of years, the funds available for the purpose of implementing SSA was much lower than what the approved AWP&B had called for, indicating a problem of resource crunch. Second, in most of the preparatory years, the actual expenditure was less than the funds

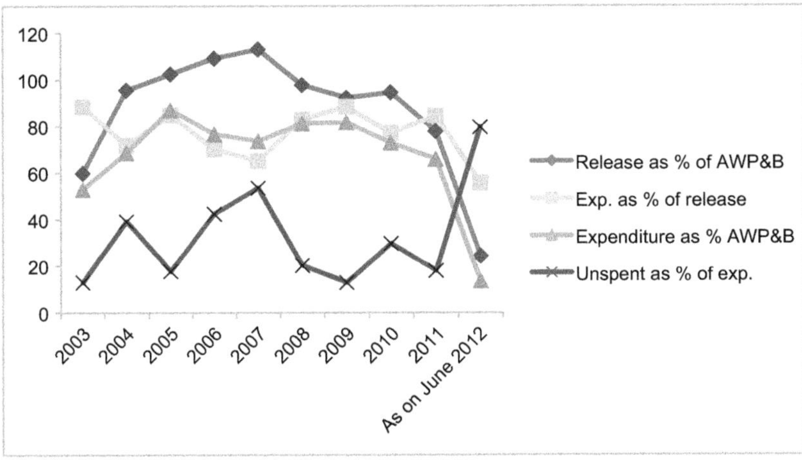


*Figure 12.1* Financial performance of SSA in Uttarakhand (including NPEGEL and KGBV)

*Source:* based on the data given in SSA (2013).

*Notes*

1 The funds include National Programme on Education for Girls at Elementary Level (NPGEL) and Kasturba Gandhi Balika Vidyalaya (KGBV).

2 Funding ratio between GOI and the State Government of Uttarakhand for the period 2002–03 to 2006–07 was 75 per cent and 25 per cent, respectively. Again for the years 2007–08 to 2008–09 the ratio was 65 per cent for GOI and 35 per cent for GOUK, respectively. For the year 2009–10, it was 60 per cent and 40 per cent and for the period 2010–11 to 2012–13, the same ratio was 65 per cent and 35 per cent.

available, which shows problems of under-utilisation. Third, the amount that remained unspent was much higher, up to 54 per cent of the actual expenditure in 2007, indicating a problem of unrealised potential achievements in elementary education, and fourth, the huge unspent balance, up to 80 per cent of funds spent in the first quarter of the financial year 2012–13 (April–June), given the significance of the beginning of the academic sessions, may indicate both issues of effectiveness of resource use as well as possible anomalies and delays in the fund flow processes. The anomalies in the implementation of SSA could also have resulted in less than desirable progress made in achieving the targets of RTE after enactment of the RTE legislation.

The financial flow for implementation of RTE in the state also deserves attention. In the year 2011 when RTE was implemented in the state, the

*Table 12.2* Financial flows under SSA–RTE in Uttarakhand

| *Year* | *Approved work plan and budget* | *Balance from previous year* | *Total amount released* | *Total expenditure* | *Expenditure as % of amount approved* | *Expenditure as % of amount released* |
|---|---|---|---|---|---|---|
| 2001–02 | 25.6 | — | 13.11 | 0.09 | 0.4 | 0.7 |
| 2002–03 | 55.83 | 13.02 | 46.77 | 19.03 | 34.1 | 40.7 |
| 2003–04 | 125.77 | 27.74 | 75.27 | 66.59 | 52.9 | 88.5 |
| 2004–05 | 141.17 | 8.68 | 134.97 | 96.93 | 68.7 | 71.8 |
| 2005–06 | 168.52 | 38.04 | 172.84 | 146.68 | 87.0 | 84.9 |
| 2006–07 | 248.21 | 26.16 | 271.1 | 190.28 | 76.7 | 70.2 |
| 2007–08 | 252.84 | 80.82 | 285.84 | 186.12 | 73.6 | 65.1 |
| 2008–09 | 272.96 | 99.72 | 266.88 | 221.67 | 81.2 | 83.1 |
| 2009–10 | 330.57 | 45.21 | 305.18 | 270.15 | 81.7 | 88.5 |
| 2010–11 | 501.33 | 35.03 | 474.4 | 365.54 | 72.9 | 77.1 |
| 2011–12 | 605.23 | 108.86 | 471.52 | 399.36 | 66.0 | 84.7 |
| 2012–13 (as on June 2012) | 569.32 | 72.16 | 138.86 | 77.28 | 13.6 | 55.7 |
| Total | 2,728.03 | 555.44 | 2,656.74 | 2,039.72 | 74.8 | 76.8 |

*Source:* Prepared based on the data given in SSA (2013).

total expenditure under SSA was only around 66 per cent of what was budgeted for in the state, compared to around 87 per cent in the year 2005–06. As we can notice from the trend of expenditure in the state on education, in terms of utilization of budgetary resources, the state maintains a cycle of better expenditure in a couple of years followed by large unspent balances in other years. Coincidentally, the better performing years are those preceding the state elections (Table 12.2).

Though the overall absorptive rates has improved, the component-wise absorptive rates ranged from 23 per cent (for the component on residential schools for specific category of children) to 98 per cent in the component school grant, with highest utilisation rates in 2011–12. Many components report more than 75 per cent utilisation rates. However, these components relate to civil works and teacher salary-related expenditures. But some of the out-of-school children activities, such as residential schools, reported very low utilisation rates (Figure 12.2).

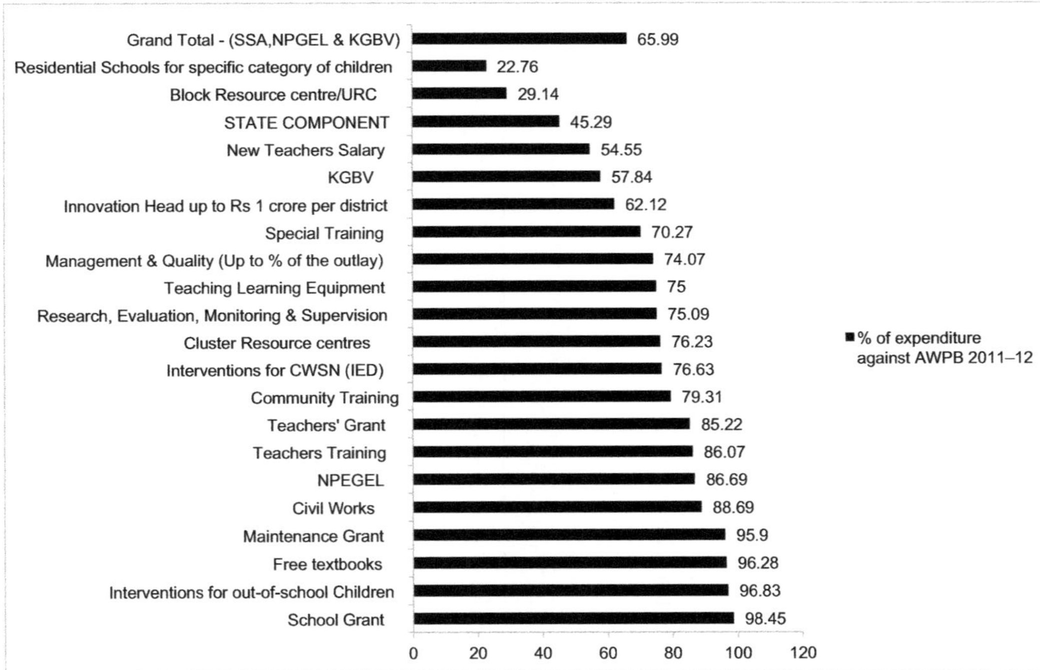


*Figure 12.2* Component-wise SSA expenditure as percentage of annual work plan and budget, 2011–12

*Source*: Prepared based on the data given in SSA (2013).

## RTE in Uttarakhand and the hill-plain divide

A district-wise comparison of some basic RTE norms suggest that most of the mountain districts are lacking in making provisions of adequate teachers to adhere to the RTE norms. Even in Dehradun district, which also hosts the capital city of the state, nearly three-fourth of primary schools and 93 per cent upper primary schools failed to comply with the RTE norms in this respect. A closer look at the provision of basic facilities presented in Table 12.3 also suggests a clear regional discrepancy in terms of hill-plain divide in infrastructure.

The RTE Act in Uttarakhand, and amendments in it, took care of incorporating some relevant state-specific concerns. For example, the Act provided for lower pupil–teacher ratio in mountain regions, transportation facility for children owing to distance from the school and so on. However, the ground realities in terms of making provisions for those concerns do not yet confirm that these are real concerns for the region. As can be seen from Figure 12.3, only around 24 per cent of all primary

*Table 12.3* District-wise availability of some basic infrastructure in government schools, Uttarakhand, 2010–11

| *Districts* | *Schools* | *Girls toilet* | *Electricity* | *Ramp* | *Playground* | *Drinking water* | *Book bank* | *Kitchen shed* |
|---|---|---|---|---|---|---|---|---|
| | (*In nos*) | | | | (%) | | | |
| Almora | 1,848 | 70.0 | 46.6 | 7.0 | 47.7 | 90.8 | 27.9 | 67.7 |
| Bageshwar | 805 | 83.1 | 68.0 | 24.0 | 34.7 | 92.0 | 48.9 | 68.0 |
| Chamoli | 1,392 | 87.7 | 17.5 | 26.0 | 77.7 | 97.9 | 34.6 | 80.7 |
| Champawat | 707 | 73.3 | 45.5 | 60.5 | 55.0 | 94.8 | 26.6 | 54.0 |
| Dehradun | 1,329 | 96.0 | 84.5 | 92.6 | 59.3 | 99.4 | 28.8 | 61.6 |
| Pauri | 2,231 | 58.0 | 16.3 | 29.6 | 38.9 | 91.6 | 61.1 | 67.6 |
| Hardwar | 907 | 76.2 | 30.9 | 77.9 | 67.7 | 96.7 | 32.4 | 68.9 |
| Nainital | 1,367 | 62.9 | 58.4 | 40.1 | 47.9 | 99.4 | 61.7 | 64.1 |
| Pithoragarh | 1,628 | 59.5 | 27.0 | 81.4 | 47.9 | 97.2 | 61.4 | 68.2 |
| Rudraprayag | 795 | 72.6 | 36.1 | 80.0 | 29.3 | 99.0 | 29.2 | 55.1 |
| Tehri | 2,031 | 97.7 | 62.3 | 100.0 | 47.9 | 93.3 | 24.1 | 74.9 |
| US Nagar | 1,088 | 36.9 | 64.8 | 73.3 | 32.8 | 73.8 | 92.6 | 18.8 |
| Uttarkashi | 1,108 | 45.5 | 48.5 | 50.2 | 42.4 | 90.4 | 25.7 | 64.7 |
| All districts | 17,236 | 72.9 | 46.8 | 55.2 | 51.1 | 95.2 | 39.6 | 68.0 |

*Source*: Prepared based on the data given in SSA (2013).

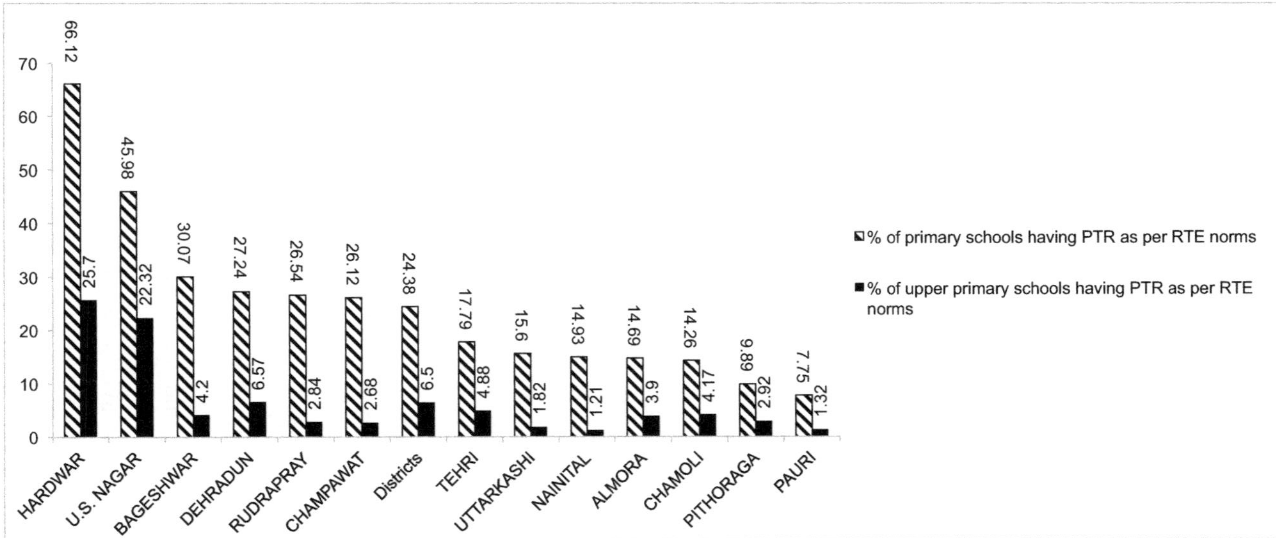


*Figure 12.3* District-wise comparison of schools adhering to PTR norms as per RTE Act in primary and upper primary levels in Uttarakhand, 2011–12

*Source:* Prepared based on the data given in SSA (2013).

*Table 12.4* Concentration of schools in plain districts

| *Areas* | *Geographical area covered* | *Composition of total schools* | *Composition of private schools* | *Proportion of private schools in total schools of the region* |
|---|---|---|---|---|
| Hill districts | 77 | 65 | 46 | 16.03 |
| Plain districts | 23 | 35 | 54 | 36.04 |
| Uttarakhand | 100 | 100 | 100 | 22.95 |

*Source:* Based on SSA (2013).

schools and 6.5 per cent of all upper primary schools holds a pupil–teacher ratio as per the RTE norms.

While plain districts cover only 23 per cent of the total geographical area of the state, around 35 per cent of all schools and around 54 per cent of all private schools are located in plain districts (Table 12.4). Since hilly districts do not attract private school managements much, it is necessary that the infrastructure to be provided in hilly regions will have to be borne largely by the government. Unfortunately, the infrastructural deficits in government schools are acute in hilly districts rather than in plain districts.

The hill-plain divide is also clearly visible in fund utilisation pattern towards RTE. As we can notice from Figure 12.4, plain districts have more unspent balance vis-à-vis their hilly counterparts.

*Hilly districts have high degree of fund utilisation, both in terms of expenditure as per cent of release and approved budget.* In order to understand the possible reasons behind better utilisation in hilly districts than the plain districts, we analysed item-wise budgets under provisioning for RTE. As presented in Figure 12.4, we find higher utilisation of funds in interventions like school grant, out-of-school children, free text books, maintenance grants, civil works, etc., for which the fund absorption capacity in the hilly districts might be higher owing to higher demands for these interventions. The tentative explanations for comparatively higher demand for public services, like education in rural, hilly and backward areas, are simple. Owing to lack of availability of alternatives like private education systems and the low paying capacity of the people in general make them depend more on public services such as government schools. Moreover, given the gap in infrastructure base in hilly areas, the fund absorption capacity may be higher in rural and hilly areas than urban areas.

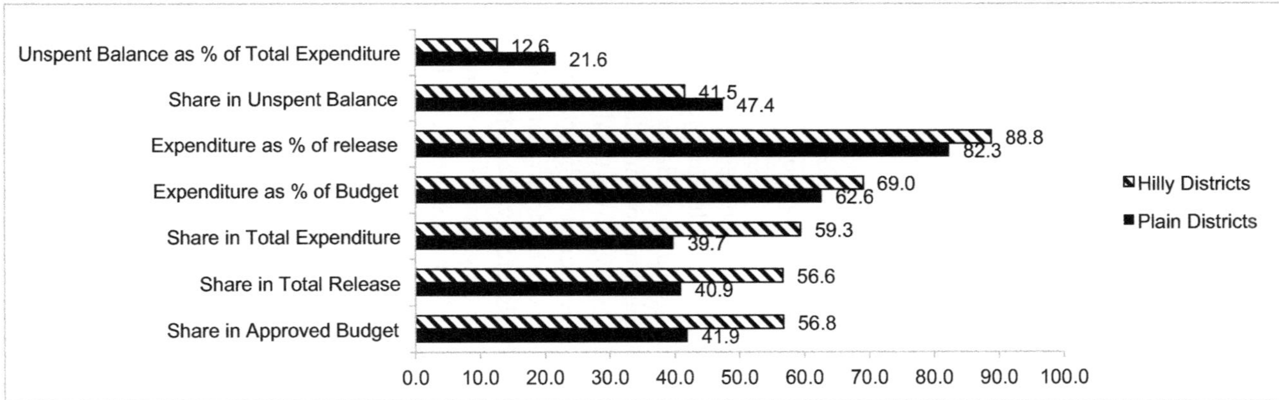


*Figure 12.4* Pattern of expenditure under SSA in plain and hill districts, 2011–12

*Source:* Based on SSA (2013).

An interesting extension of the hill-plain divide in educational outcomes in the era of both SSA and RTE in Uttarakhand may be the study of the trends in Gender Parity Indices (GPIs) in enrolment. Gender Parity Index in enrolment as defined by the United Nations Statistics Division is a ratio of girls to boys at different levels of education. As we may recall, India is a signatory to the global declaration called Millennium Development Goals (MDGs) since 2000. MDGs among other goals for development also called for achievements in universal primary education and promotion of gender equality and empowerment of women (United Nations, New Delhi). Probably, the MDG declaration of 2000, in which 189 countries including India made such commitments at global level was also one of the driving forces behind initiation of SSA and subsequently RTE in India. Although, the SSA intervention is commonly believed to have its roots in the District Primary Education Programme (DPEP) run in selected states of the country in early 1990s (GOI 2012), one cannot undermine the influence of MDG declaration in the way SSA was introduced in the country in 2001.

Not only in India, but in many countries of Africa and Asia, several interventions such as universal enrolment programmes, school feeding programmes (something similar to mid-day meal under SSA), civil society collectives under the platform of the Right to Education Project that undertakes global advocacy on institutionalisation of formal legislations towards recognising education as a basic human right, interventions related to removal of gender-based and language-based hindrances in retaining children in schools, etc. evolved effectively after the MDG declaration, and the initial funding for the interventions were provided by global communities under the banner of World Bank (IBRD), International Monetary Fund (IMF) and other multilateral agencies (United Nations n.d.). Even in India, the central share under SSA was initially mobilised through supports from IBRD, IMF, Department for International Development (DFID) and many such agencies (Jalan and Glinskaya, undated). The influence of time-bound targets under MDGs might have motivated the government as well as the watchdog civil society groups to keep a track of the progress made under SSA towards universalisation and gender equality in education. The monitoring mechanism under the purview of DISE also started keeping a track of GPI in enrolment at the district level. GPI in enrolment is a simple measure represented through the ratio of female to male enrolment in schools. One of the major causes of finding higher GPI in rural and hilly districts of Uttarakhand may be the issue of migration of male members of the family (Acharya 2000; Bose 2000).

Hill to plain migration is identified as one of the major causes of socio-cultural and political disturbances in Uttarakhand. Migration (both out of state and within the state from hilly to plain and from rural to urban areas) in Uttarakhand occur due to myriad reasons; but the most prominent among them are possibilities of better employment opportunities and better educational facilities. In Uttarakhand, drive for better education facilities and employment opportunities do claim more than 80 per cent of all migration cases among male migrants in the state (Singh 2012: 49). Migration in any society does come with a cost of loss of social capital and also the pecuniary burdens of supporting the newly migrated individuals in their pursuit in the aftermath of migration, more so in case of those going out for studies. This might have resulted in lesser resources left for education of '*lesser*' (emphasis ours) members in the family, especially the girls (Singh 2012: 47). Only a few migrants are resourceful enough to take their entire family along with them. Given the fact that often girls do not migrate at a scale their male counterparts do, for reasons associated with financial needs to support out-migrants in their initial stages of migration and also because of their requirement at home primarily for agricultural support in hilly terrains, they largely end up in schools in nearby localities, within walkable distances. The study by Desai and Banerjiin on women folk who stayed back after migration of their male family members highlight such issues in the context of two main outcomes. First, the autonomy of women increases to take decisions related to upbringing of their children along with other decision making at the household level. Second, the transformation of women from a passive homemaking role to a role of head of the households albeit, with scant resources (Desai and Banerji 2008: 340). This might have been the reason why even in cases where private alternatives are available, demand for public goods is higher among the poorer sections of the society. The situation in Uttarakhand might have been taken shape along these outcomes highlighted by Desai and Banerji. On one hand, we see a greater participation of girls to boys in the hilly districts of the state and on the other hand, we also notice a better fund absorption rate, indicating higher demand for government funded programmes in education of children. Numerous studies on contemporary discussions on development do highlight these issues (Bray 1996; Fernandez and Rogerson 1996; Acharya 2000; Bruslé 2014).

As presented in Figure 12.5, the GPI in hill districts have been in favour of girls since 2004, indicating a higher proportion of girls enrolled in schools of the hill districts. However, the trend over years shows that there is a deterioration in the index value (ratio of girls to

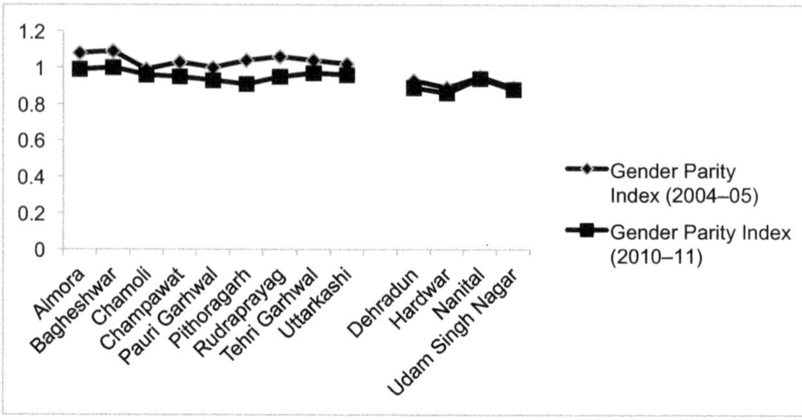


*Figure 12.5* GPI in hill and plain districts of Uttarakhand, 2004–05 and 2010–11
*Source:* DISE (2013).

boys enrolled in schools), although hill districts are still able to attain a higher GPI than their plain counterparts. While higher GPI in hilly districts only reinforce our earlier inference about higher demand for public provisioning for education owing to limited opportunities for education, a decline in the trend may indicate a loss of trust on the government schools.

Another issue of critical significance is the increasing prevalence of out-of-school children in Uttarakhand. Although, in contemporary policy circles, the potential factors contributing high dropout rates are largely linked with demand-side issues, many scientific studies and analysis consider this primarily as a supply-side phenomenon. These studies, based on primary inputs from the field, have highlighted issues such as high pupil–teacher ratio, involvement of teachers in non-academic activities, lack of suitable follow-up and monitoring activities to deal with dropout cases individually, child labour, issues related to teaching methods and school environment, issues related to physical ability of students and many other relevant issues (PROBE 1999; Jha *et al.* 2008; De *et al.* 2011). Although not specific to the state of Uttarakhand, both PROBE report of 1999 and the PROBE Revisited of 2011(De *et al.* 2011) have highlighted withdrawal by family as primary factor contributing to non-enrolment and dropout that result from complex supply-side factors.

Even in non-Indian contexts, supply-side issues such as infrastructure both in terms of physical and human capital do play a role in reducing dropout rates in schools (Scales 1969 and Belknap 1954). In the following section, we have cited a few excerpts from both the PROBE reports published at a decadal interval.

> The villages were socially and culturally diverse, but reasons why children had dropped out bore remarkable similarities. . . . The reasons for dropping out turned out to be very different for boys and girls . . . girls had dropped out due to some domestic crisis or parental pressure. Boys, on the other hand, had usually abandoned their studies owing to their own disinterest, illness or failure in examinations: parents had rarely pressed their sons to drop out . . . girls are more easily withdrawn from school for a combination of social and economic reasons. To start with, household work and child-care are seen as the responsibility of daughters. Secondly, the economic returns to education are perceived to be high . . . girls are also victims of parental anxiety. According to parents, daughters study only as far as school facilities within the village permit, because it is not safe to send a girl out of the village to study.
>
> (PROBE 1999: 34)

> Over one-third of those who had dropped out of school without completing class 8 had dropped out after completing class 5 and before enrolling in class 6. Such dropping out tends to occur when children have to transit after primary school to another school, and particularly among girls when the middle school is not in the same village.
>
> (PROBE Revisited, De *et al.* 2011)

The situations in Uttarakhand are no different. Although, performing better than the national average, the schools in Uttarakhand have not only experienced dropouts, the figures have increased after the implementation of the RTE Act. Probably owing to better fund absorption rates in hilly regions and recently built up public infrastructure in education, the dropout situation is still better in hilly regions than the plains. As presented in Figure 12.6, not only is the proportion of 6–14-year-old children, who are out of school in Uttarakhand, higher in plain districts than the hill districts, the proportion for the entire state have gone up from 1.1 per cent in 2011 to 1.9 per cent in 2013.

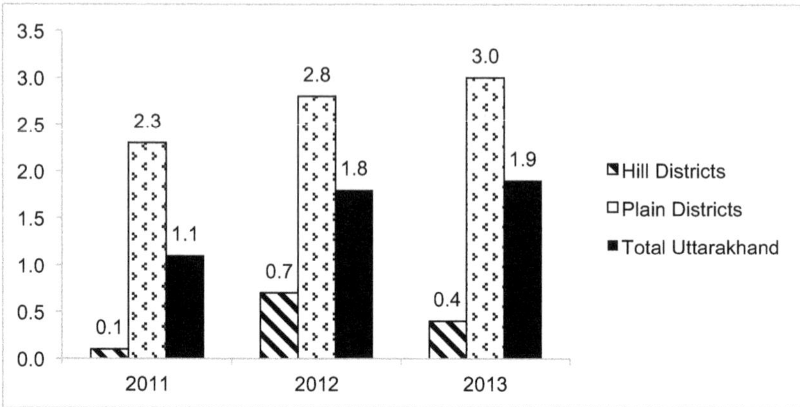


*Figure 12.6* Proportion of out-of-school children in Uttarakhand during RTE implementation period

*Source:* PEF (2012, 2013, 2014).

## Quality of education: evidences from the field

The analysis so far can be summarised as a situation of non-conformity to RTE norms in the state and lack of prioritisation towards removal of regional imbalances therein. In this section, we have made an attempt to present the issue of overall quality of education post-RTE implementation in the state. On the basis of the survey data presented in the Annual Status of Education Report (ASER) of the PEF for the year 2011, 2012 and 2013 for the state of Uttarakhand, we have compiled the district-level information on six different indicators that may be considered as proxies indicating quality of education provided in the state public education system. These include (a) % children (6–14 years) out of school; (b) % children (6–14 years) in private schools; (c) % children (standards I and II) who can read letters, words or more; (d) % children (standards I and II) who can recognise numbers (1–9) or more; (e) % children (standard III–V) who can read standard I text or more; and (f) % children (standard III–V) who can do subtraction or more (PEF 2012, 2013, 2014). In order to put these indicators in the context of hill and plain regions of Uttarakhand, we have clubbed together information from nine hill districts and four plain districts of the state.

The survey conducted by the ASER team of PEF involved different tests to assess reading, writing and mathematical ability of standard I–III and standard IV–V students on questions expected to be correctly answered by

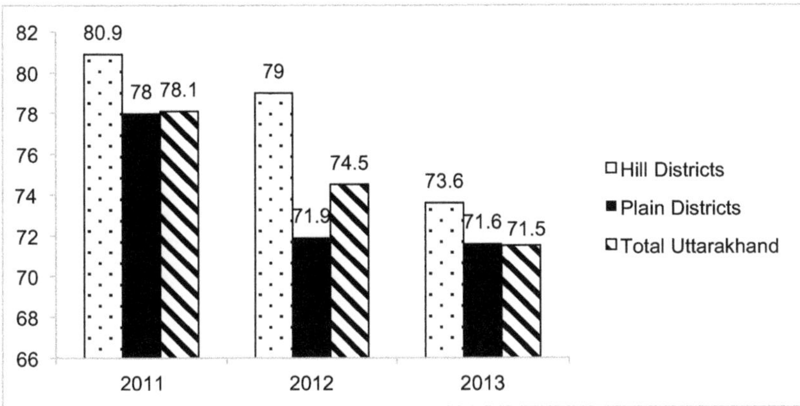


*Figure 12.7* Percentage of children (I–III) who can read letters, words or more
*Source:* PEF (2012, 2013, 2014).

students in the preceding levels. The findings of ASER not only show glaring gaps in delivery of education in the government schools, as far as learning outcomes are concerned, they also show a deterioration of standards in recent years. As can be seen in Figure 12.7, around 81 per cent learners in hilly districts of standards I–III could read simple letters, words or more, in the year 2011. By 2013, the situation worsened with around 73 per cent children with such ability. Moreover, the situation in plain districts is worse than their hill counterparts.

In all the six indicators, the districts in the plain region have performed worse than the hill districts (Tables 12.5 and 12.6). While the ASER reports of PEF clearly established a regional imbalance and deterioration of educational attainments in the state, it is also pertinent to study the situation at the sub-district level. In the forthcoming paragraphs, we have presented an analysis of the primary data collected from the Vikashnagar Block of Dehradun district for evaluating the performance of Read India Progamme run by PEF. The analysis provided some more insights into the concerns presented above.

Vikashnagar is considered one among the most developed administrative blocks of Dehradun in terms of concentration of medical and educational facilities as well as quality of other public amenities like approach road, drinking water, power supply, etc. (Gupta *et al.* 2000). Read India Programme is a pioneering activity by PEF to improve the learning skills of children enrolled in government schools vis-a-vis a

*Table 12.5* Quality of education in government schools of Uttarakhand

| *Indicators/regions* | *2011* | *2012* | *2013* |
|---|---|---|---|
| % of children in private school | | | |
| Hill districts | 21.6 | 27.6 | 25.0 |
| Plain districts | 44.2 | 46.1 | 49.7 |
| Total | 31.3 | 36.6 | 39.4 |
| % of children (standards I–III) who can read letters, words or more | | | |
| Hill districts | 80.9 | 79.0 | 73.6 |
| Plain districts | 78.0 | 71.9 | 71.6 |
| Total | 78.1 | 74.5 | 71.5 |
| % of children (standards III–V) who can read standard 1 text or more | | | |
| Hill districts | 71.8 | 68.0 | 73.1 |
| Plain districts | 59.8 | 59.7 | 59.0 |
| Total | 64.2 | 63.3 | 64.2 |

*Source:* PEF (2012, 2013, 2014).

*Table 12.6* Mathematical skills of students in government schools in Uttarakhand

| | *2011* | *2012* | *2013* |
|---|---|---|---|
| % of children (standards I–III) who can recognise numbers | | | |
| Hill districts | 79.7 | 78.7 | 72.2 |
| Plain districts | 76.7 | 78.2 | 79 |
| Total | 76.6 | 77.6 | 76.3 |
| % of children (standards III–V) who can do subtraction or more | | | |
| Hill districts | 54.6 | 53.5 | 47.6 |
| Plain districts | 49.8 | 46.3 | 44.1 |
| Total | 50.9 | 49.7 | 45.1 |

*Source:* PEF (2012, 2013, 2014).

benchmark baseline performance. Under this programme, a team of two volunteers per village school work on a target of improving the learning levels of lagging students. The team assesses the initial level of learning through a baseline survey and keeps on making efforts towards improvement of learning skill objective that a child up to standard II should be able to read, comprehend and communicate, and a child from class III to class V should have some additional expected skills in computing and mathematical reasoning. It was observed that apart from the envisioned task of improving the standard of learning of the lagging students in the schools, volunteers were also taking regular classes in the school and performing other responsibilities like overseeing the daily tasks like Mid-Day Meal Programme, etc. That is to say, the volunteers in many instances were working as substitutes to regular recruits in the government schools rather than complementing them. In the schools, children were found to be very fond of Pratham volunteers and responding to them in free, fearless manner, while they were found to be lacking confidence in front of regular government teachers.

Most of the classes were being taken by single volunteers with students of diverse learning levels. In some classes, even those students who were not covered in the baseline were attending the classes, as in many schools the volunteers were conveniently substituted for regular teachers due to lack of teachers in the class. The available information shows that the attendance of students who were covered in the baseline was 65 per cent for the block under study with the attendance ratio as low as 26 per cent in Vikashnagar village and 93 and 100 per cent in Mengwala and Bhoor villages, respectively. The incidence of non-baseline children attending classes of the volunteers was highest (37) in Vikashnagar. Overall, more than 57 per cent children tested have shown one or more levels of improvement in basic mathematics and 37 per cent have shown improvement in reading English. Unfortunately, around 7 per cent children in the study area were also found to have deteriorated in their level of learning as far as basic mathematics is concerned. One needs to discount for the fact that variations in the performance in calculations involved in mathematics is subject to many factors and while judging the performance, the investigators were very objective as to whether the answers obtained by the children are correct or not. It is possible that the same child may perform differently on a same question even if the process he/she adopts in both the classes was similar.

The overall infrastructure situation in the government schools was problematic. To cite a case, all the students of classes III–V and I–II in the school of Barhwala village (the village was not a part of five study villages, namely Bulakiwala, Vikasnagar, Magri, Mengwala and Bhoor of Vikashnagar block) were cramped into one classroom. The level of learning of the students was very poor. It was observed during the study that while measuring the level of learning was unique and interesting, the typical progress made by the students, after they attended the classes of the volunteers, was sort of rote learning. Students over time try to memorise specific words, processes and paragraphs. They failed to understand very similar but other words which were not written in the tool text books.

The regular teachers appointed in the payroll of the government seemed to be happy with the programme, as it gave them substantial support in terms of managing classes. However, their support to volunteers was negligible. In most cases, they had just handed over the classes to the volunteers irrespective of whether the concerned students were selected through the baseline survey or not. As a result, the classes in most cases were overcrowded with more than 25 numbers of students, which is the desired size.

In the study villages, many parents were sending their girl children to government schools, whereas they used to send their boys to private schools. There was a predominant view among the parents that the government-run schools are qualitatively inferior, although none referred to such issues very explicitly. Many parents were not aware of the fact that the levels of learning of their wards are measurable.

The survey of students, teachers and parents revealed discrepancies in achievement of the targets of RTE, not only in terms of their low standards than expected but also in terms of their progress over the years. Table 12.7 shows a brief overview of situation at the ground level. The figures presented in the table are only indicative of what we see today as some of the major problems confronting education sector in Uttarakhand.

*Table 12.7* Performance of children in Vikash Nagar Block, Dehradun

| *Indicators* | *Bulakiwala* | *Vikash Nagar* | *Magri* | *Mengwala* | *Bhoor* |
|---|---|---|---|---|---|
| Enrolment in government schools as % of total number of children in village in 6–11 years age (standard I–V) | 60 | 91 | 100 | 92 | 84 |
| Children identified as weak learners (baseline) who needed special attention (% of total) | 99 | 41 | 50 | 65 | 69 |
| Children who are regularly attending school (%) | 80 | 63 | 68 | 100 | 100 |
| Children tested who showed one or more level improvement (%) | 30 | 70 | 79 | 68 | 88 |

*Source*: PEF (2012).

## Concluding remarks

The analysis in the foregoing section highlights many issues relating to the implementation of Right to Education Act in the state. The number of schools providing elementary education to a unit child population in Uttarakhand is much higher than the national average. However, given the peculiar geographic location of majority of the districts, such numbers are inadequate. The progress towards building schools and efforts towards providing more infrastructure lagged vis-à-vis the national scenario. In terms of human resources too, majority of the schools do not comply with the RTE norms as far as the pupil–teacher ratios are concerned. In hilly districts like Pauri and Pithoragarh, the proportion of primary schools complying the PTR norms were even less than 3 per cent. Pupil–teacher ratio is a critical indicator for assessing the infrastructural base in terms of human resources. Many studies (Jha *et al.* 2008) on state level educational indicators have highlighted the impact of a decent PTR on quality of education.

Since the state formation, there has been an upsurge of private schools in the state. Moreover, there is a high concentration of private schools in the plain districts, representing a regional imbalance in the state. As far as financing and budgets are concerned, in almost all counts, the performances of hilly districts were better than their plain counter parts. Among all interventions under the SSA and RTE compliant efforts, specific interventions that were useful for a state like Uttarakhand such as residential schools for specific category of children, functioning of the BRC, utilisation of the state component, new teacher's salary and so on, the expenditure as per cent of Annual Work Plan and Budgets was much lower than for activities like construction. Over the last decade, the GPI also deteriorated in the state, although the situation is still better in hill districts than the plain districts. As far as quality of learning is concerned, the performance of plain districts was poorer than their hilly counterparts. There seem to be a lot of tasks that need to be completed for successful implementation of the Act in the state. For example, the RTE notification of 2013 itself suggested some relaxations and internalised some procedural delays in compliance with the RTE norms. The primary information collected from Vikashnagar Block of Dehradun district also revealed the gaps in enrolment and quality of learning of children in the government schools. Clearly, the lack of adequate infrastructure and inadequate awareness had led to a deterioration of learning levels in the block. One may therefore conclude that the size of the requirement of provisioning in a state like Uttarakhand is huge and immediate attention towards enhancement of infrastructure, improvements in the fund utilisation patterns, strengthening of the governance structures and removal of regional imbalances may result in successful implementation of the Right to Education Act.

## Notes

1 Primary inputs were collected through a fieldwork conducted by Pratham Education Foundation during 2012–13 as a part of an external evaluation process undertaken by the corresponding author.
2 These figures are indicative only in a sense that the Mehta reports covered less numbers of districts than the existing districts in the country and there were many cases of non-response in the survey.

## References

Acharya, Akash. 2000. 'Migration from Hilly Areas, Letters to the Editor'. *Economic and Political Weekly*, 35(34) (August 19–25): 2986.

Belknap, Leora E. 1954. 'Decreasing the Drop-Out Rate'. *The American Journal of Nursing*, 54(7) (July): 838–39.

Bose, Ashish. 2000. 'Demography of Himalayan Villages: Missing Men and Lonely Women'. *Economic and Political Weekly*, 35(27) (July 1–7): 2361–3.

Bray, Mark. 1996. 'Equity Issues in Local Resourcing of Education: Community Financing of Primary Schools in Bhutan'. *International Review of Education/ Internationale Zeitschrift für Erziehungswissenschaft/Revue Internationale de l'Education*, 42(5): 495–514.

Brighouse, H. 2000. *School Choice and Social Justice*. Oxford: Oxford University Press.

Brighouse, H. 2004. 'What's Wrong with Privatising Schools?' *Journal of Philosophy of Education*, 38(4), 617–31.

Bruslé, Tristan. 2014. 'Choosing a Destination and Work: Migration Strategies of Nepalese Workers in Uttarakhand, Northern India'. *Mountain Research and Development, International Mountain Society*, 28(3/4) (August–November 2008): 240–7.

Cuyvers, K., Weerd, G., Sanne, D., Mols, S., and Nuytten, C. 2011. 'Well-being at School: Does Infrastructure Matter?' *CELE Exchange*, Volume-10.http://www.oecd.org/edu/innovation-education/centreforeffectivelearningenvironments-cele/49167628.pdf (Accessed on 20 November 2014).

De, A., Khera, R., Samson, M., Kumar, A. K. Shiva. 2011 *PROBE Revisited: A Report on Elementary Education in India*, Oxford University Press.

Desai, Sonalde, and Banerji, Manjistha. 2008. 'Negotiated Identities: Male Migration and Left-Behind Wives in India'. *Journal of Population Research*, 25(3) (October): 337–55.

DISE .2013. *District Information System for Education*, National University of Educational Planning and Administration (NUEPA), New Delhi.

Fernandez, R., and Rogerson, R. 1996. 'Income Distribution, Communities, and the Quality of Public Education'. *The Quarterly Journal of Economics*, 111(1) (February): 135–64.

GOI. 2010, April 8. *The Right of Children to Free and Compulsory Education Rules 2010. The Gazette of India: Extraordinary*. New Delhi: Ministry of Human Resource Development.

GOI. 2012. *District Primary Education Programme (DPEP)*. http://india.gov.in/my-government/schemes/district-primary-education-programme-dpep (Accessed 12 July 2014).

GOI. 2001 and 2011. *Census of India: Single Year Age Data – C13 Table (India/States/UTs)*. New Delhi: Office of the Registrar General and Census Commissioner, Ministry of Home Affairs.

GOUK. 2011. Uttarakhand Right of Children to Free and Compulsory Education Rules, 2011. New Delhi: Government of Uttarakhand. 31 October 2011. http://mhrd.gov.in/sites/upload_files/mhrd/files/upload_document/Uttarakhand_Notified_RTE_Rules_English(2010)_1.pdf (Accessed 12 July 2014).

GOUK, G. O. (2 July 2013). *Amended RTE Rules 2013*. Retrieved from SSA Uttarakhand: http://ssa.uk.gov.in/files/RTE_English_2.pdf (Accessed 12 July 2014).

Gupta, R. D., Garg, P. K., and Arora, M. 2000. *Analysis of Intra-district Disparities for Dehradun District using GIS Technique*. Retrieved from GIS Development: http://www.geospatialworld.net/Paper/Application/ArticleView.aspx?aid=1403 (Accessed 15 July 2014).

Jalan, J., and Glinskaya, E. (n.d.). *Improving Primary School Education in India: An Impact Assessment of DPEP I*. Retrieved from Siteresources.worldbank.org: http://siteresources.worldbank.org/INTISPMA/Resources/Training-Events-and-Materials/india_primaryschool.pdf (Accessed 1 August 2014).

Jha, P. K., Das, S., Jha, N., and Mohanty, S. S. 2008. *Public Provisioning for Elementary Education in India*. New Delhi: SAGE Publications India Private Ltd.

Kalama, J., Etebu, C. E., Martha, C. A., and John, S. M. 2011. 'Impact of Unregulated Privatization of Education in Nigeria: An Appraisal of the Lead City University- National Universities Commission Dispute'. *Mediterranean Journal of Social Sciences*, 2(7): 117–21.

Mehta, A. C. 2009. *Elementary Education in India: Analytical Report 2009*. New Delhi: National University of Educational Planning and Administration (NUEPA) and Department of School Education and Literacy, Ministry of Human Resource Development, Government of India.

Mehta, A. C. 2013. *Elementary Education in India: Analytical Report 2012–13*. New Delhi: National University of Educational Planning and Administration (NUEPA) and Department of School Education and Literacy, Ministry of Human Resource Development, Government of India.

Mehta, A. C. 2003, 2009 and 2012–13. *Elementary Education in India: Analytical Report 2003*. New Delhi: National University of Educational Planning and Administration (NUEPA) and Department of School Education and Literacy, Ministry of Human Resource Development, Government of India.

Mohanty, D. 2012. *Economic and Financial Developments in Uttarakhand*, Reserve Bank of India: http://rbidocs.rbi.org.in/rdocs/Speeches/PDFs/SGBPU310812.pdf (Accessed on 13 August 2014).

Mohanty, S., and Chaturvedi, M. 2012.*Uttarakhand: Diagnostic Study of Building a Mountain State 2000–2010*. Dehradun: GIZ-Germany, Doon University.

Mohanty, S. S., Singh, A., and Sharma, P. 2014. 'A Decade of Tryst with Development Aspirations in Building Uttarakhand State'. *Asian Journal of Research in Social Sciences and Humanities*, 4(5): 363–84.

Pratham Education Foundation (PEF). 2012. *External Evaluation of Read India Programme in Vikash Nagar Block of Dehradun District*. Pratham Education Foundation.

Pratham Education Foundation (PEF). 2012, 2013, 2014. Annual Status of Education Report-ASER 2011, 2012, 2013. Pratham Education Foundation.

PROBE Team. 1999. *Public Report on Basic Education in India*. PROBE Team and Centre for Development Studies.

Scales, Harry H. 1969. 'Another Look at the Drop Out Problem'. *The Journal of Educational Research*, 62(8) (April): 339–43.

Singh Atul. 2012. Role of Government Policies in Addressing the Issue of Out-Migration in Uttarakhand, Unpublished Master Thesis, Doon University, Dehradun, Uttarakhand, India.

SSA. 2013. *Progress Overview & Basic Statistics- Analytical Tables based on DISE 2011–12*. Dehradun: SSA.

United Nations. (New Delhi). *UN Millennium Project*. UN Millennium Project: http://www.unmillenniumproject.org/reports/costs_benefits2.htm (Accessed 29 July 2014).

United Nations. (Undated). *United Nations Millennium Development Goals*. http://www.un.org/millenniumgoals/poverty.shtml (Accessed 21 July 2014).

# 13

# COMMUNITY MONITORING OF RIGHT TO EDUCATION

## A case of Udaipur district

*Nesar Ahmad, Mahendra S. Rao and Hariom Soni*

### Introduction

The right to education (RTE) is a fundamental right of the children in the age group 6–14 years, recognized by the Indian Constitution through an amendment in the year 2002. Further, there is now a Right to Education (RTE) Act, which ensures free and primary education to all children in the age group 6–14 years, till completion of elementary education in a neighbourhood school. The RTE Act, enacted in 2009, is in effect from 1 April 2010. This act envisages community monitoring of implementation of RTE through the mechanisms such as School Management Committee (SMC). The idea of community monitoring of education was also present in the Sarva Shiksha Abhiyan (SSA, meaning 'Education for All Campaign') and National Curriculum Framework (NCF), which were the precursors to the RTE act (Kapoor 2010). For example, under SSA, the schools used to have the School Development Committee (SDC), headed by the school head teacher. The RTE act, however, gives greater emphasis on community participation by empowering the SMCs to make school development plan, have financial powers on the grants received by the schools and monitoring the day-to-day functioning of the school.

In practice, however, the situation on the ground is quite different. The SMCs have not been constituted or/and are not functional in many cases. For example, according to the District Information System for Education (DISE) data, the SMCs are not constituted in more than 10 per cent of the schools in the country (in 2012–13). In Rajasthan, the percentage of such schools is less than 7 per cent. However, the situation on the ground suggests that the formation of the SMCs is not a guarantee of proper functioning of the SMCs. Therefore, there is a need for the active engagement of civil society organizations to make the community monitoring a reality on the ground. There are various examples of such civil society engagements to facilitate the civil community monitoring of implementation of RTE in various parts of the country (see Kapoor 2010 for examples). This chapter presents the experience of one such engagement by an organization called Astha, actively working in Southern Rajasthan.

## *Profile of Southern Rajasthan*

Rajasthan is the largest state by area, with a population of 68.58 million (Census data 2011) in the country. Southern Rajasthan mainly covers five districts namely Udaipur, Banswara, Dungarpur, Pratapgarh, and Sirohi. These districts have tribal majority, about 60 per cent tribal people of the total state population. According to the census 2011, tribal population in the state is about 9.24 million, which is about 13.5 per cent of the total state population (Table 13.1).

The major distribution of tribal population is in the southern part of the state with composition of various ethnic and cultural patterns comprising the Bhil, Damor, Meena, Garasia, Kathodi and Saharia. Saharia is the only Particularly Vulnerable Tribal Group (PVTG) in the state.

The educational status of these districts is presented in Table 13.1. It shows that status of education in most of the Southern Rajasthan districts is very low compared to the state average. Though the urban literacy among these districts is higher than the state average, with only one exception; the region lags behind the state average in terms of the overall literacy, rural literacy and female literacy rates

*Table 13.1* Educational status in Southern Rajasthan

| *Districts* | *Total population (in millions)* | *Tribal population (in millions)* | *Tribal population (%)* | *Literacy rates (%)* | | | *Female literacy (%)* |
|---|---|---|---|---|---|---|---|
| | | | | *Rural* | *Urban* | *Total* | |
| Udaipur | 3.07 | 1.52 | 49.7 | 54.9 | 87.5 | 61.8 | 39.8 |
| Dungarpur | 1.39 | 0.98 | 70.8 | 57.6 | 84.4 | 59.5 | 44 |
| Banswara | 1.80 | 1.38 | 76.4 | 54 | 85.2 | 56.3 | 40.1 |
| Pratapgarh | 0.87 | 0.55 | 63.4 | 53.2 | 84.8 | 56 | 39 |
| Sirohi | 1.03 | 0.29 | 28.2 | 49 | 78.7 | 55.3 | 32.7 |
| Total | 8.16 | 4.72 | 57.9 | — | — | — | — |
| Rajasthan | 68.58 | 9.24 | 13.5 | 61.4 | 79.7 | 66.1 | 45.8 |

*Source:* Census data, 2011.

## Right to education

Education is essential for development of any society or nation. At the time of independence, the status of education among the various regions in India was very low. The right to education had been put under Article 41 of the Indian Constitution under the directive principles for the state. Education as a subject has been placed under the state list of the constitution, making the state governments responsible for providing educational services. In the year 2002, by the Indian Constitution through the 86th amendment to, the right to education was made a fundamental right for all children in the age group 6–14 years, by adding Article 21a to the Indian Constitution. With the same amendment, Article 45 of the Indian Constitution under the directive principles of state policies was also amended, directing the state to provide early childhood care, and free and compulsory education to all children between the age group 0 and 6 years.

After seven years of this amendment, after many rounds of drafting and redrafting, the Right to Education Act was passed in 2009. According to the RTE Act, every child aged 6–14 years in the country has a right to free and compulsory education till completion of elementary education in a neighbourhood school.

In 2010, the Government of Rajasthan made a draft of rules for RTE, namely 'Rajasthan Right of Children to Free and Compulsory Education Rules, 2010', which was finalized in March 2011 as 'Rajasthan Right of Children to Free and Compulsory Education Rules, 2011' for proper implementation of RTE in the state. The Right to Education Act, however, had come into effect in India on 1 April 2010, and from this date, every state government was given a period of three years to establish proper human and physical infrastructure for the implementation of right to education in the state. But almost all the state governments have failed to establish infrastructure and facilities required as per the Right to Education Act (Pratham 2013). Many states face shortfalls in education infrastructure in the country (Jha and Parvati 2014). Main features of RTE Act related to infrastructure and other facilities are described in the following section.

### *Main features of Right to Education Act*

Main features of the RTE Act are as follows:

- Every child in the age group 6–14 years has the right to free and compulsory education in a neighbourhood school for completing his/her elementary education.

- Government must ensure a primary school within 1 km radius and middle school within 3 km radius of all the habitations to ensure 100 per cent enrolment.
- Private schools should ensure that 25 per cent of their total students of every class are from the poor, weaker and disadvantaged sections of the society, and the fund for these students will be granted by the government. Seats reserved in this quota should not remain vacant. These children should be treated the same as other children.
- Provision for establishment of a commission to supervise the implementation of right to education.
- No donation and capitation fees should be levied.
- No admission test or interview for children as well as for parents.
- All the schools except private and unaided schools must be managed by the School Management Committees (SMCs) and 75 per cent of SMCs' member should be parents and guardians of the students.

The Rajasthan RTE Rules, 2011, has some features which are at variance with the National RTE Act and in some cases they go beyond the National RTE Act. The National RTE Act provides for a middle school within a radius of 3 km, while according to the Rajasthan RTE rules, middle school must be ensured within a radius of 2 km of all the habitations. The RTE rules of Rajasthan have provisions of the Executive Committee (*Karyakarini*) and General Assembly of SMCs while the National RTE Act talks only about Executive Committee of SMCs. On the other hand while National RTE act provides uniform/dress to children, the RTE rules of the state remain silent about the uniform/dress.

According to the Rajasthan RTE rules, local authority is authorized or responsible for the proper implementation of right to education, but it does not clarify which local authority is responsible at various levels. The local authority as per the Indian Constitution is the panchayats (rural local bodies) and the municipalities (urban local bodies). These constitutional bodies, however, are not specifically mentioned in the Rajasthan rules.

### *Norms and standards for a school according to the RTE Act*

Norms and standards of the RTE rules of Rajasthan are similar as national RTE Act. All the schools have to ensure the norms and standard relating to pupil–teacher ratio, building and other facilities according to the RTE Act. Norms and standards for a school according to the RTE Act are described in Table 13.2.

*Table 13.2* Norms and standards for a school according to the RTE Act

| *Item* | *Norms and standard* |
|---|---|
| 1. Number of teachers | 30:1 (for class I–V)<br>35:1 (for class VI–VIII)<br>At least three subject teachers (for class VI–VIII) |
| 2. Building | One teacher per classroom; one office-cum-store for headmaster; Separate toilet facilities for girls and boys Facility of drinking water; Kitchen for midday meal preparation; Playground, boundary wall and ramp. |
| 3. Minimum number of working days in an academic year. | 200 (for class I–V)<br>220 (for class VI–VIII) |
| 4. Minimum number of workinghours per week for a teacher | 45 hours (including preparation hours) |
| 5. Teaching/learning equipment | Provided to each class. |
| 6. Library | Provided to each school. |
| 7. Play material and equipmentfor games and sports | Provided to each school. |

*Source:* Right to Education Act, 2009.

## Schools lacking in facilities mandated by the RTE

Similar to the other backward states of India, Rajasthan also lacks in basic education infrastructure facilities both in terms of human resources and physical infrastructure. According to DISE data for 2012–13, there are a large number of unqualified teachers, working as contract teachers. The state has high percentage of schools with single classroom (2.9 per cent) and single teacher (14 per cent). Pupil–teacher ratio (22 per cent) and student–classroom ratio (23 per cent) are quite good in terms of state average, but there are huge urban and rural disparities.

There are about 97 per cent of the schools having toilet facilities for girls', 77.6 per cent for boys and about 94.8 per cent of the schools with drinking water facility; however field studies suggest that most of them are unusable, either functional or locked. In the state, only about 48 per cent schools have playground and only in 93.4 per cent of the schools, SMCs have been constituted.

### *Rajasthan government's initiative for ensuring physical infrastructure in the schools*

Department of Administrative Reforms of the state government issued an order on 15 June 2012 to form the committees at the district level to ensure physical infrastructure in the school as per the RTE Act. District Collector is the chairperson of these committees and District Education Officer (DEO) is the member secretary and additional project officer (SSA) is the nominated member of the committee. Other members of the committees include Chief Executive Officer (Zila Parishad), Commissioner (Nagar Parishad/Municipal council), all the Subdivisional Officers (SDOs) and Block Education Officers (BEOs) of the district. The committee will identify land for the schools (without building) and will be coordinating with concerned departments to ensure required facilities in the school.

### *Monitoring mechanism for the implementation of RTE*

Monitoring the implementation of RTE in the RTE Act 2009 has been entrusted to the National Commission for Protection of Child Rights (NCPCR) and the State Commission for Protection of Child Rights (SCPCR) in the respective states. The Act also envisages the formation of the School Management Committee (SMC) for every school which will monitor the functioning of the school at school level.

### *School Management Committees (SMCs)*

Role of community in monitoring the RTE Act is specified in Article 21 of the Right to Education Act, 2009, and in the section 2 of National notified rules, 2010. The School Management Committee specified under RTE Act is called its backbone. This committee is established at the school level and 11 out of 15 members are from the community, and chairperson as well as vice chairperson would also be selected from the community (parents). Before the implementation of the Act, these committees were referred to as School Development Committees (SDCs), and the chairperson and the secretary were head teacher and the other teachers from the school only. The roles and responsibilities of the SMCs include having financial powers for the grants received by the school, making the school development plan, monitoring the day-to-day functions of the school, including midday meal (MDM) and monitoring the implementation of RTE.

### *School Management Committees in Rajasthan*

In compliance with the same, the Rajasthan government has also notified the rules for the state in 2011 and the School Management Committee has been given an even wider form. The committee has both the General Assembly and executive body according to the Rajasthan RTE Rules.

***General Assembly***: All parents/Guardians, all people representatives, all teachers of the schools are members of the General Assembly. Chairperson and vice-chairperson are from among parents/guardians only. The head teacher of the school is the secretary of the committee. Quarterly meeting of the General Assembly is held, and only here the selection of executive committee members, which is 15 in total, is done. The executive committee is responsible for the agenda/issues emerged during the General Assembly meeting and is accountable to the General Assembly.

***Executive committee is a 15-member body*:** Out of 15 members, 11 are parents/guardians. The chairperson and vice-chairperson are also selected from among the parents/guardians. Rest of four members selected for the committee are the head master of the school who is also designated as secretary, one teacher (male/female) from the school, one ward panch from the community and one student from the school/ one educated individual from the community. The committee deals with matters related to proper functioning, coordination, management and monitoring of the school.

Though the School Management Committee has been given a vital role in the notified rules by the state government and the constitution of executive committee has also been completed, the regular meeting of the committees remains an issue and their roles and responsibilities are still not taken seriously on the ground. The quarterly meeting of the General Assembly rarely happens, which results in weakening of the SMC itself.

Creating yearly sub- plans[1] and three-year plan for the school development is also one of the important roles of the committee under the RTE Act. Unfortunately, no technical training has been given to the committees nor the issue is seriously taken in the programme area; also, no guideline has been issued on the same by the state government.

Active role of the General Assembly, therefore, is crucial aspect of the functioning of the SMCs in the state, which according to the Rajasthan RTE rules has power to make the executive committee of the SMCs accountable. Hence, there is a need to strengthen the General Assembly of the SMCs and provide them necessary training at local level for establishing the community monitoring.

### *Rajasthan government's other initiatives for monitoring the RTE*

Apart from the constitution of SMCs, the government of Rajasthan has taken following initiatives to develop a mechanism for ensuring compliance with the right to education in the state.

### *Grievance redressal matrix to ensure RTE*

On September 2011, the state government came out with a grievance redressal matrix on 27 points (Appendix) related to RTE to redress the grievances in the implementation of the RTE Act. Under this mechanism, the education department has identified officials at various levels to redress the grievances regarding the RTE within a given time frame. In this matrix, authorities and officer incharge are nominated for various grievances related to admission, school and teacher as per the RTE. Again, similar to the Rajasthan RTE rules, the Grievance redressal mechanisms also ignore the role of the local bodies such as panchayats and the municipalities. The redressal matrix also names all the officials who are responsible and accountable for various entitlements at various levels. Disregarding the local bodies, especially the panchayats, in the monitoring process of the RTE is surprising, considering that the Rajasthan government claims to have devolved the primary education completely to the panchayats.

### *Shikhsa Samwad*

On the instructions of the Ministry of Human Resource Development, Government of India, the Department of Education of the state government issued a circular on 5 January 2012 to organize *Shiksha Samwads* (education dialogues) for grievance redressal at the district and below levels. The circular instructed to form committees at the district and block levels to organize *Shiksha Samwad* for grievance redressals regarding RTE at both the levels. These committees have members from the civil society organizations as well.

However, the execution of these mechanisms is far from perfect, and the *Shiksha Samwad* has not produced desired results. The *Shiksha Samwads* could not attract participation of the community people and other stakeholders at large. The *Shiksha Samwads* are held like any other formal meetings of the government, where general discussions on RTE take place.

## Community monitoring of right to education initiated by Astha Sansthan, Udaipur

National Commission for Protection of Child Rights (NCPCR) supported Astha to initiate a pilot project in Udaipur district for monitoring of right to education in Southern Rajasthan. Main objective of the project was to build a community-led monitoring mechanism to ensure the effective implementation of right to education in the schools. For the purpose of monitoring the RTE Act, Astha initiated concurrent monitoring of the schools and post facto social audits. For the pilot project, about 257 schools were selected from 25 Gram Panchayats (GPs) from five blocks namely Jhadol, Kotra, Rishabdev, Salumber and Girva of Udaipur district. Main tools applied for the community monitoring of RTE were social audits and public hearings (PHs) led by the community.

***Social audit as a monitoring tool*:** Social audit is a process of community monitoring of the government programmes, which is recognized as an effective way of ensuring community participation in monitoring of the government programme for their effective implementation. The social audit now has a legal status for one government scheme namely Mahatma Gandhi National Rural Employment Guarantee Act (MGNREGA), in which the act envisages for mandatory social audits twice a year. The operational manual of the MGNREGA defines social audit as, 'a continuous and ongoing process, involving public vigilance and verification of quantity and quality of works at different stages of implementation' (MoRD 2013). Among the civil society groups, the social audit as a monitoring tool has been quite successfully used in Rajasthan by Mazdoor Kisan Shakti Sangathan (MKSS) (IBP 2012). The MKSS social audit exercise includes social audit as well public hearing, where the findings of the social audit are shared with the concerned authorities in a public meeting, and the community members also express their views and put forward their complaints (IBP 2012).

### *Social audits: conducted in four phases*

To monitor the implementation of RTE Act, Astha facilitated community-led social audits followed by public hearings in the programme area. Based on findings of the social audits, one district-level and 10 block-level public hearings were organized. The social audits were conducted in four phases. In the first phase, the social audits were conducted for 257 schools during January–March 2012. This was followed by five block-level public hearings organized in March 2012. Second phase of social audit was

*Table 13.3* Number of social audits conducted and public hearing organized

| *Phase* | *Social audit* | | *Public hearing* | |
|---|---|---|---|---|
| | *No. of schools* | *Period* | *Level* | *No.* |
| First | 257 | January–March 2012 | Block level | 5 (March 2012) |
| Second | 145 | April–October 2012 | Block level | 5 (January 2013) |
| Third | 277 | March 2013 | – | – |
| Fourth | 124 | September 2013 | District level | 1 (September 2013) |

*Source:* Records of Astha Sansthan.

conducted during April–October 2012 in 145 schools from among the initial 257 schools, and was followed by five block-level public hearings in January 2013. Third phase of the social audits was conducted in March 2013 in 277 schools, including all 257 schools of first phase (March 2012). Fourth phase of the social audits was conducted in September 2013 in 124 schools, which was followed by a district-level public hearing organized in September 2013 (Table 13.3).

This paper is based on the data collected from the first phase of the social audit (for 257 schools), third phase of the social audits (for 277 schools) and fourth phase of the social audits (for 124 schools). Also some case studies have been presented showing the improvements in the status of RTE implementation which can be attributed to the community-based monitoring pilot project by Astha.

### *Findings of the first phase of social audit (January–March 2012)*

Before conducting the process of social audits, quality and quantitative information for the selected 257 schools were collected by Astha's volunteers from the district offices. Physical verification of the data provided by the district offices was done by conducting the social audits of the schools and in the meetings with community people during January–March 2012. This provided the baseline information for the pilot project. Data collected in this process is presented in Table 13.4.

The data in Table 13.4 shows that the status of basic amenities and facilities mandated by the RTE norms were very poor at the time of data

*Table 13.4* Situation of RTE norms in various indicators, January–March 2012

| *Indicator* | | *District administration* | | | *School level* | | | *Community* | | | | *Total* |
|---|---|---|---|---|---|---|---|---|---|---|---|---|
| | | *Yes* | *No* | *n/a* | *Yes* | *No* | *n/a* | *Yes* | *No* | *Do not know* | *n/a* | 257 |
| SMC | Constituted | 200 (77.82) | – | 52 | | 16 (6.23) | 11 | 84 (32.68) | 24 (9.33) | 95 | 38 | 257 |
| | Member elected | | 7 (2.72) | 243 | | 27 (10.51) | 50 | | 85 (33.07) | 73 | 53 | 257 |
| | Training for SMC | 122 (47.47) | – | 133 | | 55 (21.40) | 36 | 65 (25.29) | 59 (22.95) | 81 | 50 | 257 |
| Building | Ramp | 60 (23.34) | 80 (31.12) | 22 | | 133 (51.75) | 13 | | | | | 257 |
| | Boundary wall | 97 (37.74) | 136 (52.91) | 24 | | 162 (63.04) | | | | | | 257 |
| | Room for head teacher | 95 (36.96) | 135 (52.52) | 31 | | | | | | | | 257 |
| Other Facilities | Toilet facility | 244 (94.94) | 6 (2.33) | 14 | | 209 (81.32) | | | | | | 257 |
| | Useable toilet | 170 (66.14) | 4 (15.56) | 85 | | 141 (54.86) | 24 | | | | | 257 |
| | Kitchen for MDM | 167 (64.98) | 34 (13.22) | 60 | | 86 (33.46) | | | | | | 257 |
| | Drinking Water | 202 (78.59) | 43 (16.73) | 16 | | 97 (37.74) | 8 | | | | | 257 |
| Library | | 49 (19.06) | 76 (29.57) | 132 | | 205 (79.77) | | | | | | 257 |
| Parent–teacher meeting | | | | 251 | | 52 (20.23) | 36 | 80 (31.12) | 81 (31.5) | 39 | 51 | 257 |
| Play materials and equipment for sports and games | | 8 (3.11) | 133 (51.75) | 116 | | 164 (63.81) | | | | | | 257 |

*Source:* Based on data provided by the education resource unit, Astha Sansthan.

*Notes:* Figures in brackets are percentage to total schools (257); n/a, not available.

collection. According to the data collected from the schools and according to the community people, most of the schools had unusable toilets, which were either soiled or locked. However, as per the data provided by the district administration, situation is good in the schools as per some indicators, including constitution of SMCs, toilet facilities for boys and girls, drinking water and kitchen shed for MDM. But the data provided by the district administration does not match with the actual situation at the school level and there were also differences between what the schools claimed and what the community people observed. On the other hand, facilities in terms of ramp, equipment for games and playing, library, status of training for SMC members and room for head teacher were not good as well.

If we look at the information and data provided by the schools, condition of almost all the facilities were poorer; about 63 per cent of the schools had no boundary walls, while more than 50 per cent of the schools did not have a ramp. About 81 per cent of the selected schools had no toilet facilities and about 38 per cent schools had no drinking water facility.

According to the community, many schools had not constituted School Management Committees (SMCs). Near about 80 per cent of the schools had no library, and parent–teacher meetings were not held in 20 per cent schools and more than 60 per cent of the schools did not have equipment for games and playing. In this situation, Astha decided to strengthen and empower the SMCs and bring awareness to the community people to monitor the schools in the area. Main focus of the project was to empower the community for the monitoring of right to education through strengthening the SMCs.

### *Actions taken by the community*

Astha team constituted 31 volunteers under the project to collect data and organize regular meetings with community people. The team had 25 panchayat facilitators (PFs), five block monitors (BMs) and a district coordinator (DC) from the project area. Community people were regularly contacted to develop a monitoring mechanism over the RTE and SMCs. Various activities such as participation in *Shiksha Samwads* organized by the government, social audits and public Hearings (Jansunwai) were organized at block and the district levels under the project.

**Participation in *Shiksha Samwads* organized by the government:** *Shiksha Samwads* were organized by the district administration at the district and block levels. But these *Shiksha Samwads* did not produce expected results. A couple of *Shiksha Samwads* were organized after the order passed by the Government of Rajasthan, which mandated monthly *Shiksha Samwads*

*Figure 13.1* District-level education dialogue on grievance redressal of RTE, organized by government and Astha Sansthan in Udaipur

with participation of local NGOs. However, participation of the local NGOs was very limited and *Shiksha Samwads* could not attract community participation at large. The *Shiksha Samwads* turned into formal meetings, where general discussions on RTE took place. For all these reasons, Astha decided to conduct public hearings (*Jansunwai*) to ensure proper community participation in monitoring the RTE. Before organizing the public hearing, Astha team also conducted social audits of the schools.

**Public hearing (*Jansunwai*):** The idea behind the public hearing (PH) is providing people and community with a platform to raise the problems related to implementation of RTE. Before holding the public hearings, it was publicized through pamphlets (parcha) distribution, wall writings, organizing Jeep Yatra and meetings with community members. Public hearings were organized twice at block levels (in five blocks) and once at the district level. At the block level, 450–550 people from the community participated in each of the public hearing and at the district level, more than about 400 people participated. Representatives of NCPCR and RSCPCR, government officials CEO-Zilla Parisad, District Education Officers, Additional District Education Officers, Block Development Officers, Block Education Officers, as well as head teachers, teachers, and members and chairperson of the SMCs also participated in the public hearings. Community people shared their complaints regarding the schools in their

*Figure 13.2* Block-level public hearing on RTE in Kotda block, Udaipur

villages and concerned officials responded to the people's problems. The increased awareness among community people has made people to raise their concerns in dealing with problems related to facilities such as drinking water, MDM, absenteeism of teachers, toilet facilities, closed schools, corporal punishment, collapsed school buildings, quality of education, lack of teachers and role of SMCs.

**Other initiatives of community monitoring:** Besides this, many initiatives have taken place for community monitoring over RTE such as formation of Panchayat Nigrani Samiti, Yuva manch, Bal manch and Use of Media.

Panchayat Nigrani Samiti was formed by 12–13 community people including ward panch, village head, women and elders in Salumber block. This committee regularly monitored the quality of teaching and status of facilities in the schools.

Yuva manch (Youth Forum) and Bal manch (Children's Forum) were formed in one panchayat of Salumber block. Yuva manch consists of 10–12 youth from the local community and a member of the manch regularly monitored the schools, while Bal manch consists of 10–15 children who organized meeting with panchayat facilitator and shared the problems in their schools.

*Situation of RTE implementation after community monitoring initiative*

**Improvement in physical infrastructure:** In third round of the social audit conducted by the Astha team in March 2013, data were collected from 277 schools including the initial 257 schools covered in March 2012. The smaller difference in number of schools and similarity in the indicators taken in social audit in March 2012 and March 2013 allow us to compare the situations of RTE in these schools and understand the changes, which the public hearings in between might have caused. Table 13.5 provides the comparative data for these schools for March 2012 and March 2013.

Table 13.5 shows the progress as well as impact of community monitoring programme in the area for some selected indicators. According to data collected during January–March 2012, about 87.5 per cent of the selected schools did not have any playground, which came down to 70.4 per cent

*Table 13.5* Comparison of some indicators for March 2012 and March 2013

| *Indicator* | *March 2012* | | *March 2013* | | | | |
|---|---|---|---|---|---|---|---|
| | *As % of total selected schools (257)* | | *Response of the school* | | | *As % of total selected schools (277)* | |
| | *Yes* | *No* | *Yes* | *No* | *Total* | *Yes* | *No* |
| Water | | 97 (37.14) | 170 | 101 | 271 | 61.37 | 36.46 |
| Toilet facilities | | 141 (54.86)* | 56** | 215^ | 271 | 20.22 | 77.62 |
| Boundary | | 162 (63.04) | 113 | 153 | 266 | 40.79 | 55.23 |
| Playground | | 225 (87.54) | 70 | 195 | 265 | 25.27 | 70.40 |
| Constitution of SMC | | 16 (6.23) | 245 | 32 | 277 | 88.45 | 11.55 |
| Training of SMC | | 55 (21.40) | 245 | 32 | 277 | 88.45 | 11.55 |
| Getting MDM as per menu | | 99@ (38.52) | 227 | 43 | 270 | 81.95 | 15.52 |

*Source:* Based on data collected by the education resource unit, Astha Sansthan.

*Notes:* *indicates no toilet facilities, ** indicates useable toilets, ^ indicates closed toilets and @ indicates MDM menu in school.

by March 2013. As far as water and toilet facilities are concerned, there was no visible change as more than 37 per cent of the schools did not have water facility in March 2012, which came down slightly to 36.4 per cent in March 2013. For the toilet facilities, we do not have comparable data. While nearly 55 per cent of the schools did not have toilet facilities in March 2012, it was found that more than 20 per cent of the schools had useable toilets in March 2013. If we look at the training of SMCs, near about 21.4 per cent of SMCs in the selected schools had not received training for strengthening their SMCs, which came down to 11.5 per cent in March 2013. Therefore during the year, nearly 10 per cent more SMCs got training. On the other hand, nearly 38.5 per cent of the schools were not providing MDM as per menu in March 2012 and after a year, the respective percentage of the schools came down to 15.5 per cent in March 2013.

The aforementioned data reveal that the status of the schools has improved for some selected indicators in March 2013 (Table 13.5). However, for some indicators, there was not much improvement as well.

## Strengthening of SMCs

The SMCs are most important institutions for the effective functioning and implementation of RTE act. Under this project, also the focus was on formation of SMCs in the general meeting of the villagers and also on the regular meetings of the SMCs thereafter. In November 2012, when the term of most of earlier formed SMCs expired, Astha project team got the responsibility of formation of new SMCs in one selected block (Girva) of Udaipur district. It was made sure that the new SMCs of all 48 schools in the block are formed in general meeting of villagers. Also, efforts were made that regular meetings of the SMCs are held in all the five selected blocks.

The last social audit was conducted and a district-level public hearing was organized in September 2013, for 124 schools from among the 277 schools, focusing mainly on functioning of SMCs, meeting and planning for schools and other qualitative indicators, i.e. activity-based teaching, teachers' training, etc.

The last social audit conducted in 2013 (March and September) shows the impact of the community monitoring programme conducted over the course of about one and half years. Though these detailed questions about the functioning of the SMCs were not asked during the earlier social audits, there is no recorded data to make any comparisons in this regard. Table 13.6 presents the data collected in September 2013 for 124 schools, focusing mainly on the functioning of the SMCs.

*Table 13.6* Situation of RTE norms in various indicators, September 2013

| *Indicator* | | *Yes* | *No* | *Don't know* | *Total* |
|---|---|---|---|---|---|
| SMC constituted | (Parents) | 113 (93.39) | 8 (6.4) | | 124 |
| | (Teacher) | 123 (99.19) | 1 (0.8) | | 124 |
| SMC constituted in general meeting | (Parents) | 100 (65.36) | 32 (25.8) | 21 | 124 |
| | (Teacher) | 122 (98.39) | 2 (1.6) | | 124 |
| Meeting within three months of General Assembly (GA) | (Parents) | 24 (19.35) | 97 (78.22) | 3 | 124 |
| | (Teacher) | 47 (37.9) | 77 (62.09) | | 124 |
| Taking decision and proposal for schools | (Parents) | 78 (66.10) | 40 (32.25) | | 124 |
| | (Teacher) | 116 (95.08) | 6 (4.83) | | 124 |
| Providing information of general meeting to members before 15 days | (Parents) | 35 (28.23) | 89 (71.77) | | 124 |
| | (Teacher) | 72 (58.06) | 52 (41.93) | | 124 |
| Regular meeting of SMC | Members | 51 (42.15) | 70 (56.4) | | 124 |
| | | 90 (72.58) | 34 (27.4) | | 124 |
| Continuous and comprehensive evaluation (CCE) in school | | 21 (16.94) | 103 (83.06) | | 124 |
| Activity-based teaching | | 73 (58.87) | 51 (41.13) | | 124 |
| Teacher's regularity | | 115 (92.75) | 9 (7.25) | | 124 |
| Teacher's training | | 15 (12.09) | | | 124 |
| Baseline training | | 12 (9.68) | | | 124 |
| Forward planning | | 11 (8.87) | | | 124 |

*Source:* Based on data provided by the education resource unit, Astha Sansthan.

The data provided in Table 13.6 has been collected from parents and teachers for 124 schools of five blocks from Udaipur district, and there is a gap between the information provided by the teachers and parents for all the indicators. According to schoolteachers, more than 98 per cent of schools had constituted SMCs, while parents said about 93 per cent of schools had SMCs (Table 13.6). Most of these SMCs were conducted in general meeting of the villagers. Regular meetings of SMCs were being conducted in 42 per cent of the schools according to the SMC members, while according to teachers, more than 70 per cent of schools started regular meeting for the SMCs. Though quarterly meeting of general body is still low, the practice of taking decision and proposals for the schools in the general body started in at least 66 per cent of the schools. Overall, Table 13.6 suggests an improved functioning of the SMCs of these 124 schools. Activity-based teaching (59 per cent) and teachers' regularity (93 per cent) were also reported from a high percentage of schools. However, majority of these schools were still not practicing continuous and comprehensive evaluation (CCE) or forward planning. The schools were also low in terms of training of the teachers.

**Impact of community monitoring programme in the area:** Impacts of the community monitoring programme could be seen at the levels of government administration, line department, schools and community in the area. After holding public hearings (PHs) in the area, community people started to raise their problems regarding the school as per right to education. Parents and community people started monitoring the schools. Meetings and interaction with teachers and SMC members by the community could be seen in the area. The Astha team also documented some case studies, which show the impacts of the community monitoring programme. Few of the case studies as successful examples of community monitoring in the area are presented as follows:

**Case 1: schools gets proper building:** This is the case of a school in Kemari in Pai gram panchayat of Girva block, where the school had no building and it was run in a hut. During the community monitoring visit, it was found that the situation of various facilities in the school was extremely poor and the attendance rate of children was also very low. Following this, a meeting was organized with the community people to make them aware of the Right to Education Act. Then the community people raised the demand of proper building with proper road to reach the school at the block-level public hearing organizsed in March 2012. The District Education Officer present in the public hearing promised to construct proper building for the school. But no action was taken up to July 2012 and again public hearing was organized for the implementation of right to education in Pai *panchayat*. District project officer of SSA was invited to that public hearing, and once again a promise was made regarding the same. And finally, Rs. 1.5 million were sanctioned and the school building was being constructed and road was also constructed within a month for access to the school.

**Case 2: school opens regularly:** Another case is of Guniyafala school of Kotda where a school was closed for quite some time. School used to open only twice in a month and because of this the students were irregular. About 90 children of the village were deprived of their right to education due to the school not opening regularly. After complaining the officials, no action was taken on that issue. The issue was raised by the villagers in public hearing organized in Kotda in March 2012 and again in July 2013. Report of the public hearings including this issue was submitted to the district administration. After a month of holding the public hearing, the action report was sent by the Zila Parishad, reporting that school was opening regularly. After that, physical verification was done by the project team whether school was opening regularly or not. Team found that school was regular but presence of children was very low. Then door-to-door campaign was run to motivate the community to send their children to the school. After some days, number of children rose to more than 90. Since then, this school has been regularly monitored by the community people.

**Case 3: school reopens in Kotda:** During the monitoring programme in *Kotda*, a primary school of Obara village in Kotda Block was found to be closed. The school building infrastructure was in a very bad condition and the classrooms had become a shelter for goats. When enquired about the school from the community people, it was reported that the school remained closed for the last two years, and even when rarely opened, no children attended. The matter was raised by the community people during the public hearing held in Kotda and the administration was prompted to visit the school. During the public hearing, officials of the education department promised that the school would be regularly opened. After that implementation observed within a week, the school building was renovated and two new teachers were appointed to replace those who were transferred. Now, 30–40 children are continuously attending the school, with midday meal provided to the children. Blackboard and other teaching aids have been provided to the school.

These are the some success stories of the community monitoring for the betterment of right to education. Implementation of the right to education has been improved due to community monitoring mostly in quantitative terms. Level of infrastructure, whether in terms of physical and human, has been improved.

## Success, failure and lessons

The RTE Act is an important piece of legislation and its success depends as much on the participation of the parents and community in the process as on the efforts of the government machinery to provide quality education to all children. The efforts made by the Astha and the people of the selected blocks with support of NCPCR has produced some successes and some failures as well as some lessons for the effective implementation of the RTE Act. In a short period of one and half years, the people of these tribal villages have been able to shake the administrative inertia by conducting the social audits of the schools and organizing the public hearings which provided people a platform to raise their grievances before the government officials in presence of large number of villagers. This helps in making the schools and government officials more accountable, which can be gauged in improvement of physical infrastructure in the schools, reopening of the closed or defunct schools as presented in cases studies, and regularity of high percentage of teachers.

Though the functioning of the schools and the SMCs in the area are far from perfect, the ownership shown by the parents by participating in general bodies, constitution of SMCs and participating in large number in the public hearings organized by Astha is of extreme importance as it shows that they have a stake in the process of RTE implementation. Some of the lessons learnt from this process can be summarized as follows:

### *Lessons learnt*

Some of the learnings obtained from the process of community monitoring are as following:

- Establishment of better coordination and continuous dialogue between schools, community and the administration is very necessary for ensuring the effective implementation of the Right to Education Act.
- It has been felt that administration/government or non-governmental organizations cannot monitor every school all the time. Therefore, only the parents/community or institutions such as SMCs can monitor the functioning of the schools.
- Hence the community should have such platforms where they can raise their concerns and share their problems as well as can make suggestions on proper functioning of the schools. Public hearings provided people with such platforms.
- There is no doubt that the SMCs can play active and important roles in strengthening the community monitoring of the schools. Therefore, transparency should be adopted in the process of constituting the SMCs and the proposals, decisions and schemes made by the SMCs should get recognition at each level.
- Schools are facing many problems and many of those have been raised during the public hearings and education dialogue by community before the concerned officials, but many of those problems remain unresolved and the local administration maintains that these are policy issues or issues to be taken at the state level. Therefore, there should be proper ways to resolve the issues which are ignored or sidelined by the local administration.
- We have clearly visualized and experienced that we should make efforts towards strengthening the community monitoring in place of resolving the problems directly through administrative interference.

# APPENDIX

*Table A13.1* Matrix for grievance redressal

| *S. No.* | *Legal entitlement* | *Authority/ officer charged with provision* | *Authority/ officer charged with redressal* | *Time frame for redressal* | *Appellate authority/ process* |
|---|---|---|---|---|---|
| | **Admission-related grievances** | | | | |
| 1 | Admission without documents | HM/ Principal | BEEO/ DEO(s) | 7 days | DEEO/ DD(s) |
| 2 | Age appropriate admission | HM/ Principal | BEEO/ DEO(s) | 7 days | DEEO/ DD(s) |
| 3 | Any time admission | HM/ Principal | BEEO/ DEO(s) | 15 days | DEEO/ DD(s) |
| 4 | Timely public display for all admission-related information | HM/ Principal | BEEO/ DEOs | 1 months | DEEO |
| 5 | No screening test | HM/ Principal | BEEO/ DEO(s) | 7 days | Dy. Dir. Elementary/ Sec. |
| 6 | 25% reservation in private schools | HM/ Principal | DEEO/ DEOs | 1 months | DEEO/ DD(E)/(s) |
| | **School-related grievances** | | | | |
| 7 | Availability of neighbourhood schools | BEEO | DEEO | 1 year | Dir. Elementary |
| 8 | Transport, where required | BEEO | DEEO | 2 months | Dy. Dir. Elementary |
| 9 | Other specific entitlements (such as aids and appliances), where required | HM/ Principal | BEEO/ DEO(s) | 6 month | DEEO/DD/ (s) |

(*Continued*)

*Table A13.1* (Continued)

| S. No. | *Legal entitlement* | *Authority/ officer charged with provision* | *Authority/ officer charged with redressal* | *Time frame for redressal* | *Appellate authority/ process* |
|---|---|---|---|---|---|
| 10 | Special training | HM/ Principal | BEEO/ DEO(s) | 1 months | DEEO/DD/ (s) |
| 11 | No tuition fees/ no fees/fund/no application form fees/no capitation fees/no entrance fees | HM/ Principal | BEEO/ DEO(s) | 15 days | DEEO/DD/ (s) |
| 12 | Corporal punishment/ discrimination | HM/ Principal | SMC | 7 days | DEEO/ DEO(s) |
| 13 | Textbooks/workshops | HM/ Principal | BEEO/ DEO(s) | 15 day | DEEO/DD/ (s) |
| 14 | Scholarship | HM/ Principal | BEEO/ DEO(s) | 3 months | D.D.Ele./ Sec. |
| 15 | Mandated working days/instructional hours | HM/ Principal | SMC | 15 days | BEEO/ DDO/(s) |
| 16 | Pupil–teacher ratio | HM/ Principal | BEEO/ DEO(s) | As per RTE Rules | Dy. Dir. Elementary |
| 17 | Requisite classrooms | SMC | BEEO/ DEO(s) | 1 year | DEEO/DD/ (s) |
| 18 | Usable toilets/ drinking water | SMC | BEEO/ DEO(s) | 2 month | DEEO/DD/ (s) |
| 19 | Misuse of school building/infrastructure | SMC | BEEO/ DEO(s) | 7 days | DEEO/DD/ (s) |
| 20 | No striking off rolls | HM/ Principal | SMC | 7 days | BEEO/ DEEO(s) |
| | **Teacher-related grievances** | | | | |
| 21 | Non-compliance of teachers with duties | SMC | BEEO/ DEO(s) | 15 days | DEEO/DD/ (s) |
| 22 | Private tuition by teachers | HM/ Principal | SMC | 15 days | DEEO/ DEO(s) |
| 23 | No failure and no detention | HM/ Principal | BEEO/ DEO(s) | 15 days | DEEO/ DD(s) |
| 24 | Non-teaching duties | SMC | BEEO/ DEO(s) | 1 month | DEEO/DD/ (s) |
| 25 | Issuance of transfer certificate | HM/ Principal | BEEO/ DEO(s) | 7 days | DEEO/DD/ (s)) |
| 26 | Issuance of completion certificate | HM/ Principal | BEEO/ DEO(s) | 1 month | BEEO/ DEO(s) |
| 27 | No segregation of reserved children in private schools | HM/ Principal | DEEO/ DEO(s) | 1 month | DEEO/ DD(E)/(S) |

## Note

1 The School Development Plan is a three-year plan comprising three annual sub-plans.

## References

Annual Report of the community monitoring project. 2012–2013. Astha Sansthan, Udaipur, Rajasthan.

Census of India. Population Enumeration. Chapter 2: Scheduled Cast and Scheduled Tribe Population, Report. 2011. Directorate of Census Operation Rajasthan.

Census of India, Population Enumeration. Chapter 3: Literates and Literacy Rates, Report. 2011. Directorate of Census Operation Rajasthan.

DISE, State Report Card, 2012–13. National University of Education Planning Administration, New Delhi.

IBP (International Budget Partnership), 2012. 'Social Audits as Budget Monitoring Tool', available on: http://internationalbudget.org/wp-content/uploads/Social-Audits-as-a-Budget-Monitoring-Tool.pdf (accessed on 5 August 2014).

Jha, Praveen; Parvati, Pooja; 2014. 'Assessing Progress on Universal Elementary Education in India: A Note on Some Key Constraints', EPW, xlIX(44) 16 April 2014.

Kapoor, Richa. 2010. 'Essential Services: Community Based Management for Right to Education', Oxfam India, available on: http://www.oxfamindia.org/sites/default/files/II.%20Essential%20ServicesCommunity%20Based%20Management%20for%20Right%20to%20Education.pdf (accessed on 5 August 2014).

MoRD, 2013. 'Mahatma Gandhi National Rural Employment Guarantee Act, 2005', *Operation Guideline*, available on: http://nrega.nic.in/netnrega/WriteReaddata/Circulars/Operational_guidelines_4thEdition_eng_2013.pdf (accessed on 5 August 2014).

Pratham, 2013. 'Annual Status of Education Report', ASER, available on: http://www.asercentre.org/ (accessed on 14 March 2014).

## Acts and Rules

Right to Education Act, 2009, Govt. of India.

Draft Rules of Rajasthan Right of Children to free and compulsory education, 2010, Govt. of Rajasthan.

Rajasthan Right of Children to free and compulsory education Rules, 2011, Govt. of Rajasthan.

# 14

# FINANCING ELEMENTARY EDUCATION

## Induce or reduce interstate disparity?

*P. Geetha Rani*

*Not everything that counts can be counted; and not everything that can be counted counts.*

–Albert Einstein

## Introduction

States in a quasi federal set up like India are entrusted a critical role in the growth process. States, thereby play a vital role in economic and social development and hence most developmental functions are assigned to them. Social sector programmes and their implementation fall largely under the jurisdiction of the state governments. This is due to the fact that most of these functions have a direct interface with the public. All these responsibilities increase their expenditure obligations. Besides, inter-regional disparity in levels of development and incomes is a major issue of economic, social and political significance in India. Several mechanisms and instruments have been used to reduce these disparities. In India, fiscal transfers between the central and the state governments[1] occur via a complex system in two main channels: (i) Finance Commission, the Constitutional authority to 'decide' centre-state transfers, through tax-sharing and grants-in-aid and (ii) Planning Commission, a regular body which makes grants and loans for 'development' purposes. In addition, the central ministries provide project-based, specific purpose grants to states.

In recent years, the central government has also been spending directly on various services which are primarily in the functional domain of the states such as health, education and rural development. Although direct central spending are technically not transfers, they have significant impact in equalizing the quality of public service delivery across states. Other methods are grants to states, which could be tied or untied to overcome the cost and fiscal disabilities so that individual states are able to provide comparable levels of public services. Offsetting fiscal disabilities through direct central spending over the years have become an important policy tool, which is reflected in the proliferation of various centrally sponsored schemes (Chakraborty *et al.* 2010).

In this discourse, the present chapter examines the resource allocation under Sarva Shiksha Abhiyan (SSA) and its impact on development of elementary education. First, we describe current educational disparity across states in terms of funding. Second, we show that education resources have more to do with the capacity of states to finance elementary education. For this, we examine the funding mechanism under SSA focusing on the principles of adequacy, predictability and absorption. Third, we demonstrate how funding under SSA reinforces interstate inequality in school funding. Finally, we analyse the impact of additional funding on the progress of elementary education.

## Review of earlier studies

Diverging income growth performance across states is a concern in India.[2] Studies find regional disparity increased after economic reforms, but human development indices depict decline in regional inequality. Dholakia (2003) found that during the 1990s, a mixed result was shown in regional disparity in human development. Later Dholakia (2005) in a detailed assessment indicates that disparities in social and human development have declined except in education, where it remained stable. Earlier studies convey few significant trends: (i) government allocation towards social sector has been on the decline, indicating 'state's withdrawal ensuing more private sector participation and privatization of social services (Panchamukhi 2000; Mooij and Dev 2004; Pal and Ghosh 2007); (ii) economic divide between states have been accentuating during economic reforms resulting in widening of uneven development in economic and social sectors (Sridhar and Reddy 2011); (iii) distinct divide between educationally better-off states; educationally worse off; and a middle category is apparent. Kerala, Himachal Pradesh, Tamil Nadu and Goa, needless to say fall in first category, attained threshold levels of educational development and moving ahead. Conversely, educationally worse-off states such as Bihar, Uttar Pradesh, West Bengal, Orissa, Rajasthan, Madhya Pradesh, Andhra Pradesh and Assam continue to persist (Bashir 2000; Filmer and Pritchett 2001; Kulkarni 2002). Despite handicaps,

Rajasthan and Madhya Pradesh perform better due to states' commitment. Medium developed yet economically better-off states, such as Maharashtra, Gujarat, Punjab, Haryana and Karnataka neither allocate a higher share of expenditures on education nor signal a strong commitment. (iv) Few fundamental causes identified for development include fiscal capacity; inclination and/or capability of state governments to ensure good governance in delivery of quality government schooling (Mehrotra *et al.* 2005); (v) major education sector development programme, SSA has failed to allocate resources where it was required the most as evidenced from a mid-course review during the middle of 2000s (Geetha Rani 2007; Chakraborty 2009; Jhingran and Shankar 2009). Building on these arguments, this chapter advances to examine interstate disparity in education funding and its impact.

## Data

The study uses secondary data, namely Selected Education Statistics, Selected School Statistics, Analysis of Budgeted Expenditure on Education, 7th All India Education Survey (AIES) of NCERT, Economic Surveys, DISE, SSA Annual Reports, website of SSA, etc. Time period covered include from 1980–81 to 2011–12 for the analysis on state education funding, with selected point of time, namely 1980–81, 1990–91, 1995–96, 2000–01, 2005–06, 2009–10 and 2011–12. Fifteen major states[3] are covered in this analysis. The analysis on SSA funding and its impact covered the latest decade of 2000s, with time series data either from 2002–03 or 2003–04 to 2010–11, depending on consistent availability of data across states. In this analysis, all states and union territories (UTs) are covered. The primary data sources used are from NSSO surveys of 61st, 64th and 66th rounds. The study uses box plots[4] for illustrating interstate disparity across various indicators. In addition, coefficient of variation (CV) is estimated.

## Interstate disparity in education funding

Relationship between education and measures of well-being is borne out by theory and history. Human capital theory entail educational contributes to economic development of both individuals and nations. Instrumental value of education enables people to make use of economic opportunities available in the growth process. The best example is Kerala with a high literacy rate of 90 per cent has underlined India's successful performance in poverty reduction. In contrast, Bihar, the weakest of the large Indian states

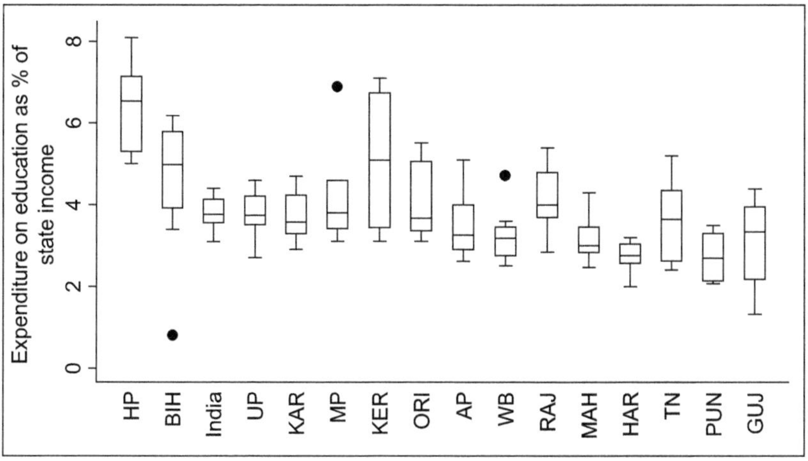


*Figure 14.1* Total expenditure on education as percentage of state income
*Source:* Based on Analysis of Budget Expenditure, various issues; EPWRF (2003), www.cso.org.

in terms of long-term poverty reduction is characterized by an abysmally low literacy rate (Dreze and Sen 2002). Education is critical in enhancing the quality of this asset through improved productivity, employment, and wages. Hence, increasing the productivity of labour through government investing in education provides sustainable means of poverty reduction, besides many other benefits. Yet, the government expenditures on education range from an average of 6.4 per cent in Himachal Pradesh to a minimum of 2.7 per cent in Punjab over three decades from 1980s to 2000s (Figure 14.1).

Another indictor to examine government's commitment to invest on education is state government expenditures on education in state budgets. This displays a different pattern altogether. Kerala is highly committed to investing on education consistently with an average of 27.7 per cent of education expenditures in state budget (Figure 14.2).

Intra-sectoral allocation indicates the level of educational development and portrays the degree of state commitment toward elementary education vis-a-vis post-elementary levels of education. Highest expenditure share to elementary education was reported in Bihar, followed by Madhya Pradesh during the last three decades (Figure 14.3).

The analysis on interstate disparity in education funding from Figures 14.1 to 14.3 signify a couple of pointers.

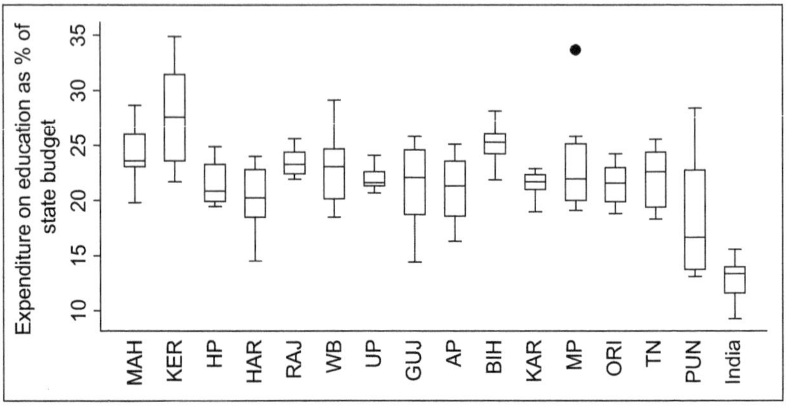


*Figure 14.2* Total expenditure on education as percentage of state budget

*Source:* Based on Analysis of Budget Expenditure, various issues; EPWRF(2003), www.cso.org.

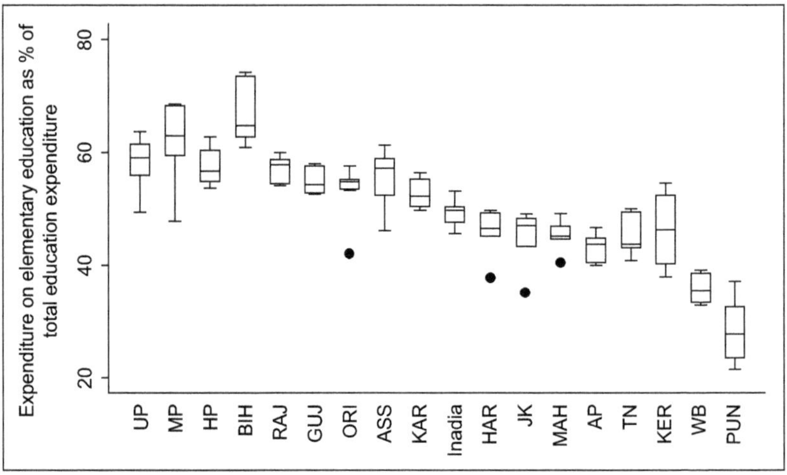


*Figure 14.3* Expenditure on elementary education as percentage of total education expenditure

*Source:* Based on Analysis of Budget Expenditure on Education.

(i) As per human capital theory, direct relation between education and economic development signifying economically developed states spend higher resources on education at the initial stages of development. Once the states attain certain threshold levels of educational attainment, such states either sustain or reduce their allocation to education as a share of national income. This is found to hold good in Kerala and Tamil Nadu. It is because other subsectors of education need more allocation representing next stage in development. On the contrary, economically and educationally backward states due to their fiscal capacity allocate lesser resources to education. Invariably these states do have bulk of child population that is to be brought into school. Unexpectedly, this does not hold true in many educationally and economically backward states such as Bihar, Madhya Pradesh, Rajasthan and Uttar Pradesh.

(ii) Intra-sectoral allocation to elementary education is improving across educationally backward states than in educationally better-off states, indicating their early phase of education development. Impact of SSA on induced state allocation towards elementary education is discernible in few educationally backward states, namely Bihar, Madhya Pradesh, Uttar Pradesh, Rajasthan, Assam and Orissa. In addition to these states Himachal Pradesh allocated consistently higher share towards elementary education. On the contrary, this does not hold true in Punjab and West Bengal which retained their allocation to elementary education at pre-SSA level. Punjab being an agriculturally prosperous state spent very less on education.

## Interstate disparities in funding SSA

SSA brings in additional resources from the centre to achieve universal elementary education across states. Basic economic case for such horizontal equalization is that such a transfer is needed to enable poorer state governments – poorer in terms of their capacity to raise resources out of local resources to respond adequately to central transfers intended to generate the appropriate level of public goods. Hence, it is argued that interstate disparities in educational resources though have to do with the capacity of states to finance education, yet is influenced by a number of non-monetary factors. To explicate this resource base argument, we apply the principles of adequacy, predictability and absorptive rates across states.

### *Adequate funds*

Two questions – whether approved budget is released to states, and whether the funds available under SSA are related to states' requirement – are raised to ensure the adherence of adequacy principle. The first question is examined by looking at the discrepancy between the funds released in the approved outlay under SSA. Karnataka is the only state to lie above this horizontal line, which indicates 80 per cent of released money in the approved outlay, of course with an outlier (Figure 14.4). Karnataka is

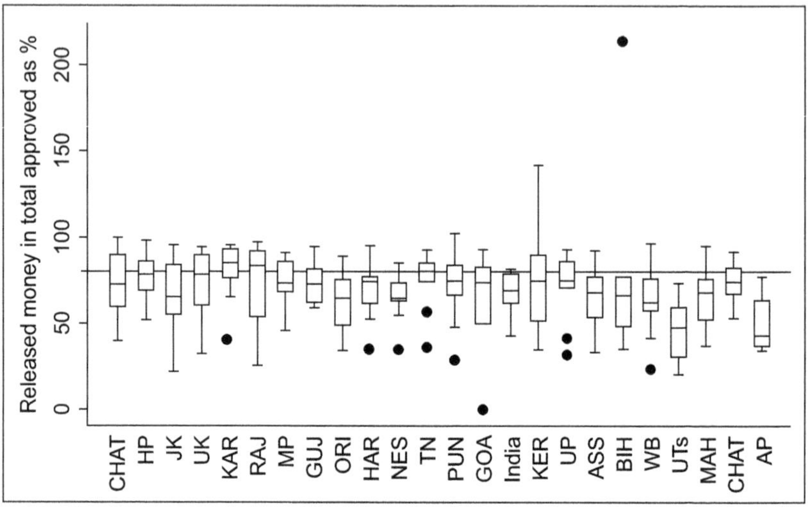


*Figure 14.4* Adequacy of SSA funds: released money as percentage of approved outlay under SSA

*Source:* Based on www.ssa.nic.in downloaded as on 22 February 2013; Ed. Cil TSG.

followed by Himachal Pradesh, Tamil Nadu and Rajasthan getting on an average of 80 per cent of approved outlay. *Educationally better-off states except Rajasthan get allocated consistently better.* On the contrary, on an average 60 per cent and less were given to Andhra Pradesh, UTs and north-eastern states (NES) excluding Assam. However, Goa and Delhi came into the orbit of SSA in 2006–07. Extreme variation within states is found in Kerala, ranging from 35 per cent in 2005–06 to 142 per cent in 2007–08 as has been the case in Figures 14.2 and 14.3 as well. However, the explanation here is quite different that in the two previous consecutive years, Kerala got allocated a much lesser share and hence this 142 per cent in 2007–08. Next highest within state variation is reported in Bihar, ranging from 35 to 214 per cent allocations, indicating the backlog being allocated in the coming years during the initial phase of SSA. Least variation within states is reported in Karnataka, followed by Uttar Pradesh. The allocations ranged between 41 and 93 per cent with an outlier at 32 per cent level. Unlike the earlier figures, *extent of variation within states over the years as well as across states is considerably higher in this figure.*

Relative frequency of fund availability vis-a-vis child population, enrolment, schools and teachers is analysed to know whether funds available under SSA is related to states' requirement (the second question). The idea of looking at relative shares of child population, enrolment, schools and teachers is because much of SSA allocations are based on covering out of school children, number of government and government aided schools, children enrolled in these schools and teacher grants for teachers employed in government and government funded schools. It is expected that states with a large infrastructure gap, greater shortage of teachers, high proportion of children not attending schools, high dropout rates or high gender gaps in enrolment would need proportionately higher financial resources to make up for greater distance they need to cover for achieving the right to education. Uttar Pradesh, Bihar, Madhya Pradesh, West Bengal, Rajasthan and Jharkhand together got 54 per cent of total allocations, which occupy 45.7 per cent of child population (appendix Figures A14.1 and A14.2). *In a way, it appears that educationally backward states are getting the highest shares and also as per the relative requirement of the child population.*

However, it may be noted that Maharashtra seems to have got lesser allocation compared to its child population and enrolment shares (Figure A14.3). But the relative share of government and private aided schools depict a different picture that Uttar Pradesh, Madhya Pradesh, Orissa, Maharashtra, Andhra Pradesh and Bihar occupy 56 per cent of total schools. It can be noted that Orissa and Andhra Pradesh have more share of schools compared to their child population and enrolment. Although Bihar has more proportion of child population and enrolment, it reports less proportion of schools. Investments under SSA have not yet built the proportionate physical infrastructure in Bihar (Figure A14.4). The relative share of government and private aided teachers depict yet another pattern that Uttar Pradesh, Maharashtra, Bihar, Karnataka, Rajasthan, Gujarat and Madhya Pradesh occupy 56 per cent of total teachers in India. States such as Karnataka and Gujarat occupy a much lesser share of child population, enrolment and schools compared to teachers share (Figure A14.5). In each Figures from A14.1 to A14.5, within state variation is found to be highest among teachers' relative share. This is found in Bihar, followed by Uttar Pradesh and Madhya Pradesh. *The analysis here somewhat indicate that the allocations under SSA are not fully synchronized with their requirements as observed in relation to their enrolment, school and teachers.*

### *Predictability*

On designing intergovernmental fiscal transfers, one of the desirable qualities is predictability. Intergovernmental fiscal transfer mechanisms should ensure predictability of sub-national government shares from year to year to permit strategic planning (Parker 1995). We examined the predictability by looking at timing and share of release of funds from (i) Government of India (GoI) to State Implementation Society (SIS) in Uttar Pradesh and (ii) state governments of Uttar Pradesh to SIS. Budget Calendar in India runs from April to March. In principle, appraisal of the annual work plans and budget at the national capital to be done by 1st April by the Appraisal Mission and plans are to be approved by 15th April. The *Manual on Financial Management and Procurement* (MFM&P) stipulated that the release of funds to SIS are to be carried out in two installments in April and September every year (MHRD 2004, 2010). Similarly, the state governments are to transfer matching shares on approved outlay in two installments to SIS.

Table 14.1 specifies the pattern of fund flow by quarters. Fund flow from centre to SIS does not follow any clear pattern in Uttar Pradesh. More than 20 per cent of the funds reach SIS by fourth quarter in many years. Though there are improvements in 2006–07 that within third quarter all money is

*Table 14.1* Fund flow from government of India to SIS in Uttar Pradesh

| | *April–June* | *July–Sep* | *Oct–Dec* | *Jan–March* | *Total (Rs. in lakhs)* | *No. of installments* |
|---|---|---|---|---|---|---|
| | *Quarter I* | *Quarter II* | *Quarter III* | *Quarter IV* | | |
| 2002–03 | 5.8 | 39.0 | 55.2 | 0.0 | 12,820 | 4 |
| 2003–04 | 0.0 | 61.4 | 0.0 | 38.6 | 42,135 | 5 |
| 2004–05 | 5.7 | 60.1 | 0.0 | 34.2 | 87,761 | 5 |
| 2005–06 | 10.9 | 42.4 | 31.1 | 15.5 | 182,799 | 6 |
| 2006–07 | 61.3 | 0.0 | 38.7 | 0.0 | 206,654 | 4 |
| 2007–08 | 21.7 | 7.9 | 48.9 | 21.4 | 204,758 | 5 |
| 2008–09 | 25.5 | 18.8 | 27.4 | 28.3 | 200,959 | 4 |
| 2010–11 | 67.8 | 0.0 | 41.9 | 44.8 | 310,463 | 7 |
| | | **Fund flow from Govt. Uttar Pradesh to SIS** | | | | |
| 2003–04 | 5.2 | 47.7 | 7.7 | 39.4 | 11,348 | 7 |
| 2004–05 | 5.7 | 40.4 | 19.7 | 34.2 | 29,254 | 11 |
| 2005–06 | 35.0 | 16.3 | 29.4 | 19.3 | 60,933 | 13 |
| 2006–07 | 33.4 | 27.9 | 38.7 | 0.0 | 68,886 | 12 |
| 2007–08 | 19.5 | 31.4 | 0.0 | 49.1 | 114,140 | 11 |
| 2008–09 | 75.9 | 14.4 | 4.1 | 5.5 | 114,630 | 14 |
| 2010–11 | 25.4 | 25.4 | 25.4 | 23.9 | 157,728 | 21 |

*Source:* calculated by author based on Audit Reports of SSA, Lucknow; Institute of Public Auditors of India (IPAI) Report, 2009.

released, providing some time if not adequate time to spend the money. But such a scenario is not followed in the later years. As per the provisions of the *Manual on Financial Management and Procurement* (MFM&P), GoI was to release its share in two installments, in April and September each year, whereas funds were released in four to six installments during 2002–03 to 2010–11.

Indeed, for many years, release of fund from GoI took place till February just leaving hardly a month to spend the allocation in Uttar Pradesh. The issue of receiving funds with considerable time gap is not only specific to these states. MHRD (2008a) reports that the releases of funds during 2007–08 have been reasonable, although the Joint Review Mission (JRM) observed certain delays in releases from GoI and states to the SISs in almost all states the team visited, namely Orissa, Rajasthan and West Bengal. Next, we compare the pattern and timing of fund flow from GoUP to SIS (see Table 14.1 and Figure 14.5).

Similar to the fund flow from GoI to SIS in Uttar Pradesh, no specific pattern of fund flow was observed during the four quarters from 2003–04 to 2010–11. It can be noted that in 2007–08, almost 50 per cent of the money is released during the fourth quarter. This hardly leaves adequate time for the SIS for proper implementation of the allocated money on various interventions. However, 60 per cent of state allocations have been released before October during 2008–09. This has been an improved situation than previous years that around 60 per cent of the allocations were made in January. Such transfers not only mean that senior officers at SIS are constantly busy with releases but it also increases the load on accounting system manifold and delays transfers at districts. Besides the delayed release, fragmented release by both MHRD and states make the State Implementing Societies unable to adhere to the schedule of releasing funds within 15 days of their receipt. MHRD (2008b) notes that all states/UTs have been instructed to release funds in two installments to avoid delay in execution of works (MHRD 2008b). State governments are to release the matching share within 30 days of receipt of GoI share and in maximum two installments. But the GoUP funds were released to SIS in 7, 11, 13 and 21 installments by GoUP during 2003–04, 2004–05, 2005–06, 2010–11, respectively.[5] These delays are observed even after electronic transfer of funds commenced in 2004.

A major bottleneck relating to fund flow and financial management is delay of funds reaching SIS, most of the money coming in the last two quarters and in fragmented installments. The delay in sending both by the centre and state governments and the receipt of it by SIS delays the whole process of planning and implementing the planned programme interventions.

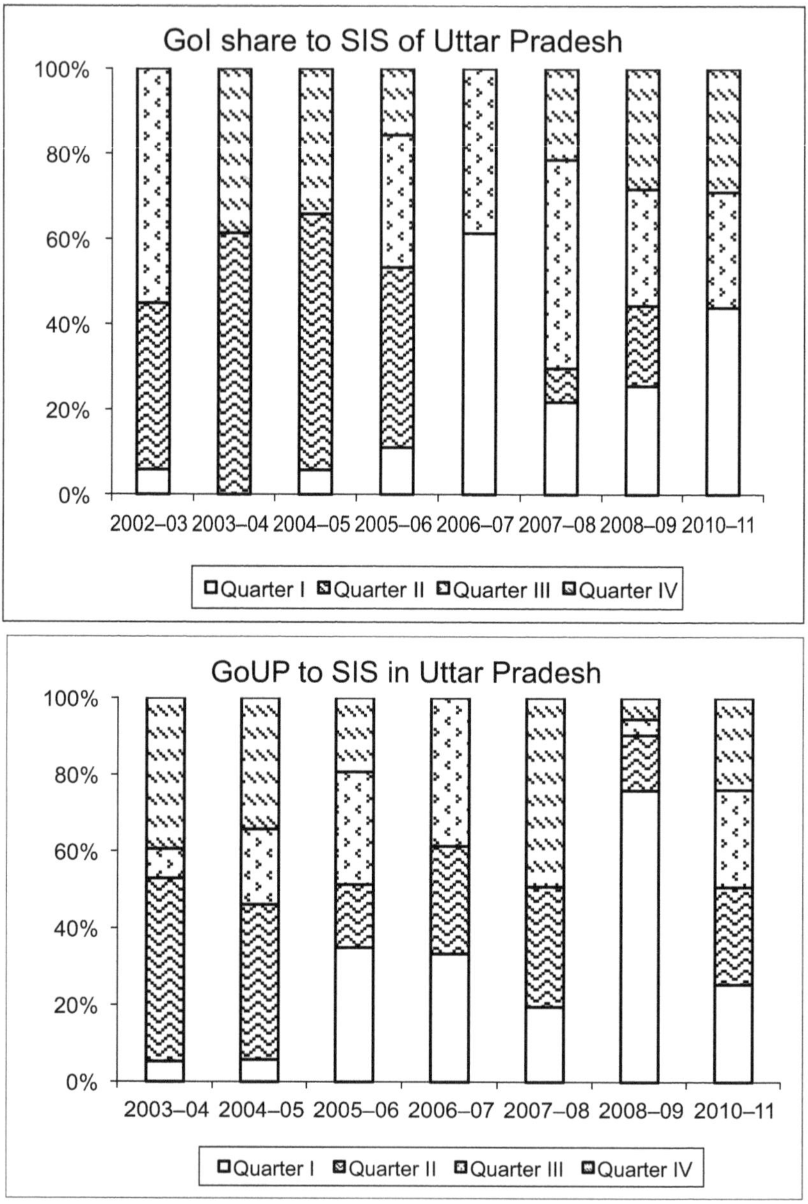


*Figure 14.5* Fund flow from Government of India and GOUP to SIS in Uttar Pradesh (by quarters)

*Source:* Based on Table 14.1.

*The resource allocation mechanism neither seem to ensure predictability and transparency that how much of resources are sanctioned to state governments nor sanctions the available resources within the stipulated time period and in fewer installments.*

### Absorptive capacity

Expenditure on education empowers people with skills, knowledge and abilities and is obviously an investment in human capital. If properly utilized, it has the potential of lifting millions out of poverty. The efficiency with which resources are utilized has an impact on economic growth. If resources maximize the useful goods and services derived from those resources, then we may expect greater economic growth to occur. This section attempts to examine apparent verses actual absorptive rates of funds allocated under SSA across states. Apparent absorptive rates are measured as expenditure on SSA as a percentage of total funds available in a year. While the actual absorptive rates are measured as reverse of unspent balance[6] as percentage of total funds available.

#### *Apparent verses actual absorptive capacity*

On an average, above 80 per cent apparent absorptive rate is found in Rajasthan, Uttar Pradesh, Andhra Pradesh, Tamil Nadu, Karnataka, Madhya Pradesh, Himachal Pradesh, Goa and Haryana. As noted earlier, few educationally backward states are consistently performing better than Rajasthan and Madhya Pradesh. In addition to these states, Uttar Pradesh[7] and Andhra Pradesh do report better apparent absorptive rates (Figure 14.6a). On the contrary, the lowest utilization rate was found in Bihar with less than 50 per cent. And the next lowest was among UTs, followed by Jharkhand and Punjab, however with much higher above 60 per cent average absorptive rates. Within state variation, the highest variance is found in Jammu Kashmir, followed by Bihar. In Jammu Kashmir, apparent absorptive rates ranged between 37 and 137 per cent during the first decade of the new millennium. In Bihar, the apparent absorptive rates ranged between as low as 10 to 102 per cent during the same period. Though it indicates erratic pattern of absorption in few states, absorptive rates improved across states over the period. On the contrary, few states such as Rajasthan and Tamil Nadu display relatively acceptable pattern of absorptive rates. Such an acceptable pattern of apparent absorptive rates were found across many states almost from Rajasthan to Orissa (Figure 14.6a).

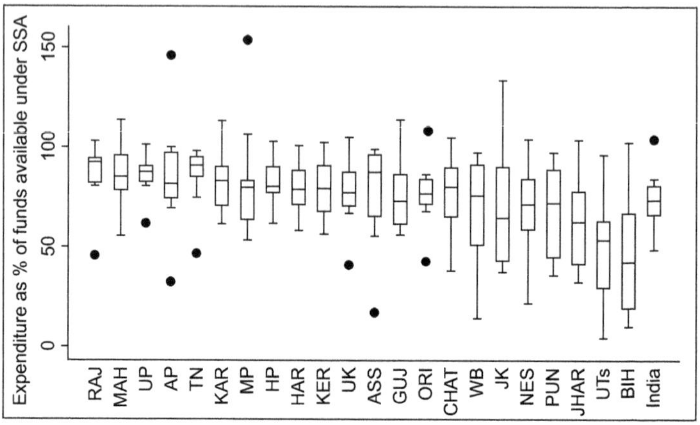


*Figure 14.6a* Apparent absorptive rates across states under SSA

*Source:* Based on www.ssa.nic.in downloaded as an 22.2.2013; Ed. Cil TSG.

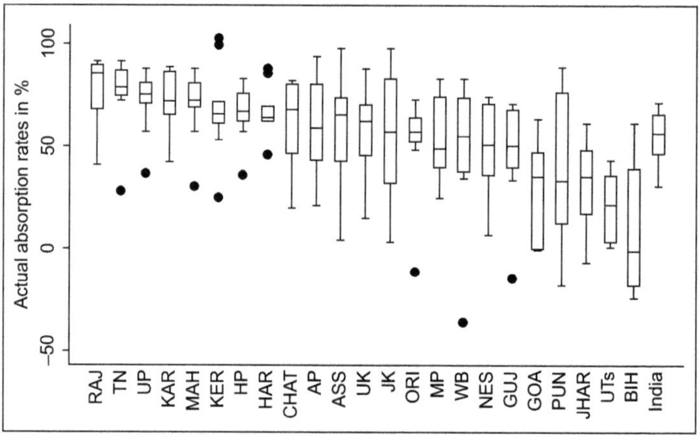


*Figure 14.6b* Actual absorptive rates across states under SSA

*Source:* Based on www.ssa.nic.in downloaded as an 22.2.2013; Ed. Cil TSG.

Almost 14 states boxes lie above 50 per cent absorptive rates and their extent of variation across the years is at relatively reasonable levels, though with outliers on both sides. In terms of actual absorptive rates as well as almost the same set of states, Rajasthan, Tamil Nadu, Uttar Pradesh and Karnataka spent on an average more than 70 per cent (a 10 percentage point lesser than apparent absorptive rates) (Figure 14.6b).

Same set of states – Bihar, UTs, Jharkhand and Punjab – reported their actual absorptive rates as the least as that of apparent absorptive rates. Bihar could spend on an average less than 10 per cent of allocated resources only with reporting negative absorptive rates in four years in the total analysis of nine years data. Though the relative position of states has not changed a great deal, yet one can find the reduction in the absorptive rates varying from as low as 8.3 percentage points in Rajasthan to 39 percentage points in Bihar. Within states, extreme variation can be found in Punjab ranging from a negative 20 per cent to a positive 89 per cent. It is followed by Jammu & Kashmir, ranging from 3 to 98 per cent. Though the extent of variance is quite extreme in many states, yet in few other states, within state variation is relatively minimum.

For instance, Tamil Nadu reports consistent spending pattern though with an outlier. Unlike, many other Figures, many states report outliers. *Yet another revelation is the actual absorptive rates are much less than apparent absorptive rates*. Bihar reporting low utilization rate of the funds is not something new under SSA, even in DPEP it persisted (Karan and Pushpendra 2005). For instance, Bihar spent a mere 30 per cent of its budget allocation in 2000–01 under the Bihar Education Project. It is important to explore what are the factors behind this scenario. This is definitely an inequitable and undesirable situation. Since the utilization of funds is often lower in states that are educationally disadvantaged, this disconnect between need and allocation becomes further distorted for some states when actual expenditures are taken into account. Disparity between apparent and actual expenditure comes out even more starkly. *It becomes unambiguous that additional resources coming from the centre for development of education can have a positive influence on states only after states have achieved a certain threshold level of absorptive capacities*.

An important guiding principle in allocating financial resources in a federal system is to enable the states to provide comparable levels of public services at comparable tax effort. When the states are at different levels of fiscal capacity, they can incur comparable levels of expenditures on social and physical infrastructure only when central transfers offset the fiscal disability of states with low fiscal capacity. As argued by Chakraborty *et al.* (2010), in this sense, the issue of designing a transfer system is critically important in offsetting the fiscal disability of the states. *As can be evidenced in the absorptive rates, fiscal disability is not compensated by the transfers via SSA as the matching shares are uniform across states*. It undoubtedly conveys that SSA financial allocations are not strongly linked to not only educational but also fiscal disadvantage of states. On the other hand, though the proportion of central revenues transferred to states had increased substantially over the years and dependence of relatively backward states on transfers had sharply risen (Jha *et al*. 2008).

## Impact of SSA funding on elementary education

Transfers in themselves are neither good nor bad; what matters from a policy perspective are their effects on the outcomes of interest such as allocative efficiency, distributional equity and macroeconomic stability (Shah 1991). In the current context in the case of non-economic well being indictors, in elementary education, impact of SSA funding on the progress of elementary education across states is analysed by examining the Gross Enrolment Ratio (GER) in upper primary, dropout rates, per-student expenditures with and without SSA expenditures. Besides, children outside formal schooling across gender and rural and urban areas from the household surveys of NSSO is examined. Every state has moved upwards in terms of enrolling more number of children at primary and upper primary levels. However, the major goal of SSA in terms of universal elementary enrolment is yet to be attained (Figure 14.7). Unlike the finance indicators that fluctuate up and down, the education indicators such as GER will only move upwards. Hence, whiskers at the upper end in each box representing

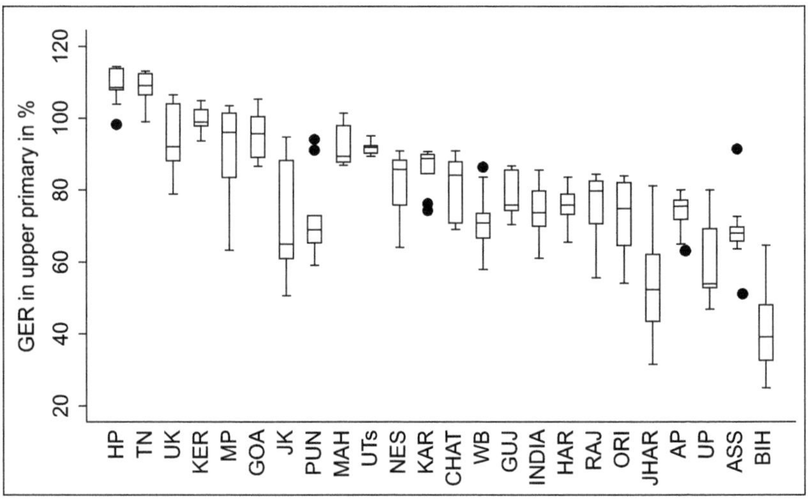


*Figure 14.7* Gross Enrolment Ratio at upper primary level by states

*Source:* Based on MHRD (2005, 2006); www.ssa.nic.in downloaded as on 22 February 2013; Ed. Cil TSG.

indicate the latest years GER and similarly whiskers at the lower end indicate the place from where each began in 2002–03. Above 100 per cent GER is reported in Himachal Pradesh, Tamil Nadu, Uttarakhand, Kerala, Madhya Pradesh and Goa. Among them, Himachal Pradesh and Tamil Nadu already attained universal upper primary enrolment by 2002–03.

On the contrary, Bihar reports 64 per cent GER in 2010–11 which was treated at par with other states with the GER of 25 per cent at upper primary level in 2002–03. *The first and foremost problem with SSA funding being treating educationally backward and better-off states on an equal footing. It is because all states are to provide equal matching shares irrespective of their achievement or non-achievement in elementary education except the north eastern or special category states*. Within state variation, each box indicates the extent of coverage each state has made from the beginning in 2002–03 with the bottom line whisker to the current level of GER at upper most whisker. Highest variation can be found in Jharkhand and Madhya Pradesh, followed by Jammu Kashmir. For instance, Jharkhand started with 31 per cent GER in 2002–03 improved to cover 82 per cent by 2010–11.

On the contrary, the least within state variation is reported in Kerala, followed by Himachal Pradesh and Tamil Nadu. The larger issue still remains that, except these three states, the GER at upper primary is not yet attained in many states. Nonetheless, irrespective of their educational attainment or economic position, states have improved in terms of Gross Enrolment Ratio at upper primary levels over the first decade of the new millennium. Yet in many respects, upper primary level remains the unfinished access agenda for SSA and should continue to receive the highest attention. In terms of the efforts made by states, by improvement in terms of the percentage points from 2002–03 to 2010–11, Madhya Pradesh has made tremendous efforts in attaining almost universal enrolment at upper primary level. Madhya Pradesh is followed by Rajasthan, Jammu & Kashmir and Orissa. Though elementary school enrolment may have increased steadily over the years, it is low even by South Asian standards. Countries such as Sri Lanka and Bangladesh have higher school enrolment rates than India.

Intergovernmental transfers is expected to enable the states to operate in such a way that it leads to efficiency in the use of resources, both in terms of quality of services provided and resource use efficiency (Rangarajan 2004). Dropout rates, an indicator on quality of elementary education, are very high, especially in educationally backward states. On the contrary, a zero dropout rate of children is reported in Kerala, Himachal Pradesh, Goa and Punjab. Among these states, Kerala has been consistently reporting zero dropout rates. Kerala is followed by Goa and Himachal Pradesh (Figure 14.8). Conversely, states such as Bihar, Orissa,

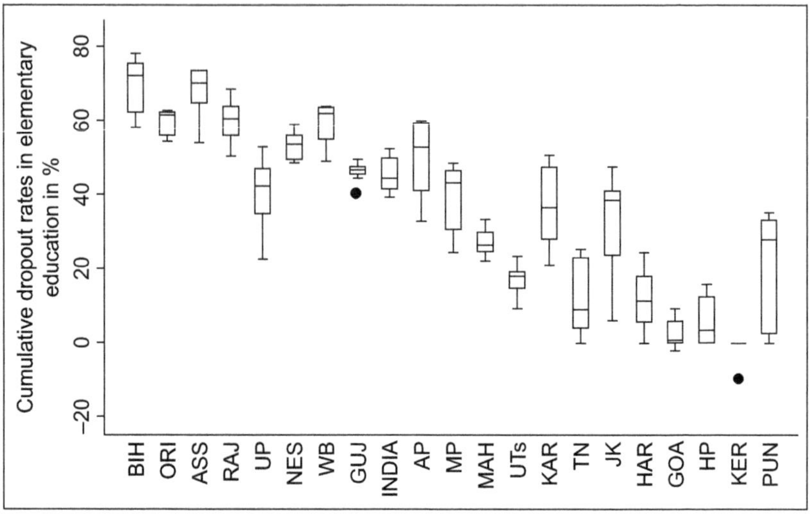


*Figure 14.8* Cumulative dropout rates at elementary level by states

*Source:* Selected Educational Statistics, Selected School Statistics, various issues.

Assam, Rajasthan and Uttar Pradesh report 50 per cent and above dropout rates, indicating that though their enrolment levels are rapidly improving their retaining capacity of children in schools are yet to be developed. Unlike GER, dropout rates fluctuated over the years within a state. However, few states display consistently declining dropout rates such as Bihar, Orissa, Andhra Pradesh, Karnataka, Goa and Punjab. Within state variation is the highest in Punjab, followed by Karnataka. Both states have improved their internal efficiency by bringing down their dropout rates. On the contrary, least variation indicating no efforts to reduce internal inefficiency can be found in Gujarat, followed by Maharashtra.

*The analysis on enrolment ratio and dropout rates across states clearly brings out not only the uneven development to start with in terms of access and internal efficiency indictors, but also uneven efforts by the states to overcome the handicaps in not only merely attaining UEE but also retaining the enrolled children in the school system.* Such imbalances further exacerbate with similar unit cost norms and uniform matching shares in allocation of resources under SSA.[8] Different states have different capacities to translate certain financial resources into well-being outcome. This results in differential expenditures per child across states. A noteworthy issue arises of how equally or unequally money is spent on each child across states. Ensuring of regional balance has been constantly underlined in all plan documents. Hence, per-student expenditures on elementary education are compared to per-student expenditures without SSA expenditure.

First, let us examine the interstate variation in per-student expenditure on elementary education with SSA expenditures. Per-student expenditure pertains to children studying in government and government funded called private aided schools.[9] Per-student expenditures ranged between Rs. 4,556 in Bihar to more than four times higher – Rs. 21,177 in Himachal Pradesh during 2010–11 (Figure 14.9).

Bihar though allocated higher shares to total education and elementary education. It also allocated a relatively appropriate share as per their child population, enrolment, school shares under SSA, yet could not absorb the allocation and hence spent one of the least per child expenditures. On the contrary, Himachal Pradesh allocated higher share but spent effectively and hence one of the highest per-student expenditures. Equally important to note, since Himachal Pradesh report zero dropout rates, this per-student cost can be considered as effective unit cost. The states that could gain more in terms of increase in per-student cost from 2002–03 to 2010–11 are

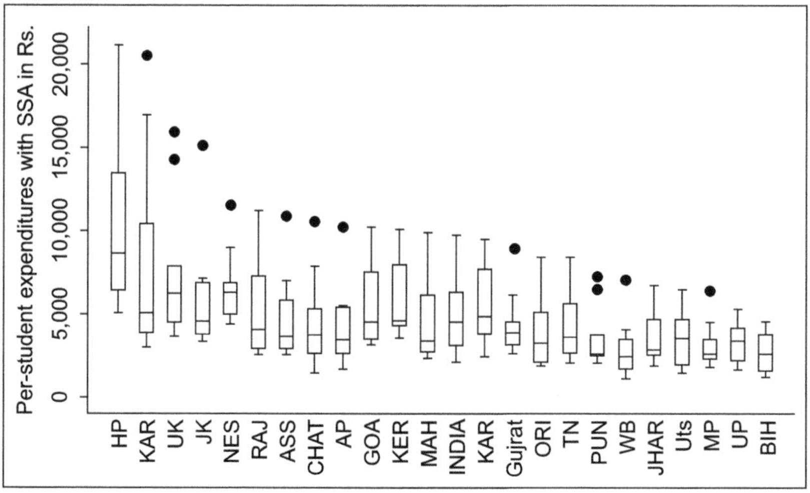


*Figure 14.9* Per-student government expenditures on elementary education with SSA expenditures

*Source:* Based on Analysis of Budget Expenditure on Education and Selected Educational Statistics, (various issues); www.ssa.nic.in downloaded as an 22.2.2013; Ed. Cil TSG; Selected Educational Statistics, Selected School Statistics, various issues; 7th AIES, NCERT, 64th Round NSSO.

Andhra Pradesh, Haryana and West Bengal. Within state variation is the highest among Himachal Pradesh followed by Haryana. The outliers are many in almost all states except Himachal Pradesh, Goa, Kerala, Maharashtra, Tamil Nadu, Orissa, Uttar Pradesh and Bihar.

The least variation within state is found in Bihar, where per-student cost in 2002–03 was Rs. 1,238 and improved to Rs. 4,556 by 2010–11. It is quite straightforward to notice the uneven growth of per-student cost across state and it emerges that SSA allocations have helped in reinforcing this disparity than to reduce them. Comparison of per-student cost without SSA expenditures would further add on this. Himachal Pradesh reported the highest per-student expenditure of Rs. 18,509 and Bihar spent Rs.2,684 in 2010–11 (Figure 14.10). The increase in per-student cost additionally on account of SSA was Rs. 2,668 in Himachal Pradesh, while this amount itself was the per-student cost in Bihar. Additional per-student cost that Bihar could reap was Rs. 1,872. This clearly brings out the extent of disparity in per-student cost. This further raises the question to what extent the current allocations of SSA can ensure the balance. Nevertheless, there are few states, Haryana, Gujarat and Andhra Pradesh report the highest increase in per-student cost without SSA expenditures between 2002–03 and 2010–11. Within state variation is

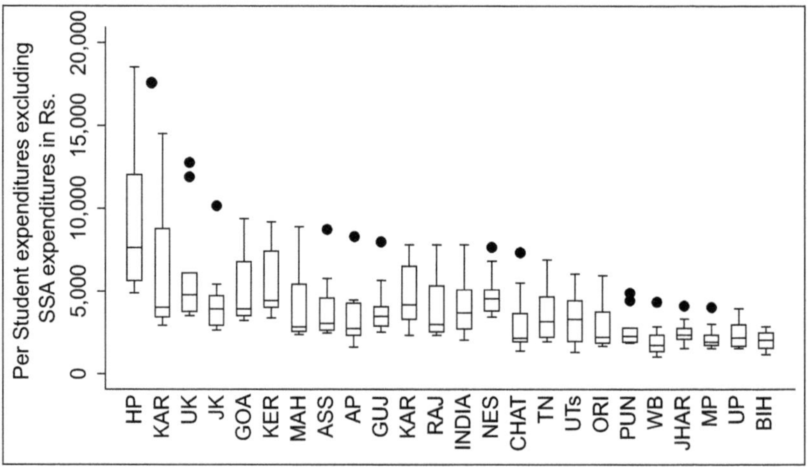


*Figure 14.10* Per-student government expenditures on elementary education excluding SSA expenditures

*Source:* Based on Analysis of Budget Expenditure on Education and Selected Educational Statistics, (various issues); Selected Educational Statistics, Selected School Statistics, various issues; 7th AIES, NCERT, 64th Round NSSO.

the highest in Himachal Pradesh as in the earlier case with SSA expenditure. Similarly, the least within state variation was found in Bihar. So, the relative position of states did not change much with and without SSA expenditures.

It clearly emerges that states with initial advantages of both educational development and fiscal advantage along with state commitment toward not only financing but also better public delivery system gained out of additional allocations under SSA. *While the states suffering with handicaps of all these are not the gainer but at the same time not the losers as well.* However, the fact remains that the developed states improved their elementary education delivery and quality faster than educationally and economically backward states, widening the interstate disparity.

An attempt is made here to examine interstate disparity by rural urban locations and by gender using the NSSO data for 2004–05 and 2009–10. Bringing all children in the age group 6–14 years into the formal schooling system is one of the foremost goals of SSA. Differences in boys-girls and rural-urban children outside formal schooling persist after implementing SSA for more than a decade. In 2009–10, more than 20 per cent girls in the age group 5–14 years who have received formal schooling are found in Bihar, Rajasthan, Jharkhand and Gujarat. They are educationally backward except Gujarat. States performing better with 4 per cent or less than 4 per cent of girl children outside formal schooling are Himachal Pradesh, Kerala, Tamil Nadu and Goa (Figure 14.11).

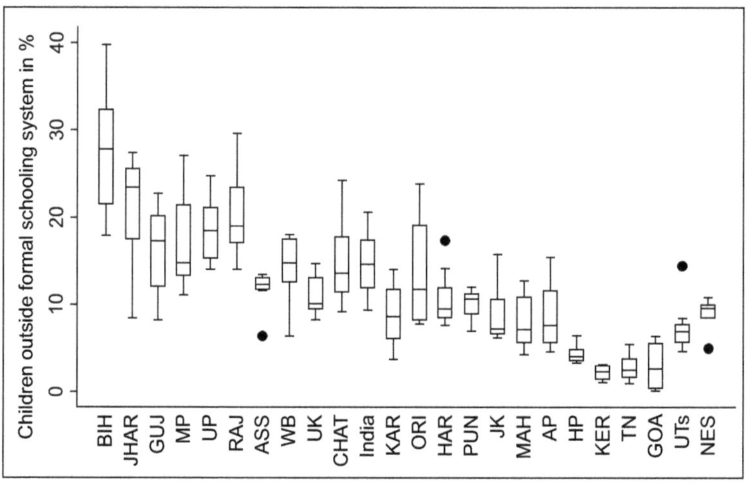


*Figure 14.11* Children outside formal schooling system in age group 5–14

*Source:* Kundu, Moahanan and Varghese (2013)

More than 20 per cent of children outside the formal schooling in rural areas include Bihar, Jharkhand and Gujarat. These are almost the same states as having poor performance in terms of more than 20 per cent of girls not in the formal schooling. The better performers with less than 4 per cent of rural children outside the formal schooling are the same educationally better-off states such as Goa, Tamil Nadu, and Kerala. The analysis suggests that there will be significant deficit in attaining the SSA goals of universal elementary education and eliminating gender disparity in all levels of education by 2015. By both the indicators, one would, however, argue that the situation has improved during 2005–10. What is disturbing is that inequality across states has gone up in urban and rural areas.

Despite the improvements during 2004–05 to 2009–10, interstate disparity remained considerably high across groups and predominant among girls with 54 per cent in 2009–10. The decline in interstate disparity is marginal among girls between the two periods. While the disparity marginally improved among the rural children, it remained the same among urban children. Though SSA attempts to iron out regional imbalances in UEE, it is yet to be realized. This analysis indicates that there is a significant correlation between economic deprivation and educational deficiency. This corroborates commonly held viewpoint that various kinds of inequalities interact with and reinforce each other. Multidimensional deprivation operates to confine some geographical pockets and social groups in 'inequality traps'. In other words, the regions that were poor (rich) earlier are the ones that continue to be poor (rich) now. At the end of more than a decade of implementing SSA, the distance to reach not only to universal upper primary enrolment but also retaining children in the system would remain a challenge for many educationally backward states.

## Induce interstate disparity

The empirical analysis in earlier section clearly bring out how funding under SSA reinforces interstate inequality in school funding. An attempt is made here to look at the extent of disparity as measured through coefficient of variation (CV) in selected SSA-funding indictors, namely adequacy of SSA funds, apparent absorptive rates and actual absorptive rates and the impact of SSA captured through GER at upper primary, cumulative dropout rates, per-student expenditures on elementary education with and without SSA expenditures (Figure 14.12). Disparities in apparent absorptive rates have consistently declined over the years from

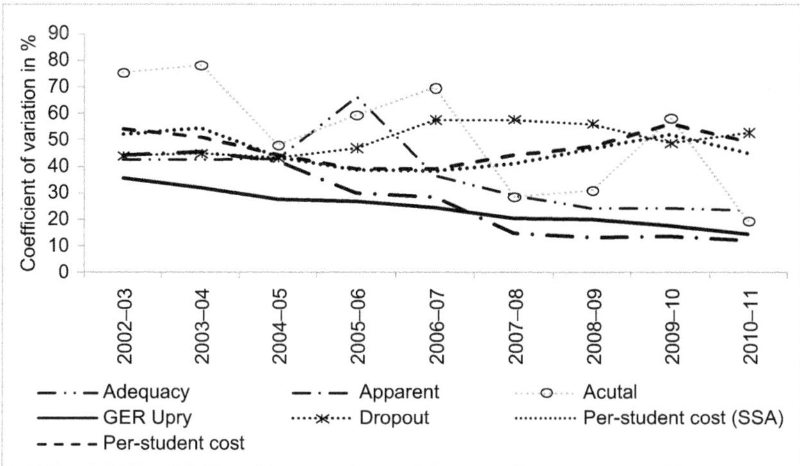


*Figure 14.12* Interstate disparity in SSA funding and impact of SSA funding

44 per cent in beginning phase to 12 per cent by 2010–11. But in terms of actual absorptive rates, it fluctuates without indicating any discernible declining or increasing trend. In terms of adequacy of funds CV stagnate at 24 per cent during 2008–09 and 2009–10 and marginally declined in 2010–11. Though no patterns emerge on SSA funding, yet it would be worthwhile to examine interstate disparity on the impact of SSA funding.

Interstate disparity across GER at upper primary declined drastically like apparent absorptive rates. But on dropout rates, per-student cost with and without SSA expenditures, it widened across states over time.

Although it is clear that interstate disparity with SSA funding has widened, an attempt is made to examine average annual growth rates of critical inputs – schools, enrolment, teachers and per-student cost with and without SSA expenditures excluding private unaided sector. Growth rate of enrolment has been the highest in Jharkhand, followed by Bihar and Madhya Pradesh (Table 14.2). Another interesting trend that spans out is the negative growth rates in 13 states ranging from 0.4 per cent to –4.4 per cent. This could be on account of a couple of reasons: (i) Child population in these states is declining and (ii) demand for government schools is declining, thereby indicating the demand for private unaided education. This has been another contributing factor to increased inequality in education.

*Table 14.2* Average annual growth rates of educational indicators

| | *Elementary enrolment** | *Elementary schools** | *Elementary education teachers** | *Per-student expr. without SSA* | *Per-student expr. (with SSA)* |
|---|---|---|---|---|---|
| Jharkhand | 7.8 | 7.17 | 10.9 | 9.3 | 16.5 |
| Bihar | 6.2 | 5.09 | 13.6 | 11.6 | 19.2 |
| Madhya Pradesh | 5.4 | 3.70 | –2.3 | 9.5 | 14.7 |
| Uts | 2.6 | –4.04 | 2.1 | 16.6 | 17.6 |
| Uttar Pradesh | 2.4 | 6.35 | –3.5 | 13.2 | 16.9 |
| Jammu & Kashmir | 2.2 | 5.76 | 9.8 | 12.0 | 16.7 |
| Gujarat | 1.7 | 4.96 | 2.0 | 13.9 | 14.6 |
| Chhattisgarh | 1.6 | 2.89 | 9.3 | 22.7 | 27.4 |
| NES | 1.0 | 5.68 | 1.7 | 8.1 | 9.6 |
| **INDIA** | 0.7 | 3.03 | 0.5 | 17.7 | 20.3 |
| Goa | 0.6 | 10.03 | 13.0 | 15.5 | 17.2 |
| Orissa | –0.4 | 4.18 | 6.5 | 17.2 | 21.7 |
| Rajasthan | –0.6 | 0.60 | 2.6 | 17.1 | 21.9 |
| Tamil Nadu | –0.9 | –0.10 | –2.1 | 18.2 | 19.6 |
| Uttaranchal | –1.0 | 1.52 | 1.9 | 18.2 | 20.2 |
| Karnataka | –1.4 | 1.12 | 2.7 | 16.7 | 18.8 |
| Assam | –1.9 | 3.34 | 1.8 | 14.5 | 17.2 |
| West Bengal | –2.1 | 1.56 | 2.4 | 17.5 | 23.8 |
| Maharashtra | –2.4 | 1.83 | –1.5 | 18.3 | 20.0 |
| Himachal Pradesh | –3.2 | 3.50 | 7.7 | 18.4 | 19.1 |
| Haryana | –3.5 | 3.07 | –3.1 | 26.5 | 28.1 |
| Punjab | –3.8 | 2.25 | 6.2 | 11.2 | 15.8 |
| Andhra Pradesh | –4.1 | –0.13 | –0.4 | 18.6 | 21.3 |
| Kerala | –4.4 | 1.94 | –0.6 | 12.9 | 13.8 |

*Source:* Estimated based Selected Educational Statistics; Analysis of Budgeted Expenditure on Education, various issue; 7th AIES, NCERT and 64th round of NSSO, unit records DISE, 2004–05 and 2005–06.

*Note:* *Excluding PUA share.

Over the years, shares of private unaided schools have gone up significantly at primary, upper primary and secondary levels. These private unaided schools are mostly located in urban areas, and charge much higher fees than government or local body schools. Since these private schools mainly cater to richer sections of the population, their rapid growth is indicative of increasing education inequality in India.[10] The growth of government and aided schools is highest among Jharkhand, Uttar Pradesh, Jammu & Kashmir and Bihar.[11] Negative growth rates of government and private aided schools are reported only in Andhra Pradesh and Tamil Nadu. Disconnect between negative growth rates in enrolment and increasing growth rates in schools in Kerala and Himachal Pradesh needs to be explored further and is a cause for concern. This is true in other states reporting negative growth rates in enrolment and positive growth rates in schools. This would result in many uneconomic or unviable schools.

With regard to teachers in government and private aided schools,[12] the highest growth rates are reported in Bihar, Goa and Jharkhand. Unexpectedly many states registered negative growth rates, namely Uttar Pradesh, Haryana, Madhya Pradesh, Tamil Nadu, Maharashtra, Kerala, and Andhra Pradesh. States such as Andhra Pradesh, Tamil Nadu and Kerala registering negative growth rate of teachers would be considered as a normal process of educational development and an aftermath of demographic transition. But negative growth rates of teachers in Madhya Pradesh and Uttar Pradesh is on account of the highest recruitment of para-teacher in these states. However, this issue needs to be explored further.

Per-student expenditures on elementary education without SSA expenditures report the highest growth in Haryana, where enrolment and teachers reported negative growth rates. Above 18 per cent growth is reported in states such as Chhattisgarh, Andhra Pradesh, Himachal Pradesh, Maharashtra, Tamil Nadu and Uttaranchal. Except Chhattisgarh, rest of the states are either economically or educationally better off. On the contrary, less than 10 per cent growth was reported in Jharkhand and Madhya Pradesh. While per-student expenditures with SSA expenditures report the highest growth rates of above 20 per cent in Haryana, Chhattisgarh, West Bengal, Rajasthan, Orissa and Andhra Pradesh. Conversely, below 15 per cent growth rate is reported in Madhya Pradesh, Gujarat and Kerala. Though the spending with SSA somewhat tries to address interstate disparity, huge initial disadvantage plays a much bigger role. In the same spirit, Rao, Shand and Kalirajan (1999) argue that intergovernmental transfers cannot remove such inequalities. However, they can be designed to more clearly meet Musgravian horizontal equity objectives, without reducing incentives for fiscal discipline, than is the case now. Streamlining the centre-state transfer system can only help isolate any interstate disparities that are likely to cause political tensions, and make clear the redistributive effort that is politically necessary. In this respect, it is important to recognize that implicit financial transfers by central government have often favoured higher income states.

Transfer system via centrally sponsored schemes like SSA has adopted a different funding mechanism with the transfers going outside the statutory channels. The effect of these changes through multiple channels of transfers is mixed in achieving horizontal equity. The analysis brings out that one is in conflict with the other. In addition, the overall effect appears to be highly regressive. In this context, Chakraborty *et al* (2010) argue that any design of transfers would remain cosmetic, unless drastic redistribution takes place in the horizontal allocation of resources. Differences in initial conditions do matter. *Hence, we argue that though SSA attempt to address interstate disparity yet, the accumulated initial advantage of the better-off states with uniform norms under SSA funding induce interstate disparity rather than reducing it.*

## Summing up

This chapter signifies a couple of cursors: (i) Direct relation between education and economic development, as per the human capital theory, suggest economically developed states might spend higher resources on education at the initial stages of development. Once the states attain certain threshold levels of educational attainment, such states either sustain or reduce their allocation to education. It is because other subsectors of education need more allocation representing next stage of development. This is found to hold good in Kerala and Tamil Nadu. On the contrary, economically and educationally backward states due to their fiscal capacity allocate lesser resources to education. Inevitably these states do have bulk of child population that is to be brought into school. However, what is observed is contrary to this proposition that many educationally and economically backward states such as Bihar, Madhya Pradesh, Rajasthan and Uttar Pradesh spend relatively more of their state budget on education.

(ii) Intra-sectoral allocation to elementary education is improving across educationally backward states than educationally better-off states, indicating their early phase of education development. That the induced impact of SSA on increased state allocation towards elementary education is discernible in few educationally backward states, namely Bihar, Madhya Pradesh, Uttar Pradesh, Rajasthan, Assam and Orissa. In addition to these educationally backward states Himachal Pradesh allocated consistently higher share towards elementary education. On the contrary, this does not hold true in Punjab and West Bengal which retained their allocation to elementary education at pre-SSA periods.

Funding under SSA exhibit that educationally backward states getting the highest shares and as per child population, but not essentially so in terms of their relative proportions of enrolment, schools and teachers. Resource allocation mechanism neither seem to ensure predictability and transparency that how much of resources are sanctioned to state governments nor sanctions the available resources within the stipulated time and in fewer installments. Yet another revelation is the actual absorptive rates are much less than apparent absorptive rates. It becomes unambiguous that the additional resources coming from the centre for development of education can have a positive influence on states only after states have achieved a certain threshold level of absorptive capacities. As can be evidenced, fiscal disability is not compensated by the transfers via SSA as matching shares are uniform across states.

Though SSA attempts to address interstate disparity, yet the accumulated initial advantage of the better-off states with uniform funding norms under SSA widens interstate disparity. Hence, at the end of more than a decade of implementing SSA, the distance to reach not only to universal upper primary enrolment but also retaining children in the system would remain a challenge for many educationally backward states. Hence, any design of transfers would remain cosmetic, unless drastic redistribution takes place in the horizontal allocation of resources. It would be apt to quote here 'Not everything that counts can be (is) counted; and not everything that can be counted counts'.

# APPENDIX

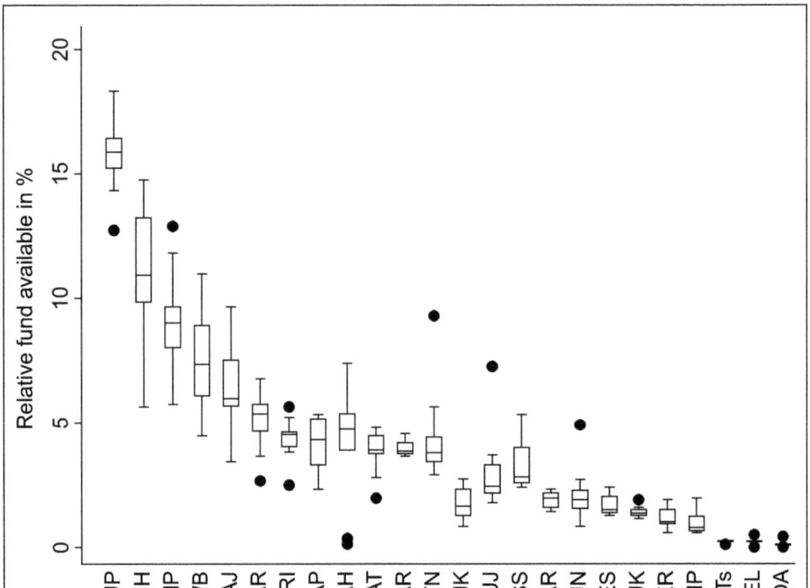


*Figure A14.1* Relative share of total funds available under SSA

*Source:* www.ssa.nic.in downloaded as an 22.2.2013; Ed. Cil TSG.

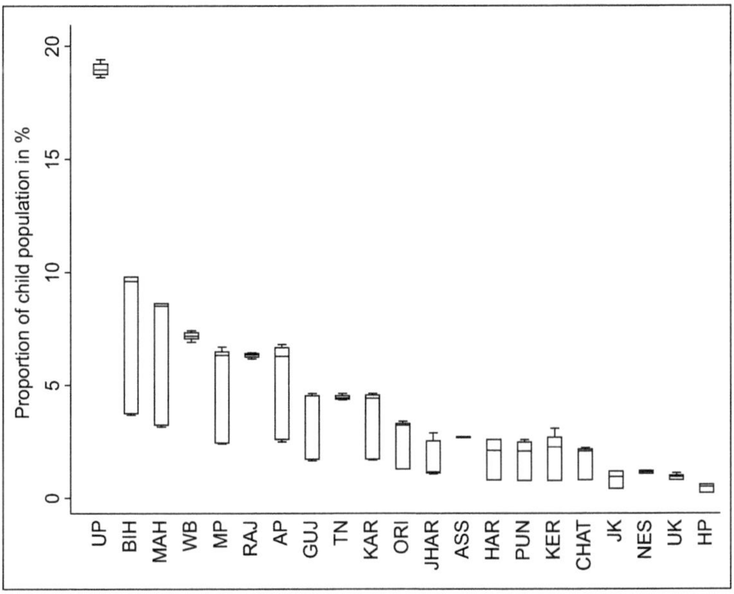


*Figure A14.2* Relative share of child population across states

*Source:* Based on Census Projection, Census of India (2006).

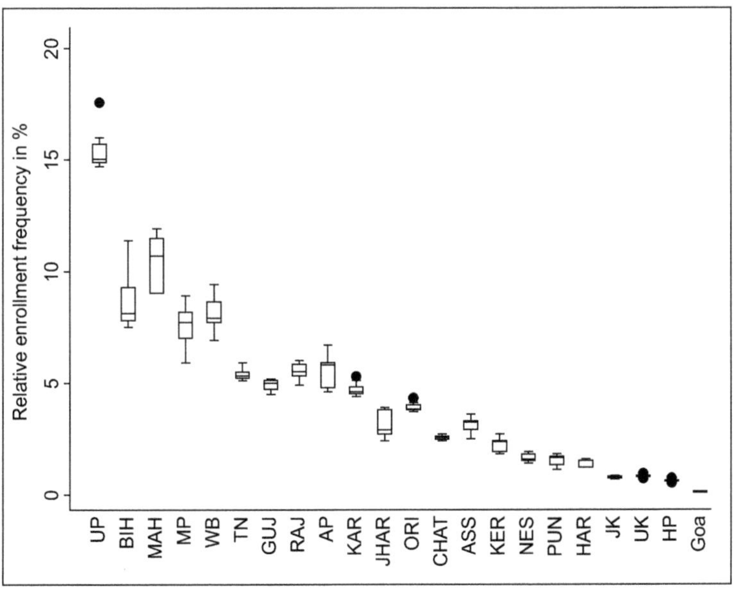


*Figure A14.3* Relative share of enrolment across states

*Source:* Based on Selected Educational Statistics, Selected School Statistics, various issues, 7th AIES of NCERT, 64th round of NSO.

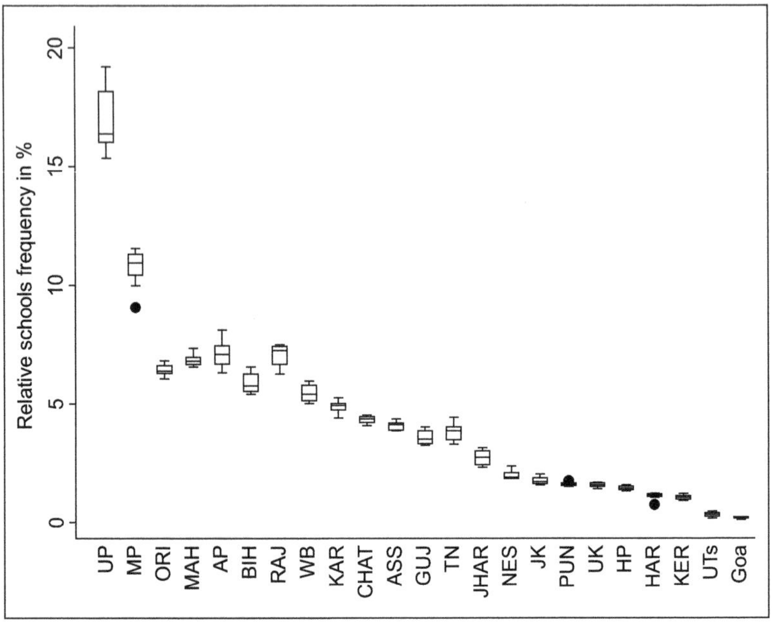


*Figure A14.4* Relative share of schools across states

*Source:* Based on Selected Educational Statistics, Selected School Statistics, various issues.

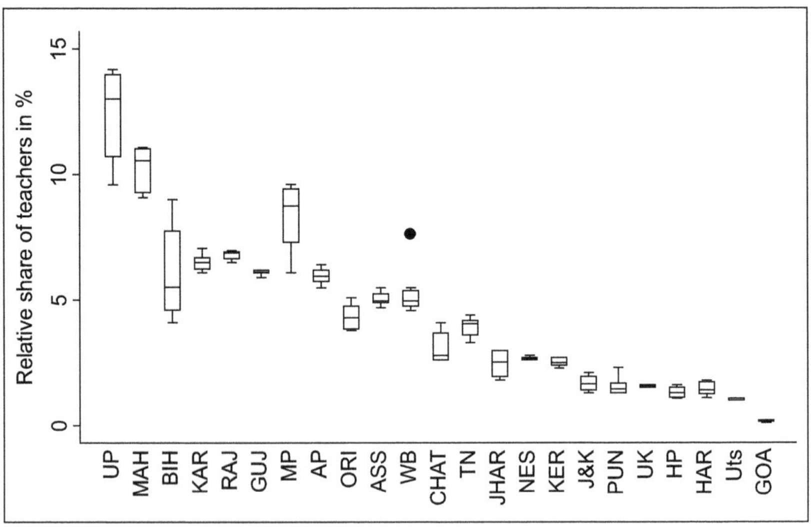


*Figure A14.5* Relative share of teachers across states

*Source:* Based on Selected Educational Statistics, Selected School Statistics, various issues, DISE unit level data 2004–05 and 2005–06.

## Notes

1 India consists of 28 states and seven union territories as per Census, 2011.
2 This concern is supported by various statistical analyses. Yet, conclusions are sensitive to what measures of attainment are used. Review of studies here cover recent studies published since 2000.
3 Inter-sectoral allocation is examined in 15 major states, namely, Andhra Pradesh, Bihar, Gujarat, Haryana, Himachal Pradesh, Karnataka, Kerala, Madhya Pradesh, Maharashtra, Orissa, Punjab, Rajasthan, Tamil Nadu, Uttar Pradesh and West Bengal. Two more states, Assam and Jammu & Kashmir are added in intra-sectoral allocations.
4 Graphical representation showing a data set's lowest value, highest value, median value, and size of the first and third quartiles.
5 Number of installments through which money was transferred indicate the extent of fragmentation in allocations.
6 Actual absorptive rates = 100 – (Unspent balance/Total funds available). Unspent balance is the sum of opening and closing balance in a year.
7 Uttar Pradesh report the allocation as expenditure as noted in many JRMS. Hence, apparent absorptive rates needs to be interpreted cautiously.
8 The setback in this illustration is, it does not factor in enrolment and dropout by private unaided schools.
9 Time series information on enrolment by type of management is not available. Hence, enrolment share of private unaided obtained using 7th All India Educational Survey (NCERT) for the year 2002 is factored in by assuming that share of PUA enrolment would remain the same from 2002–03 to 2006–07. Share of PUA enrolment estimated from 64th round of NSSO is applied to arrive at enrolment in government and private aided schools for 2007–08 and assumed that the share would remain the same from 2008–09 to 2010–11. We are aware that the assumption of keeping the same share would probably underestimate the growing share of PUA enrolment. However, this is the next best alterative as there is no data on enrolment by type of management.
10 However, this aspect has not been analysed in detail as this is outside the scope of this paper.
11 Though Goa reports the highest growth rates among all state this needs to be interpreted cautiously given its low base of just 953 schools in 2003–04 to 1533 schools by 2009–10.
12 Share of teacher working in private unaided school is computed using DISE data for 2004–05 and 2005–06. An average of these two years is applied to arrive at teachers working in government and private aided schools. Teachers by management type by states is unavailable from NCERT.

## References

Bashir, S. 2000. Government Expenditure on Elementary Education in the Nineties. The European Commission, New Delhi.

Chakraborty, A. 2009. 'Some Normatively Relevant Aspects of Inter-State and Intra-State Disparities', *Economic and Political Weekly*, xliv (26 & 27):179–184.

Chakraborty, P., Anit, N. M., and Amar Nath, H. K. 2010. 'Interstate Distribution of Central Expenditure and Subsidies', Working Paper No. 2010–66, National Institute of Public Finance and Policy, New Delhi, http://www.nipfp.org.in (accessed on 20 March 2011).

Dholakia, R. 2003. 'Regional Disparity In Economic And Human Development In India', *The Journal of income and wealth*, 25(1 & 2):115–128.

Dholakia, R. 2005. 'Trends in Regional Disparity in Human and Social Development in India', Working Paper No; 2005–09–07, Indian Institute of Management, Ahmadabad.

Dreze, J. and Sen, A. K. 2002. *India: Development and Participation*, Oxford University Press, New Delhi.

Dreze, J. and Sen, A. K. 2013, *The Uncertain Glory: India and its Contradictions*, Allan Lane, New Delhi.

Filmer, D. and Lant, P. 1999. 'Estimating Wealth Effects Without Expenditure Data – or Tears: An Application To Educational Enrollments in States of India' *Demography*, 38 (1): 115–132.

Geetha, R. P. 2007. 'Every Child in School: The Challenges of Attaining and Financing Education for All in India' in *Education for All: Global Promises, National Challenges*, Alex Wiseman and David Baker (ed.), International Perspectives on Education and Society, 8: 207–264.

Jha, P., Subrat, D., Siba, S. M., and Nandan, K. J. 2008. *Public Provisioning for Elementary Education in India*, Sage, New Delhi.

Jhingran, D. and Deepa, S. 2009. Addressing Educational Disparity: Using District Level Education Development Indices for Equitable Resource Allocations in India, Policy Research Working Paper, WPS, 4955, World Bank, South Asia Region, New Delhi.

Karan, A. K. and Pushpendra. 2005. 'Bihar: Including the Excluded and Addressing the Failures of Public Provision in Elementary Education', in *The Economics of Elementary Education in India: The Challenge of Public Finance, Private Provision and Household Costs*, Santosh Mehrotra (ed.), Sage, New Delhi.

Kulkarni, P. M. 2002. Inter-State Variations in Human Development Differentials among Social Groups in India, NCAER Working Paper, New Delhi.

Kundu, A., Moahanan, P. C. and Varghese, K. 2013. Spatial and Social Inequalities in Human Development: India in the Global Context, UNDP India.

Mehrotra, S. et al. 2005. Universalizing Elementary Education in India: Uncaging the Tiger Economy, Oxford University Press, New Delhi.

MHRD, 2004. *Sarva Shiksha Abhiyan: A Programme for Universal Elementary Education; Manual on Financial Management and Procurement*, Department of Elementry Education and Literacy, Ministry of Human Resources Development, Government of India, New Delhi.

MHRD, 2005. *Report of Committee on National Common Minimum Programs Commitment of Six Per cent of GDP to Education*, National Institute of Educational Planning and Administration, New Delhi.

MHRD, 2006. Report of Fourth Joint Review Mission of Sarva Shiksha Abhiyan, Government of India, 17–27 July 2006, New Delhi.

MHRD, 2008a. Seventh Joint Review Mission, Government of India 21st January to 5th February 2008, New Delhi.

MHRD, 2008b. Eighth Joint Review Mission of *Sarva Shiksha Abhiyan*, Government of India, 21–31 July 2008, New Delhi.

MHRD, 2010. *Sarva Shiksha Abhiyan: A Programme for Universal Elementary Education; Manual on Financial Management and Procurement*, Revised, Department of Elementary Education and Literacy, Ministry of Human Resources Development, Government of India, New Delhi.

Mooij, J. and Mahendra Dev, S. 2004. 'Social Sector Priorities: An Analysis of Budgets and Expenditures in India in the 1990s', *Development Policy Review*, 22(1): 97–120.

Pal, P. and Jayati, G. 2007. Inequality in India: A Survey of Recent Trends, *Social Affairs*, pp. 1–28.

Panchamukhi, P. R. 2000. 'Social Impact of Economic Reforms in India: A Critical Appraisal', *Economic and Political Weekly*, XXXV(10): 853–866.

Parker, A. N. 1995. Decentralisation: The Way Forward for Rural Development? Policy Research Working Paper No. 1475, World Bank, Washington, DC.

Rangarajan, C. 2004. 'Issues before Twelfth Finance Commission', *Economic and Political Weekly*, XXXIX(26): 2707–2794.

Rao, M. Govinda, Shand, Ric and Kalirajan, K. P. 1999. 'Convergence of Incomes across Indian States: A Divergent View,' *Economic and Political Weekly*, March 27–April 2, 769–778.

Shah, A. 1991. Perspectives on the Design of Intergovernmental Fiscal Relations, Policy, Research and External Affairs Working Paper, No.726, World Bank, Washington, DC.

Sridhar, K. S. and Venugopala Reddy, A. 2011. 'Investment and Economic Opportunities: Urbanization, Infrastructure and Governance In The North and South of India', *Asia-Pacific Development Journal*, 18(1):1–46.

# INDEX